Emma Phipson

The Animal-lore of Shakspeares Time

including quadrupeds, birds, reptiles, fish and insects

Emma Phipson

The Animal-lore of Shakspeares Time
including quadrupeds, birds, reptiles, fish and insects

ISBN/EAN: 9783337815981

Printed in Europe, USA, Canada, Australia, Japan

Cover: Foto ©ninafisch / pixelio.de

More available books at **www.hansebooks.com**

THE ANIMAL-LORE

OF

SHAKSPEARE'S TIME

INCLUDING

QUADRUPEDS, BIRDS, REPTILES, FISH AND INSECTS

BY

EMMA PHIPSON

LONDON
KEGAN PAUL, TRENCH & CO., 1, PATERNOSTER SQUARE
1883

(The rights of translation and of reproduction are reserved.)

PREFACE.

THE object of the following compilation is to bring together in an accessible form waifs and strays of information, collected from various sources, relating to medieval natural history, so far as animal life is concerned. Descriptions, more or less accurate, of the birds and quadrupeds known in the Middle Ages are to be found in the writings of Gesner, Belon, Aldrovandus, and other naturalists. A knowledge of the state of natural science during the period in which our great dramatist lived may be gained, not only from the writings of naturalists and antiquaries, but from similes, allusions, and anecdotes introduced into the plays, poems, and general literature of England during the latter half of the sixteenth and the beginning of the seventeenth centuries.

The chief works already published on this branch of Shakspearian literature are *The Insects mentioned in Shakspeare's Plays*, by Robert Patterson, 1848, a series of letters on entomology with a sprinkling of quotations from Shakspeare to add to the interest; a *Natural History of Shakespeare*, by Bessie Mayou, 1877, in which passages relating to flowers, fruits and animals are quoted without comment; and *The Ornithology of Shakespeare*, by Edmund Harting, 1871, a very valuable work.

I have endeavoured to keep the book as much on a chronological level as possible, chiefly referring to ancient authors in order to trace the origin of some fable or myth, and to modern writers when they explain or correct an erroneous impression.

As Mrs. Cowden Clarke's *Concordance* renders reference to Shakspeare's pages so easy, I have thought it unnecessary to increase the size of the volume by numerous passages from his works. The text of the "Globe" edition is that from which I have quoted.

Relinquishing all claim to originality, I have given, in most cases, the actual words of the authors quoted, in preference to incorporating their facts and ideas into the body of the book. I trust that the advantage of being able to refer to the original sources will compensate the reader for the tiresome interruptions that constant quotation entails. The quaint phrases employed by many of the early writers seem also to harmonize with the antiquarian nature of the subject.

In consequence of the charming indifference displayed by older writers on natural history to the necessity for any system of animate nature, I have followed the modern classification of the animal kingdom, although I have purposely avoided introducing scientific nomenclature. The plan of arrangement is that adopted by Dr. Percival Wright, in his recent work, *Animal Life*.

I must express my thanks to Mr. F. J. Furnivall, Dr. Brinsley Nicholson, Dr. J. E. Shaw and other friends, who have kindly assisted me in various ways; and, in conclusion, I may add that I shall be much indebted to any reader who will point out mistakes or give me suggestions for a future edition.

5, *Park Place,*
Upper Baker Street, N.W.

CONTENTS.

	PAGE
INTRODUCTION	1

CHAPTER I.
Monkey—Bat—Hedgehog—Mole—Shrew 8

CHAPTER II.
Lion—Tiger—Jaguar—Leopard—Panther—Puma—Ounce—Cat—Lynx—Hyæna—Civet—Ichneumon—Wolf—Jackal ... 17

CHAPTER III.
Dog 40

CHAPTER IV.
Fox—Ermine—Miniver—Marten—Sable—Ferret—Polecat—Weasel—Wolverine—Skunk—Coati—Otter—Badger—Bear 62

CHAPTER V.
Walrus—Seal—Whale—Dolphin—Narwhal—Porpoise—Ork—Grampus—Manatee 87

CHAPTER VI.
Horse—Ass—Zebra—Rhinoceros—Hippopotamus—Pig—Camel—Llama—Deer—Giraffe—Bison—Buffalo—Ox—Antelope—Sheep—Elephant 104

CHAPTER VII.
Rat—Mouse—Beaver—Squirrel—Marmot—Chinchilla—Porcupine—Hare—Rabbit—Sloth—Armadillo—Iguana—Ant-eater—Opossum 149

CHAPTER VIII.

Thrush — Missel Thrush — Redwing — Fieldfare — Nightingale — Robin — Wheatear — Wren — Titmouse — Oriole — Magpie — Crow — Raven — Jackdaw — Chough — Bird of Paradise — Swallow — Finch — Siskin — Canary — Linnet — Bulfinch — Crossbill — Ortolan — Starling — Lark — Wagtail — Sparrow — Yellow-hammer 169

CHAPTER IX.

Woodpecker — Toucan — Cuckoo — Kingfisher — Hoopoe — Goat-sucker — Humming-bird — Parrot — Pigeon — Dodo — Capercaillie — Quail — Partridge — Pheasant — Cock — Turkey — Guinea-fowl ... 203

CHAPTER X.

Vulture — Condor — Eagle — Kite — Hawks — Osprey — Owl ... 230

CHAPTER XI.

Water-rail — Land-rail — Coot — Snipe — Woodcock — Redshank — Curlew — Ruff — Knot — Godwit — Dunlin — Plover — Oyster-catcher — Bustard — Crane — Heron — Bittern — Spoonbill — Stork — Flamingo 255

CHAPTER XII.

Goose — Swan — Duck — Teal — Sheldrake — Gull — Petrel — Cormorant — Pelican — Tropic Bird — Penguin — Auk — Grebe — Puffin — Ostrich — Emeu 273

CHAPTER XIII.

Tortoise — Crocodile — Lizard — Chameleon — Blindworm — Adder — Asp — Snake — Newt — Salamander — Frog — Toad 297

CHAPTER XIV.

Stickleback — Perch — Ruffe — Mullet — Gurnet — Miller's Thumb — Mackerel — Tunny — Bonito — Sword-fish — Sea-angler — Cod — Haddock — Whiting — Hake — Ling — Plaice — Flounder — Turbot — Sole — Brill — Dory 325

Contents.

CHAPTER XV.

Salmon—Trout — Charr — Gwiniad — Grayling — Smelt — Pike—
Flying-fish—Carp — Bream—Tench—Barbel—Roach—Dace—
Chub—Bleak—Loach—Gudgeon—Minnow 349

CHAPTER XVI.

Pilchard—Herring—Sprat—Sardine—Anchovy—Eel — Sturgeon—
Shark — Pilot-fish — Remora — Dog-fish — Monk-fish —
Torpedo—Thornback—Skate—Lamprey 369

CHAPTER XVII.

Cochineal—Cicada — Cricket — Grasshopper — Locust — Mantis —
Cockroach—Beetle—Glow-worm—Fire-fly—Ladybird—Ant —
Bee—Wasp—Hornet—Fly —Gnat — Butterfly — Moth — Silk-
worm—Spider—Scorpion 389

CHAPTER XVIII.

Lobster—Crayfish—Shrimp—Crab—Polypus—Nautilus—Cuttlefish
—Scallop—Oyster—Mussel—Snail—Leech—Coral 434

CHAPTER XIX.

Unicorn—Dragon—Basilisk—Cockatrice—Wyvern — Fire-Drake—
Griffin—Sphinx—Harpy—Minotaur—Centaur —Satyr— Chimæra — Mantichor — Phœnix—Caladrius — Hircinie — Memnonides—Liver—Sea-Serpent 452

AUTHORS AND EDITIONS QUOTED.

Anderson (A.), Origin of Commerce. 4 vols. 4to. 1801.
Ancient British Drama. Edit. Sir W. Scott. 3 vols. 8vo. 1810.
Antiquarian Repertory (The). Edit. Grose, Astley, etc. New edition. 4 vols. 4to. 1807.
Arber (E.), An English Garner. Vols. 1–5. 1877–1882.
Archæologia. Published by Society of Antiquaries of London. 45 vols. 4to. 1770.
Ascham (R.), Toxophilus. 1515. Twelfth edition, reprint. 1868.
Astley (T.), Collection of Voyages. Edit. J. Green. 4 vols. 4to. 1745.

Babees Book (The), etc. Meals and Manners in Olden Time. Edit. F. J. Furnivall. 8vo. 1868.
Bacon (F.), Works. Vol. 4. Edit. Montagu. 4to. 1825.
Baring-Gould (Rev. S.), Book of Were-wolves. 8vo. 1865.
Barrington (D.), Miscellanies. 4to. 1781.
Bartas (Guillaume de Saluste du), Divine Weekes and Workes. Trans. by Joshua Sylvester. Fol. 1633.
A learned Summary upon the Poeme. Trans. by T. L. D., M.P. Fol. 1637.
Batman uppon Bartholome. Fol. 1582.
Beaumont and Fletcher, Dramatic Works. Edit. Dyce. 11 vols. 8vo. 1843.
Beckmann (J.), Inventions and Discoveries. Trans. by Johnson. Third edition. 4 vols. 8vo. 1817.
Bennett (E. T.), Gardens and Menagerie of the Zoological Society. 2 vols. 8vo. 1830.
Tower Menagerie. 8vo. 1829.
Benzoni (G.), History of the New World. Edit. W. H. Smyth. 8vo. (*Hakluyt Society*). 1857.
Berners (Dame Juliana), Treatise of Fysshynge with an Angle. 8vo. 1827.
Blount (T.), Ancient Tenures of Land. Edit. W. C. Hazlitt. 8vo. 1874.

Boorde (A.), Introduction and Dietary. Edit. F. J. Furnivall. (*Early English Text Society.*) 8vo. 1870.
Brady (J.), Clavis Calendaria. Second edition. 2 vols. 8vo. 1812.
Brand (Rev. J.), Popular Antiquities. Edit. Sir H. Ellis. 2 vols. 4to. 1841.
Brayley (E. W.), Londiniana. 4 vols. 12mo. 1828.
Brewer (Rev. Dr. E. C.), Dictionary of Phrase and Fable. 8vo. 1875.
Browne (Sir T.), Works. Edit. S. Wilkins. 4 vols. 8vo. 1835.
Browne (W.), Poetical Works. Edit. W. C. Hazlitt. 3 vols. Small 4to. 1868.
Buchner (L.), Mind in Animals. Trans. by A. Besant. 8vo. 1880.
Buckland (F.), Curiosities of Natural History. 4 vols. 12mo. 1873.
Burney (A.), Collection of Travels. 4 vols. 4to. 1803.
Burton (R.), Anatomy of Melancholy. New. edit. 2 vols. 8vo. 1837.

Camden (W.), Britannia. Trans. by Holland. Fol. 1610.
Camden Miscellany (The), 6 vols. 4to. (*Camden Society.*) 1847-1859.
Carew (R.), Survey of Cornwall. Edit. Lord de Dunstanville. 4to. 1811.
Champlain (S.), Voyage to the West Indies (1599-1602). Edit. Shaw. 8vo. (*Hakluyt Society.*) 1859.
Chester (R.), Love's Martyr. Edit. Grosart. (*New Shakspere Society, reprint.*) 1820.
Churchill (Messrs.), Collection of Travels. Third edition. 6 vols. Fol. 1744.
Collier (J. P.), Poetical Decameron. 2 vols. 8vo. 1820.
Conway (M. D.), Demonology and Devil-lore. 2 vols. 8vo. 1879.
Coryat (Tom.), Crudities (1611). 3 vols. 8vo. 1776.
Couch (J.), History of Fishes of the British Islands. 4 vols. 8vo. 1877.
Cromwell (T.), History of Colchester. 8vo. 1825.

Daniel (S.), Poems. 2 vols. 12mo. 1753.
Daniel (Rev. W. B.), Rural Sports, with Supplement. 3 vols. 4to. 1812.
Dawson (J. W.), Archaia. 8vo. 1860.
Day (J.), Works. Edit. E. H. Bullen. (*Reprint.*) 4to. 1880.
Derricke (J.), The Image of Ireland. (*Somer's Tracts*, i.) 1581.
Digby (Sir K.), Two Treatises on the Nature of Bodies. Fol. 1644.
Dodsley (R.), Old English Plays. Edit. W. C. Hazlitt. 15 vols. 8vo. 1874-76.
    Fugitive Pieces. 2 vols. 8vo. 1761.
Drake (N.), Shakspeare and his Times. 2 vols. 4to. 1817.
Drayton (M.), Works. 4 vols. 8vo. 1753.
Dyer (T. F. T.), English Folk-lore. 8vo. 1878.

Earle (Bishop), Microscomography. Edit. Bliss. 8vo. 1811.
Elvin (C. N.), Anecdotes of Heraldry. 8vo. 1864.
English Poets. Edit. Dr. Johnson. Vols. 1-6. 8vo. 1810.

Authors and Editions quoted. xiii

Fleming (A.), Of Englishe Dogges (1576). *Reprint.* 8vo. 1880.
Folkard (H. C.), The Wild Fowler. 8vo. 1859.
Ford (J.), Dramatic Works. Notes by Gifford. New edition. 3 vols. 8vo. 1869.
Fosbroke (Rev. T. D.), Encyclopædia of Antiquities. 2 vols. 8vo. New edition. 1843.
Fuller (J.), Worthies of England. 2 vols. 4to. Edit. Nicholls. 1811.

Garner (R.), Natural History of Stafford. 8vo. 1844.
Gascoigne (G.), Poems. Edit. W. C. Hazlitt. 2 vols. 8vo. (*Roxburgh Library.*) 1870.
Giraldus Cambrensis, Historical Works. Edit. Wright. 8vo. 1863.
Gordon (Pat.), Short Abridgement of Britane's Distemper. 1639–49. 4to. (*Spalding Club.*) 1844.
Green (H.), Shakspeare and the Emblem Writers. 8vo. 1870.
Greene (R.), Dramatic Works. Edit. Dyce. 2 vols. 8vo. 1831.
Grieve (J.), History of Kamschatka. 4to. 1764.
Guillim (J.), Display of Heraldry. Sixth edition. Fol. 1744.

Hakewill (Rev. Dr. G.), Apologie. Fol. 1630.
Hakluyt (R.), Collection of Voyages. 5 vols. 4to. 1810.
Hall (J.), Satires. Notes by Singer. 12mo. 1824.
Harleian Miscellany. 10 vols. 4to. New edition. 1808.
Harting (J. E.), Ornithology of Shakespeare. 8vo. 1871.
British Animals extinct within Historic Times. 8vo. 1880.
Harris (J.), Collection of Travels. 2 vols. Fol. New edition. 1764.
Hazlitt (W. C.), Shakspeare's Jest Books. 8vo. 1864.
Herbert (Sir Thos.), Travels. Fol. 1677.
Herrera (A. de), History of America. Trans. by Stephens. Second edition. 1740.
Heywood (J.), Dramatic Works. 6 vols. 8vo. 1874.
Holinshed, Chronicles of England. Vols. 1, 2 (1577). 4to. 1807.
Houghton (Rev. W.), Gleanings from the Natural History of the Ancients. 8vo. 1879.
Howell (J.), Familiar Letters. Eleventh edition. 8vo. 1754.
Hyll (Thos.), Art of Gardening. 4to. 1593.

Jesse (G. R.), Researches into the History of the British Dog. 2 vols. 8vo. 1866.
Jonson (Ben.), Works. Notes by Gifford. Edit. Cunningham. 3 vols. 8vo. (No date.)

Kennett (Bp. W.), History of England. Second edition. 3 vols. Fol. 1719.

Lambarde (W.), Perambulation of Kent, 1570. Third edition. 8vo. 1656.

Leigh (Dr. C.), Natural History of Lancashire, etc. Fol. 1700.
Leland (J.), The Itinerary. Published by T. Hearne. 9 vols. 8vo. 1744.
Lord Mayors' Pageants, (Collection of). (*Percy Society.*) 8vo. 1843.
Low (D.), Domesticated Animals of the British Islands. 8vo. 1846.
Lower (M. A.), Curiosities of Heraldry. 8vo. 1845.
Lubbock (Rev. R.), Fauna of Norfolk. 8vo. 1845.
Lyly (J.), Euphues. Edit. E. Arber. 12mo. (*Reprint.*) 1868.
    Dramatic Works. Edit. F. W. Fairholt. 2 vols. 1858.

Mandeville (Sir John), Travels. Edit. Halliwell. 8vo. 1839.
Manley (J. J.), Fish and Fishing. 8vo. 1877.
Manningham (J.), Diary. Edit. Bruce. (*Camden Society.*) 4to. 1868.
Marco Polo, Travels in the East. Edit. Marsden. 4to. 1817.
Marlowe (C.), Works. Edit. Cunningham. 8vo. (No date.)
Massinger (P.), Dramatic Works. Edit. Giffard. 4 vols. 8vo. 1805.
Miller (S. H.), and S. B. J. Skertchley. The Fenland, Past and Present. 8vo. 1878.
Minsheu (J.), Guide unto the Tongues. Fol. 1617.
Mirror (The), for Magistrates. Edit. Haslewood. 3 vols. 4to. 1815.
Mitchell (J. M.), The Herring, its Natural History and National Importance. 8vo. 1864.
Montaigne (M. de), Essays. Trans. by Cotton, 1700. 1870.
Morgan (J.), Phœnix Britannicus. Vol. 1. 4to. 1732.
Moryson (F.), History of Ireland, 1599–1603. 2 vols. 8vo. 1735.
    Itinerary. Fol. 1617.
Muffett (T.), Healths Improvement. Enlarged by Dr. C. Bennett. Sm. 4to. 1655.
    Theater of Insects. Printed with Topsell. Fol. 1658.
Munday (A.), Briefe Chronicle of the Successe of Times. 8vo. 1611.

Nares (R.), Glossary. Edit. J. O. Halliwell and T. Wright. 2 vols. 8vo. 1876.
Nicander Nucius (Travels of). Edit. Cramer. (*Camden Society.*) Sm. 4to. 1840.
Nichols (J.), Progresses of Queen Elizabeth. New edition. 3 vols. 4to. 1823.
Nicolas (Sir H.), Testamenta Vetusta. 2 vols. 8vo. 1826.
Norden (J.), Description of Essex. (*Camden Society.*) Sm. 4to. 1840.
Northumberland Household Book (1512). Edit. Percy. Second edition. 8vo. 1827.
Notes and Queries. 64 vols. Sm. 4to. 1850–82.

Olaus Magnus, Compendious History of the Goths, Swedes, and Vandals, and other Northern Nations. (Trans. by J. S.) Fol. 1658.

Palliser (Mrs. B.), Historic Devices, Badges, and War Cries. 8vo. 1870.
Patterson (R.), Natural History of the Insects mentioned in Shakspeare's Plays. 12mo. 1842.
Peele (G.), Dramatic Works. Edit. Dyce. Second edition. 3 vols. 8vo. 1822-39.
Pegge (Rev. S.), Anonymiana. 8vo. 1809.
    Curialia. 4to. 1782.
    Curialia Miscellania, or Anecdotes of Old Times. 8vo. 1780.
Pennant (T.), History of Quadrupeds.
Planché (J. R.), Cyclopædia of Costume. 2 vols. 4to. 1876-79.
Poole (J.), English Parnassus. 8vo. 1657.
Privy Purse Expenses of Henry VIII. (No date.)
Purchas (Rev. S.), His Pilgrimes. 5 vols. Fourth edition. Fol. 1625.

Quarles (F.), Emblems. 12mo. 1736.

Raleigh (Sir W.), Works. 8 vols. 8vo. 1829.
Reynard the Fox, (Pleasant History of). Edit. W. J. Thoms. (*Percy Society.*) 8vo. 1844.
Russel (A.), The Salmon. 8vo. 1874.

Selden (J.), Works. Fol. 1726.
Scot (Reginald), Discovery of Witchcraft. Second edition. 4to. 1634.
Shakspeare (W.), Works. Edit. Clarke and Wright. (*Globe edition.*) 1873.
    Edit. Singer. 11 vols. 8vo. 1875.
Shakspere, (New) Society Transactions. 1874-82.
Shepherd (C. W.), North-West Peninsula of Iceland. 8vo. 1867.
Shirley (J.), Works. 6 vols. 8vo. Notes by Gifford. 1833.
Sidney (Sir P.), Works, in Prose and Verse. Fourteenth edition. 3 vols. 8vo. 1725.
Six Ballads, with Burdens. Edit. J. Goodwin. (*Percy Society.*) 8vo. 1845.
Spenser (E.), Poetical Works. Edit. Aikin. 5 vols. 8vo. 1842.
Stanley (Bp. of Norwich), Familiar History of Birds. Sixth edition. 12mo. 1854.
Stapfer (Paul), Shakespeare and Classical Antiquity. Trans. by E. Carey. 8vo. 1880.
Starkey (T.), England in the reign of Henry VIII. (*Early English Text Society.*) 8vo. 1871.
Stevenson, Birds of Norfolk. 8vo. 1866.
Stow (J.), Chronicle of England, continued by Howes. Fol. 1632.
    Survey of London. 4to. 1598.

Taylor (J.), Works. Edit. Hindley. 8vo. 1872.
Timbs (J.), Eccentricities of the Animal Creation. 8vo. 1869.
Topsell (Ed.), Historie of Foure-footed Beastes. Fol. 1607.

Topsell, with Muffett's Theater of Insects. Fol. 1658.
Tristram (Canon), Natural History of the Bible. 8vo. 1873.
Tusser (T.), Five Hundred Points of Good Husbandry. 4to. 1812.

Virgil, Works. Edit. Singleton. 2 vols. 1859.

Walton (Izaak), and Cotton. Complete Angler. Edit. Sir H. Nicolas. 1875.
Warner (Rev. R.), Antiquitates Culinariæ. 4to. 1791.
Webster (J.), Dramatic Works. Edit. Dyce. 4 vols. 8vo. 1830.
Wilson (A.), Leisure Time Studies. 8vo. 1879.
Wright (E. P.), Animal Life. 4to. (No date.)

Yarrell (W.), History of British Birds. 3 vols. 8vo. 1837–43.
    History of British Fishes. 3 vols. 8vo. 1836.
Yonge (W.), Diary of. Edit. Roberts. (*Camden Society*). 4to. 1848.

THE ANIMAL-LORE

OF

SHAKSPEARE'S TIME.

INTRODUCTION.

FEW subjects have more frequently occupied the attention of man than that of his own relation to the animal life around him. The classic writers delighted to note the various points of contact and the joint ownership of qualities which man and animals possessed. In the time of Shakspeare this question of kinship seems to have been studied with renewed interest. Montaigne labours long and earnestly to prove the "equality and correspondence betwixt us and the beasts." In Essay liv. he refuses to allow to man the sole possession of any faculty, or to debase the intelligence of animals with the name of instinct. He draws illustrations of the employment of such mental attributes as prudence, ingenuity, foresight, memory, from many beasts and birds.

"Why," he writes, "does the spider make her web streighter in one place and slacker in another? why now make one sort of knot, and then another, if she has not deliberation, thought, and conclusion? We sufficiently discover in most of their works how much animals excel us, and how unable our art is to imitate them. We see, nevertheless, in our more gross performances, that we employ all our faculties, and apply the utmost power of our souls; why do we not conclude the same of them? Why should we attribute to I know not what natural and servile inclination the works that excel all we can do by nature and art? Wherein, before we are aware, we give them a mighty advantage over us, in making nature, with a maternal sweetness, to accompany and lead them, as it were, by the hand to all the actions and commodities of their life, whilst she leaves us to chance and fortune, and to seek out, by art, the things that are necessary to our conservation, at the same time denying us the means of being able, by any instruction or contention of understanding, to arrive at the natural sufficiency of beasts; so that their brutish stupidity surpasses, in all conveniences, all that our divine intelligence can do. Really, at this rate, we might with great reason call her an unjust step-mother; but it is nothing so, our polity is not so irregular and deform'd. Nature has been generally kind to all her creatures, and there is not one she has not amply furnished with all means necessary for the conservation of his being."

A little further on, he writes—

"All this I have said to prove the resemblance there is in human things, and to bring us back and joyn us to the crowd. We are neither above nor below the rest. All that is under heaven (says the wise man) runs one law, and one fortune."

The Rev. J. Kirkman has recently shown, in an essay written for the New Shakspere Society, how, in almost every one of Shakspeare's plays, the tone of the drama is reflected by the animal life introduced. In *Midsummer Night's Dream*—

"the season and atmosphere of exuberant life, joy, and fun, show almost all creatures but serpents under their genial light. There is a very delight even in naming things, because of their song, their beauty, their innocent, or quaint, or industrious ways. It is exactly the opposite condition of things that rules in *King Lear*. Here the darker purpose of the play, which throws its shadow over human nature, shrouds in its gloom animal nature as well. A greater number of animals are mentioned in *King Lear* than in any other play, and with scarcely an exception the references are unfavourable. Their cruelty, treachery, and deceit are dwelt upon, and withal the terrible fact of the similar villainy of man. We have to ask," Mr. Kirkman continues, "what beautiful or sad law was it that was like the igneous rock ever beneath us, cropping up through all sedimentary strata here and there, often commanding attention by the height and sharpness of its peaks? Mr. Darwin would answer infallibly, without a moment's hesitation, I would venture to predict, 'Because of the common nature of man and his lower progenitors in the scale of creation.' I mean, without any allusion to Shakspere being of 'Darwin's views,' Darwin would state on biological grounds precisely the same fact in nature as Shakspere has worked out on moral or psychological principles." (*New Shakspere Society's Transactions*, 1879.)

The question has been asked,—How is it that the number of animal metaphors and similes in Shakspeare's works so greatly exceeds that of any other of his brother dramatists? The answer is to be found mainly in his larger sympathy with nature; but it may be that his deeper study of the problems concerning man's origin and destiny, led him thus closely to connect man with his fellow-denizens of the earth.

However great the interest in external nature felt by our forefathers may have been, the scientific knowledge they possessed was still but slight. Natural history, according to Pliny, was the authorized version of the gospel of nature. The most absurd theories and statements concerning animal life put forth by this classical authority remained uncontradicted down to the time of Shakspeare. The method of interpreting natural phenomena which was founded by Lord Bacon, of substituting patient observation of facts for reliance on speculation and tradition, gave a fresh impulse to the study of natural history.

Another source from which writers of this time derived their notions of animal life was the Bible, which, recently translated, was eagerly read from one end of the country to the other. Unfortunately, this rather retarded than advanced their knowledge of the subject. The crude notions of the ancient Hebrews about beasts and birds, the very names of which were sometimes changed by the translators, were accepted as undoubted truths, and many errors were thus perpetuated. Guillim, the quaint old herald, quotes texts to prove the correctness of his descriptions of various animals, in the same way that modern writers quote the investigations and experiments of Darwin or Huxley.

The myth-making tendency of the human mind has also had an effect on man's study of nature. What Mr. Tylor calls "myths of observation," arose from a laudable anxiety to account for certain known phenomena. When fossil ammonites were found in the solid rock, miles away from the sea-shore, how was it possible to explain their presence better than by the statement that they were snakes turned into stones by the prayers of some local saint? Huge bones of fossil mammals, far exceeding in size those of living men, were obviously the limbs of some giant warrior slain in combat. These theories once started, poetry and imagination were ready to clothe the bare statement with ornament, and legends of early heroes, Guy of Warwick, Bevis of Southampton, and their compeers in might, grew with rapidity, and were universally believed.

It does not follow that all the absurd notions connected with animals that are found in the works of this period were generally credited at the time an author wrote. These fanciful theories were often merely adopted as metaphors and similes; but at the same time writers would not care to be behind the age, and would not willingly use expressions which could only provoke ridicule on the part of their readers. For example, the nightingale is invariably spoken of in the time of Elizabeth as of the feminine gender, while in our own day the knowledge that it is the male bird which sings is reflected in the poetry of our time.

Opportunities for the study of the habits of animals were by no means frequent. Although menageries have existed from the earliest times, they were chiefly used as places of temporary confinement for such wild beasts as were likely soon to be required for sport or war. Instances where animals have been kept for the purpose of observation are rare. Aristotle gained the materials for his work on animals in great measure from the large collection formed by Alexander the Great during his expedition made in search of conquest into distant countries. Pliny had an opportunity of drawing from life in his descriptions of beasts and birds, as there were several private collections made by wealthy Romans of his time; that he did not fully avail himself of this chance is evident from the strange mistakes and absurdities that crowd his pages.

The first English menagerie, according to Mr. Bennett (*Tower Menagerie*, 1829, p. xii.), was at Woodstock, in the time of Henry I. This collection, which consisted of lions, leopards, and other wild animals, was transferred to the Tower of London in the reign of Henry III. There it remained till it was superseded by the establishment of the Zoological Gardens in the Regent's Park. Paul Hentzner, in an account of a journey into England in 1598, gives a list of the various animals which formed the Tower menagerie at that date:—

"On coming out of the Tower we were led to a small house close by, where are kept a variety of creatures, viz. three lionesses, one lion of great size, called Edward VI., from his having been born in that reign; a tiger, a lynx; a wolf excessively old—this is a very scarce animal in England, so that their sheep and cattle stray about in great numbers, free from any danger, though without anybody to keep them; there is, besides, a porcupine, and an eagle. All these creatures are kept in a remote place, fitted up for the purpose with wooden lattices, at the queen's expense." (*Dodsley's Fugitive Pieces*, vol. ii. p. 244.)

Fynes Moryson, in the account of his tour through Europe, 1591, describes a menagerie on a small scale at Prague in Bohemia.

"The Emperour hath two inclosures walled about, which they call gardaines, one of which is called *Stella*, because the trees are planted in the figure of starres, and a little faire house therein is likewise built, with six corners in forme of a starre. And in this place be kept 12 cammels, and an Indian oxe, yellow, all over rugged, and hairy upon the throate, like a lyon; and an Indian calfe; and two leopards, which were said to be tame, if such wild beasts may be tamed. They were of a yellow colour, spotted with blacke, the head partly like a lyon, partly like a cat, the tayle like a cat, the body like a greyhound, and when the huntsman went abroad, at call they leaped up behind him, sitting upon the horse like a dog on the hinder parts, being so swift in running, as they would easily kill a hart" (*Itinerary*, p. 15).

In Italy, again, Moryson meets with a similar collection :—

"'The Duke of Florence kept fierce wilde beasts in a little round house, namely, five lyons, five wolves, three eagles, three tygers (of blacke and gray colour, not unlike cats, but much greater), one wilde cat (like a tyger), beares, leopards spotted with white, black and red, and used sometimes for hunting, an Indian mouse (with a head like our mise, but a long hairie taile, so fierce and big, that it would easily kill one of our cats), and wilde boares." (Page 151.)

This last-named animal may have been an ichneumon, sometimes called Pharaoh's rat.

Herrera, in his *History of America* (vol. ii. p. 348), gives an account of a menagerie in Mexico, far exceeding in magnitude any European collection. When the Spaniards visited Mexico, about the year 1500, they found a zoological garden sustained by Montezuma with right royal magnificence. This menagerie contained many varieties of beasts, birds, and serpents. These last were fed sometimes on human diet; persons sacrificed were afterwards given to the snakes and alligators. According to Herrera, five hundred cocks were daily given to the eagles, and three hundred men were appointed to attend in the house of birds. There were also large ponds for salt and fresh water birds, the water of which was frequently renewed. These birds were

Introduction.

kept chiefly for the sake of their feathers, which formed an article of commerce of considerable importance.

The universal fondness for hunting, hawking, and other field sports, gave rise to a great number of technical expressions connected with the chase, which perpetually occur in the writings of the Elizabethan dramatists. Guillim, in his *Display of Heraldry*, 1610 (p. 15), gives a list of phrases, many of which are in use at the present day:—

"The tayl of a hart is termed the tayl; of a buck, roe, or any other deer, the single; of a boar, the wreath; of a fox, the brush, or holy water sprinkler; of a wolf, the stern; and of a hare or coney, the scut. You shall say that a hart harboureth; a buck lodgeth; a roe beddeth; a hare seateth or formeth; a coney sitteth; a fox is uncased. You shall say dislodge a buck; start a hare; unkennel a fox; rowse a hart; bowlt a coney. A hart belloweth; a buck groaneth; a roe belleth; a hare beateth; a coney tappeth; a fox barketh; a wolf howleth. You shall say a herd of harts, and all manner of deer; a bevy of roes; a sounder of swine; a rowt of wolves; a riches of marternes; a brace or lease of bucks, of foxes, or hares; a couple of rabbets or conies."

Mr. Daniel, in his *Rural Sports*, 1812 (vol. ii. p. 480), quotes from *The Book of Saint Albans* a long list of nouns of multitude:—

"A sege of herons and of bitterns; an herd of swans, of cranes, and of curlews; a dopping of sheldrakes; a spring of teales; a covert of coots; a gaggle of geese: a padelynge of ducks; a bord or sute of mallards; a muster of peacocks; a nye of pheasants; a bevy of quailes; a covey of partridges; a congregation of plovers; a flight of doves; a dule of turkies; a walk of snipes; a fall of woodcocks; a brood of hens; a building of rooks; a murmuration of starlings; an exaltation of larks; a flight of swallows; a host of sparrows; a watch of nightingales; and a charm of goldfinches. A pride of lions; a lepe of leopards; an herd of harts, of buck, and of all sorts of deer; a bevy of roes; a sloth of bears; a singular of boars; a sounder of wild swine; a dryft of tame swine; a route of wolves; a harrass of horses; a rag of colts; a stud of mares; a pace of asses; a baren of mules; a team of oxen; a drove of kine; a flock of sheep; a tribe of goats; a sculk of foxes; a cete of badgers; a riches of martins; a fesynes of ferrets; a huske or a down of hares; a nest of rabbits; a clowder of cats, and a kendel of young cats; a shrewdness of apes; and a labour of móles."

CHAPTER I.

<small>Quadrupeds.
Monkey.</small> The Monkey order is generally spoken of in mediæval times under the three broad names of ape, baboon, and monkey or marmoset, though various kinds are described by the early explorers of Africa and South America under the native names.

The chief sources from which we derive our information respecting the different species of animals found in various parts of the globe are the collections of travels made by Hakluyt and Purchas. The Rev. Samuel Purchas published the first volume of his work in 1613, and the last four volumes in 1625. He gave to his compilation the long title of *Purchas his Pilgrimage; or Relations of the World and the Religions observed in all Ages and Places.* He appears to have been more credulous than Hakluyt, or perhaps he took a stronger interest in natural history, for to him we are chiefly indebted for strange adventures and marvellous descriptions of animal life.

One of the most intelligent of the pilgrims whose peregrinations are recorded in this collection was Andrew Battell, an English sailor, who was taken prisoner by the Portuguese and sent to Angola, on the West Coast of Africa, where he lived nearly eighteen years. This writer gives a tolerably correct account of the largest species of ape, known in modern times as the Gorilla. He says :—

"The largest of these ape monsters is called *Pongo*, in their language, and the lesser is called *Engeco*. This pongo is in all proportion like a man, but that he is more like a giant in stature than a man; for he is very tall and hath a man's face, hollow-eyed, with long haire upon his browes. His face and eares are without haire, and his hands also. His bodie is full of haire, but not very thicke, and of a dunnish colour. He differeth not from a man but in his legs, for they have no calfe. Hee goeth alwaies upon his legs, and carrieth his hands clasped on the nape of his necke, when he goeth upon the ground. They sleepe in the trees, and build shelters for the raine. They feed upon the fruit that they find in the woods, and upon nuts, for they eate no kind of flesh. They cannot speake, and have no more understanding than a beast. The people of the countrie, when they travaile in the woods, make fires where they sleepe in the night; and in the morning, when they are gone, the pongoes will come and sit about the fire till it goeth out, for they have no understanding to lay the wood together. They goe many together, and kill many negroes that travaile in the woods. . . . When they die among themselves, they cover the dead with great heapes of boughs and wood, which is commonly found in the forrests." (*Purchas*, vol. ii. p. 982.)

The engeco here mentioned is possibly the Chimpanzee. The gorilla was known to the Carthaginians. It is mentioned under this name in a Greek translation from the *Periplus*, or circumnavigation of Hanno the Carthaginian.

A Portuguese resident in Brazil, whose observations on that country are also recorded in Purchas's collection (vol. iv. p. 1302), gives a curious account of an ape king.

"The *Aquiqui* are very great apes, as bigge as a good sized dog, blacke, and very ougly, as well the male as the female. They have a great beard onely in the lower chap. Of these come sometimes a male one so yellow that it draweth toward red, which they say is their king. This hath a white face, and the beard from eare to eare as cut with the scissers; and it hath one thing much to be noted, namely, that he goeth into a tree, and maketh so great a noise that it is heard very farre off, in the which he continueth a great while without ceasing, and for this, this kind hath a particular instrument; and the instrument is a certaine hollow thing, as it were made of parchment, very strong, and so smooth that it serveth to burnish withall, as big as a duckes egge, and beginneth from the beginning of the gullet, till very neere the palate of the mouth betweene both the cheekes, and it is so light that as soone as it is toucht it moveth as the key of a virginals."

This species has been identified by modern travellers as the Mycetes, or Howling Monkey. According to some writers, the peculiar cry from which it derives its name may be heard at a distance of two miles.

Antonio de Herrera, in his description of the West Indies (*Purchas*, vol. i. p. 966), tells us that—

"throughout all the mountaines, either of these ilands of the firme land, or of the Andes, there are infinite numbers of *micos*, or monkeys, which are a kinde of apes, but very different, in that they have a taile, yea a very long one. And amongst them there are some kindes which are thrice, yea foure times bigger than the ordinarie; some are all blacke, some bay, some grey, and some spotted. Their agilitie and manner of doing is admirable, for that they seeme to have reason and discourse to goe upon trees, wherein they seeme to imitate birds."

John Leo, in his account of travels in Africa, says that the native name for the small kinds of apes which have tails is *Monne*, which may be the origin of the English name monkey; those without tails are called *Babuini* (*Purchas*, vol. ii. p. 847).

Another traveller, Wilson, who returned from Guiana in the year 1606, reports (*Purchas*, vol. iv. p. 1261), that "there are many monkies, great and small, blacke and greene, which sorts are called Marmosites."

Small monkeys seem to have been rather fashionable as pets, as well as forming a necessary part of the outfit of the itinerant showman. Ben Jonson has several allusions to them :—

"'Tis like your clog to your marmoset."
(*The Poetaster*, iv. 1.)

"He past, appears some mincing marmoset,
Made all of clothes and face."
(*Cynthia's Revels*, iii. 2.)

Drayton writes—

"What sports have we whereon our minds to set,
Our dog, our parrot, or our marmoset?"
(*England's Heroical Epistles.*)

Tubal sticks a dagger into his friend *Shylock* by telling him of a ring that a sailor had obtained from *Jessica* in exchange for a monkey:—

"*Shylock.* Out upon her! Thou torturest me, Tubal: it was my turquoise; I had it of Leah when I was a bachelor: I would not have given it for a wilderness of monkeys." (*Merchant of Venice*, iii. 1, 125.)

A monkey was also a common appendage of the domestic fool, or jester, and an appropriate companion in his gambols.

The wing-handed animal, the Bat, known also as the rere-mouse, or still more appropriately as the flitter-mouse, was a great puzzle to our forefathers. It was classed by them as *avis, non avis*, "bird and not bird." Nor was it until the close of the seventeenth century that it was placed with viviparous animals. It shared with the owl and the raven the reputation of foreboding misery and death to the inmates of the house where it entered, and was classed with these birds by Spenser:—

Bat.

" The ill-faste owle, death's dreadfull messengere;
The hoars night-raven, trump of dolefull drere;
The lether-winged bat, dayes enimy;
The ruefull strich, still waiting on the bere."
(*Faerie Queene*, ii., xii., 36.)

Ben Jonson speaks of—

"The giddy flitter-mice with leather wings!"
(*The Sad Shepherd*, ii. 2.)

And again—

"Once a bat, and ever a bat! a rere-mouse,
And bird of twilight."
(*The New Inn*, iii. 1.)

In 1626 Sir Thomas Herbert accompanied Sir Dodmore Cotton in an embassage to the Shah of Persia, and was so delighted with the strange scenes he witnessed in that country that he extended his visit, and spent four years in exploring the southern portion of Asia and part of Africa. On his return he published his travels. He is an amusing writer, and gives some lively descriptions of the curious sights he witnessed, and the difficulties he met with. In his account of certain strange creatures found in the island of Mauritius, he writes:—

"Bats are here in great numbers; but if my stomach deceive me not, worse meat cannot be tasted: a fierce ill-favour'd carrion, ever squeeking, and in offensive noise calling to one another, make bad melody. This is the onely four-footed beast that's volant, and therefore whether more properly to be raukt amongst birds or beasts, as yet undecided. . . . Bats, flying-fish and seals be participles of nature and species of a doubtful kind, participating both of bird and beast: these vespertilios, a large foot in length, hang in swarms upon the boughs of trees, by claws two inches long, fixed at the extream part of their wings, which are above twenty inches in length, their monkey faces in that posture ever turning downwards." (*Travels*, p. 385.)

The worthy knight was somewhat of an epicure, as appears from his constantly expressed opinion as to the flavour of the new dishes he was compelled by necessity to investigate, but he may be excused in this instance for not relishing his repast.

Sir Francis Drake, in his voyage into the South Seas, 1577 (*Hakluyt*, vol. iv. p. 244), finds, in an island southward of Celebes, a wonderful store of bats as big as large hens.

Bats were given to hawks as a remedy for certain maladies.

Of insect-eating animals, which are placed by modern naturalists next in order to the bats, only three representatives appear to have been known to our mediæval ancestors, the hedgehog, mole, and shrew.

Hedgehog.

The Hedgehog.

The Hedgehog, echinus, or urchin, is often mentioned by Shakspeare and other poets. Lyly declares of this little animal that he "evermore lodgeth in the thornes bicause he himself is so full of prickells" (*Euphues*, p. 373); and Chester, whose singular poem, *Love's Martyr*, has recently been edited by Dr. Grosart for the New Shakspere Society, says of him :—

> "The hedgehogge hath a sharpe quicke thorned garment,
> That on his backe doth serve him for defence :
> He can presage the winds incontinent,
> And hath good knowledge in the difference
>   Betweene the southerne and the northern wind,
>   These vertues are allotted him by kind.
>
> Whereon in Constantinople, that great city,
> A marchant in his garden gave one nourishment :
> By which he knew that winds true certainty,
> Because the hedgehogge gave him just presagement :
>   Apples, or pears, or grapes, such is his meate,
>   Which on his backe he carries for to eate."
>   (*Love's Martyr*, p. 111.)

Thomas Fuller, in his work, *The Worthies of England*, alludes to a superstition which has not yet died out in rural districts. Describing the county of Hertfordshire, he writes :—

"Plenty of hedgehogs are found in this high-woodland county, where too often they suck the kine, though the dayry-maids coune them small thanks for sparing their pains in milking them. A creature alwayes in his posture of defence, carrying a stand of pikes on his back, so that if as well victualled as armed, he may hold out a siege against any equal opposition." (Vol. ii. p. 426.)

Amongst other miseries inflicted upon him by his harsh taskmaster, *Caliban* complains of spirits—

> "Like hedgehogs which
> Lie tumbling in my barefoot way and mount
> Their pricks at my footfall."
>   (*Tempest*, ii. 2, 10.)

The Mole, moldwarp, or mouldiwarpe, as it is frequently called, must have been as common in earlier times as at present. The Rev. Edward Topsell was chaplain in the Church of Saint Botolph, Aldersgate, and the author of one of the most remarkable books of his age. He called his work *A Historie of Foure-Footed Beastes*, and added, that it was "necessary for all divines and students, because the story of every beast is amplified with narrations out of scriptures, fathers, phylosophers, physitians, and poets, collected out of all the volumes of Conradus Gesner and all other writers to this present day." This book was published in 1607. Though it abounds with marvellous stories, farfetched derivations of names, and absurd recipes, yet it is no mere compilation from the writings of others. Notwithstanding his amazing credulity on many points, the author is independent enough to decline to accept statements which are contradicted by his own observations. As regards the place of the mole in nature, he writes :—

"I do utterly dissent from all them that holde opinion that the mole or want is of the kinde of myse, for that all of them in generall, both one and other have two longe crooked fore-teeth which is not in moles, and therefore wanting those as the inseparable propriety of kind; we wil take it for graunted that it pertaineth not to that ranke or order of four-footed beasts." (Page 499.)

With respect to the name, he informs us that—

"the Italians retaine the latine word *talpa*, the Spaniards *topo*, by which word the Italians call a mouse. The French call it *taulpe*, the Germaines *mulwerf*, and in Saxon *molwurffe*, from whence is derived the English mole and molewarpe."

Topsell gives it as his opinion that though moles want their sight, yet they possess eyes, or rather, they have where the eyes should be, "a plaine and bald place of the skin." As a further proof of the perversity of this little animal, he adds that, though they have no ears, yet they hear perfectly in the earth.

The idea of the mole's blindness, still lingering in country districts, is often referred to by the Elizabethan poets. *Caliban* warns his companions to be silent:—

"Pray you, tread softly, that the blind mole may not
Hear a foot fall: we now are near his cell."
(*Tempest*, iv. 1, 195.)

"Ye work and work like moles, blind in the paths
That are bor'd thro' the crannies of the earth."
(FORD, *The Lover's Melancholy*, ii. 2.)

Sylvester, in his translation of Du Bartas' great work, *Divine Weekes and Workes*, published 1605, introduces the following simile:—

"Even as the soft, blinde, mine-inventing moule,
In velvet robes under the earth doth roule,
Refusing light, and little ayre receives,
And hunting worms her moving hillocks heaves."
(Ed. 1633, p. 186.)

In Burton's *Anatomy of Melancholy*, published 1621, we read:—

"Comfort thyself with other men's misfortunes, as the mouldiwarpe in Æsope told the fox for complaining of want of a tail, You complain of toies, but I am blind, be quiet." (Page 310, ed. 1837.)

Owen Glendower probably employed these little animals in his incantations. *Hotspur* replies to his uncle's lecture upon the impropriety of petulant impatience:—

"I cannot choose: sometime he angers me
With telling me of the moldwarp and the ant,
Of the dreamer Merlin and his prophecies."
(1 *Henry IV.*, iii. 1, 148.)

To Topsell we are indebted for an account of the Shrew, or the erdshrew:— Shrew.

"The word *hamaka* of the Hebrewes remembred in the second

chapter of Leviticus, is diversely interpreted by the translators, some call it a reptile beast which alwaies cryeth: some a reptile-flying beast, some a horse-leach, or bloud-sucker, some a hedghog, and some a beaver, as we have shewed before in the hedghog. But the Septuagints translate it *mygale*, and S. Jerom *mus araneus*, that is, a shrew. The Hollanders call it *moll musse*, because it resembleth a mole. . . . And concerning the description of this beast, it may be taken from the words of an auncient English phisition, called doctor William Turner. I have seene, saith he, in England, the shrew-mouse of colour blacke, having a taile very short, and her snout very long and sharp, and from the venomous biting of this beast, we have an English proverb or imprecation, I beshrow thee, when we curse or wish harm unto any man, that is, that some such evil as the biting of this mouse may come upon him. . . . It is a raveuing beast, feynging it selfe to be gentle and tame, but being touched it biteth deepe, and poisoneth deadly. It beareth a cruell minde, desiring to hurt any thing, neither is there any creature that it loveth, or it loveth him, because it is feared of all. The cats as we have saide do hunt it and kill it, but they eat not them, for if they do they consume away in time." (*Historie of Foure-Footed Beasts*, pp. 534–536.)

The character here attributed to this harmless little animal is not unlike that bestowed by the old chroniclers upon *Richard III*. It is quite undeserved by the British shrew, which feeds only on insects and grain. Some European varieties are more destructive, and will even eat small birds if opportunities offer.

CHAPTER II.

DEPOSED as he is by modern classification from the first place in the ranks, the Lion has from the earliest times reigned supreme and undisputed monarch of the animal kingdom. He has been endowed by poets with many virtues, most of them quite imaginary. Unlike some beasts of prey, he does not destroy for the mere pleasure of killing, and this forbearance has perhaps gained for him a reputation for clemency and magnanimity beyond his merits. Possibly one reason why the lion was credited with this generosity by the early intruders into his domain, was that his supply of provisions was still plentiful, and his larder in no danger of becoming empty; he could therefore afford to be generous, and he had not learned to fear man both on his own account and as a rival in the chase.

Lion.

Chester, writing in the time of Elizabeth, rather goes beyond the truth when he represents other animals deliberately giving up their prey to the animal monarch:

> "The princely lion, king of forrest-kings,
> And chiefe commaunder of the wildernesse,
> At whose faire feete all beasts lay down their offrings,
> Yielding allegiance to his worthinesse:
>   His strength remaineth most within his head,
>   His vertue in his heart is compassed."
>   (*Love's Martyr*, p. 112.)

Shakspeare seems to have completely adopted the

popular view of the lion's noble qualities, and to hold him in high estimation. *Richard's* queen tries to rouse her husband to more dignified conduct by reminding him that—

> " The lion dying thrusteth forth his paw,
> And wounds the earth, if nothing else, with rage
> To be o'erpower'd ; and wilt thou, pupil-like,
> Take thy correction mildly, kiss the rod,
> And fawn on rage with base humility,
> Which art a lion and a king of beasts ? "
> *(Richard II.,* v. 1, 29.)

And *Troilus* taunts *Hector* by aid of a comparison which is decidedly complimentary to the animal :—

> " Brother, you have a vice of mercy in you,
> Which better fits a lion than a man."
> *(Troilus and Cressida,* v. 3, 37.)

Ben Jonson introduces the lion occasionally :—

> " The Libyan lion hunts no butterflies,
> He makes the camel and dull ass his prize."
> *(Epigram on Inigo Jones.)*

By painters and writers on religious subjects the lion was employed as a symbol of strength, courage, nobility, and other lofty qualities, of which the companion and protector of Una is the personification.

In heraldry the lion was more frequently utilized than any other member of the animal kingdom, and it has from the earliest period been claimed as an appropriate emblem by English sovereigns. As denoting fortitude, it was usually placed, in Christian art, at the feet of martyrs, and was sculptured on the tombs of crusaders.

The frequent mention of the lion in English literature may arise from the fact that the somewhat mythical character attributed to him is exactly the same with which the English have always invested their heroes. This union of strength and courage with clemency and tenderness was the secret of Richard Cœur de Lion's popularity; and Shakspeare's lines on Edward the Black Prince—

"In war was never lion raged more fierce,
In peace was never gentle lamb more mild,
Than was that young and princely gentleman,"

may serve for a description of the men whom England in all times has delighted to honour.

Lions were kept in the Tower for the purpose of affording entertainment to the court by their combats. As they were expensive both to obtain and to keep, lion-baiting was a sport chiefly reserved for royalty. John Stow, in his record of the reign of James I., considers the birth of a young lion an event of sufficient importance to enter with great gravity in his *Chronicle* (p. 844): "Sunday, fift of August [1604], a lionesse named Elizabeth, in the Tower of London, brought forth a lyons whelpe, which lyons whelpe lived not longer than the next day." The next year he tells of a similar arrival, and gives as a reason for chronicling it that this was the first time that young lions had been born in Great Britain.

Topsell (p. 475) quotes from Crantzius a notable story of a lion in England, who by evident tokens was able to distinguish betwixt the king, nobles, and vulgar sort of people. Patrick Gordon of Ruthven, in a work, written about the year 1647, and reprinted by the Spalding Club in 1844, entitled, *A Short Abridgement of Britane's Distemper*, tells a story which, if it could only be believed, would confirm the theory that there was a close connexion between kings and lions:—

"It is constantly related by all, nor could I ever find it contradicted by any, that some little time after the kinges death [Charles I.] there ware sevin or eight gentlemen that went to the Towre to sie the lyons.... They were brought by the keiper near to their caiges, that they might looke in throw the barrs and sie them; when upon a sudden the *Old Harie*, a lyone called so after Henrie the Eight, because he had brought him their, began to blow, to snort, and to brissell his haire, and then to roare with such a terible and furious countenance, tearing the grats with his paws, as if he would have devored or torne them all in pieces; which made all to recoill bak, much affrighted, the keeper telling them seriously that he had never done the lyk befor, altho all sorts came daylie and saw him, and therefore he was perswaded that some one of them had done him ane injurie. They all swore they had not come near the grats of his cabin by more then a yeare: wherefor sieing him still to roare, to bray, and to become more furious, the keeper tells them that they must all goe furth, and he would call them in one by one, to sie if that way he could find furth the reasone. This was done; and behold, when they ware all gone, he groaned a little while and then was peaceable. Wherefor the keiper would neids try this conclusion; he bringes first in one of them and leids him to the grats, whereat the lyon made no sturre till one gentleman came in, whom he no sooner espyes, when he begines againe to raige, and become more furious than befor; wherefor the keiper, with an angrie countenance, beseeches him to tell what he had done. The gentleman, avoueing his owne innocencie, was yet much confounded to sie that terrible beast angrie with non but him; and having ruminate within himselfe of his former lyfe, at last he tells the keiper that he knew himself guiltie of nothinge except that he was on the skafold when the kinge was execute, and had dipt ane handkirtcheff in his blood, which he had yet in his pocket; and drawing it furth, gives it to the keiper, who threw it to the lyone; and he no sooner gets it, when, leaving his former roaring, he takes it betwixt his former feit, and fallinge growfflings to the ground, he laid his head on it, and never rose from that posture till hee died, which was the third day after. This discourse, because it seemed so onprobable, I kept up two years, before I would insert it in my Abridgment, yet could never find anie that opposed the trueth of it, but everie man avoued it to be reallie true." (Page 221.)

The sensitive nature of this centenarian lion must have been sorely tried by the frequent "deaths of kings" he had bewailed. We are not told of any acts of kindness on the part of English sovereigns which could account for this one-sided affection.

The Tiger was generally considered the personification of remorseless cruelty. *Lear* calls *Regan* and *Goneril* "tigers, not daughters;" and *York* calls his unrelenting foe, *Queen Margaret*,—

Tiger.

"O tiger's heart wrapt in a woman's hide!"

and declares that she is—

"More inhuman, more inexorable,
O, ten times more, than tigers of Hyrcania."
(3 *Henry VI.*, i. 4.)

The distinction drawn between the natures of the lion and tiger has little foundation in fact. The habits of both species are very similar. The tiger does occasionally destroy more than is sufficient to satisfy its hunger, but in general it is content with a single victim. The name Tiger was given by travellers and early writers on natural history to many species, some of which, like the jaguar, are undoubtedly more bloodthirsty than others. The character of the natives of the countries which these animals inhabit may have something to do with their respective attributes.

Oviedo, in an account of the West Indies, sent by him to the Emperor Charles V., in 1525 (*Purchas*, vol. iii. p. 990), describes the jaguar under the name of tiger. His misgivings as to the correctness of the name are well founded, as the range of the tiger is confined exclusively to Asia. He writes—

"In the Firme Land [S. America] are found many terrible beasts, which some think to be tigres. Which thing nevertheless I dare not affirme, considering what authors doe write of the lightnesse and agilitie of the tigre, whereas this beast, being otherwise in shape very like a tigre, is notwithstanding very slow."

The stealthy motion it frequently adopts in order to approach its victim, probably gave this writer the idea that the jaguar was a slow animal. Oviedo proceeds to point out that many creatures of undoubtedly the same species vary considerably in different parts of the world:—

"The sheepe of Arabie draw their tailes long and bigge on the ground, and the bulls of Egypt have their haire growing toward their heads, yet are those sheepe, and these buls. . . . Men, likewise, which in some countries are blacke, are in other places white: and yet are both these and they men.... My intent is onely to proove that this beast may be a tigre, or of the kinde of tigres, although it bee not of such lightnesse and swiftnesse, as are they whereof Plinie and other authors speake, describing it to bee one of the swiftest beasts of the land, and that the river of Tygris, for the swift course thereof, was called by that name. The first Spaniards, which saw this tygre in the Firme Land, did so name it. Of the kind of these was that which Don Diego Columbo, the admiral, sent your majestie out of New Spaine to Toledo. Their heads are like to the heads of lions, or lionesses, but greater: the rest of their bodies and their legs are full of black spots, one neere unto another, and divided with a circumference, or fringe of red colour, shewing (as it were) a faire work and correspondent picture. About their croopes or hinder parts they have these spots biggest, and lesse and lesse toward their bellies, legs, and heads. I have seen some of three spans in height, and more than five in length. They are beasts of great force, with strong legs, and well armed with nayles and fanges which we call dog-teeth: they are so fierce that in my judgment no reall lyon of the biggest sort is so strong or fierce."

As this author is so precise in his description, it is somewhat strange that he should fail to notice the chief difference between this animal and the tiger. Even the rudest and the most heraldic drawing of a tiger must have had stripes and not spots.

By early writers the Leopard, pard, or pardale, and the Panther, were considered to be two distinct animals, though these authors made no attempt to show in what particulars the difference existed. Modern naturalists are of opinion that there is but one species. Leopards may no doubt vary in size and shape according to the locality in which they are found. In Christian art the leopard was symbolized as the representative of perseverance in evil. This idea is prominent in the interpretations of the passage in *Jeremiah*, "Can the Ethiopian change his skin, or the leopard his spots?" It may be that Shakspeare had this verse in mind when he wrote—" Lions make leopards tame," " Yea, but not change their spots." (*Richard II.*, i. 1, 175.)

The conventional lion of heraldic artists was supposed

to exist in a chronic state of dignified rage. This condition could be best depicted by the attitude known in heraldry as *rampant*. In profile only could due prominence be given to teeth, claws, and tail. When for the sake of variety or economy of space the lion was represented as *passant gardant*, or walking, with his face turned to the spectator, he was called a *lion-leopardé*, to denote that his ferocity was partially subdued. When *rampant gardant* he was a *leopard-lionné*. The charge of *three lions leopardé*, which now appears on the escutcheon of England, was first borne by *Richard I*. This nomenclature gave rise to some confusion, and for a time the notion existed that leopards had a place in the English arms. It was not until the middle of the fifteenth century that the animals on the royal shield were blazoned as " lions."

The leopard, or panther, of antiquity was chiefly remarkable for the sweetness of his breath, which was supposed to have an attraction for other animals. Ben Jonson has several allusious to this fancy:—

" You have a tongue steeped in honey, and a breath like a panther."
(Cynthia's Revels, v. 2.)

Other poets write :—

" The panther so,
Breathes odors pretious as the sarmaticke gums
Of Easterne groves, but the delicious sent,
Not taken in at a distance, choakes the sense
With the too muskie savour."
(GLAPTHORNE, *The Hollander.*)

" Your grace is bound
To hunt the spotted panther to his ruin,
Whose breath is only sweet to poison virtue."
(SHIRLEY, *The Royal Master.*)

Sir William Segar (Harleian MS. 6085) tells us:—

" The panther is admired of all other beasts for the beauty of his skyn, being spotted with variable colours, and beloved and followed of them for the sweetness of his breath, that streameth forth of his nostrils and ears like smoke, which our paynters mistaking, corruptly doe make fire."

By painters this author probably meant heraldic artists. The correct blazonry of a panther has flames issuing from the mouth and ears. When thus depicted it is termed "incensed." The looks of this animal were supposed to have a most baneful influence.

> " The panther, knowing that his spotted hyde
> Doth please all beasts, but that his looks them fray,
> Within a bush his dreadful head doth hide,
> To let them gaze while he on them may prey."
> (SPENSER, *Sonnet* 53.)

Mr. Elvin, in *Anecdotes of Heraldry*, 1864 (p. 59), tells the following story :—

"In the early part of the reign of Henry VIII. a leopard, which had been presented to Sir John Giffard of Chillington, escaped from her cage, and was pursued by the knight, bow in hand, accompanied by his son. Having hurried to the top of a steep ascent, nearly a mile from his house, Sir John overtook the beast as it was about to spring upon a woman with an infant; and as, in his still breathless state, he was preparing to shoot at it, his son, fearing his haste might weaken the force of the shot, called out, 'Preigne haleine, tire fort.' Sir John paused, took breath, drew his bow strongly with a sure aim, killed the leopard, and saved the woman. To this day the Giffards of Chillington bear as their crest a leopard's head and an archer with bended bow, whilst the words ' Preigne haleine, tire fort,' form the family motto."

Sir John Mandeville, in his *Travels*, written about the year 1350, mentions the small hunting leopard, or cheetah, employed in Cyprus :—

"In Cipre men hunten with papyonns, that ben lyche lepardes, and thei taken wylde bestes right welle, and thei ben somdelle more then lyouns; and thei taken more scharpely the bestes and more delyverly than don houndes." (Page 29.)

Puma.

The Puma was considered by the early colonists of the New World to be merely a degenerate variety of the lion, and was spoken of by them under that name. The puma is especially to be met with in the more tropical regions of America, though its range extends over the whole continent.

The Ounce, a native of some parts of Asia, according to modern authorities, is mentioned as an inhabitant of Brazil by a Portuguese who had long lived there. With that confusion of pronouns which characterizes writers of the Elizabethan period, he says:—

Ounce.

"There are many ounces, some blacke, some grey, some speckled. It is a very cruell beast, and fierce. They assault men exceedingly, that even on the trees they cannot escape them, especially if they be bigge. When they are flesht there is none that dare abide them, especially by night. They kill many beasts at once, they spoile a whole hen-house, or a heard of swine; and to open a man, or whatsoever beast, it sufficeth to hit him with one of his clawes. . . . The Indians use the heads for trumpets, and the Portugall women use the skinnes for rugs or coverlets." (*Purchas*, vol. i. p. 1301.)

The early explorers seem to have been somewhat puzzled by the different varieties of the leopard tribe, and this much-dreaded animal may have been the jaguar or puma. Du Bartas, in his poem on the Creation, alludes to—

"The cat-fac'd ounce, that doth me much dismay,
With grumbling horror threatens my decay."
(*Divine Weekes and Workes*, 6th day, p. 50.)

Shakspeare has but one reference to this animal:—

"Be it ounce, or cat, or bear,
Pard, or boar with bristled hair."
(*Midsummer Night's Dream*, ii. 2, 30.)

Topsell says that he can follow no better author in the description of this animal than Dr. Caius, who evidently wrote from personal observation:—

"The ounce is a most cruel beast, of the quantity of a village or mastiffe dog, having his face and ears like to a lyons, his body, taile, feet, and nails like a cat, of a very terrible aspect, his teeth so strong and sharpe that he can cut wood in sunder with them."

After a long description of the appearance of the ounce, and the exact place and number of most of his spots, the doctor proceeds:—

"It liveth on flesh, and the female is more cruell then the male, though lesser, and one of either sex was brought out of Mauritania into England in a ship, for they are bred in Libia. When they are angry they utter a voice like an angry dog, but they double the arr twice, and also bigger then any dogs, proceeding out of a large breast and wide arteries, much like to the howling of a great mastive, that is shut up in a close roome alone against his will. Some say that it is longer then a dog, but it did not so appeare in England, for we had many mastive dogs as long as it, but yet was it every way greater then any other kind of dogs." (*Historie of Four-Footed Beasts*, 1607, p. 570.)

Cat. The Wild Cat is the true English cat. It was common in this country in the Middle Ages. Its fur was much used as a trimming for dresses and other articles of clothing. Like the marten it was frequently hunted for the sake of its skin, and so long ago as the time of Richard II. an abbot of Peterborough obtained a charter granting him permission to hunt cats. It has now become entirely extinct in England, though in the wilder parts of Scotland it is not uncommon.

The domestic "harmless necessary cat" has no connexion with the above, and was introduced to us from the East in early times. Some varieties may have been brought over by the Crusaders, but the original home of the species seems to have been Persia. In Wales the cat was held in great estimation. It was enacted by Howel Dha, "the Good," that the price of a kitten before it could see was to be a penny; if it caught a mouse its value was raised to twopence, and afterwards to fourpence. If any one stole or killed a cat that guarded the prince's granary, the offender was compelled either to forfeit a ewe, or as much wheat as would cover the cat when suspended by its tail.

Topsell (p. 106) writes of the cat with the interest of intimate personal acquaintance:—

"It is needlesse to spend any time about her loving nature to man, how she flattereth by rubbing her skinne against ones legges, how she whurleth with her voyce, having as many tunes as turnes; for she hath one voice to beg and to complain, another to testifie her delight and pleasure, another among hir own kind by flattring, by hissing, by spitting, insomuch as some have thought that they have a peculiar intelligible language among themselves."

Topsell also notices the various peculiarities of the cat, her dislike to water, her fondness for dwellings rather than persons:—

"Although their maisters forsake their houses yet will not these beastes heare them company, and being carried forth in close baskets or sackes, they will yet returne againe or loose themselves. As this beaste has beene familiarly nourished of many, so have they payed deare for their love, being requited with the losse of their health, and sometimes of their life for their friendship; and worthily, they who love beasts in a high measure, have so much the lesse charity unto man."

This last remark is not without truth; but the author is somewhat vague as to the injuries inflicted by the cat on its benefactor.

It has been said that the cat owed the consecration and divine honours it received among the Egyptians to a peculiar physical attribute, the power of contracting and dilating the pupil of the eye, exhibiting so mysterious a representation of the moon's changes, as to give rise to the notion that the animal was in some degree under the influence of that luminary, and therefore to be propitiated.

The absence of any mention of the cat in the Bible, except in the Apocrypha, is probably owing to the veneration of this animal by the Egyptians. The Jews would naturally have unpleasant associations both with dogs and cats, as animals that they had seen idolized during their captivity in the land of Pharaoh. But fondness for animals of any kind seems to have been entirely wanting among the Jews. In every early history, except the Bible, we meet with some allusion to a favourite horse, or dog, or tame gazelle. No wonder Jessica, freed from the trammels of her Jewish home, could give a turquoise ring for a monkey!

Another explanation as to the singular scarcity of allusions to animal life in the Bible may be suggested. The Jews appear to have been quite indifferent to the beauties of nature. The only traces of admiration of the external world are found in the writings of Job and Solomon. Job was not of Hebrew birth, and Solomon had by his large knowledge gained a wider sympathy with nature than his compatriots. It is almost incredible that a nation should wander for forty years through lands rich enough to furnish pasture for vast flocks and herds, materials for clothing, ornament, and manufactures, and that the chronicle of their Exodus should be absolutely deficient in a single reference to the rich animal life around them. Many species of birds and animals are indeed mentioned, but only to be avoided as unclean. From the list of creatures that might not be used as food, we gather the only information from a Jewish source respecting the fauna of Arabia or Palestine.

A similar disregard of natural beauty exists in the Mohammedan scriptures. The poetry of nature animates every other mythology. Love of beauty led the Greeks to personify the waterfall and the rainbow, to find dryads in trees, nereids in running brooks, altars in stones, and gods in everything. The Grecian deities were surrounded in the imagination of their worshippers with all that was strong or lovely in nature. Zeus had his princely eagle; Phœbus, his dappled coursers; ox-eyed Hera, her peacock train; whilst Aphrodite was born of the ocean froth, and Pan sat hidden in the tangled thickets. Even in the religion of the frozen North we find a loving sympathy with external nature. The sacred ash-tree that spread its roots to encircle the world; the frisking squirrel; the croaking raven, whispering tidings into Odin's ear; the ferocious wolf; even the little mistletoe that was "too young to swear,"—all were woven into the Scandinavian mythology, and added a reality and beauty to the Norse belief.

The pertinacity of the cat in contending fiercely against all efforts to deprive it of liberty caused this animal to be chosen by the Dutch as their ensign. It was an appropriate emblem for a nation that so long and so valiantly struggled for independence.

The cat plays a conspicuous part in the story of *Dick Whittington*. Modern folk-lore Dryasdusts would have us believe that the ship which contained the merchandise of the young City apprentice was called *The Cat*, and that thence arose the legend. Something of this sceptical spirit is to be found in the writings of Shakspeare's time: "When the famous fable of *Whittington and his Puss* shall be forgotten." (*Eastward Hoe*, v. 1.)

Both Shakspeare and Lyly use the proverbial comparison, "As melancholy as a cat," though it does not seem a specially appropriate simile.

In *Jacob and Esau*, an interlude, 1568, we find the nickname *Puss*. Mido exclaims—

"But Esau beguil'd me, I shrew him for that,
And left not so much as a lick for Puss our cat."

This name occurs again in Middleton:—

"I shall be moused by puss-cats, but I had rather die a dog's death: they have nine lives apiece, like a woman, and they will make it up ten lives, if they and I fall a scratching." (*Blurt, Master Constable*, iv. 2.)

Tib, from the French Thibert, and *Gib* from Gilbert, the Northern name for a male cat, were as usual names for the cat, as *Tom* is in our own time.

Though the strange cures and remedies attributed by

mediæval physicians to various animals have no rightful place in natural history, yet the account of the medicinal virtues of the cat, as recorded by Topsell, is too grotesque to be omitted. He writes—

"For the pain and blindness in the eye, by reason of any skins, webs, or nails, this is an approved medicine : take the head of a black cat, which hath not a spot of another colour in it, and burn it to powder in an earthen pot, leaded or glazed within; then take this powder and, through a quill, blow it thrice a day into thy eye; and if in the night any heat do thereby annoy thee, take two leaves of an oke, wet in cold water, and bind them to the eye, and so shall all pain flie away, and blindness depart, although it hath oppressed thee a whole year: and this medicine is approved by many physicians both elder and later." (Page 83.)

Lynx. The Lynx has a wide range. It is met with in Asia, Africa, and America. The European lynx is an animal of Northern origin. It is mentioned under the name of lyserne, by Doctor Giles Fletcher, in his account of Russia in 1588 (*Purchas*, vol. iii. p. 417). In a description of the device of a pageant borne before Woolstone Dixi, Lord Mayor of London, 1585, a speech is given that is "spoken by him that rid on a luzarne, before the pageant, apparelled like a More.

"'From where the sun dooth settle in his wayn
And yoakes his horses to his fiery carte,
And in his way gives life to Ceres corne,
Even from the parching zone, behold, I come,
A straunger, straungely mounted, as you see,
Seated upon a lusty luzern's back;
And offer to your honour, good my lord,
This emblem thus in showe significant.'"
(*Harleian Miscellany*, vol. x. p. 351.)

The lynx is here called a tropical animal. The name *luzarne*, or *lozarde*, is derived by Minsheu from the French "loup cervier." Olaus Magnus (*History of Scandinavia*, p. 182) has a short account of the lynx:—

"In the northern woods the lynxes are not so commonly bred as wolves, though they are as greedy as these. The nature of the lynx is never to look back, but he always runs and leaps forward. The meat he commonly or chiefly eats is wild cats; and as he most willingly feeds on them, so he always lyes in wait about their holes to catch them. The skins of them, as they are framed with light down, and rare spots, are sold very dear, especially such as are taken in the most sharp winter, for then their colour and virtue is best, but in summer they are far worse."

The fur of this animal was held in high estimation in England. In the inventory of the goods of the Duke of Richmond, 1527, occurs mention of a gown of crimson damask, furred with luzardes.

The lynx was credited by ancient writers with such wonderful acuteness of vision that it could see through a stone wall. If, as Magnus asserts, its principal diet was wild cats, the powers of sight and agility possessed by the lynx must have been fully exercised.

Topsell (p. 490) quotes from Dr. Caius a description of an individual of this species, which, at the time the latter wrote (1550), was in the Tower collection.

" In the top of his eares there are placed some blacke haires, as it were a foretop or tuft. The colour of this beast in the outmost parts is red, in the innermost white, but sprinkled here with blacke spots and almost by rowes, and there with spots somewhat lighter then the other, all his haire being for the most part white all over all his body except the aforesaid spottes, as it is in certaine skinnes of young conies. And on both the sides of his nose there are foure spots set in order. . . . He doth climbe wonderfully, so that what he may be able to do in that thinge, either in his cave or den, nature her selfe doth teach : he is a quicke-mooving creature, and cannot stand still in a place, so that except, by meer chance, the voice of a woodpecker in the basket of a certaine country man, who came then onely to see the lyone, had made him quiet and attentive, there had bene no hope of the portraiting out the picture of his body. He being present he was most quyet : but he going away, hee would never stande still : wherefore I was constrained to send my man after the countrey man to buy the birde, which beeing present, he stood very still until the busines was dispatched and the worke absolutely performed. . . . Our country men call it luzarne, it is doubtfull whether we should call it leunce, or lynx, in the affinity of the words. His skinne is used by noblemen, and is sold for a great price. He is angry at none but them which offer him injury. His voice is like a cat's, when he would snatch away the food from his fellow. He is loving and gentle unto his keeper, and not cruell unto any man."

Civet. The Civet was found in Africa and India. By some writers it was called the hyæna, by others the musk cat. The only resemblance between the civet and a cat lies in the shape of the ears and some strong whisker-like hairs. A Frenchman, who wrote a *Commentary on Du Bartas* (p. 264), tells us that—

"Belon, in the second booke of his singularities, the twentieth chapter, holdeth that the hyena of the ancients is the civet, which is somewhat greater then a badger, with a pointed muzzell, having mustachies, her eyes shining and red, her eares round, with two black spots, her body spotted with black and white, her feete and tayle blacke: she liveth upon flesh, and is very nimble, but that which Pliny saith, seemeth to allude to some beast more strange and savage."

The perfume obtained from the civet was formerly valued as a medicine, and realized a high price. It was also an indispensable article in the toilet of a fop. Among the other changes in *Benedick's* appearance, *Don Pedro* notices, "A' rubs himself with civet: can you smell him out by that?" to which *Claudio* adds, "That's as much as to say, The sweet youth's in love." (*Much Ado*, iii. 2, 50.)

Ichneumon. The Ichneumon was sometimes called the Indian mouse, or Pharaoh's rat. Its life history is so closely connected with that of the crocodile that nothing further need be said of it in this place.

Hyæna. The Hyæna was the scavenger of the East, and from its fondness for carrion, which led it to rifle graveyards, it was always regarded with feelings of horror and disgust. There was a notion that it could imitate the voice of a man. Lyly (*Euphues*, p. 110) writes, "Hiena, when she speaketh lyke a man deviseth most mischief."

Sir Kenelm Digby, who is somewhat of a Darwinian in his suggestions as to the mode in which various creatures may have acquired their different ways of escaping capture and obtaining food, thus accounts for the hyæna's mode of proceeding :—

"That the jaccatray, or hyæna, when he is hungry, should have his fantasy call out from his memory the images of those beasts which use to serve him in that occasion, is the ordinary course of nature : and that together with those images, there should like wise come along the actions and soundes which used to accompany them, and are lodged together with them in the memory, is also naturall; then, as little strange it is, that by his owne voice he should imitate those soundes, which at that time do so powerfully possesse his imagination : and having a great docility in those organes which forme the voice, like a parrat, he representeth them so lively, that the deceived beasts flock to him, and so are caught by him: which at the first happeneth by chance, but afterwardes by memory." (*A Treatise of Bodies*, ed. 1644, p. 314.)

Hence it would follow that the hyæna which had the best memory, and could imitate the largest number of beasts, would have the greatest chance of a dinner.

Topsell (p. 434) has, as usual, something marvellous to add as to the structure of this animal :—

"Their back bone stretcheth it selfe out to the head, so as the necke cannot bend except the whole body be turned about, and therefore whensoever he hath occasion to wry his necke, he must supply that qualitie by removing of his whole bodie."

Mr. Harting, in his *Extinct British Animals*, 1880, has completely refuted the popular notion that Wolves were exterminated in England and Wales in consequence of the tribute imposed upon the latter country by King Edgar in the year 965, and has traced the history of the wolf in Great Britain. From his account, which is derived both from historical evidence and from tradition, we find that no wolf is reported to have been seen in England later than the reign of Henry VII. In Scotland wolves were plentiful till the beginning of the seventeenth century, and stray specimens were killed in that country at a still more recent date. In Ireland these animals were so numerous, that as late as Cromwell's time a law was passed prohibiting the exportation of wolf-dogs.

Of all evils that from time to time have sprung from purely imaginary sources, none was more terrible in its results than the strange hallucination known as lycanthropy (from *lycos*, a wolf, and *anthropos*, a man), or wolf-madness. Men and women believed that by supernatural agency they could transform themselves for a certain period into wolves. Human beings, when under this delusion, roamed through forests and desert places actuated by the same passions as the wild beasts whose name they bore. They howled, walked on all fours, tore up graves in search of prey, attacked unarmed passengers, devoured children, and committed the wildest excesses. Mr. Baring-Gould, in his *Book of Were-Wolves*, 1865, has traced this frightful superstition back to the very earliest times. The origin of the were-wolf myth may be found in the dread of wolves experienced by the early pastoral inhabitants of various countries, and in the natural tendency of the human mind to attribute every physical evil to superhuman power. The hurricane, the waterspout, the volcano, were universally supposed to be animated by some demon; consequently, we find werewolf legends in countries as far asunder as Norway and India, and they may be discovered in almost every country whose forests were extensive enough to harbour wolves in formidable numbers. The myth varies, indeed, among different nations according to the particular animal by which the flocks were molested. That it is seldom alluded to in English folk-lore is due to the early destruction of wolves, and the consequent cessation of dread on their account. The more harmless cat and dog are substituted for the wolf in the various witchcraft stories.

In the Middle Ages lycanthropy seems to have spread like an epidemic. In the year 1600 the inhabitants of the Jura were attacked by this disease, and numbers of men and women formed themselves into packs and hunted through the country, spreading terror and destruction. This superstition lingers to-day among the ignorant peasantry in Southern France, where the "loup garou" is still an object of intense alarm to the belated traveller. A modified form of this disease still exists as hydrophobia.

A curious account is given of the midnight meetings and orgies of were-wolves by the Norwegian chronicler, Olaus Magnus:—

"In the feasts of Christ's nativity, in the night, at a certain place that they are resolved upon amongst themselves, there is gathered together such a huge multitude of wolves changed from men that dwell in divers places, which afterwards the same night doth so rage with wonderful fiercenesse, both against mankind and other creatures that are not fierce by nature, that the inhabitants of that country suffer more hurt from them than ever they do from true natural wolves. . . . They go into beer-cellars, and there they drink out some tuns of beer or mede, and they heap all the empty vessels one upon another in the midst of the cellar, and so leave them: wherein they differ from natural and true wolves. And it is constantly affirmed that amongst that multitude there are the great men and chiefest nobility of the land. The reason of this metamorphosis, that is exceeding contrary to nature, is given by one skilled in this witchcraft, by drinking to one in a cup of ale, and by mumbling certain words at the same time, so that he who is to be admitted into that unlawful society do accept it. Then, when he pleaseth, he may change his human form into the form of a wolf entirely. Again, he can alter the form he had before at his pleasure. It is fresh in memory how the Duke of Prussia, giving small credit to such a witchcraft, compelled one who was cunning in this sorcery, whom he held in chains, to change himself into a wolf, and he did so. Yet, that he might not go unpunished for his idolatry, he afterwards caused him to be burnt." (*History of Scandinavia*, p. 193.)

The Norwegian word "berserker," meaning a man possessed of superhuman powers and subject to accesses of diabolical fury, was originally applied to doughty champions who went about wrapped in bear-skins, or who wore habits made of bear-skin over their armour. These warriors, writes Mr. Baring-Gould (p. 45), were often dressed in wolf-skins, and it was an easy transition to imagine these unscrupulous destroyers of the public peace as possessing the strength as well as the ferocity of the animals whose skins they wore. Among the Anglo-Saxons an outlaw was said to have the head of a wolf, and the legal form of sentence against the offender was that "he shall be driven away as a wolf and chased so far as men chase wolves farthest."

Reginald Scot, in his work on witchcraft, 1584, relates some stories as to the power of men to change themselves into wolves and other animals, but treats them with great ridicule. He concludes his chapter on these transformations with the remark—

"But I have put twenty of these witchmongers to silence with this one question, to wit, whether a witch that can turn a woman into a cat, etc., can also turn a cat into a woman?" (*Discovery of Witchcraft*, ed. 1654, p. 70.)

There are numerous stories of unfortunate men and women being hanged or burnt for ravages imagined to be committed by them in their lupine shape. In France and Italy these executions occurred even so late as the year 1684.

Trials of animals for crimes and misdemeanors prompted by simple natural depravity were also frequent in Europe in the Middle Ages. According to a writer in *Notes and Queries* (3rd series, vol. v. p. 218), a sow, in 1403, killed and devoured a child at Meulan. All the forms of law were carried out, and the bill of costs was duly chronicled. A treatise was published so late as 1668, by Gaspard Bailly, a lawyer at Chambery, on legal proceedings against animals, with forms of indictments and modes of pleading. Nothing corresponding to this occurs in English tradition, but, in one sense, animals here were proceeded against in cases of their killing, accidentally or otherwise, a human being. For instance, if a horse should strike his keeper, and so kill him, the horse was to be a deodand. He was to be sold, and his price given to the poor in expiation of the calamity and for the appeasing of the Divine wrath. It is curious to note that these statutes have only been repealed in the present century.

These trials probably had their origin in the Levitical law, as propounded in the twenty-first chapter of Exodus. Here we find that the punishment of the owner of an ox that had gored a man or a woman varied according to the rank of the individual, but in every case the ox was to be put to death by the cruel process of stoning, and its flesh was prohibited as food.

Topsell tells how some lions, which had grown so bold that they would attack men, were turned into scarecrows as a warning to their fellows:

"Polybius affirmeth that he saw them besiege and compasse about many citties of Affricke, and therefore the people tooke and hanged them up upon crosses and gallowses by the high waies to the terror of others." (Page 464.)

The following passage in *The Merchant of Venice* (iv. 1) suggests the inquiry whether Shakspeare wittingly or by error of memory applied this punishment to man-eating wolves:—

"*Gratiano.* O, be thou damn'd, inexecrable dog!
And for thy life let justice be accus'd.
Thou almost mak'st me waver in my faith,
To hold opinion with Pythagoras,
That souls of animals infuse themselves
Into the trunks of men: thy currish spirit
Govern'd a wolf, who, hang'd for human slaughter,
Even from the gallows did his fell soul fleet,
And, whilst thou lay'st in thy unhallow'd dam,
Infus'd itself in thee; for thy desires
Are wolfish, bloody, starved, and ravenous."

Shakspeare may have had the passage from his great authority, Holinshed, in his mind when he wrote thus:—

"For, said they [Plato and others] (of whom Pythagoras also had, and taught this errour), if the soule apperteined at the first to a king, and he in this estate did not leade his life worthie his calling, it should, after his decease, be shut up in the bodie of a slave, begger, cocke, owle, dog, ape, horsse, asse, worme, or monster, there to remaine as in a place of purgation and punishment, for a certcine period of time. Beside this, it should peradventure susteine often translation from one bodie to another, according to the quantitie and qualitie of his dooings here on earth, till it should finallie be purified and restored againe to an other humane bodie." (*Chronicles*, vol. i. p. 35.)

James Howell, in his *Familiar Letters*, 1624 (p. 169, ed. 1754), tells the following anecdote of a Scotch piper and wolves:—

"A pleasant tale I heard Sir Thomas Fairfax relate of a soldier in Ireland, who having got his passport to go for England, as he passed through the wood with his knapsack upon his back, being weary, he sat down under a tree, where he opened his knapsack, and fell to some victuals he had; but on a sudden he was surprized with two or three wolves, who coming towards him, he threw them scraps of bread and cheese, till all was gone; then the wolves making a nearer approach to him he knew not what shift to make, but by taking a pair of bagpipes which he had, and as soone as he began to play upon them, the wolves ran all away as if they had been scared out of their wits: whereupon the soldier said, A pox take you all, if I had known you had loved music so well, you should have had it before dinner."

The habit of the wolf of howling by moonlight is alluded to by Shakspeare, "'Tis like the howling of Irish wolves against the moon" (*As You Like It*, v. 2, 118), and by Lyly, "I am none of those wolves that barke most when thou [the moon] shinest brightest" (*Endimion*).

The Jackal is not often mentioned in old writings.

Jackal. Richard Jobson, in some observations touching the river Gambia (*Purchas*, vol. ii. p. 1575), describes this animal's mode of hunting:—

"They have many lions, hardly seene by day, easily knowne by night, by reason of his ushers or fore-runners the jackall, sometimes two or three, which is a little blacke shag-haired beast, of the bignesse of a small spaniell; which when evening comes hunts for his prey, and comming on the foote, followes the scent with open crie : to which the lion as chiefe hunt, gives diligent eare, following for his advantage. If the jackall set up his chase before the lion comes in, he howles out maynly, and then the lion seiseth on it, making a grumbling noyse, whiles his servant stands by barking (as we not onely heard of the countrey people, but might heare our selves riding at anchor by night in our passing up the river). When the lion hath done, this attendant feeds on the relikes."

CHAPTER III.

Dog. WHILE Shakspeare has admiration to bestow on the "awless lion" and the "princely eagle," he has in no one instance mentioned with appreciation the moral qualities of the dog. Sporting dogs he certainly describes with spirit, if not affection; but "to snarl, and bite, and play the dog," appears to him the normal condition of the domestic animal. The poet must have been singularly unfortunate in his experience of the canine race, for his allusions are almost all of an unfavourable nature. Sir Henry Holland, in his *Recollections of Past Life* (p. 254), tells us that Lord Nugent, the greatest Shakspearian scholar of his day, declared that no passage was to be found in Shakspeare, "commending, directly or indirectly, the moral qualities of the dog." A bet of a guinea was made, which Sir Henry, after a year's search, paid. This was before the publication of Mrs. Cowden Clarke's concordance. The only passage which could have had a chance of winning the wager is the speech of *Timon* :—

"*Tim.* Who, without those means thou talk'st of, didst thou ever know beloved ?
Apem. Myself.
Tim. I understand thee ; thou hadst some means to keep a dog."
(*Timon of Athens*, iv. 3, 113.)

Lear asks of *Gloucester*—

"*Lear.* Thou hast seen a farmer's dog bark at a beggar?
Glou. Ay, sir.
Lear. And the creature run from the cur? There thou might'st behold the great image of authority : a dog's obeyed in office."
(*King Lear*, iv. 6, 158.)

Professor Huxley, sad to say, in his recent work on Hume, endorses Shakspeare's opinion as to the total depravity of dog nature. He writes :—

"One of the most curious peculiarities of the dog mind is its inherent snobbishness, shown by the regard paid to external respectability. The dog who barks furiously at a beggar will let a well-dressed man pass him without opposition. Has he not then a 'generic idea' of rags and dirt associated with the idea of aversion, and that of sleek broadcloth associated with the idea of liking?" (*Hume*, 1879, p. 106.)

May not this distinction of persons be due to snobbishness on the part of the owners of dogs, to education, rather than to any natural tendency? A lady, who was in the habit of giving food to all who asked, saw her dog go to the open bread-pan, take out half a loaf, and give it to a beggar. What had become of this dog's "inherent snobbishness"?

The beautiful description of Argus in the *Iliad*, so pathetic in its simplicity, shows that appreciation of the good qualities of the dog is not entirely of modern origin. Chester, a writer contemporary with Shakspeare, pays the following tribute to the attachment of the animal to its master :—

"The dogge, a naturall, kind, and loving thing,
As witnesseth our histories of old :
Their master dead, the poore foole with lamenting
Doth kill himself before accounted bold :
 And would defend his maister if he might,
 When cruelly his foe begins to fight."
(*Love's Martyr*, ed. New Shak. Soc., 1878, p. 110.)

Doubtless some of the evil report attaching to dogs

has descended to them in consequence of certain passages in the Bible. In the Old Testament this animal is generally spoken of as being, what he still is in Oriental countries, a shy, greedy, mean-spirited creature, uncared for, and left to dwell among the refuse of the city. Had he been in any way the companion of man, the dog must have been more favourably mentioned.

Ben Jonson is not much more complimentary to the dog than Shakspeare. In one play he writes:—

> " O, 'tis an open-throated, black-mouthed cur,
> That bites at all, but eats on those that feed him;
> A slave, that to your face will, serpent-like,
> Creep on the ground, as he would eat the dust,
> And to your back will turn the tail, and sting
> More deadly than a scorpion."
> (*Every Man out of his Humour*, i. 1.)

But in another play he makes some amends by reporting how, when *Sabinus*, by order of the tyrant, *Sejanus*, was thrown into the river Tiber,—

> "His faithful dog, upbraiding all us Romans,
> Never forsook the corpse, but seeing it thrown
> Into the stream, leaped in, and drowned with it."
> (*Sejanus*, iv. 5.)

The writer Churchyard thus classifies the dog:—

> "A Turk, a Jew, a Pagan, and a dog."

Sir John Davies, in an epigram, ridicules the prevalent fancy for making unmeaning comparisons between unpopular individuals and dogs, and shows a truer appreciation of the "friend of man" than his contemporaries.

> "Thou doggèd Cineas, hated like a dog,
> For still thou grumblest like a mastiff dog,
> Compar'st thyself to nothing but a dog:
> Thou say'st thou art as weary as a dog,
> As angry, sick, and hungry as a dog,
> As dull, and melancholy as a dog,

As lazy, sleepy, and as idle as a dog;
But why dost thou compare thee to a dog,
In that for which all men despise a dog?
I will compare thee better to a dog:
Thou art as fair and comely as a dog,
Thou art as true and honest as a dog,
Thou art as kind and liberal as a dog,
Thou art as wise and valiant as a dog."
(*Marlowe's Works*, ed. Cunningham, p. 265.)

In the play by Thomas Nash, *Summer's Last Will and Testament*, printed in the year 1600, *Orion*, the hunter, thus answers a tirade of *Autumn* against his hounds:—

"A tedious discourse built on no ground,
A silly fancy, Autumn, hast thou told,
Which no philosophy doth warrantise,
No old-received poetry confirms.
I will not grace thee by refuting thee;
Yet, in a jest, since thou rail'st so 'gainst dogs,
I'll speak a word or two in their defence.
That creature's best that comes most near to men;
That dogs of all come nearest, thus I prove:
First, they excel us in all outward sense,
Which no one of experience will deny:
They hear, they smell, they see better than we.
To come to speech, they have it questionless,
Although we understand them not so well,
They bark as good old Saxon as may be,
And that in more variety than we.
For they have one voice when they are in chase:
Another when they wrangle for their meat:
Another when we beat them out of doors."
(*Dodsley's Old Plays*, ed. Hazlitt, vol. 8.)

Dogs seem to have been sufficiently plentiful in number and variety in England at this period. Fynes Morrison, in his *Itinerary*, writing about 1591, tells us:—

"England hath much more dogges, as well for the severall kinds as the number of each kind, then any other territorie of like compasse in the world, not onely little dogges for beauty, but hunting and water-dogges, whereof the bloudhounds and some other have admirable qualities." (Ed. 1617, p. 148.)

Amoretto, in the play *The Return from Parnassus*, enumerates some of the different varieties :—

"He hath your greyhound, your mungrell, your mastiff, your leurier, your spaniell, your kennets, terriers, butchers dogges, bloudhoundes, dunghill-dogges, trindle tailes, and prick-eard curres."

Orion concludes his defence of dogs by the following list of their acquirements :—

"Yea, there be of them, as there be of men,
Of every occupation more or less :
Some carriers, and they fetch ; some watermen,
And they will dive and swim when you do bid them ;
Some butchers, and they worry sheep by night ;
Some cooks, and they do nothing but turn spits.
Cynics they are, for they will snarl and bite ;
Right courtiers to flatter and to fawn ;
Valiant to set upon their enemies ;
Most faithful and most constant to their friends."

Shakspeare was perhaps indebted to this passage.

"*First Murderer.* We are men, my liege.
Macbeth. Ay, in the catalogue ye go for men :
As hounds, and greyhounds, mongrels, spaniels, curs,
Shoughs, water-rugs, and demi-wolves, are clept
All by the name of dogs : the valued file
Distinguishes the swift, the slow, the subtle,
The housekeeper, the hunter, every one
According to the gift which bounteous nature
Hath in him clos'd ; whereby he does receive
Particular addition, from the bill
That writes them all alike : and so of men."

(*Macbeth,* iii. 1, 91.)

Dr. John Kaye, or Caius, as he called himself, was physician to three sovereigns of England, Edward VI., Mary, and Elizabeth. Amongst other works, Dr. Caius wrote, about the year 1550, a short treatise in Latin on English dogs, which was translated into English by Abraham Fleming in 1576. This hitherto scarce work has recently been reprinted, and published at a moderate price. Mr. Jesse, in his *History of the British Dog*, has drawn largely upon the pages of this pamphlet, which is indeed the chief authority on the subject.

The translator, in his preface, informs his readers that this little treatise was written by Dr. Caius at the request of Conrad Gesner, a Swiss naturalist, one of the most learned men of his time.

The most formidable of our English dogs was the Bloodhound. This dog was sometimes called limier, or limehound, from the leash, lyme, or line, by which he was held while tracking the deer. Bloodhound. He was employed to find the stag, but did not as a rule run with the pack. His superior sense of smell made him the most valuable addition to a hunting establishment. Dr. Caius distinguishes between the bloodhound and the limier. According to him the limier was a hound remarkable for quick running as well as for his scent, in size between a harrier and a greyhound. Other names for the bloodhound were slough, sleuth, slow, or slug hound; he was not unfrequently employed for tracing thieves and cattle-stealers through the mosses and bogs, impassable save to those intimately acquainted with them. Mr. Jesse quotes from Nicolson and Burn's *History of the Antiquities of Westmoreland and Cumberland*, published 1777, a warrant, dated September, 1616, from Sir Wilfride Lawson and Sir William Hutton, two of his Majesty's commissioners for the government of the middle shires of Great Britain, to the garrison of Carlisle, ordering that in consequence of the numerous robberies slough dogs should be provided, and kept at the charge of the inhabitants, at nine parishes in the neighbourhood of the Marches. A more formidable ally could scarcely be given to a pursuer.

Shakspeare has only one allusion to this variety by name: "Ay, come, you starved blood-hound" (2 *Henry IV.*, v. 4, 31). Ben Jonson writes, "A good bloodhound,

a close-mouthed dog, he followeth the scent well"
(*Every Man out of his Humour*, iv. 4). And again, "No,
an I had, all the lime hounds o' the city should have
drawn after you by the scent rather" (*Bartholomew
Fair*, i. 1).

Mr. Low, in his work *The Domesticated Animals of
Great Britain*, 1846 (p. 739), is of opinion that the
hounds described by *Theseus*, in *Midsummer Night's
Dream*, were talbots. The talbot, he tells us, was a
breed of bloodhound, differing in some slight peculiarities
from the ordinary type. Unfortunately the author gives
no authorities for his information.

"The hounds employed in England for the chase of the wild deer
were generally termed raches. They likewise received the name of
talbots—a word of uncertain origin, perhaps merely the proper name
of some person, or of some place where a good breed was reared.
They were a race of large dogs, nearly of the size of mastiffs, and with
something of the same aspect. They had the muzzle broad, the
upper lip hanging over the lower, the ears long and pendulous, the
chest wide, with a kind of dewlap, and the limbs muscular and
crooked. Their voice was deep and sonorous, and they were endowed
with an exquisite sense of smell. They were far inferior in speed to
the modern hunting dogs, but excelled them in their adherence to the
track of the game, and their pertinacity in pursuing it. At first only
a few of the more experienced hounds were let into the covert, in
order to find the game, when they manifested unrivalled sagacity and
powers of scent. Disregarding all inferior quarry, they could discriminate, by the smell alone, what was called the warrantable game
from the fawns which were not to be hunted, and the hinds when
out of season for the chase. The instant a dog caught the scent
he opened mouth, and was joined in chorus by his fellows. A few
lines, often quoted, of our great dramatic poet, describe to the life the
ancient stag-hounds of England:—

"'My hounds are bred out of the Spartan kind,
So flew'd, so sanded, and their heads are hung
With ears that sweep away the morning dew;
Crook-knee'd, and dew-lapp'd like Thessalian bulls;
Slow in pursuit, but match'd in mouth like bells,
Each under each. A cry more tuneable

Was never holla'd to, nor cheer'd with horn,
In Crete, in Sparta, nor in Thessaly,
Judge when you hear.'"
(*Midsummer Night's Dream*, iv. 1, 124.)

Topsell writes (p. 149) :—

"There are in England and Scotland two kinds of hunting dogs, and no where else in the world. The first kind they call in Scotland ane *rache*, and this is a foot-smelling creature, both of wilde beasts, birds, and fishes also which lie hid among the rockes; the female hereof in England is called a *brache*. The second kind is called in Scotland a *sluth-hound*, being a little greater than a hunting hound, and in colour for the most part browne or sandy-spotted."

In the *Mirror for Magistrates*, vol. ii. p. 74, ed. Haslewood, 1815, we read :—

"For as the dogges pursue the seely doe,
The brache behinde, the houndes on every side,
So traste they mee among the mountaynes wide."

When told to keep silence and listen to *Lady Mortimer's* Welsh song, *Hotspur* uncivilly replies, "I had rather hear Lady, my brach, howl in Irish" (1 *Henry IV.*, iii. 1, 240).

Buckhounds and harriers were frequently called "running-hounds." The Harrier, a very different animal from the small foxhound known by that name at the present day, is described by Caius as having "long, large, and bagging lippes, hanging eares, reachyng downe both sydes of their chappes." The word "heirers," or harriers, is as old as the time of Henry V. Though used for hunting the hart as well as the hare, harriers were distinct from "herte-hounds," or "greyhoundes." The fondness of James I. for hunting may be gathered from the many allusions in the State Papers of his reign to the various requirements for that sport.

Harrier.

Beagle. The Beagle was another kind of sporting dog. Markham speaks of the little beagle, which may be carried in a man's glove, and of—

"the little small mitten-beagle, which may be companion for a ladies kirtle, and in the field will run as cunningly as any hound whatever, only their musick is very small like reeds, and their face like their body only for exercise and not for slaughter." (*Jesse*, vol. ii, p. 330.)

Much attention was paid to the cry of the pack. Hounds were selected, not only for the more useful qualities of scent and speed, but for the various tones of their voice, ranging from base to treble, so as to form a complete choir. *Hippolyta* replies to her lover's proposal to hunt :—

> "I was with Hercules and Cadmus once,
> When in a wood of Crete they bay'd the boar
> With hounds of Sparta: never did I hear
> Such gallant chiding; for, besides the groves,
> The skies, the fountains, every region near
> Seem'd all one mutual cry: I never heard
> So musical a discord, such sweet thunder."
> (*Midsummer Night's Dream*, iv. 1, 117.)

Roderigo complains—

> "I do follow here in the chase, not like a hound that hunts,
> But one that fills up the cry."
> (*Othello*, ii. 3, 369.)

On one occasion the cry of the pack would seem to have constituted the chief part of the entertainment. Sir John Savile gives an account of festivities on the occasion of the arrival of James I. at London. After the customary addresses and congratulations had been graciously received and acknowledged, his loyal subjects proceeded to indulge their sovereign after a somewhat cockney fashion, with his favourite recreation of hunting.

"From Stamford Hill to London was a train made with a tame deer, with such turnings and doubles that the hounds could not take it faster than his majesty proceeded; yet still by the industry of the huntsman and the subtilty of him that made the train in a full mouthed cry all the way, it was never further distant that one close from the highway whereby his highness rode, and for the most part directly against his majesty; who, together with the whole company, had the lee wind from the hounds; to the end they might the better receive and judge of the uniformity of the cry." (*Arber's English Garner*, 1882, vol. v. p. 631.)

Commentators have been sorely puzzled by an expression that occurs in *Coriolanus*, iv. 5. The servants of Aufidius are discussing the news, just brought by one of their fellows, of the intention of their master and *Coriolanus* to march against Rome: "1*st Servant*. Let me have war, say I; it exceeds peace as far as day does night; it's spritely, waking, audible, and full of vent." The phrase "full of vent" is explained by the writer of an article on *Shakespeare's Knowledge of Field Sports*, contributed to the *Edinburgh Review*, October, 1872, to be a technical term in hunting, to express the scenting of the game by the hounds employed in the chase. War is thus personified as a trained hound, "keenly excited, full of pluck and courage, of throbbing energy and impetuous desire, in a word, full of all the kindling stir and commotion of anticipated conflict."

Terriers, which Dr. Caius rather curiously classes with hounds, were employed in hunting "the foxe, and the badger or greye only." According to this author they were called—

Terrier.

"Terrars, because they (after the manner and custome of ferrets in searching for connyes) creepe into the grounde and by that meanes make afrayde, nyppe, and byte the foxe and the badger in such sort, that eyther they teare them in peeces with theyr teeth beying in the bosome of the earth, or else hayle and pull them perforce out of their lurking angles, darke dongeons, and close caves, or at the least through conceaved feare, drive them out of their hollow harbours, in so much that they are compelled to prepare speedy flight, and being desirous of the next (albeit not the safest) refuge, are otherwise taken and

E

intrapped with snarre and nettes layde over holes to the same purpose."
(*Reprint*, p. 5.)

Turbervile, in his *Noble Art of Venerie*, translated from Du Fouiloux, mentions two kinds of terriers. One sort he imagines to have come from Flanders, or the Low Countries: "They have crooked legges and are shorte-heared most commonly. Another sorte there is which are shagged and streight-legged." The former variety was probably the progenitor of the long-bodied dachshund, or badger-hound, so popular in modern times.

Of the Gazehound, Camden writes, "That very dog which of the old name, agasæus, we call yet at this day a gazehound, those ancient Greeks both knew and had in great price." Caius says (*Reprint*, p. 9) this variety is called a gazehound—

Gazehound.

"because the beames of his sight are so stedfastly and unmouveably fastened. These dogges are much and usually occupied in the northern partes of England more then in the southern parts, and in fealdy landes rather then in bushy and wooddy places. Horsemen use them more then footemen, to th' intent that they might provoke their horses to a swift galloppe (wherewith they are more delighted then with the pray it selfe)."

Mr. Low (*Domesticated Animals*, p. 722) says:—

"This dog was employed in the pursuit of the stag or fallow-deer. The great Irish wolf-dog was of this class. He was one of the tallest dogs of Europe, measuring from three to four feet high at the shoulder. He approached to the general conformation of the ancient deerhound, but his muzzle was broader, his neck relatively thicker, his breast proportionably wider, and his limbs were more muscular. He followed the game chiefly by the eye, grasping it in the manner of the greyhound with his long and powerful jaws. He was a dog of amazing courage, and could destroy unaided the fiercest wolf."

Poor Gelert, of ballad celebrity, was probably a gazehound. Mr. Baring-Gould and other myth-students, who have an unhappy knack of destroying some of our most cherished and earliest beliefs, assure us that this noble dog, whose tragic fate has been mourned for centuries, and whose monument is still to be seen, never existed.

The Greyhound was also used in—

"taking the bucke, the harte, the dowe, the foxe, and other beastes of semblable kindes ordained for the game of hunting. But more or lesse, each one according to the Greyhound. measure and proportion of theyr desire, and as might and habilitie of theyr bodyes will permit and suffer. For it is a spare and bare kinde of dogge (of fleshe but not of bone). Some are of a greater sorte, and some of a lesser, some are smooth skynned and some are curled, the bigger therefore are appointed to hunt the bigger beasts, and the smaller serve to hunt the smaller accordingly." (*Reprint*, p. 10.)

The greyhound was an object of value and esteem, not only to the sportsman, but also to men of birth and means. According to Mr. Jesse, "the famous Shane O'Neill wrote to Lord Robert Duddeley, in 1562, with a present of two horses, two hawks, and two greyhounds, requesting his interest with Queen Elizabeth" (vol. ii. p. 218). The passion of James I. for sport of all kinds rendered a good hunting establishment essential to any nobleman or country gentleman who was desirous of entertaining the "British Solomon."

At the time of which we write, horse-racing, as now practised, was unknown, and all coursing-matches were dog to dog, in manner thus described by Mr. Tomlins (*Shakspere Society Papers*, 1844, vol. i.) :—

"In the paddock were two harriers. At one end was kept a buck educated for the purpose; he was let go from the other and to go home as fast as he could; after a little law given him, the greyhounds were slipped, and the dog first in won the prize. 'Hay! voux!' is dog-language to this day with harriers. In the *Book of Sports*, or *Laws of the Paddock*, published the end of King James I., are these directions: 'No keeper shall slip his greyhound till the warden throws down his wardour and cries, Hay! voux!' Is not this," asks Mr. Tomlin, "the meaning of the passage in *Julius Cæsar* (iii. 1)?—

' And Cæsar's spirit, ranging for revenge,
With Até by his side, come hot from hell,
Shall in these confines, with a monarch's voice,
Cry ' Havoc,' and let slip the dogs of war.' "

No material alterations have been made in the rules and laws of coursing since they received the fiat of the Duke of Norfolk, in the reign of Elizabeth. The man who slipped the greyhounds was called a fewterer, a term that frequently occurs in the dramas of the time.

The naturalist Buffon is of opinion that the modern greyhound is derived from what he calls the "matin," but in its descent the variety has become finer, more slender, and more delicate in shape and skin, from climate, care, and attention to breeding only with its own species. In Wynkyn de Worde's *Treatise on Hawking*, 1496, the properties of a good greyhound are thus given:—

> "A greyhounde should be headed lyke a snake, and
>   neckyd like a drake,
> Fotyd lyke a cat: taylyd lyke a ratte:
> Syded like a teme: and chyned lyke a bream."

Thomas Fuller derives the word "greyhound" from the *gray* or *badger*, from a theory that this dog was employed in hunting grays, that is, brocks or badgers. This derivation is manifestly incorrect, as the badger is far too sagacious an animal to come above ground in order to provide sport for such a swift-footed antagonist.

Ben Jonson speaks of some one who—

> "Restrained, grows more impatient; and in kind
> Like to the eager, but the generous greyhound,
> Who ne'er so little from his game withheld,
> Turns head, and leaps up at his holder's throat."
>   (*Every Man in his Humour*, i. 1.)

Lyly has a similar comparison: "You resemble the grayhounde, that seeing his game, leapeth upon him that holdeth him, not running after that he is held for." (*Ephues*, p. 420.)

Dr. Nathan Drake (*Shakspeare and His Times*, 1817, vol. i. p. 252) informs us that—

"a very popular diversion was celebrated, during the age of Shakspeare, and for more than twenty-five years after, on the Cotswold

Hills in Gloucestershire. It has been said that the rural games which constituted this anniversary were founded by one Robert Dover, on the accession of James I., but it appears to be ascertained that Dover was only the reviver, with additional splendour, of sports which had been yearly exhibited, at an early period, on the same spot, and perhaps only discontinued for a short time before this revival in 1603."

In the *Merry Wives of Windsor*, Slender asks Page, "How does your fallow greyhound, sir? I heard say he was outrun on Cotsall?" (i. 1).

Joshua Sylvester interpolates into his translation of Du Bartas a simile drawn apparently from his personal recollection of these games:—

> "So have I seen on Lamborn's pleasant douns,
> When yelping begles or some deeper hounds
> Have start a hare, how milk-white Minks and Lun
> (Gray-bitches both, the best that ever run)
> Held in one leash, have leapt and strain'd, and whin'd
> They might be slipt, to purpose; that (for sport)
> Watt might have law neither too-long nor short."
>
> (Page 182.)

Tumbler. The Tumbler was principally used in taking rabbits. It acquired this name from the eccentricity of its movements. It ran in a circle, and then suddenly turned upon its prey, in the manner thus described by William Browne in his pastorals:—

> "As I have seene
> A nimble tumbler on a burrow'd greene
> Bend cleane awry his course yet give a checke,
> And throw himself upon a rabbet's necke."
>
> (*Britannia's Pastorals*, book ii., song 4.)

These dogs, according to Caius,—

"are somewhat lesser then the houndes, and they be lancker and leaner, beside that they be somwhat prick eared. A man that shall marke the forme and fashion of their bodyes, may well call them mungrell greboundes if they were somwhat bigger. But notwithstanding they countervaile not the grehound in greatnes, yet will he take in one dayes space as many connyes as shall arise to as bigge a burthen, and as heavy a loade as a horse can carry, for deceipt and guile is the instrument wherby he make this spoyle, which pernicious properties supply the place of more commendable qualities." (*Reprint*, p. 12.)

Caius mentions also a light dog of the lurcher type, used for poaching, which will not bark "least he shoulde bee prejudiciall to his owne advantage."

Spaniel. Spaniels were employed in falconry to rouse the herons, ducks, etc., from the reeds and marshy ground frequented by them. Spenser writes:

" Like as a fearfull partridge that is fledd
From the sharpe hawke which her attacked neare,
And falls to ground to seeke for succor theare,
Whereas the hungry spaniells she does spye,
With greedy jawes her ready for to teare."
(*Faerie Queene*, b. 3, c. 8, s. 33.)

Shakspeare's allusions to the spaniel, if taken literally, seem to show that the affection which this dog so often displays was scarcely appreciated by the poet. *Cæsar*, when he rejects the suit of *Metellus Cimber*, warns him to avoid vain adulations:—

" I mean, sweet words,
Low-crooked court'sies and base spaniel-fawning.
Thy brother by decree is banished;
If thou dost bend, and pray, and fawn for him,
I spurn thee like a cur out of my way."
(*Julius Cæsar*, iii. 1, 42.)

Launce, however, who was fond of dogs, says in praise of his mistress, "She hath more qualities than a water-spaniel, which is much in a bare Christian" (*Two Gentlemen of Verona*, iii. 1, 271).

Caius declines to undertake the task of enumerating the many varieties of dogs used in fowling. He says they are called after the birds that they are trained to take. Some are called dogs for the falcon, dogs for the pheasant, and such like:—

The Spaniel.

"The common sort of people call them by one general word, namely spaniells, as though these kinde of dogges came originally and first of all out of Spaine. The most part of their skynnes are white, and if they be marcked with any spottes, they are commonly red, and somewhat great therewithall, the haires not growing in such thicknesse but that the mixture of them maye easely be perceaved. Other-some of them be reddishe and blackishe, but of that sorte there be but a very few. There is also at this day among us a newe kinde of dogge brought out of Fraunce (for we Englishe men are marvailous greedy gaping gluttons after novelties, and covetous cormorauntes of things that be seldom, rare, straunge, and hard to get). And they bee speckled all over with white and black, which mingled colours incline to a marble blewe, which bewtifyeth their skinnes and affordeth a seemely show of comelynesse." (*Reprint*, p. 15.)

Topsell writes :—

"Unto all those smelling dogs, I may also adde the water spagnell, called in French *barbati*, and in Germany *wasserhund*: who is taught by his maister to seeke for thinges that are lost by words and tokens. These also will take water-foule, and hunt otters and beavers, and watch the stroke of the gun when the fouler shooteth. They use to sheare their hinder parts, that so they may be the lesse annoyed in swimming; whose figure is in the bottome of the former page described." (Page 154.)

The picture referred to represents a spaniel clipped after the fashion of the French poodle of our own day.

The Setting-dogge, or Setter, was a large land spaniel, probably similar in appearance to his modern namesake. His mode of action is thus described by Caius :— **Setter.**

"When he hath founde the byrde, he keepeth sure and fast silence, he stayeth his steppes and wil proceede no further, and with a close, covert, watching eye, layeth his belly to the grounde, and so creepeth forward like a worme. When he approcheth neere to the place where the birde is, he layes him downe, and with a marcke of his pawes, betrayeth the place of the byrdes last abode, whereby it is supposed that this kinde of dogge is called *index*, setter, being indeede a name most consonant and agreable to his quality." (*Reprint*, p. 15.)

The smallest variety of this class of dogs was the

Spaniel Gentle, Comforter, or Fisting Hound, of which
Dr. Caius speaks with great contempt. According to this writer, an animal whose chief purpose in life was to enliven the solitude of his mistress, to amuse her, to give her pleasure, instead of assisting her to destroy some other creature, was a mere "instrument of follie, to plaie and dally withall, to trifle away the treasure of time." In the dedication of *Euphues* to the ladies of England, Lyly speaks less harshly :—

<small>Spaniel Gentle.</small>

"It resteth ladies, that you take the paines to read it [his book], but at such times, as you spend in playing with your little dogges: and yet will I not pinch you of that pastime, for I am content that your dogges lye in your laps, so *Euphues* may be in your hands, that when you shall be wearie in reading of the one, you may be ready to sport with the other." (*Euphues and his England*, Arber's Reprint, p. 220.)

According to Ben Jonson, a fashion prevailed of scenting these small pets :—

"From perfumed dogs, monkies, sparrows, lildoes, and paraquettoes,
Good Mercury defend us."
(*Cynthia's Revels*, v. 3.)

Mary Queen of Scots had one of these little favourites, so despised by the worthy doctor. After her execution the animal refused to leave the dead body of its mistress, and had to be forcibly removed. That dogs were the pets not only of women but, on occasion, of men, is shown by the following anecdote. Manningham writes in his dairy, 1602 :—

"Mr. Francis Curle told me howe one Dr. Bullein, the queenes kinsman, had a dog which he doted on, soe much that the queene understanding of it requested he would graunt hir one desyre, and he should have what soever he would aske : shee demaunded his dogge ; he gave it, 'And now, madame,' quoth he, 'you promised to give me my desyre.' 'I will,' quothe she. 'Then, I pray you give me my dog againe.'" (*Diary of John Manningham*. Reprinted by Camden Society, 1868.)

Mr. Kirkman, in a very interesting paper on *Animal Nature versus Human Nature in King Lear* (*New Shakspere Society's Transactions*, 1877), comments on the infinite pathos of the last touch of humiliation which the old king endures when he fancies that the—

"defection and disaffection of the palace has *spread to the dogs.*

'The little dogs and all,
Tray, Blanche, and Sweetheart, see, they bark at me.'
(*Lear*, iii. 6, 65.)

It has a deep touch of human distress and disgrace equal to the bitterness of *Anthony's* humiliation when the servant *Thyreus* derides his orders, and he feels the vile sting which a contemptible nature can so easily dart."

Edgar, his voice broken with tears, keeps up the delusion:

"'Tom will throw his head at them.
Avaunt, you curs!
Be thy mouth or black or white,
Tooth that poisons if it bite;
Mastiff, greyhound, mongrel grim,
Hound or spaniel, brach or lym;
Or bobtail tike, or trundle-tail,
Tom will make them weep and wail:
For, with throwing thus my head,
Dogs leap the hatch, and all are fled:'

as if *Lear's* uncontrollable mortification at the disaffection of the three pampered pets caught from their mistresses' laps, had touched one of those cerebral chains of association we all know we possess, and he must needs run over the links."

Of domestic dogs the Mastiff, Ban-dog, or Tie-dog, was the largest and most powerful. Mr. Jesse quotes the following passage from a translation, by Barnaby Googe, of Conrad Heresbach's *Whole Art of Husbandry*:—

Mastiff.

First the mastie that keepeth the house: for this purpose you must provide you such a one, as hath a large and a mightie body, a great and a shrill voyce, that both with his barking he may discover, and with his sight dismay the theefe, yea, being not seene, with the horror of his voice put him to flight; his stature must neither be long nor short, but well set, his head great, his eyes sharpe, and fiery, either browne or grey, his lippes blackish, neither turning up, nor hanging too much downe, his mouth black and wide, his neather jawe fat, and comming out of it on either side a fang, appearing more outward then his other teeth; his upper teeth even with his neather, not hanging too much over, sharpe, and hidden with his lippe. His countenance like a lion, his brest great and shaghayrd, his shoulders broad, his legges bigge, his tayle short, his feet very great; his disposition must neither be too gentle, nor too curst, that he neither fawne upon a theefe, nor flee upon his friends; very waking, no gadder abroad, not lavish of his mouth, barking without cause; neither maketh it any matter though he be not swift: for he is but to fight at home, and to give warning of the enemie."

Mr. Jesse remarks that although this description is taken from a foreign work, it probably gives a correct portrait of the mastiff, or rather of the bull-mastiff of the England of that period. Shakspeare makes the "repining enemy" commend the English breed of this variety. *Rambures* admits, "That island of England breeds very valiant creatures; their mastiffs are of unmatchable courage" (*Henry V.*, iii. 7, 150).

Lyly also writes—

"They excel for one thing there [England] dogges of al sortes, spaniels, hounds, maistiffes, and divers such, the one they keepe for hunting and hawking, the other for necessarie uses about their houses, as to draw water, to watch theeves &c., and thereof they derive the word mastiffe, of mase and thiefe." (*Euphues*, p. 438.)

Dr. Caius give the mastiff a variety of names: the dog-keeper, or watch-dog, from his usefulness in guarding houses; the butcher's dog, from the help he affords to the butcher, both in following and in driving the cattle; the carrier, because he was occasionally employed as a messenger with letters carefully sewn up inside his collar; the mooner, because he does nothing but watch, wasting the wearisome night season without sleeping, "bawing and wawing at the moone;" the water-drawer, because he was made to turn the wheel of the well in courtyards; and the tinker's cur, from his use in drawing trucks and barrows. Our word *bulldog* may come from the employment of the mastiff in driving cattle, as well as from the pertinacity with which the bulldog attacks his bovine enemy. The first line of the following quotation suggests yet another etymology :—

> " Than came one with two bolddogges at his tayle,
> And that was a bocher, without fayle,
> All be gored in red blode."
> (*Cocke Lorelles Bote*, about 1520, Percy Society, vol. v. p. 2.)

After the various uses enumerated by Caius, the many accounts of the misuse of this noble dog in baiting lions, bears, horses, and asses fall harshly on the ear. These sports have been so fully described by authors that there is no occasion to dwell on them.

Thomas Fuller writes of mastiffs :—

> "They are not (like apes) the fooles and jesters, but the useful servants in a family, viz. the porters thereof. Pliny observes, that Brittan breeds cowardly lions and courageous mastiffes, which seems to me no wonder; the former being whelped in prison, the latter at liberty. An English mastiff, anno 1602, did in effect worst a lion, on the same token that Prince Henry allowed a kind of pension for his maintenance, and gave strict orders, 'that he that had fought with the king of beasts should never after encounter any inferior creatures.'"
> (*Worthies of England*, ed. Nichols, 1811, vol. 2, p. 276.)

The ban-dog, or tie-dog, was probably a small variety of the mastiff.

> " Whose noise, as me-thinketh, I could best compare
> To a cry of hounds, following after the hare,
> Or a rabblement of bandogs barking at a bear."
> (*New Custom, an Interlude*, 1573.)

> " I know the villain is both rough and grim;
> But as a tie-dog I will muzzle him.
> I'll bring him up to fawn upon my friends,
> And worry dead my foes."
> (H. CHETTLE, *The Death of Robert Earl of Huntingdon*.)

The Sheep Dog, or Ramhundt, was employed then as now to guard the flock. According to Caius it was a dog of medium size, and exceedingly intelligent.

Iceland Dogs were kept as pets by ladies, and are often mentioned. The dramatist Shirley seems to consider them as a necessary part of the establishment of a woman of fashion :—

> " You have a waiting-woman,
> A monkey, squirrel, and a brace of Islands,
> Which may be thought superfluous in your family
> When husbands come to rule."
>
> (*Hyde Park*, i. 2.)

Pistol exclaims : " Pish for thee, Iceland dog ! Thou prick-ear'd cur of Iceland!" (*Henry V.*, ii. 1, 43). Drayton declares, in one of his minor poems, that in consequence of the prevalent fashion for light hair among ladies—

> " Our water-dogs and Islands here are shorn,
> White hair of women here so much is worn."
>
> (*Mooncalf.*)

From the description of these little favourites by Dr. Caius, they would seem to have been long-haired, white, sharp-eared dogs, not unlike the Skye terriers of the present day, though of a less amiable disposition. Caius writes :—

" Use and custome hath intertained other dogges of an outlandishe kinde, but a few of the same beying of a pretty bygnesse; I mean Iseland dogges, curled and rough all over, which by reason of the length of their heare make showe neither of face, nor of body. And yet these curres, forsoothe, because they are so straunge, are greatly set by, esteemed, taken up, and made of, many times in the roome of the spaniell gentle or comforter."

Then follows the usual sneer of the author at the eagerness of the English people for foreign novelties :—

" A beggerly beast brought out of barbarous borders, from the uttermost countryes northward, &c., we stare at, we gase at, we muse, we marvaile at, like an asse of Cumanum, like Thales with the brasen shancks, like the man in the moone." (*Reprint*, p. 37.)

Topsell mentions some varieties of performing dogs. One is the Mimicke or Getulian dog :—

" There is also in England two other sorts of dogs, the figure of which is here expressed, being apt to imitate al things it seeth, in face sharpe and blacke like a hedgehog, having a short recurved body, very long legs, shaggy haire and a short taile. These being brought up with apes in their youth learne very admirable and strange feats." (Page 161.)

In the next page he describes some miniature dogs, artificially dwarfed :—

" Now a daies, they have found another breede of little dogs in all nations, beside the Melitean [Maltese] dogs, either made so by art, as inclosing their bodies in the earth, when they are whelpes, so as they cannot grow great by reason of the place, or els, lessening and impayring their growth, by some kind of meat or nourishment. . . . They are not above a foot or half a foote long, and alway the lesser the mor delicate and precious. Their head like the head of a mouse, but greater, their snowt sharpe, their eares like the eares of a cony, short legs, little feete, long, and white colour, and the haire about the shoulders longer then ordinary is most commended. They are of pleasant disposition, and will leape and bite without pinching, and barke prettily, and some of them are taught to stand upright, holding up their fore legs like hands, other to fetch and cary in their mouths that which is cast unto them."

The little toy Maltese dog, here referred to, is now almost extinct. The useful little Whappet, or Turnspit, needs no description.

To write a full description of the various dogs known at this period would require, not a chapter, but a volume. Many interesting particulars, as well as numerous anecdotes of the different varieties, are to be found in Jesse's *History of the British Dog*, already quoted. The concluding sentence of the description of the mastiff by Dr. Caius, sums up the good qualities of the dog :—

" Who by his barcking (as good as a burning beacon) foreshoweth hassards at hand ? what maner of beast stronger ? what servant to his master more loving ? what companion more trustie ? what watchman more vigilant ? what revenger more constant ? what messinger more speedie ? what water-bearer more painefull ? finally, what packhorse more patient ? And thus much concerning English dogges." (*Tract on Dogs*, tr. Fleming, 1576; Reprint, 1880.)

CHAPTER IV.

Fox. The Fox is seldom mentioned as an animal of chase by early writers. As rabbits were most abundant in all parts of England, foxes were probably numerous. Olaus Magnus (p. 193) informs us that in Scandinavia—

"There are in the Northerne woods foxes, white, black, red, crosse-bearers on the back, and others of a blew colour, spotted, but they all partake of the same malice and fraud; the black skins are dearest because the Emperours of Moscovie use these often; next are the crosse-bearing skins, that is, such as are marked on the back with a black crosse by nature, because they are more adorned, and the skins are greatest; for the foxes have not this crosse till they grow of a full age."

The fox has always been considered the personification of craft and cunning. *Edgar* declares that he has been "a hog in sloth, a fox in stealth, a wolf in greediness" (*Lear*, iii. 4, 195). *Venus* attempts to dissuade *Adonis* from his intention to pursue the boar:—

"But if thou needs wilt hunt, be ruled by me;
Uncouple at the timorous flying hare,
Or at the fox which lives by subtlety."
(*Venus and Adonis*, l. 673.)

The skin of a fox, hare, or rabbit was called its case. The *Duke* thus reproaches *Viola* for her supposed deception,—

'O thou dissembling cub! what wilt thou be
When Time hath sow'd a grizzle on thy case?
Or will not else thy craft so quickly grow,
That thine own trip shall be thine overthrow?"
(*Twelfth Night*, v. 1, 167.)

At the period of which we write dress was regulated by strict sumptuary laws, according to the rank or profession of the wearer. Lawyers were prohibited from wearing any fur except fox or lamb skin. Shakspeare has an allusion to this regulation,— **Furs in Dress.**

" 'Twas never merry world since, of two usuries, the merriest was put down, and the worser allowed by order of law a furred gown to keep him warm; and furred with fox and lamb-skins too, to signify, that craft, being richer than innocency, stands for the facing."
(*Measure for Measure*, iii. 2, 10.)

Fur was largely used as an ornament in dress by all classes, so much so that the importation of skins threatened to interfere with cloth and woollen manufacture in England. To encourage the sale of materials of home growth, restrictions were placed upon the use of foreign furs. According to a law passed in the reign of Queen Mary, no one below the rank of an earl was allowed to wear sable; fur of black genet, or luserne, was prohibited to all under the degree of knight, and no one was permitted to wear any fur, "whereof the like groweth not within the queenes dominions, except foynes, gray jenet, calaber, budge, outlandish hare, or fox, except he have 100 marks by the year."

Dr. Giles Fletcher was sent to Russia as ambassador from Queen Elizabeth to the Czar Vasilievitch, and in 1591 he published a full account of the manners and customs, commodities and government of the country. The internal arrangements of Russia were not sufficiently satisfactory to be thus exposed to the common gaze, and the Government despatched a remonstrance to the English

Court against the publication of the book. The work was accordingly suppressed. The report of Dr. Fletcher to Queen Elizabeth from Russia, is printed in Hakluyt's collection of voyages (vol. i. p. 538, ed. Evans, 1810). He gives a list of the various fur-producing animals of that part of the country :—

"The chiefe furres are these, blacke fox, sables, lusernes, dun fox, martrones, gurnestalles or armins, lasets or miniver, bever, wulverins, the skin of a great water rat that smelleth naturally like muske, calaber or gray squirrel, red squirrel, red and white fox. The blacke foxe and red come out of Siberia, white and dunne from Pechora, whence also come the white wolfe and white beare skin. The best wulverin also thence and from Perm. The best martrons are from Siberia, Cadam, Morum, Perm, and Cazan. Lyserns, minever, and armins, the best are out of Gallets, and Ouglits, many from Novogrod, and Perm. The beaver of the best sort breede in Murmonskey by Cola."

The Ermine, though one of the smallest of the animals hunted for the sake of their skins, takes precedence of others from the fact that its fur was chiefly worn by royal personages. From the snowy whiteness of its coat, and perhaps from the dislike it has to any substance that can soil it, this animal was considered as the emblem of purity and stainless honour. As such it has been, as accurate students of history would naturally expect, appropriated by sovereigns to their peculiar use—

Ermine.

"Whose honour, ermine like, can never suffer
  Spot, or black soil."
    (BEAUMONT and FLETCHER, *Knight of Malta*.).

The ermine, or armin, is the Siberian stoat. The name is a corruption of Armenia, in the woods of which country the animal abounded.

Olaus Magnus gives a strange account of the Norwegian ermines :—

"These small beasts, for the most part, every three years, for the merchants exceeding great gain, grow to have their skins very long,

The Ermine's Spots. 65

because they eat so much: which after the same manner happens not onely in Norway, but in the forcsaid Helsingia, and provinces that are near to it in the diocess of Upsal, namely, that small beasts with four feet, that they call lemmar, or lemmus [Norwegian rat or lemming], as big as a rat, with a skin diverse coloured, fall out of the ayr in tempests, and sudden showres; but no man knows from whence they come, whether from the remoter islands, and are brought hither by the wind, or else they breed of seculent matter in the clouds: yet this is proved, that so soon as they fall down, there is found green grass in their bellies not yet digested. Those, like locusts, falling in great swarms, destroy all green things, and all dyes they bite on, by the venome of them. This swarm lives so long as they feed on no new grass: also they come together in troops like swallowes that are ready to fly away; but at the set-time they either dye in heaps, with a contagion of the earth, or they are devoured by beasts, called commonly lekat, or hermelin, and these ermins grow fat thereby, and their skins grow longer. And these skins also are sold by tens, especially fourty in a bundle, as sabel,' or martins, fox, beaver, squirrel, or hares skins are, and are carryed forth by shipping into far distant countries." (Page 185.)

The ermine, in its brown summer coat, was called the rosetel. The English stoat is called in Norfolk the lobster. In his account of English dogs Dr. Caius tells us that harriers were trained to hunt, besides the hare and the fox, the polecat, lobster, and weasel.

Some poets of the time were wont to imagine that the spotted appearance of the ermine's fur was natural, but this ignorance was possibly feigned for the sake of the illustration. Greene says:—

"The manners and the fashions of this age
Are like the ermine's skin so full of spots."
(James IV.)

And Randolph informs us that—

"Nature adorns
The peacock's tail with stars; 'tis she attires
The bird of Paradise in all her plumes;
She decks the fields with various flowers; 'tis she
Spangled the heavens with all those glorious lights
She spotted the ermin's skin; and arm'd the fish
In silver mail."
(The Muse's Looking-Glass, iv. 1.)

F

Lettice. The laws that regulated the costume of both ladies and gentlemen at this period were so arbitrary, that even in matters so trifling as the spots on their fur no scope was allowed for the fancy of the wearer. It was ordered that none should appear in an ermine, or lettice-bonnet, unless she were a gentlewoman born, having the right to bear arms.

"Item, a gentleman's wife, she being a gentlewoman born, shall wear an ermine or lettice bonnet, having one powdering to the top. And if she be of honourable stock, to have two powderings, one before another in the top. Item, an esquire's wife to have two powderings." (S. PEGGE, *Curialia Miscellania*, 1818, p. 313.)

In other articles of dress the numbers of spots varied according to the wearer's rank. A knight's wife might wear seven powderings or spots, a baron's wife thirteen, a viscount's wife eighteen, a countess twenty-four, and after that estate as many as convenient. On the occasion of Anne Boleyn's coronation the queen was followed by ladies—

"being lordes wives, which had circotes of scarlet, with narrow sleeves, the breast all lettice, with barres of pouders, according to their degrees." (NICHOLS, *Progresses of Queen Elizabeth*, vol. i. p. 12.)

The word Lettice has been variously explained. By some authors it is considered to mean lattice, or network. Mr. Planché, in his *Cyclopædia of British Costume*, adopts the explanation of Cotgrave, that it was the fur of a small animal of a whitish grey colour. It evidently resembled ermine, but it is impossible that ermines could be supplied in sufficient quantities for ornamenting robes on state occasions. In the account given in Wriothesley's *Chronicle* of the procession of Henry VIII. to open Parliament in 1536, we find that the bishops were attired in—

"robes of scarlett furred with white lettis with hoodes of the same. Then my Lord Chauncelor of Englande, in his perliment robe of scarlett with a hood to the same furred with white lettis, with the kinges great seale borne before him; ... the king following in a robe of crimson velvet furred with poudre ermyns, with a hood of the same. Then after the king followed the Duke of Suffolke, and all erles, marques, and lordes, all in their perliament robes of scarlett furred with white, and their hoodes about their neckes, which were fortie in number; everie duke having fower barres of white furre alongest the right side of their robes, and everie earle having three barres of white furre alongest the right side of their robes, and everie lord two barres in likewise." (Ed. Hakluyt Society, 1875, p. 45.)

The Marten, martern, martron, or marten-cat, was hunted for the sake of its skin, which in good specimens is little inferior to that of the sable. Topsell divides martens into two varieties —the "beech-martin" and the "fir-martin." He writes (p. 496):—

Marten.

"Princes and great nobles are clothed therewith, every skinne being woorthe a French crowne, or foure shillings at the least. And they are so much the better when there are more whit haires aspersed among the yellowe. By inspection of the *foines*, that is, the martins of the beech, for the Frenchmen called a beech *fau*, from whence cometh the word *foines*, you may see that their skins are more dusky, having a tail both greater and blacker then the martins of the firres. And therefore you must understand that they of the firs, are by way of excellency called *martins* and the other of the woods called *foines*. In France there are no martins of the wall; but these martins live in hollow beaches. There are also woods full of these beastes in Brussia, which the people there call *gayns*. There are also store of martins near Bragansa, and generally in all parts of Europe except in England."

We learn from the account of a Lord Mayor's pageant (*Percy Society*, vol. ix. p. 14) that when Sir William Draper served the office of Lord Mayor, in 1566–1567, the Ironmongers exerted themselves to their utmost ability in honouring the procession, as he was what is termed "free of the company." Forty-six persons, bachelors, were nominated, whose drapery was composed of satin cassocks, gowns furred with *foynes*, and crimson satin hoods.

Olaus Magnus distinguishes between martens and sables :—

"Martins and sables are creatures of cold countries. All know them by their names, but few by their virtues, unless by the quality of their skins a man may know what creatures they are. . . . They will bite terribly for their bigness, for they have teeth naturally as sharp as razours, and exceeding small and sharp nails. But as their flesh is said to be nothing worth, so their skins are of huge prices, especially among forrainers, that use them more for their pleasure than commodity. The difference between them is this, that the martins are of a grosser fur from the crown of their head to their tail, but not if you rub them the contrary way : but the sabels are not so; for if you stroak them with your hand from their tail to their crowns, they are equally smooth, because they are furry, and their hair is thicker; and therefore they are sooner eaten by the worms then other skins are, unless they are constantly used, or wormwood leaves put between them to preserve them. And if sable skins are laid in the sun to dry, they will consume more in one day than if they were worn a whole year. When the beast is alive he always lyes in some shady grove, and gets his living by lying in wait for small birds." (Page 184.)

Topsell (p. 755) writes thus

Sable.
"Of the zebel, commonly called a sabell.—Among all the kindes of weasels, squirrels, wood-mice, wilde-mice, or other little beasts of the world, there is none comparable to this zebeth. It is bred in Muscovia and the northerne partes of the worlde, among the Lapones, but no where more plentifull then in Tartaria, Scythia, and Sarmasia ; and it is therefore called by some *Mus Scythicus*, the Scythian mouse. In the furthest part of Lithuania they have little or no mony, and therefore the marchants which traffick thither do exchange their wares for zebel or sabel skins. Those are the best which have most white and yellow haires mingled in them, and the garments of princes are onely fringed and lined with these sabel skinnes ; and honorable matrons, auncient noble men and their wives, doe likewise use two or three of these to weare about their neckes. For it is certaine that a garment of these skinnes is much deerer then cloth of gold ; and I have heard, and also read, that there have beene two thousand duckets payed for so many as were put in one cloake."

As a besant is supposed to have been equivalent to a ducat, the following passage from Marco Polo's *Travels*, which were written about the year 1300, may possibly be Topsell's authority for his assertion as to the value of the sable. Describing the tents of some grand khan of Tartary, Marco Polo says :—

"Withinside they are lined with the skins of ermins and sables, which are the most costly of all furs; for the latter, if of a size to trim a dress, is valued at two thousand besants of gold, provided it be perfect, but if otherwise, only one thousand. It is esteemed by the Tartars the queen of furs. The animal, which in their language is named *rondes*, is about the size of a polecat." (*Travels*, ed. Marsden, 1817, p. 344.)

The following letter from the Muscovite Company in London to their agents in Russia, in 1560, shows that at that date foreign furs were already going out of fashion. The ladies of the period had, no doubt, exerted their influence in support of the development of British woollen manufactures :—

"The sables which you sent this yeere be very base. Among them all we could not make one principall timber. We have always written unto you to send them that bee good or else none. The wolverings were indifferent, and some of the wolves; the rest verie base, the lusernes but meane, the lettes not so large skinnes as we have had: the best is, they were of a new death. As for the ermines, they cost more there with you then we can sell them for here. Therefore buy no more of them, nor of squirrels, for wee lost the one halfe in the other. The wares that we would have you provide against the comming of the shippes are waxe, tallowe, trayne oyles, flaxe, cables and ropes, and furres, such as we have written to you for in our last letters by the shippes: and from henceforth not to make any great provision of any rich furres except principal sables and lettes; for now there is a proclamation made that no furres shall be worne here but such as the like is growing here within this our realm. The sables that you doe mind to send to us let them be principall and fayre, and not past foure or five timbars; for they will not be commonly worne here as they have bin with noble men: and likewise of luserns send fewe and principal good." (*Hakluyt's Voyages*, vol. i. p. 342, ed. Evans, 1810.)

A timber, or timmer, of sables, martens, or ermines, was a bundle of 40 skins; of other furs it included 120 skins.

The animal lette here mentioned probably supplied the lettice fur already referred to.

The wearing of sable was prohibited by statute in the reign of Queen Mary, to any one below the rank of earl. Gowns furred with sable were deemed of sufficient value to be bestowed as presents, and to be mentioned as rich legacies by the possessors unto their heirs. Sir John Wallop, in 1551, bequeaths to different friends gowns furred with sable, lucerns, and black coney. In the collection of wills, *Testamenta Vetusta*, by Sir H. Nicolas, 1826, we find many such bequests.

Hamlet's exclamation, "Let the devil wear black, for I'll have a suit of sables," has given rise to much controversy. The only passage in Shakspeare's plays where the word *sable* may be understood to mean the fur is in the same play:—

"For youth no less becomes
The light and careless livery that it wears
Than settled age his sables and his weeds,
Importing health and graveness."

(*Hamlet*, iv. 7, 79.)

But in these latter lines the meaning may well be the dark and sombre costume appropriate to advanced years, in contrast with the more lively colours and the paler tints preferred by youth. If *Hamlet*, after speaking of his "inky cloak," professes his intention of going into mourning, the announcement is certainly unnecessary. At the same time, there is no reason why he should array himself in a costume so expensive as a suit of sables. Warburton, the commentator, suggested a plausible reading—"Let the devil wear black, 'fore [before] I'll have a suit of sables." Mr. G. Wightwick, in *The Critic*, declares that *Hamlet* meant to say, "I'll have a suit of sabell," *i.e.* of flame colour. A misspelling, this writer considers, has caused the confusion. There would certainly be a novelty in *Hamlet's* making his appearance in a brilliant red costume.

Ferret and Polecat. 71

In *The Seven Days of the Week*, an interlude performed at Oxford in 1607, the word *sable* occurs in connexion with mourning. But as the rhyme is evidently the author's first consideration, it is not easy to decide whether a noun or an adjective is intended by the name. *Night* enters, and thus announces himself:—

> "Blacke Night, as black as any mourninge sable is,
> Comes for to prompt the actors if they stumble;
> For who can see what Night doth say, or able is
> To heare how Night doth walke about and mumble."

The Ferret, originally a native of Africa, was brought into Spain with the design of freeing the latter country from the multitudes of rabbits that infested it. Thence the whole of Europe was in time stocked.

Ferret.

The solitary reference to this animal by Shakspeare is more expressive than polite. *Brutus* describes *Cicero* as looking—

> "With such ferret and such fiery eyes
> As we have seen him in the Capitol,
> Being cross'd in conference by some senators."
> (*Julius Cæsar*, i. 2, 186.)

The Polecat was called also, on account of its strong scent, the foulmartin or foumart, and fitchet or fitchew.

Polecat.

The first name is derived by some authorities from the French words, *poule* and *chat*, and has been bestowed on this animal on account of the destruction it works in hen-roosts. Shakspeare uses the word *polecat* only as a term of abuse. The foul-mouthed *Thersites* exclaims:—

> "To be a dog, a mule, a cat, a fitchew, a toad, a lizard, an owl, a puttock, or a herring without a roe, I would not care: but to be Menelaus! I would conspire against destiny." (*Troilus and Cressida*, v. 1, 64.)

The animals of the weasel tribe found in England are

known under a variety of names, and do not appear to have been clearly distinguished one from another. Harrison, in his description of England (*Holinshed's Chronicles*, vol. i. p. 377, ed. 1577), says, "I might here entreat largelie of other vermine, as the polcat, the miniver, the weasell, stote (fulmart), squirrell, fitchew, and such like."

A correspondent in *Notes and Queries*, 1853, started a somewhat unprofitable discussion by an inquiry as to the meaning of the word *mousehunt* in *Romeo and Juliet* (iv. 4, 11):—

Mousehunt.

> "Ay, you have been a mousehunt in your time;
> But I will watch you from such watching now."

One suggestion was that the Mousehunt was a little animal of the weasel species, about the length of a rat, with a long and hairy tail, bushy at the tip. Another, quoting Fennell's *Natural History*, asserted that the reference was to the beech-marten. A third considered that this was a mistake, and that the mousehunt, if any actual animal of that name exists, is only the young of the common weasel. In *The Storye of Reynard the Foxe*, as it was printed by Caxton in 1481, an animal named the *mousehunt* appears in the list of Master Reynard's relations:—

> "Rukenawe [the she-ape, Reynard's aunt] called hem [them] forth and sayde, Welcome, my dere chyldren; come forth and stande by Reynard your der nevew. Thenne sayd she, Come forth, alle ye that ben of my kynne and Reynarts; and late us praye the kynge that he wille doo to Reynard ryght of the lande. Tho cam forth many a beest anon, as the squyrel, the musehont, the fychews, the martron, the bever wyth his wyf Ordegale, the genete [wild cat], the ostrole, the boussyng and the fyret." (Ed. Percy Society, 1844, vol. xii. p. 109.)

In explanation of the appearance of the beaver in such disreputable company, it is stated that he only attended in deference to the command of Dame Rukenawe. Reynard's aunt had the reputation of great wisdom, and was much dreaded on account of her unlimited power of mischief. That *mousehunt* was at a much later period the name of an animal is evident from a passage in Milton :—

> "Although I know that many pretend to be great rabies in these studies, have scarce saluted them from the strings to the title page; or to give them more, have been but the mousehunts and ferrets of an index." (*Of Reformation in England, etc.*)

The Weasel, like the polecat, was a great enemy to poultry. Shakspeare compares England's invading neighbour to this little intruder :— *Weasel.*

> "For once the eagle England being in prey,
> To her unguarded nest the weasel Scot
> Comes sneaking, and so sucks her princely eggs,
> Playing the mouse in absence of the cat,
> To tear and havoc more than she can eat."
> (*Henry V.*, i. 2, 169.)

Pisanio warns *Imogen* that if she assumes male attire she must adopt the manners "should attend it." She must be—

> "Ready in gibes, quick-answer'd, saucy, and
> As quarrelous as the weasel."
> (*Cymbeline*, iii. 4, 161.)

Owing to the want of accurate knowledge of animals great confusion exists as to the names given to the furs worn at this period. According to some authors, Miniver was the lighter portion of the skin of squirrels and weasels. According to others it was the skin of a small animal caught in Russia. Henry VII. wore at his coronation a "surcote closed, furred with menyver pure, a hode of estate furred with menyver pure and purfuld [bordered] with ermyns, a gret mantell of crymesyn saten furred also with menyver pure." From this record it would appear that the fur *Miniver.*

was without spots. In other accounts spots are mentioned. They were probably smaller in size than those on the fur called ermine. In Massinger's play, *The City Madam*, *Luke* describes the costume of a wealthy merchant's wife :—

> "He made a knight,
> And your sweet mistress-ship ladyfied, you wore
> Satin on solemn days, a chain of gold,
> A velvet hood, rich borders, and sometimes
> A dainty miniver cap" (iv. 4).

Joseph Hall satirizes some candidates for ecclesiastical honours, who—

> "Sit seven years pining in an anchores cheyre,
> To win some patched shreds of minivere."
> (*Satires*, book iv., satire 2.)

Furs. Vair was a fur largely used in heraldry. It was represented by a series of shield or bell-shaped pieces placed together alternately, commonly blue and white. Some say this form was taken from the pattern which is made by the dark fur on the back of the squirrel when entire skins of this animal are laid flat and sewn edge to edge. Mr. Planché, in his *Cyclopædia of Costume*, explains the names of other furs that were occasionally worn.

Biche, according to him, was the skin of the female deer. By statute passed in the reign of Henry IV., furs of biche were prohibited to clergymen below the dignity of resident canon.

Budge, bogy, bogys or burge, was lambskin with the wool dressed outwards. Garments were often edged and lined with this fur, and the hood of the bachelor of arts is still so ornamented. Powderings of bogy shanks, or tips cut from the legs of black lambs, were used in spotting ermine.

Calabrere, or calabar, was the summer coat of the

The Glutton.

gray squirrel of Russia. It was so called from Calabria, whence it was imported. Piers Ploughman describes a physician as clad in a furred hood and cloak of calabrere.

Chisamus, cicimus, or sismusilis was a valuable species of fur mentioned by the historians and poets of the Middle Ages. It was probably the skin of the Pontic mouse.

Lituite, a fur only used in doublings, was so called from the skin of the lituit, or white martyn cat. Jennet, or genet, was the fur of the wild cat.

Dossus, from the French *dos*, was the fur from the back of the squirrel, the same as the fur called in France *petit gris*.

Olaus Magnus describes the Wolverine, Glutton, or Wood Dog (*Gulo luscus*), one of the fur-producing animals mentioned by Dr. Fletcher in his list of Russian commodities :—

Wolverine.

"Amongst all creatures that are thought to be insatiable in the northern parts of Sweden, the gulo hath its name to be the principall; and in the vulgar tongue they call him *jerff*, but in the German language *vielfras*, in the Sclavonish speech *rossamaka*, from his much eating; and the made Latin name is *gulo*; for he is so called from his gluttony. He is as great as a great dog, and his ears and face are like a cats; his feet and nails are very sharp: his body is hairy with long brown hair, his tail is like the foxes, but somewhat shorter, but his hair is thicker, and of this they make brave winter caps. The flesh of this creature is altogether uselesse for man's food: but his skin is very commodious and pretious. For it is of a white brown black colour, like a damask cloth wrought with many figures; and it shews the more beautiful, as by the industry of the artists it is joyn'd with other garments in the likenesse or colour. Princes and great men use this habit in winter made like coats; because it quickly makes heat and holds it long; and that not only in Swethland, and Gothland, but in Germany, where the rarity of these skins makes them to be more esteemed, when it is prised in ships among other merchandise. And I do not think fit to overpasse, that when men sleep under these skins, they have dreams that agree with the nature of that creature and have an insatiable stomach." (Page 180.)

There is a delightful vagueness in the description of this animal's colour. It is a pity that the worthy archbishop's accuracy was not on a par with his credulity. The description given by Grieve, in his *History of Kamschatka*, 1764 (p. 99), of the wolverine deserves quotation, although of a more recent date, as showing the high value set by the natives upon the animal :—

"There is a creature of the weasel kind, called the glutton, whose furr is so greatly esteemed above all others, that when they would describe a man most richly attired, they say that he is cloathed with the furr of the glutton. The women of Kamtschatka dress their heire with the white claws of this animal, and reckon them a very great ornament. However, the Kamtschadales kill so few of them that they not only have not enough for exportation, but even import some from Jakutski at a very great price. They put the greater value upon the furr of the glutton the whiter and yellower it is, although everywhere else this sort is despised ; nay, they esteem it so much, that they say the heavenly beings wear no other garments than of this furr."

The general colour of the wolverine is a rich brown, deepening in parts to black; the young ones are much lighter, of a pale cream yellow. It is only the claws that are white, but they form a striking contrast with the jet black fur of the paws. Marvellous stories are told of the insatiate appetite of the glutton, but after making due allowance for exaggeration it must be admitted that its voracity entitles it to the name, "the vulture of quadrupeds."

Otter.

The Otter was in these times a denizen of most of the rivers in the north and west of England. Fuller, in his *Worthies of England* (vol. 2, p. 573, ed. Nichols, 1811), writes :—

"Plenty of these in Brecknock-meer ; a creature that can dig and dive, resident in the two elements of earth and water. The badger, where he bites, maketh his teeth to meet; and the otter leaves little distance between them. He is as destructive to fish as the wolf to sheep. See we here, more is required to make fine flesh than to have fine feeding; the flesh of the otter, from his innate rankness, being nought, though his diet be dainty."

Shakspeare has but one mention of this animal:—

"*Hostess.* Say, what beast, thou knave, thou?
Falstaff. What beast! why, an otter.
Prince. An otter, Sir John! why an otter?
Fal. Why, she's neither fish nor flesh."

(1 *Henry IV.*, iii. 3, 141.)

The doubt among learned men as to the nature of the otter, hinted at in the above passage, was not quite cleared up even in the time of Izaak Walton, who declines to commit himself by speaking positively on the subject.

Olaus Magnus writes of the otters of Norway:—

"The otters have a square mouth, and bite as beavers, they are like them in their skins but they are a third part longer. Their skins are greatly used by the northern people, to enlarge the borders of their garments, because their skin will hold fast. They are sold by tens, as beavers and foxes, and martins skins are: and they are falsified with smoke of a stone-tree upon coles, that they may appear to be of a shining black; but if you rub them presently with a white cloth, the colour is gone, and the sophistication is discovered. So wolves skins powdred, with coal and chalk, rubbed with a linnen cloth, are proved to be falsified. So squirrels skins, called in Italian *dossœ*, strewed over with chalk, are discovered to be false by a black cloth. We must search out which colour is natural, and which artificial, and so prize them." (Page 183.)

Those who talk sentimentally about the "good old times," would fain have us believe that such deceptions as are here described are inventions of a modern date.

Sir Thomas Browne records that otters were plentiful in his time: "They are accounted no bad dish by many; they are to be made very tame; and in some houses have served for turnspits" (vol. iv. p. 336, ed. Wilkins). They could hardly have been trusted when fish formed part of the meal.

The Badger was also known by the names bawson, brock, and gray. In Ben Jonson's *Sad Shepherd*, a country swain brings as a present to his mistress a fine—

Badger.

"Smooth bawson cub, the young grice of a gray,
Twa tyny urshins and this ferret gay" (i. 1).

The first line of this passage has given rise to some discussion. Whalley reads "bawson's cub, and the young ones of a badger." Gifford, in his edition, explains *bawson*, which, used as a substantive, is a badger, to mean here plump, sleek. This epithet cannot be applied to a full-grown badger, but might very well be said of a cub. *Grice*, he says, is a suckling of any kind. That this is the correct explanation is shown by the lines a little later on :—

"Thou woo thy love! thy mistress! with twa hedgehogs?
A stinkand brock, a polecat? Out, thou houlet!"

The only mention of this animal that occurs in Shakspeare is when *Sir Toby Belch* applies it as a term of reproach to *Malvolio* : "Marry, hang thee, brock!" (*Twelfth Night*, ii. 5, 114).

The absurd idea that the badger's right legs were of a different length from those on its left, to enable it to run with ease on the side of a hill, lasted long after this period. William Browne, in his poems on country life, is evidently a firm believer in the notion:—

"And as that beast hath legs, which shepherds feare,
Yclep'd a badger, which our lambs doth teare,
One long, the other short, that when he runs
Upon the plaines he halts; but when he wons
On craggy rocks, or steepy hills, we see
None runs more swift, nor easier than he."
(*Britannia's Pastorals*, book i., song 4.)

Topsell writes of the badger,—

"His back is broad, his legs as some say longer on the right side then on the left, and therefore he runneth best when he getteth to the side of a hill or a cart road way." (Page 34.)

To correspond with this statement, the badger in the woodcut which accompanies it is represented as using the legs on the same side together instead of alternately. Sir

Thomas Browne, in his *Enquiry concerning Vulgar Errors*, ridicules this idea, and points out that as, like other animals, it uses its legs diagonally, the brevity had been more tolerable in the cross legs.

Drayton, in his poetical account of the Flood, probably refers to the use made of the skin of this animal as the outer covering for the Jewish tabernacle :—

> "Th' uneven-legg'd badger, whose eye-pleasing skin
> The case to many a curious thing hath been,
> Since that great flood, his fortresses forsakes
> Wrought in the earth, and tho' but halting, makes
> Up to the Ark."
>
> (*Noah's Flood.*)

Canon Tristram, however, considers that though the badger is found commonly in Palestine, it was not likely to have been attainable in sufficient numbers in the Sinaitic wilderness to have furnished skins to the amount required. He imagines that the animal referred to in the Bible was the seal, or dugong; both of which animals, together with the dolphin, are found in considerable abundance in the Red Sea. The badger is also spoken of as furnishing the sandals of the Jewish women (*Natural History of the Bible*, 1873, p. 44).

Topsell mentions two kinds of badgers—

"one resembling a dog in his feet, which is cald canine, the other a hog in his cloven hoofe, and is cald swinish: also these differ in the fashion of their snowt, one resembling the snowt of a dog, the other of a swine, and in their meat, the one eating flesh and carrion like a dogge, the other roots and fruits like a hog; both kinds have bene found in Normandy and other parts of France and Sicillie. In Italy and Germany they eat grayes flesh and boile with it peares, which maketh the flesh tast like the flesh of a porcupine. The flesh is best in September if it be fat, and of the two kindes, the swinish badger is better flesh then the other." (Page 34.)

For this distinction Topsell is probably indebted to Olaus Magnus, who writes :—

"There are two sorts of them [badgers] one that is tame; another wilde, that hath stiffer bristles. It is also called the dog-badger, because his foot is divided like to the dogs: another is called the hog-badger, because his hoof is divided into two. There are some also greater than foxes, that have a hairy bristly skin, and the bristles are stiff, and the skin rough; and with these they cover all their quivers for war or hunting, to keep their arrows from the wet and snow. Also mens cloaths are made of them." (Page 187.)

In an early version of *Reynard the Foxe*, the badger is called "grymbart the dasse," from the German *dachs*, whence also comes the modern dachshund, or badger-hound.

Every variety of the weasel tribe possesses as a weapon of defence a disagreeable scent. The Skunk has the power of emitting, at will, a secretion so fetid that the odour thereof can put to flight both man and beast. "All the perfumes of Arabia will not sweeten" any substance that has been tainted by this "odoriferous stench." The skunk is described, though under another name, by a Portuguese resident in Brazil:—

Skunk.

"The biarataca is of the bignesse of a cat, like a ferret; it hath a white stroake and a grey along the backe, like a crosse, very well made; it feeds upon birds and their egges, and upon other things, especially upon ambar, and loveth it so well that all the night he goeth by the seaside to seeke it, and where there is any, hee is the first. It is greatly feared, not because it hath any teeth, or any other defensive thing, but it hath a certaine ventositie so strong, and so evill of sent, that it doth penetrate the wood, the stones, and all that it encountreth withall, and it is such that some Indians have died with the stench. And the dog that commeth neere it escapeth not: and this smell lasteth fifteene, twentie, or more days, and it is such that if it lighteth neere some towne, it is presently disinhabited." (*Purchas*, vol. iv., p. 1304.)

The last statement savours of exaggeration.

The same writer describes the Coati, or Coati-mundi, an animal found in Central and South America:—

Coati.

"The coaty, is of the height of an hare, with short and spotted haire, with little and sharpe eares, both of a little head, and also with an eminent snout from the eyes, more then a foote long, round like a walking-staffe, suddenly decreasing at the end, so that it is altogether of an equall thicknesse, with so narrow a mouth that it can scarce receive the little finger. None may be found more monstrous: afterward, when this wilde beast is taken, gathering her foure feet together, shee bendeth her selfe to the one side or the other, or falleth flat downe: nor can shee ever bee raised, nor compelled to eate, unlesse ants be given her, on which shee also feedeth in the woods." (*Purchas*, vol. iv. p. 1328.)

Besides ants and other insects, the coati lives on eggs and small birds.

The Bear might almost claim to be classed among the domestic animals, so familiar must it have been in Elizabeth's time to all who lived in London or any other large town. Its life, however, was far less enjoyable than that of its fellows who had been more completely domesticated by man. It was either penned up in a shed, or led about the country by a chain in company with a monkey and one or two performing dogs. Shakspeare's references to the sport of bear-baiting are numerous. *Slender* says—

Bear.

" I love the sport well; but I shall as soon quarrel at it as any man in England. You are afraid, if you see the bear loose, are you not?

"*Anne.* Ay indeed, sir.

"*Slen.* That's meat and drink to me, now. I have seen Sackerson loose twenty times, and have taken him by the chain ; but, I warrant you, the women have so cried and shrieked at it, that it passed: but, women, indeed, cannot abide 'em ; they are very ill-favoured rough things." (*Merry Wives*, i. 1.)

This bear is mentioned also by Sir John Davies, who describes a law student—

"Leaving old Ploydon, Dier, and Brooke alone,
To see old Harry Hunks and Sacarson."

(*Epigrams.*)

G

Ben Jonson mentions two of the most famous fighters who were named after their owners:—

"When *Ned Whiting* or *George Stone* were at the stake."
(*The Silent Woman*, iii. 1.)

Bear-baiting was at this time considered not only a suitable exhibition to be presented before the queen and her nobles, but the amusement was placed under the particular patronage of her Majesty. An order of the Privy Council in July, 1591, prohibited the performance of plays on Thursdays, because on Thursdays bear-baiting, and the like pastimes, had been usually practised; and an injunction to the same effect was sent to the Lord Mayor, wherein it is stated, "That in divers places the players do use to recite their plays, to the great hurt and destruction of bear-baiting, and the like pastimes, which are maintained for her Majesty's pleasure" (Nichols, *Progresses*, p. 438, note). The bears for the queen's royal pleasure were kept at the Paris Garden, Bankside, Southwark, close to the river; and as the land lay somewhat low, probably when the tide rose higher than usual the bears found their quarters rather damp.

"It was the day what time the powerful moon
Makes the poor Bankside creature wet its shoon
In its own hall."
(BEN JONSON, *Epigram* 133.)

Paris Garden was named after Robert de Paris, a nobleman of the time of Richard II., who had a house and garden on the same site. Crowley, a poet of the time of Henry VIII., describes these gardens as then existing. He says that exhibitions were held there on Sundays, and that the price of admission was one halfpenny. The popularity of the pastime in Elizabeth's time caused the entrance fee to be raised. Lambarde tells us (*Perambulation of Kent*, p. 248) that, in 1570, visitors to Paris Gardens were charged "one pennie at the gate, another to the entrie of the scaffold, and a third for quiet standing." Sunday was the day usually selected for the sport, but towards the end of the century public opinion declared against such desecration of the sabbath. An accident at Paris Gardens, Sunday, January 13, 1583, when many people were injured by the falling of the stage during a bear-baiting, was made the occasion of much moralizing in clerical pulpits.

At this period every town of importance had its bear, bearward, and set of dogs. A story is told against the people of Congleton, in Cheshire, which, though it varies in different versions, is a good illustration of the fondness of this pastime which prevailed. One version of the story is that the people of Congleton, about the year 1620, being in want of a new Bible at the chapel, laid up a sum of money for the purpose of replacing the worn-out volume. But the town bear happened to die at that time, and the bearward being unable to purchase another applied to the corporation for assistance. The corporation gave him the sum set apart for buying the new Bible, and left the minister to put up with the old one as well as he could. Others say that the authorities only gave the bearward the money arising from the sale of the old Bible, or gave him the old Bible to sell for that purpose. However it arose, the tale spread, and grew into a rhyme, which is still occasionally quoted, to the great indignation of the inhabitants of the town:—

"'Congleton rare, Congleton rare,
Sold the Bible to pay for a bear.'"
(*Notes and Queries*, 3rd series, vol. ii. p. 166.)

Bears were brought to England from various countries. In a description of a voyage to Cherie Island by Jonas Poole, 1609, the author says:—

"The thirtieth day we slue 26 whales, and espied three white beares: we went aboord for shot and powder, and comming to the ice againe, we found a shee-beare and two young ones: Master Thomas Welden shot and killed her: after shee was slayne, wee got the young ones, and brought them home into England, where they are alive in Paris Garden." (*Purchas*, vol. iii. p. 563.)

Olaus Magnus, Archbishop of Upsal, the naturalist of the North, has a good deal of information, more or less trustworthy, to give about bears and their uses. He writes:—

"The bears are huge, white, and strong, and they will break the ice with their paws. These white bears skins are wont to be offered by the hunters, for the high altars, or cathedrals, of parochial churches, that the priest celebrating Mass standing, may not take cold of his feet when the weather is extream cold. In the church at Nidrosum, which is the metropolis of the kingdom of Norway, every year such white skins are found, that are faithfully offered by the hunters devotion, whensoever they take them, and wolves-skins, to buy wax-light, and to burn them in honour of the saints." (Page 187.)

According to this author the brown varieties, which were often taught to dance and beg, were made the medium of instruction as well as amusement:—

"The master of these bears, that cannot speak the language of other countries, will get a good gain by his dumb beast. Nor doth this seem to be done onely, because that these should live by this small gain: for the bearherds that lead these bears, are at least ten or twelve lusty men; and in their company, sometimes, there go noblemens sons, that they may learn the fashions, manners, and distances of places, the military arts, and concord of princes, by these merry pastimes. But since they were found in Germany to spoil travellers and to cast them to their bears to eat, most strict laws are made against them, that they may never come there again. But that tame bears may not onely be kept unprofitably to feed and make sport, they are set to the wheels in the courts of great men, that with one or two, or more company to help them, they may draw up water out of deep wells; and that in huge vessels made for this purpose, and they do not help alone this way, but they are set to draw great waggons, for they are very strong in their legs, claws, and loins; nor is it unfit to make them go upright, and carry burdens of wood, and such like, to the place appointed, or they stand at great mens doors, to keep out other hurtful creatures. When they are young, they will play wonderfully with boys, and do them no hurt." (*History of the Goths*, p. 191.)

It is to be feared that the worthy archbishop was somewhat credulous, and listened too readily to stories of the Norwegian bears' docility, as he does not mention that he witnessed any of these feats.

The notion handed down from antiquity, notwithstanding its manifest absurdity, and the numerous opportunities that must have occurred for its disproof, that the bear's cubs are shapeless and require to be moulded into form by the mother's tongue, is referred to by Shakspeare :—

> " Like to a chaos, or an unlick'd bear-whelp,
> That carries no impression like the dam."
> (3 *Henry VI.*, iii. 2, 161.)

Chester tells us that the bear—

> " Brings forth at first a thing that's indigest,
> A lump of flesh without all fashion,
> Which she by often licking brings to rest,
> Making a formal body good and sound,
> Which often in this iland we have found."
> (*Love's Martyr*, p. 208.)

Olaus Magnus makes the same mistake. Describing the bear, he writes :—

> " For the most part she useth to bring forth five whelps not much greater than mice, without any shape: their flesh is white but they have not eyes, nor hair: yet the nails appear: the dams by degrees, lick these whelpes into form." (Page 188.)

Lyly, who delights in all the absurdities connected with ancient natural history, informs us that " where the bear cannot find origanum to heal her griefe, hee blasteth all other leaves with his breath " (*Epilogue to Campaspe*).

Mr. Furnivall notes that so early as this period bear's grease was recommended for promoting the growth of the hair. He quotes the following passage from W. Bulleyn's *Booke of Simples*, fol. 76 :—

> " The beare is a beaste whose flesh is good for mankynd: his fat is good, with laudanum, to make an oyntment to heale balde headed

men to receive the hayre agayne. The grease of the beare, the fatte of a lamb, and the oyntment of the fox, maketh a good oyntment to anoynt the feete against the payne of travell or labour of footemen." (*Notes and Queries*, 4th series, vol. ix. p. 484.)

Bear's grease is also recommended in old works on husbandry as a preventive against mildew and blight. All tools, such as rakes, spades, and shovels, were to be smeared with this substance preparatory to beginning gardening operations.

CHAPTER V.

ALTHOUGH whales, seals, and other marine inhabitants were always included among fish by writers of the Elizabethan period, yet there evidently existed in the minds of some authors a misgiving as to whether this arrangement was correct. Pious Catholics were slow to be persuaded that these aquatic mammalia were blood relations of the bear, and resolved as long as possible to take the benefit of the doubt. Harrison, in his description of England prefixed to Holinshed's *Chronicle*, decides that under the head of sea-fish should be included "the seale, the dolphin, the porpoise, the thirlepoole, whale, and whatsoever is round of bodie be it never so great and huge" (*Holinshed*, vol. i. p. 377). Pennant, writing so late as 1791, quite declines to accept the modern classification. He admits that they have in many respects the structure of land animals, but he holds that their want of hair and feet, their fish-like form, and their constant residence in the water, are arguments for separating them from this class, and forming them into another independent of the rest.

Captain John Monck, in his account of a voyage to Greenland, taken about the year 1600, thus describes the Walrus :—

"The sea horses are very strange creatures, approaching to the bigness of a moderate ox, having four legs, the two hindermost being very unshapable, and a very thick hide. Their heads are vastly large, having teeth each of about a foot long, as white as the best ivory. The English call them *sea-horses*, the Dutch *wallnissets* and the Muscovites *morse*. It was in the year 1593 that the English sent the first time their ships to catch the sea horses, and continued the trade with great advantage for several years after." (*Churchill's Voyages*, vol. i. p. 441.)

A *Briefe Note of the Morsse and the use thereof*, further explains the value of the different parts of the walrus:—

"In the voyage of Jaques Carthier, wherein he discovered the Gulfe of S. Laurance and the said Isle of Ramea in the yeere 1534, he met with these beastes, as he witnesseth in these words: About the said island are very great beasts as great as oxen, which have two great teeth in their mouthes like unto elephants teeth, and live in the sea. Wee sawe one of them sleeping upon the banks of the water, and thinking to take it, we went to it with our boates, but so soone as he heard us, he cast himselfe into the sea. Touching these beasts which Jaques Carthier saith to be as big as oxen, and to have teeth in their mouthes like elephants teeth: true it is that they are called in Latine *boves marini*, or *caccæ marinæ*, and in the Russian tongue *morsses*, the hides whereof I have seene as big as any oxe hide, and being dressed I have yet a piece of one thicker then any two oxe or buls hides in England. The leather dressers take them to be excellent good to make light targets against the arrowes of the savages: and I hold them farre better then the light leather targets which the Moores use in Barbarie against arrowes and lances, whereof I have seene divers in her majesties stately armorie in the Towre of London. The teeth of the sayd fishes, whereof I have seene a dry flat full at once, are a foote and sometimes more in length: and have bene sold in England to the combe and knife maker at 8 groats and 3 shillings the pound weight, whereas the best ivory is sold for halfe the money: the graine of the bone is somewhat more yellow then the ivorie. One M. Alexander Woodson of Bristoll, my old friend, an excellent mathematician and skilful phisition, shewed me one of these beasts teeth which were brought from the Isle of Ramea in the first prize, which was half a yard long or very little lesse: and assured mee that he had made tryall of it in ministering medicine to his patients, and had found it as soveraigne against poyson as any unicornes horne."

This note was appended to a letter sent to the "Right Honourable Sir William Cecill, Lord Burghley, from

Thomas James, of Bristoll." The letter is dated the 14th of September, 1591, and announces the discovery of the Isle of Ramea by two small ships of Saint Malo, one of which was taken as a prize by a ship of which James was part owner (*Hakluyt*, vol. iii. p. 238).

According to Olaus Magnus the walrus was a formidable antagonist of the whale, and occasionally of human beings :—

"The Norway coast, toward the more northern parts, hath huge great fish as big as elephants, which are called *morsi*, or *rosmari*, may be they are so called from their sharp biting; for if they see any man on the sea-shore, and can catch him, they come suddenly upon him, and rend him with their teeth, that they will kill him in a trice. Therefore, these fish called rosmari, or morsi, have heads fashioned like to an oxes, and a hairy skin, and hair growing as thick as straw or corn-reeds, that lye loose very largely." (Page 231.)

The Norwegian word, *rosmar*, signifies a sea-horse. Notwithstanding its size and formidable appearance the walrus is not the ferocious animal here described. It will not attack man unprovoked, and only uses its teeth when driven to extremities. The walrus is probably the same as the rosmarine mentioned by Spenser in his list of marine monsters.

Jonas Poole, in an account of a voyage to Cherie Island, in the North Seas, chronicles the capture of a young walrus, and its safe conduct to London.

"The twelfth day [July, 1608] we took into our ship two young morses, male and female, alive : the female died before we came into England, the male lived above ten weekes. The twentieth of August wee arrived at London; and having dispatched some private businesse, we brought our living young morse to the court, where the king and many honourable personages beheld it with admiration for the strangenesse of the same, the like whereof had never before beene seene alive in England. Not long after it fell sicke and died. As the beast in shape is very strange, so is it of strange docilitie, and apt to be taught, as by good experience we often proved." (*Purchas*, vol. iii. p. 560.)

Seal. Olaus Magnus has no mention of the Seal by that name, but his description of the sea-calf can apply to no other animal. He writes (p. 226):

"Because in the Bothnick and Finland Sea, there is a vast company of sea-calves: wherefore I will set down briefly the nature of them, and the way to catch them, which I have seen. The sea-calf, which also in Latine is called *helcus*, hath its name from the likeness of a land-calf, and it hath a hard fleshy body; and therefore is hard to be killed, but by breaking the temples of the head. They will low in their sleep, thence are they called calves. They will learn, and with their voyce and countenance salute the company, with a confused murmuring; called by their names, they will answer: no creature sleeps more profoundly; the fins that serve them for to swim in the sea, serve for legs on land, and they go hobling up and down as lame people do. Their skins, though taken from their bodies, have always a sense of the seas, the right fin hath a soporiferous quality, to make one sleep, if it be put under ones head. They that fear thunder, think those tabernacles best to live in, that are made of sea-calves skins, because onely this creature in the sea, as an eagle in the ayr, is safe and secure from the stroke of thunder."

Camden also uses the word sea-calf, in his notes on Sussex.

"*Selsey* befor said, is somewhat lower in the Saxon tongue, *sealsey*, that is to say, the Isle of Sea-calves, for these in our language we call seale, which alwaies seek to islands, and to the shore, for to bring forth their yong, but now it is most famous for good cockles, and full lobsters." (*Britain*, p. 308, ed. Holland, 1610.)

From Carew's *Survey of Cornwall*, published 1602, we learn that seals were no unfrequent visitors on the Cornish coast. Carew writes:—

"The seal, or soyl, is in making and growth not unlike a pig, ugly faced, and footed like a moldwarp [mole]; he delighteth in music, or any loud noise, and thereby is trained to approach near the shore, and to shew himself almost wholly above water. They also come on land and lie sleeping in holes of the cliffs; but are now and then waked with the deadly greeting of a bullet in their sides." (Page 106, ed. 1811.)

Spenser attributes combativeness to the seal, but unfortunately does not state his authority :—

> "As when a dolphin and a sele are met
> In the wide champian of the ocean plaine,
> With cruell chaufe their courages they whet,
> The masterdome of each by force to gaine."
> (*Faerie Queene*, vol. 2, 15.)

The amphibious nature of the seal caused great perplexity to Catholics, as to whether they might lawfully indulge in it during Lent. After much discussion, ecclesiastics came to the conclusion that if the creature were surprised on land, and took refuge in the woods, men must forbear to eat of it in Lent, when flesh is forbidden ; but if he should run to the waters, men may safely eat thereof. This nice distinction deserves credit for its ingenuity, and we may easily imagine that hungry sailors would take care that seals, when pursued, took the desired direction.

We find many notices and descriptions of the Whale by the early navigators. The most accurate account of the different varieties of whales is given by Thomas Edge, in a narrative of the first whaling expedition sent out by the Russian company in London to the coast of Greenland in the year 1611 :—

Whale.

"The whale is a fish or sea-beast of a large bignesse, about sixtie five foot long, and thirtie five foot thicke, his head is a third part of all his bodies quantitie, his spacious mouth contayning a very great tongue, and all his finnes, which we call whale finnes. These finnes are fastned or rooted in his upper chap, and spread over his tongue on both sides his mouth, being in number about two hundred and fiftie on one side, and as many on the other side. The longest finnes are placed in the midst of his mouth, and the rest doe shorten by their proportionable degrees, backward and forwards, from ten or eleven foot long to foure inches in length, his eyes are not much bigger then an oxes eyes. There are eight severall kinds of whales, and differing the one from the other in goodnesse, quantitie and qualitie.

"The first sort of whale is called the *grand-bay*, taking his name from Grand Bay in Newfoundland, as having there beene first killed :

he is blacke of colour, with a smooth skinne, and white underneath the chaps.

"The second sort of whale is called *sarda*, of the same colour as the former, but somewhat lesser, and the finnes likewise lesser, aud yeelds in oyle according to his bignesse. This whale hath naturally growing upon his backe white things like unto barnacles.

"The third sort of whale is called *trumpa*, being as long as the first but thicker forwards, of colour more gray then the former, having but one spoute in his head, aud the rest have all two ; he hath in his mouth teeth about a span long, and as thicke as a mans wrist, but no finnes. In the head of this whale is the permesitie, which lieth there in a hole like a well. This is the whale that is supposed to yeeld the ambergreese.

"The fourth sort of whale is called *otta sotta*, and is of the same colour of the trumpa, having finnes in his mouth all white, but not above halfe a yard long, being thicker then the trumpa, but not so long.

"The fift sort of whale is called *gibarta*, of colour blacke like the two first, saving that it hath standing upon the top of his backe, a finne half a yard long. This whale is as bigge as the first, his fins little or nothing worth, being not above halfe a yard long.

"The sixt sort is called *sedena*, being of a whitly colour, and bigger then any of the former, the finnes not above one foot long, and he yeelds little or no oyle.

"The seventh is called *sedena negro*, of colour blacke, with a bumpe on his backe ; this whale yeelds neither oyle, finnes, nor teeth, and yet he is of a great bignesse.

"The eight sort is called *sewria*, of colour as white as snow, of the bignesse of a wherrie, he yeelds not above one hogshead or two of oyle, nor any finnes, and is good meate to be eaten." (*Purchas*, vol. iii. p. 476.)

Olaus Magnus, who ought to be the chief authority on the subject of whales, owing to the opportunities he had for personal observation, gives such scope to his imagination that his account is more amusing than instructive. He writes :—

"There are many kinds of whales, some are hairy, and of four acres in bigness : the acre is 240 foot long, and 120 broad : some are smooth-skinned, and those are smaller, and are taken in the west and northern sea; some have their jaws long and full of teeth, and the teeth are 6 or 8 or 12 foot long, but their two dog-teeth, or tushes, are

Introduction of Whalebone. 93

longer than the rest, underneath like a horn, like the teeth of bores, or elephants. This kind of whale hath a fit mouth to eat: and his eyes are so large, that 15 men may sit in the room of each of them. His horns are 6 or 7 foot long, and he hath 250 upon each eye, as hard as horn, that he can stir stiff or gentle, either before, or behind. These grow together, to defend his eyes in tempestuous weather, or when any other beast that is his enemy sets upon him; nor is it a wonder, that he hath so many horns though they be very troublesome to him; when as between his eyes, the space of his forehead is 15 or 20 foot." (Page 226.)

Du Bartas is scarcely less absurd :—

"Our fear-less saylers, in far voyages
(More led by gain's hope than their compasses)
On th' Indian shore, have somtime noted som
Whose bodies covered two broad acres room :
And in the South-seas they have also seen
Some like high-topped and huge armed treen;
And other-som whose monstrous backs did bear
Two mighty wheels with whirling spokes, that were
Much like the winged and wide spreading sayles
Of any winde-mill turn'd with merry gales."
(*Divine Weekes*, p. 40.)

The whale fishery, so important a branch of maritime industry and adventure, had its rise in the time of Elizabeth. Hakluyt, 1575, reports the request of an honest merchant, by letter to a friend of his, to be advised and directed in the course of killing the whale. The oil was the only produce for which the whale was at first valued. Anderson, in his *Origin of Commerce*, 1801, traces the introduction of whalebone into England to an accident. Some English ships were sent, in 1593, to Cape Breton on a whaling expedition. At the entrance of the Bay of Saint Lawrence the sailors found no whales, but came to a store of 800 whale fins which had been left on an island by some Biscay ship, that was afterwards wrecked. Deeming the fins of some value, the sailors brought them home, and we have soon after this date the first mention of whale bones or fins being used in various articles of ladies' dress. These fins, as explained by Edge, are the horny laminæ adhering to the upper jaw of the whale, and are a substitute for teeth. They are only found in perfection in the Greenland whale and a few other varieties. The spermaceti and white whales possess teeth and no fins. The expression so often used, " white as whale's bone," arose from the supposition on the part of early English writers that ivory was a portion of the bones of the whale. The ivory of the Middle Ages was supplied chiefly by the walrus, whose teeth were brought over in considerable quantities by the Northern fishermen. Shakspeare only follows numerous examples when he writes :—

> "This is the flower that smiles on every one,
> To show his teeth as white as whale his bone."
> (*Love's Labour Lost*, v. 2, 331.)

Harrison, describing the extreme North of Scotland and the Orkney Isles, writes :—

> " Such plentie of whales also are taken on this coast that the verie tithe hath beene-knowne in some one yeere to amount unto seaven and twentie whales of one greatnesse and other." (*Holinshed*, vol. i. p. 73, ed. 1807.)

Shakspeare mentions the whale several times, and it is quite possible he may have seen a stranded specimen. Gesner tells of a whale that was cast on shore near Tynemouth Haven, in 1532, which measured ninety feet in length.

The Whirlpool is included by Harrison in his list of English fishes. The description of this creature by Olaus Magnus will, however, apply to no known species. The northern chronicler informs us that—

Marine Monsters.

> "the whirlpool, or prister, is of the kind of whales, two hundred cubits long, and is very cruel. For, to the danger of sea-men, he will

sometimes raise himself beyond the sail-yards, and casts such floods of waters above his head, which he had sucked in, that with a cloud of them he will often sink the strongest ships, or expose the mariners to extream danger. This beast hath also a long and large round mouth like a lamprey, whereby he sucks in his meat or water, and by his weight cast upon the fore or hinder deck, sinks and drowns a ship. He hath a thick black skin all his body over, long fins like to broad feet, and a forked tail, 15 or 20 feet broad, wherewith he forcibly binds any parts of the ship, he twists it about. A trumpet of war is the fit remedy against him, by reason of the sharp noise, which he cannot endure." (Page 226.)

By other writers the sawfish is called the whirlpool, or physeter. It would not, perhaps, be worth while to notice these extravagancies but that Spenser must have some authority or suggestion for his list of marine monsters in the *Faerie Queene* (xii. 23, 24) :—

> "Spring-headed hydres; and sea-shouldring whales,
> Great whirlpooles, which all fishes make to flee;
> Bright scolopendraes armd with silver scales;
> Mighty monoceros with immeasured tayles;
>
> "The dreadful fish, that hath deserved the name
> Of Death, and like him lookes in dreadfull hew;
> The griesly wasserman, that makes his game
> The flying ships with swiftness to pursew;
> The horrible satyre, that doth shew
> His fearefull face in time of greatest storme;
> Huge ziffius, whom mariners eschew
> No less than rockes, as travellers informe;
> And greedy rosmarines with visages deforme."

In these lines *scolopendra*, the name of the centipede, is probably applied to the sea-serpent; *monoceros* is the narwhal or sea-unicorn; the *dreadful fish* is the morse or walrus, so also is the *rosmarine;* the *satyr* is the merman, dreaded by sailors as foreboding tempest; *ziffius* is probably xiphias, the sword-fish.

Harrison mentions both the Dolphin and the porpoise, and they seem to have been generally recognised as distinct species, notwithstanding Dolphin.

their strong likeness. Sir Richard Hawkins, in his account of a voyage to the South Sea, writes:—

"Ordinarily such ships as navigate between the tropickes are accompanied with three sorts of fish: the dolphin, which the Spaniards call *dozado*: the bonito, or Spanish mackerill: and the sharke, *alias* tiberune. The dolphin I hold to be one of the swiftest fishes in the sea. He is like unto a breame, but that he is longer and thinner, and his scales very small. Hee is of the colour of the rain-bow, and his head different to other fishes; for, from his mouth halfe a span it goeth straite upright, as the head of a wherry, or the cut-water of a ship. He is very good meate if he be in season, but the best part of him is his head, which is great. They are some bigger, some lesser; the greatest that I have seene might be some foure foot long." (*Purchas*, vol. iv. p. 1330.)

In the city pageants a dolphin was a common device. It was sometimes crowned, and then represented the arms of the Fishmongers' Company. In allusion to the classical myth, Arion, the lyric poet of Lesbos, was often depicted seated on the dolphin's back. Ben Jonson refers twice to this device:—

"Another Orpheus, you slave, another Orpheus! An Arion riding on the back of a dolphin." (*The Poetaster*, iv. 1.)

"Give him allowance,
And that but a moderate, he will make a syren
Sing in the kettle, send in an Arion
In a brave broth, and of a watery green,
Just the sea-colour, mounted on the back
Of a grown conger, but in such a posture
As all the world would take him for a dolphin."
(*The Staple of News*, iii. 2.)

Shakspeare possibly refers to one of these city shows:—

"My gentle Puck, come hither. Thou rememberest
Since once I sat upon a promontory,
And heard a mermaid on a dolphin's back
Uttering such dulcet and harmonious breath

Arion on a Dolphin.

> That the rude sea grew civil at her song
> And certain stars shot madly from their spheres,
> To hear the sea-maid's music."
> (*Midsummer Night's Dream*, ii. 1, 148.)

Here, as elsewhere, Shakspeare confuses the mermaid of mediæval times with the siren of classical authors. The fish-like tail of the mermaid, which would have rendered her quite independent of any assistance from the dolphin, would also have caused her to have a somewhat insecure seat on so frolicsome a steed. In *Twelfth Night* (i. 2, 14) we find another allusion to this water Pegasus. The captain of the shipwrecked vessel encourages *Viola* to hope for her brother's safety by telling how he saw *Sebastian* bind himself—

> "To a strong mast that lived upon the sea;
> Where, like Arion on the dolphin's back,
> I saw him hold acquaintance with the waves
> So long as I could see."

Sir Thomas Browne treats as a vulgar error the notion that the back of the dolphin was permanently bowed, alluded to by Ford:—

> "Straight comes a dolphin playing near your ship,
> Heaving his crooked back up."
> (*The Lover's Melancholy*, i. 1.)

In art the dolphin was employed as an emblem of social feeling and affection.

The Narwhal, or Sea-Unicorn, another semi-mythical beast of the sea, was the object of much speculation, and his horn was supposed to have the same virtue as an antidote to poison as that of the land unicorn. It is described in a letter quoted from Mr. Wormen, a Danish gentleman, as having the head of a whale, with a long pointed horn, fixed to the upper part of the left jawbone. The creature is called by the Icelanders narwhall, which implies a whale living upon

Narwhal.

a dead carcase—*wall* signifying a whale and *nar* the carcase (*Churchill's Voyages*, vol. i.).

Baffin, the discoverer, writes to Sir John Wostenholme:—

"As for the sea unicorne, it being a great fish, having a long horn or bone growing forth of his forehead or nostrill, such as Sir Martin Frobisher in his second voyage found one, in divers places we saw them, which if the horne be of any good value, no doubt but many of them may be killed." (*Purchas*, vol. iii. p. 843.)

The specimen found by Frobisher is described by him in Hakluyt's *Travels*. It is a pity that the experiment recorded was not tried also on some non-poisonous insect.

"On this west shore," he writes, "we found a dead fish floating, which had in his nose a horne streight and torquet, of length two yards lacking two ynches. Being broken in the top, here we might perceive it hollow, into the which some of our sailors, putting spiders, they presently died. I saw not the triall hereof, but it was reported unto me of a truth: by the vertue whereof we supposed it to be the sea unicorne." (*Hakluyt*, vol. iii. p. 59.)

Porpoise. The appearance of the Porpoise was always held to foretell a storm:—

"Come, porpoise, where's Haterius?
His gout keeps him most miserably constant!
Your dancing shows a tempest."
(BEN JONSON, *Sejanus*, v. 10.)

Webster writes:—

"He lifts his nose like a porpus before a storm."
(*Duchess of Malfy*.)

Shakspeare's only reference to the porpoise is to the same effect. The fishermen in *Pericles* discuss the recent tempest, and one of them sagely observes:—

"Nay, master, said not I as much when I saw the porpus how he bounced and tumbled? They say they're half fish, half flesh: a plague on them! they ne'er come but I look to be washed" (ii. 1, 24).

The porpoise, though not now considered a palatable dish, was in earlier times frequently eaten. It was even thought a dainty, and was dressed in a variety of ways. Sometimes it was prepared with a sauce made of fine bread-crumbs, mixed with vinegar and sugar; at other times it was roasted or stewed with blanched almonds or onions. Andrew Boorde, in his *Dietary*, 1542, speaks contemptuously of its culinary properties: " A yonge porpesse, the which kynde of fysshe is nother praysed in the Olde Testament nor in physycke " (Early English Text Society, ed. Furnivall, 1870, p. 268.)

The Ork, or Orca, was apparently the same as the grampus, thresher, or ardluk. It is not unlike the porpoise in shape, but larger and more powerful. It has been invested by poets with mythical powers. Du Bartas writes :— Ork.

> " When on the surges I perceive, from far,
> Th' ork, whirl-poole whale, or huffing physeter,
> Methinks I see the wandering ile again
> (Ortygian Delos) floating on the main."
> *(Divine Weekes,* p. 40.)

Olaus Magnus tells us that—

"an orca is like a hull turned inside outward; a beast with fierce teeth, with which as with the stern of a ship he rends the whales guts, and tears his calves body, or he quickly runs and drives him up and down with his prickly back, that he makes him run to fords and shores. But the whale that cannot turn its huge body, not knowing how to resist the wily orca, puts all its hopes in flight : yet that flight is weak, because this sluggish beast, burdened with its own weight, wants one to guide her, to fly to the foords to escape the dangers." (Page 226.)

Jonas Poole, one of the early whalers, gives a similar, but less exaggerated, description of this cetacean. The grampus is in truth the great terror of the inhabitants of the northern seas. Not content with seals and porpoises, it will even attack large whales, and its appearance is sufficient to put whole shoals of the latter to flight.

The grampus has a fin on its back, but not of the dimensions or sharpness sometimes ascribed to it. Insatiate in its appetite, this creature may well be accounted the emblem of voracity.

" 'Twere to consider too curiously " to attempt to give an accurate scientific description of the marine monstrosity which *Lear* imagined to exceed in deformity filial ingratitude :—

> "Ingratitude, thou marble-hearted fiend,
> More hideous when thou show'st thee in a child
> Than the sea-monster."
>
> (*Lear*, i. 4, 281.)

Blefkens, whose account of Iceland in 1563 is included in Purchas's Collection, has evolved from his inner consciousness a creature of whom he might have written—

> " Which cannot look more hideously upon me
> Than I have drawn it in my fantasy : "—

"The Iseland Sea hath a monster also, whose name is unknowne. They judge it a kinde of whale at the first sight, when hee shews his head out of the sea, he so scarreth men that they fall downe almost dead. His square head hath flaming eyes, on both sides fenced with long hornes; his body is blacke, and beset with black quills. If he be seen by night his eyes are fiery, which lighten his whole head, which he putteth out of the sea. Nothing can either bee painted or imagined more fearefull. Olaus Magnus makes mention of this monster in his twentieth booke, and saith that it is twelve cubits long." (*Purchas*, vol. iii. p. 650.)

Manatee. It has been thought that the Manatee, or Dugong, a marine animal, with a round head, two finlike flappers, a long body, and a short broad tail, was the original of the strange stories that were brought home by travellers of the mermaids of the far West. Anything less like the form of a beautiful woman than this dull, shapeless creature it would be difficult to imagine. The manatee exhibited a few years ago at the

Westminster Aquarium, when seen at close quarters, was an inert, clumsy-looking animal, bearing far more resemblance to an overgrown conger than to a human being. But sailors are gifted with considerable powers of fancy, and it may be that the appearance of this creature at dusk, with rounded head lifted above the waves, and sometimes holding its young one to its breast, had a sufficiently human aspect to afford material at least for yarns.

There are some good descriptions of the manatee by some of the more accurate observers who "sailed the Spanish Main." Robert Harcourt, in his relation of a voyage to Guiana, 1608, thus describes this animal:—

"There is also a sea-fish which usually commeth into the fresh waters, especially in the winter and wet season. It is of great esteeme amongst us, and we account it halfe flesh, for the bloud of it is warm. It commeth up into the shallow waters in the drowned lands, and feedeth upon grasse and weedes: the Indians name it *coiumero*, and the Spaniards *manati*, but we call it the sea-cow. In taste it is like beefe, will take salt, and serve to victuall ships. Of this fish may bee made an excellent oile for many purposes; the fat of it is good to frie either fish or flesh. The hide, as I have heard, being dried in the sunne and kept from wet, will serve for targets and armour against the Indian arrowes. In the wet season the store of them are infinite. Some of these were heretofore brought into England by Sir Walter Rawleigh." (*Purchas*, vol. iv. p. 1275.)

Joseph Acosta, a learned Jesuit, and a careful writer, tells us in his observations on the West Indies, that—

"at the Islands which they cal Barlovente, which are Cuba, Saint Dominique, Portrique, and Jamaique, they finde a fish which they call manati, a strange kind of fish, if we may call it fish, a creature which ingenders her young ones alive, and doth nourish them with milke, feeding of grasse in the fields, but in effect it lives continually in the water, and therefore they eate it as fish; yet when I did eate of it at Saint Dominique on a Friday I had some scruple, not for that which is spoken, but for that in colour and taste it was like unto morsels of veale. . . . Manate therefore, is a fish of the sea, of the biggest sort, and much greater than the tiburon [shark] in length and breadth, and is very brutish and vile, so that it appeareth in forme like unto one of those great vessels made of goats skins, wherein they use to carry new wine in Median de Campom. The head of this beast is like the head of an oxe, with also like eyes, and hath in the place of armes, two great stumps wherewith he swimmeth : it is a very gentle and tame beast, and commeth oftentimes out of the water to the next shoare, where if he finde any herbes or grasse he feedeth thereof." (*Purchas,* vol. iii. pp. 931, 987.)

This author is much perplexed by the mode by which the various species of animals, known and unknown, could have found their way to the Indies. As it was not likely that people should have taken the fiercer kinds in ships, and as they could not have swum from the mainland, he concludes that the old and new world were once united. A separate creation in a different part of the world would destroy the value of Noah's ark; moreover, the creation could not be completed in six days if there were yet other kinds to make. It follows then, according to Acosta—

"that those beasts, of whose kindes wee finde not any but at the Indies, have passed thither from this continent, as wee have said of other beasts that are knowne unto us. This supposed, I demand, how is it possible that none of their kinde should remayne here? and how they are found there, being as it were travellers and strangers? Truly it is a question that hath long held me in suspence. Wee must then say, that though all beasts came out of the arke, yet by a naturall instinct, and the providence of heaven, divers kindes dispersed themselves into divers regions, where they found themselves so well as they would not part, or if they departed they did not preserve themselves, but in processe of time perished wholly, as we doe see it chance in many things." (Page 964.)

Robert Burton, in his *Anatomy of Melancholy* (vol. i. p. 497, ed. 1837), alludes to the difficulty suggested by the worthy Jesuit, but is equally at a loss to solve the problem of the distribution of species. He writes:—

" Why doth Africa breed so many venemous beasts, Ireland none? Athens owles, Creet none? Why hath Daulis and Thebes no swallowes, so Pausanias informeth us, as well as the rest of Greece ?—Ithaca no hares, Pontus asses, Scythia swine? Whence come this variety of complections, colours, plants, birds, beasts, metals, peculiar almost to every place? Why so many thousand strange birds and beasts proper to America alone, as Acosta demands? Were they created in six dayes, or ever in Noahs arke? If there, why are they not dispersed and found in other countries? It is a thing, saith he, hath long held me in suspence. No Greek, Latine, Hebrew, ever heard of them before, and yet as differing from our European animals, as an egg and a chesnut: and, which is more, kine, horses, sheep, etc., till the Spaniards brought them were never heard of in those parts."

The popular notion of the Mermaid owed its origin to the classical fable of the siren, a sea maiden, who sat on a rock singing sweetly, and often luring mariners to their destruction. Shakspeare's mermaids are all of the sweet-voiced siren type. Drayton also confuses the two:—

"To call for aid, and then to lie in wait,
So the hyena murthers by deceit:
By sweet enticement sudden death to bring,
So from the rocks th' alluring mermaids sing."
(*England's Heroical Epistles*.)

The mediæval mermaid was supposed to be half fish, half woman, and there are many accounts of specimens that were exhibited at shows. In the time of Elizabeth the mermaid was often adopted as a crest or charge, and was heraldically depicted as a beautiful woman, holding a mirror in her right hand and combing her long golden hair with her left. The arms of the Fishmongers' Company of London were supported most appropriately by a merman and a mermaid.

The Mermaid tavern in Cornhill was the familiar resort of Shakspeare and other writers of the time, whose wit combats are commemorated by Beaumont in his epilogue to Ben Jonson:—

"What things we have seen
Done at the Mermaid! heard words that have been
So nimble, and so full of subtile flame,
As if that every one from whence they came
Had meant to put his whole life in a jest,
And had resolved to live a fool the rest
Of his dull life."

CHAPTER VI.

Horse. However little Shakspeare cared for dogs he always writes as if he loved horses. The enthusiastic praises heaped upon his horse by the Dauphin, though spoken by a foreigner, are evidently genuine. So is the grief of the poor groom of *Richard's* stable at the degradation of "Roan Barbary."

> "*Groom.* O, how it yearn'd my heart when I beheld
> In London streets, that coronation day,
> When Bolingbroke rode on roan Barbary,
> That horse that thou so often hast bestrid,
> That horse that I so carefully have dress'd!
>   *Rich.* Rode he on Barbary? Tell me, gentle friend,
> How went he under him?
>   *Groom.* So proudly as if he disdain'd the ground.
>   *Rich.* So proud that Bolingbroke was on his back!
> That jade hath eat bread from my royal hand;
> This hand hath made him proud with clapping him.
> Would he not stumble? Would he not fall down,
> Since pride must have a fall, and break the neck
> Of that proud man that did usurp his back?"
>   (*Richard II.*, v. 5, 76.)

The description of the courser of Adonis is almost too familiar to quote. The striking resemblance the lines bear to a passage in Du Bartas may, however, be worth noting :—

Horse tamed by Cain.

" Look, when a painter would surpass the life,
In limning out a well-proportion'd steed,
His art with nature's workmanship at strife,
As if the dead the living should exceed ;
So did this horse excel a common one
In shape, in courage, colour, pace, and bone.
" Round-hoof'd, short-jointed, fetlock shag and long,
Broad breast, full eye, small head and nostrils wide, -
High crest, short ears, straight legs and passing strong,
Thin mane, thick tail, broad buttock, tender hide :
Look, what a horse should have he did not lack,
Save a proud rider on so proud a back."
    (*Venus and Adonis*, ll. 289-300.)

Du Bartas, in his sacred history of the world, tells how Cain, when preparing to found a new habitation and a colony, turns for assistance to animals, as human beings are scarce. The troops of wild horses bounding across the plains attract his attention, and—

" Among a hundred brave, light, lusty horses
(With curious eye marking their comly forces,)
He chooseth one for his industrious proof,
With round, high, hollow, smooth, brown, jetty hoof.
With pasterns short, upright, but yet in mean ;
Dry sinewy shanks ; strong, flesh-less knees, and lean ;
With hart-like legs, broad brest, and large behinde,
With body large, smooth flanks, and double-chin'd ;
A crested neck bow'd like a half-bent bowe,
Whereon a long, thin, curled mane doth flowe ;
A firm full tail, touching the lowly ground,
With dock between two fair fat buttocks drownd;
A pricked ear, that rests as little space,
As his light foot ; a lean, bare, bonny face,
Thin joule, and head but of a middle size,
Full, lively-flaming, quickly rowling eyes,
Great foaming mouth, hot-fuming nostrill wide,
Of chest-nut hair, his fore-head starrifi'd,
Three milky feet, a feather on his brest,
Whom seven-years-old at the next grass he ghest."
    (*Divine Weekes and Workes*, p. 106.)

This description would better apply to a horse competing

for a prize at a show than to the desert-born. The reference to the "next grass" is whimsically out of place. Shakspeare was doubtless too well acquainted with the points of a good horse to seek instruction from a foreigner, but less likely still is it that the gallant Huguenot, Sieur du Bartas, had ever seen the English poem. Both writers may have derived their materials from some veterinary work of the time. The date of *Venus and Adonis* is fixed by critics at about 1593. The complete translation of the *Divine Weekes* was published in 1606, but portions of the book had already appeared.

Owing to the state of the roads, which were highly unfavourable for wheeled traffic, horses were largely employed in England as a means of locomotion. Nicander Nucius, in his *Travels through England* in the sixteenth century, observes that the English horses were for the most part white.

Thomas Fuller is not particularly enthusiastic about the English breed. Our English horses, he says—

"have a mediocrity of all necessary good properties in them; as neither so slight as the Barb, nor so slovenly as the Flemish, nor so fiery as the Hungarian, nor so airy as the Spanish gennets, nor so earthly as those in the Low Countries, and generally all the German horse. For stature and strength they are of a middle size, and are bothe seemly and serviceable in a good proportion. And, whilst the seller praiseth them too much, the buyer too little, the indifferent stander-by will give them this due commendation. Yorkshire doth breed the best race of English horses, whose keeping commonly in steep and stony ground bringeth them to firmness of footing and hardness of hoof. Well may Philip be so common a name amongst the gentry of this county, who are generally so delighted in horsemanship." (*Worthies of England*, vol. ii. p. 491, ed. 1811.)

Hobby. Camden mentions an Irish variety of horse, with a special kind of pace :—

"They have likewise excellent good horses, wee terme the Hobies, which have not the same pace that other horses in their course have, but a soft and round amble, setting one legge before another very finely."

Fynes Moryson, describing the natural commodities of the Irish, says:—

"Their horses, called ¸hobbies, are much commended for their ambling pace and beuty: but Ireland yeelds few good horses for service in war, and the said hobbies are much inferior to our geldings in strength to endure long journies, and being bred in the fenny soft ground of Ireland, are soone lamed when they are brought into England." (*Itinerary*, 1617, part iii. p. 160.)

Galloway nags are said to have sprung from some Spanish stallions washed on shore at Galloway, during the wreck of the Armada. Gambalding horses were managed horses of show and parade. The gennet, which Froissart calls a light speedy pleasure horse, Cotgrave makes a Spanish horse. Hackneys, a word derived from the French *haquenée*, and the Italian *achinea*, a little nag, and not, as Maitland (*History of London*, p. 1365) supposes, from hired horses being chiefly engaged for journeys to Hackney, were ridden in marches to ease the war-horses (Fosbroke, *Enc. of Antiquities*, vol. ii. p. 1018, ed. 1843).

Galloway.

The Gennet was kept principally for display, and was a handsome showy animal. In Winwood's *State Papers* (vol. ii. p. 149) we find a letter from Sir Charles Cornwallis, 1605, to the Earl of Salisbury. He writes from Spain, of the Spaniards, "If they get but a day's rest they are not unlike your pampered gennets, which are only estimable for their outward show, nothing for service of effect." Philip Bliss, in his edition of Bishop Earle's *Microcosmography*, gives a passage from an early writer, name unknown, who enthusiastically praises this kind of horse:—

Gennet.

" When Nature first framed him she took a secret complacence in her worke. He is even her masterpeece in irracionall things, borrowing somewhat of all things to set him forth. For example, his silke bay coat hee tooke from the chesnut; his necke from the rainbow, which perhaps makes him rain so well. His maine belike he took from

Pegasus, making him a hobbie, to make this a compleat gennet, which main he wears so curld, much after the women's fashions now adayes; this I am sure of, howsoever it becomes them, it sets forth our gennet well. His legges he borrowed from the hart, with his swiftnesse, which make him a true courser indeed; the starres in his forehead hee fetcht from heaven, which will not be much mist, there being so many."

Montaigne, in his *Essays*, 1580, explains the origin of the word *Destrier*, a name sometimes given to horses employed in tournaments:—

Destrier.

"I am now become a grammarian; I who never learn'd any language but by rote, and who do not yet know adjective, conjunction, or ablative, I think I have read, that the Romans had a sort of horses by them call'd *funales*, or *dextrarios*, which were either led-horses, or horses laid in at several stages to be taken fresh upon occasion; and thence it is, that we call our horses of service *destriers*: and our romances commonly use the phrase of *destrer* for *accompagner*, to accompany. They also call'd such as were dress'd in such sort, that running full speed side by side without bridle or saddle, the Roman gentlemen arm'd at all pieces, would shift, and throw themselves from the one to the other, *desultorios equos*." (*Essay* 37.)

In the *Privy Purse Expenses of Henry VIII.*, there are frequent mentions of the king's horses, and especially of a Barbary horse, called in one place the Barra horse, and in another the Barbarista horse. This horse may have been an Arabian sent as a present from some district of Barbary. The high price of 7s. 2d. was paid at one time for a bath for him.

The drink prepared from mare's milk, now known as *koumiss*, is described by one of Purchas's pilgrims as early as the year 1253. William de Rubruquis, a French friar of the order of Minorites, went a missionary journey through Tartary and China, and sent a detailed account of his travels to King Louis IX. of France. He describes at some length the preparation of cosmos, or fermented mares' milk. As many as three thousand mares were kept on a single estate to furnish the superior article called caracosmos, or black cosmos, a

Koumiss,

beverage reserved for the nobility. The milk, according to this traveller, was poured into a bladder, and shaken till it formed a sediment as thick as butter; the clear portion of the liquid was strained off, and formed a pleasant, slightly intoxicating drink. The lees or dregs were given to servants (*Purchas*, vol. iii. p. 5).

The history of racing in England dates from the reign of James I. This monarch had a passionate fondness for field sports. Under his superintendence a code of regulations was drawn up, which served as a foundation for the laws of racing as they exist to-day. Regular courses were established, in which what were called running-horses competed. Manningham, in his *Diary*, takes notice of what was probably one of the earliest races in England :—

Racing.

"This day [April 6, 1602] there was a race at Sapley neere Huntingdon, invented by the gentlemen of that county : at this Mr. Oliver Cromwell's horse won the sylver bell; and Mr. Cromwell had the glory of the day. Mr. Hynd came behinde." (Ed. Camden Society, 1868, p. 49.)

In Baker's *Chronicle*, 1612, we read that private matches between gentlemen who rode their own horses were very common in that year. The most celebrated races of the time were called bell courses. At these races the prize of a bell was given to the winner. It has been contended that the phrase " to bear the bell " may have had its origin in this custom. It is probably to one of these matches that *Imogen* alludes :—

" I have heard of riding wagers,
Where horses have been nimbler than the sands
That run i' the clock's behalf."

(*Cymbeline*, iii. 2, 74.)

Exhibitions of animals trained to perform tricks were not unfrequent at this period. The plays of the time contain many references to Marocco, a bay gelding, fourteen years old, belonging to a Scotch-

Marocco.

man named Banks. This docile animal was taught to perform a variety of feats: among other exploits, he is reported to have climbed up to the top of St. Paul's, though whether he went up by the galleries within or over the dome is not recorded. "Could the little horse that ambled on the top of St. Paul's carry all the people?" (Webster, *Northward Hoe*, iv. 1). "He keeps more ado with this monster than ever Banks did with his horse" (Ben Jonson, *Every Man out of his Humour*, iv. 5). "I'll teach thee to turn me into Banks his horse and to tell gentlemen I am a jugler and can shew tricks" (Decker, *Satiromastix*).

Shakspeare alludes to Marocco in *Love's Labour Lost*, i. 2: "How easy it is to put 'years' to the word 'three,' and study three years in two words, the dancing horse will tell you." As to the future fate of this intelligent quadruped we read in Mr. Payne Collier's *Poetical Decameron*, 1820, that "poor Marocco and his master were many years afterwards both burnt in Portugal, or, as others say in Rome, for having dealings with the devil." Sir Walter Raleigh, in his *History of the World*, seems to have had a sort of presentiment of the fate of poor Banks, for speaking of " the divers kindes of unlawful magicke," he says,

"And certainly if Bankes had lived in elder times he would have shamed all the inchanters of the world, for whosoever was most famous among them could never master or instruct any beast as he did his horse."

Sir Kenelm Digby also mentions this animal, and observes :—

"He that should tell an Indian, what feates Banks his horse would do; how he would restore a glove to the due owner, after his master had whispered that mans name in his eare ; how he would tell the just number of pence in any piece of silver coyne barely shewed him by his master, would make him, I beleeve, admire more at this learned beast, then we do at their docile elephantes, upon the relations we have of them. Whereas every one of us knoweth by what means his painefull tutor brought him to do all his trickes: and they are no whitte more extraordinary, then a fawkeners manning of a hawke, and trayning her to kill partridges, and to fly at the retrive." (*A Treatise of Bodies*, p. 321, ed. 1644.)

Marocco's feats were apparently outdone in other countries. George Sandys, an Eastern traveller, during his residence in Cairo, seems to have been amused at the number and variety of performing animals in that city: dancing camels, talking ravens, learned dogs, and goats were exhibited. "Asses they will teach to doe such tricks, as if possessed with reason: to whom Bankes his horse would have proved but a zany" (*Purchas*, vol. ii. p. 907).

The earliest notice of Marocco's popularity occurs in a manuscript copy of one of Dr. Donne's satires, dated 1593, preserved in the Harleian manuscript, No. 5110. The best account of Bankes and his horse, says Mr. Douce, is to be found in the notes to a French translation of Apuleius's *Golden Ass*, by Jean de Montlyard, 1602.

The Ass is a native of hot countries; and though it has been in a measure acclimatized in England, the breed has degenerated in the transference. This animal does not appear to have been common in the time of Elizabeth. Nicander Nucius notes, in his travels in England in the reign of Henry VIII., that this country is deficient in the breed of asses and mules.

Ass.

Batman derives the name *ass* from *sedendo*, sitting, as it were a beast to sit on; for men sat and rode upon asses before they used horses to ride upon. Or, he suggests, this name *asinus* may come from *a*, not having, and *synos*, wit, as it were a beast without wit. Quoting Aristotle, Batman further states that as the ass feeds among thorns and briars he excites the enmity of the small birds that build in bushes. His habit of rubbing himself against the thorns causes the birds' eggs to fall out of their nests; and again, when he lifts his head, "then by a strong blast the thorns moveth and shaketh, and of the great noyse the birdes be affeard full sore and falleth out of the nest" (*Batman upon Bartholome*, p. 341). The synonym *donkey* is never used in the time of Shakspeare. It is impossible to write of this animal without recalling *Dogberry's* indignant exclamation, "O that I had been writ down an ass!" (*Much Ado About Nothing*, iv. 2, 90).

The Zebra, one of the most beautiful animals inhabiting the continent of Africa, is mentioned by early travellers, though no specimen seems to have been brought to England, at least up to the time of Shakspeare. Edward Lopes, a Portuguese, in his report of the kingdom of Congo, states that—

Zebra.

"there breedeth in this country, another creature, which they call a zebra, commonly found also in certaine provinces of Barbary and Africa. It hath a most singular skin, and peculiar from all other creatures. For from the ridge of the chin downe towards the belly it is straked with rowes of three colours, blacke, white, and browne bay, about the breadth of three fingers a piece, and so meet againe together in a circle, every row, with his owne colour."

After giving a full description of the various parts of the animal the writer goes on to admire its speed, which, he says, is admirable:—

"insomuch as in Portugall and in Castile also, it is commonly used (as it were for a proverbe) as swift as a zebra, when they will signifie an exceeding quicknesse." (*Purchas*, vol. ii. p. 1001.)

Andrew Battell, an Englishman, writing a description of the same part of Africa, also mentions the zevera, or zebra.

Rhinoceros. John Huighen van Linschoten, in his description of a voyage to Goa, informs us that—

The Armed Rhinoceros. 113

"the Abada, or Rhinoceros, is not in India, but only in Benegala and Pataue. They are lesse and lower then the elephant. It hath a short horne upon the nose, in the hinder part somewhat bigge, and toward the end sharper, of a browne, blew, and whitish colour; it hath a snout like a hog, and the skin upon the upper part of his body is all wrinckled, as it were armed with shields or targets. It is a great enemie of the elephant. Some thinke it is the right unicorne, because that as yet there hath no other beene found, but onely by hear-say, and by the pictures of them. The Portugalls and those of Bengala affirme, that by the river Ganges in the kingdome of Bengala, are many of these rhinocerots, which when they will drinke, the other beasts stand and waite upon them, till the rhinoceros hath drunke, and thrust their horne into the water, for hee cannot drinke but his horne must be under the water, because it standeth so close unto his nose, and muzzle: and then after him all the other beasts doe drinke. Their hornes in India are much esteemed and used against all venome, poyson, and many other diseases." (*Purchas*, vol. iv. p. 1773.)

Shakspeare has but one reference to this animal—
" The arm'd rhinoceros, or the Hyrcan tiger" (*Macbeth*, iii. 4). For the epithet *armed* he may have been indebted to the foregoing description.

The Indian rhinoceros is a one-horned species, and is probably the original of the unicorn of the Greeks and Romans. It is, however, distinguished from that animal by Drayton:—

" The unicorn leaves off his pride and close
There sets him down by the rhinoceros."
(*Noah's Flood*.)

In a pageant written by Thomas Heywood, on the occasion of the mayoralty of Sir Maurice Abbot, printed 1638, the following account is given of this curious animal:—

"The second show by land is an Indian beast called a rhinoceros, which being presented to the life, is for the rarenesse thereof, more fit to beautifie a triumph. His head, necke, backe, sides, and thighes, armed by nature with impenetrable skales; his hide or skinne of the colour of the boxe tree; in greatnesse equall with the elephant, but his legges are somewhat shorter; and enemy to all beasts of rapine

I

and prey, as the lyon, leopard, beare, wolfe, tiger, and the like; but to others, as the horse, asse, oxe, sheep, &c. which feede not upon the life and blood of the weaker, but of the grasse and hearbage of the field, harmlesse and gentle, ready to succour them, when they be any way distressed. Hee hath a short horne growing from his nose, being in continual enmity with the elephant before hee encounter him, he sharpeneth it against a stone." (*Lord Mayor's Pageants*, ed. Percy Society, vol. 9, p. 71.)

The enmity between these two animals, the elephant and rhinoceros, is a myth of ancient growth, which has survived to recent times. The amiability of the rhinoceros towards his weaker comrades is a trait of character for which this animal is indebted to the imagination of Heywood.

Mr. Timbs, in his *Eccentricities of the Animal Creation*, 1869, tells us that a specimen of the one-horned variety was sent from India, to Emmanuel, King of Portugal, in the year 1513 :—

"The sovereign made a present of it to the pope; but the animal being seized during the passage with a fit of fury, occasioned the loss of the vessel in which it was transported."

The first rhinoceros brought to England was in the year 1684. It is noticed by Evelyn in his *Diary* as the rhinoceros or unicorn.

Another frequenter of the mudbanks of rivers in the East, the Hippopotamus, is thus described by a Portuguese who travelled in Ethiopia and along the southern coast of Africa :—

Hippopotamus.

"In these rivers are many *zoua* or *zoo*, so they call the river-horses; greater then two of our horses together, with thick and short hinder-legs, having five clawes on each fore-foot, and foure on the hinder-foot; the footing large as it were of an elephant, the mouth wide and full of teeth, some of which are remarkable, each above two palmes or spans long, the two lower straight up, and those above turned like a bores tusks, all foure being above a great spanne eminent from the mouth. The head is as big as of three oxen. Their hides are much thicker then an oxe-hide, all of one colour, ash-coloured gray, most of them with a white strake on the face all quite downe, and a starre in the fore-head, haire rough, mane little and short." (*Purchas*, vol. ii., p. 1544.)

Edward Lopes, a Portuguese traveller, relates that one of the islands at the mouth of the river Zaire, in Congo, is called the " Ile of horses, because there are bred and brought up in it great store of these creatures that the Greekes call *hippopotami*, that is to say, water-horses." This writer is a little in error in his etymology. The name is derived from the words *hippos*, a horse, and *potamos*, a river.

There is no record of any living specimen of the hippopotamus being brought to England till the year 1850, when the arrival of a young one at the Zoological Gardens caused quite a flutter of interest.

We come now to a more familiar animal. **Boar.**

> " The great wild Bore of nature terrible,
> With two strong tushes for his armourie,
> Sometimes assailes the beare most horrible,
> And 'twixt them is a fight both fierce and deadly.
> He hunteth after marjoram and organie,
> Which as a whetstone doth his need supply."
> (CHESTER, *Love's Martyr*, p. 109.)

The Boar, once the most abundant of British wild animals, had been gradually driven by the cultivation of the forest lands into remote regions of England. According to Mr. Harting, the exact date of the extinction of the wild boar in England is uncertain. James I. was regaled with "wild boar pie" on the occasion of a visit he paid to Lancashire, 1617, and his Majesty hunted this game in Windsor Forest in the same year (*Extinct British Animals*, p. 100).

Thomas Fuller writes of the oak woods of Hampshire :

" Hantshire hogs are allowed by all for the best bacon, being our English Westphalian, and which well-ordered hath deceived the most judicious pallats. Here the swine feed in the forrest on plenty of acorns (men's meat in the golden, hog's food in this iron age;) which, going out lean, return home fat, without either care or cost to their owners. Nothing but fulness stinteth their feeding on the mast falling from the trees, where also they lodge at liberty (not pent up, as in other places, to stacks of pease), which some assign the reason of the fineness of their flesh; which, though not all glorre (where no bancke of lean can be seen for the deluge of fat), is no less delicious to the taste, and more wholsome for the stomack." (*Worthies of England*, vol. i. p. 400, ed. 1811.)

Glore is a word still used for fat in the north of England.

Venus, fearful for the safety of *Adonis*, reminds him of the dangerous nature of the beast he proposes to encounter :—

"'Thou hadst been gone,' quoth she, 'sweet boy, ere this,
But that thou told'st me thou wouldst hunt the boar.
O, be advised! thou know'st not what it is
With javelin's point a churlish swine to gore,
 Whose tushes never sheathed he whetteth still,
 Like to a mortal butcher bent to kill.

"'On his bow-back he hath a battle set
Of bristly pikes, that ever threat his foes;
His eyes, like glow-worms, shine when he doth fret;
His snout digs sepulchres where'er he goes;
 Being moved, he strikes whate'er is in his way,
 And whom he strikes his crooked tushes slay.

"'His brawny sides, with hairy bristles arm'd,
Are better proof than thy spear's point can enter;
His short thick neck cannot be easily harm'd;
Being ireful, on the lion he will venture;
 The thorny brambles and embracing bushes,
 As fearful of him, part, through whom he rushes.'"
       (*Venus and Adonis*, ll. 619–630.)

The antiquary, John Stowe, gives an account of Saint Anthony's pigs, in his *Survey of London*, written in the reign of Elizabeth :—

"Some distance from this, the Merchant-Tailors' Hall, is Finke's Lane, so called of Robert Finke, and Robert Finke his son, James

Finke, and Rosamond Finke. On the north side of this street, from over against the east corner of St. Martin's Oteswich Church, have ye divers fair and large houses till ye come to the hospital of St. Anthonie, sometime a cell to St. Anthonie's of Vienna. The proctors of this house were to collect the benevolence of charitable persons towards the building and supporting thereof. And amongst other things observed in my youth, I remember that the officers charged with oversight of the markets in this city, did divers times take from the market people, pigs starved, or otherwise unwholesome for man's sustenance; these they slit in the ear. One of the proctors for St. Anthonie tied a bell about the neck, and let it feed on the dunghills. No man would hurt or take them up, but if any gave to them bread, or other feeding, such would they know, watch for, and daily follow, whining till they had somewhat given them; whereupon was raised a proverb, 'Such an one will follow such an one, and whine as it were an Anthonie pig;' but if such a pig grew to be fat and came to good liking, as oftimes they did, then the proctors would take him up to the use of the hospital." (Page 69, ed. 1842.)

It is said that pigs were placed under the protection of Saint Anthony, but if such a precarious existence was the outcome of his favour, the poor animals might well have desired the patronage of some more kind-hearted saint. An illustration of the custom recorded by Stowe is found in Bale's comedy of *Thre Lawes*, 1538, in which play *Infedelity* begins his address:—

"Good Christen people, I'm come hyther verelye
As a true proctor of the house of S. Antonye."

He offers, among other charms—

"Lo, here is a belle to hang upon hour hogge,
And save your cattel from the bytynge of a dogge."

John Leo, in his book of the history of Africa, gives a good description of another animal most useful to man, the Camel:—

Camel.

"Camels are gentle and domesticall beasts; and are found in Africa in great numbers, especially in the desarts of Libya, Numidia, and Barbaria. And these the Arabians esteeme to bee their principall possessions and riches; so that speaking of the wealth of any of their princes, or governours, He hath, say they, so many thousand camels, and not so many thousand duckets. Of camels there are three kinds; whereof the first, being called *hugiun*, are grosse, and of a tall stature, and most fit to carrie burthens. The second kinde of camel is called *becheti*, and having a double bunch, are fit both to carrie burthens and to ride upon; and these are bred onely in Asia. The third kind, called *raguahill*, are camels of a slender and low stature, which albeit they are unfit to carry burthens, yet doe they so excell the two other kinds in swiftnesse, that in the space of one day they will travell one hundred miles, and so continue over the desarts for eight or ten dayes together with very little provender: and these doe the principall Arabians of Numidia and the Moores of Libya usually ride upon." (*Purchas*, vol. ii. p. 842.)

The kind, here mentioned, with the double bunch, is the *Bakhtee*, or Bactrian camel, found in Persia. By the third variety Leo probably means the lighter breed of camel, usually called a dromedary.

Mr. Palgrave, in his book on *Central and Eastern Arabia*, 1865, demolishes the common belief that the camel and the dromedary are distinct varieties. He says:—

"It may be well to make my readers aware, once for all, of the fact that the popular home idea of a dromedary having two humps and a camel one, or *vice versa* (for I have forgotten which of the animals is supplied with a duplicate boss in coloured picture-books), is a simple mistake. The camel and the dromedary in Arabia are the same identical genus and creature, excepting that the dromedary is a high-bred camel, and the camel a low-bred dromedary; exactly the same distinction which exists between a race-horse and a hack; both are horses, but the one of blood, the other not. The dromedary is the race-horse of his species, thin, elegant (or comparatively so), fine-haired, light of step, easy of pace, and much more enduring of thirst than the woolly, thick-built, heavy-footed, ungainly, and jolting camel. Both and each of them have only one hump, placed immediately behind their shoulders, where it serves as a fixing-point for the saddle or burden."

This modern account confirms the accuracy of Henry Timberley, a traveller contemporary with Shakspeare, who writes:—

"The dromedarie is like a camel, but that his head is lesse, his legs longer, and a very small necke, the difference being as betweene a greyhound and a mastiff." (*Purchas*, vol. ii. p. 1642.)

Shakspeare has several allusions to the camel, but none to the dromedary. Chester, in his list of animals, 1601, distinguishes between them :—

> "The bunch-back'd, big-bon'd, swift-foote dromidary,
> Of *dromas*, the Greeke word, borrowing the name,
> For his quicke flying speedy property:
> Which easily these countrymen do tame.
>   He'l go a hundred miles within one day,
>   And never seeke in any place to stay.

> "The camel is of nature flexible,
> For when a burden on his backe is bound,
> To ease the labourer, he is known most gentle,
> For why he kneeleth downe upon the ground:
>   Suffering the man to put it off or on,
>   As it seemes best in his discretion."
>   (*Love's Martyr*, p. 110.)

The camel was credited with a prodigious appetite, but considering the long fasts to which it was occasionally subjected this voracity was perhaps excusable.

> "*Anannestes.* Why, lad, they be pure cameleons, they feed only upon air.
> "*Mendacio.* Cameleons? I'll be sworn some of your fiddlers be rather camels, for, by their good wills, they will never leave eating." (Brewer, *Lingua*, iv. i.)

The Llama is the representative of the camel in the New World. There are several species, some of which are described by the early travellers. H. Brewer, in some notes on Chili and Peru, included in Churchill's collection, gives the llama the appropriate name of the camel-sheep, "whose neck is nearly four feet long, and the wool very fine." Joseph Acosta, a learned Jesuit, in his *Natural and Moral History of the East and West Indies*, writes:—

Llama.

> "There is nothing in Peru of greater riches and profit than the cattell of the country, which our men call Indian sheepe, and the Indians

in their generall language call them *lama*. For all things well considered, it is a beast of the greatest profit and least charge of any that I know; from them they draw meate and clothing, as from the sheepe of Spaine. There are two kindes of these sheepe or lamas, the one they call *pacos*, or sheepe bearing wooll, and the other are bare, and have little wooll, so are they better for burthen; they are bigger then great sheepe, and lesse then calves, they have a very long necke, like to a camel, whereof they have good need: for being high of stature, they have neede of a long necke, else should they be deformed. They are of divers colours, some all white, others all blacke, some grey, and some spotted." (*Purchas*, vol. iii. p. 968.)

The same author also describes the Vicuna, a species of llama :

"Amongst the most remarkable things at the Indies of Peru, be the vicugnes, and sheepe of the countrie, as they call them, which are tractable beasts and of great profit. The vicugnes are wilde, and the sheepe are tame. Some thinke that the vicugnes are those which Aristotle, Plinie, and other authors call *capreas*, which are wilde goats, and in truth they have some resemblance, for the lightnesse they have in the woods and mountaines, but yet they are no goates, for the vicugnes have no hornes, as those have whereof Aristotle makes mention. These vicugnes are greater then goates and lesser than calves. Their haire is of the colour of dried roses, somewhat clearer. They have no hornes like stags and goates. They feed upon the highest tops of the mountaines, which they call *Pugnas*. They are accustomed to sheere these beasts, and of their fleece to make coverings and rugge of great value, for that this wooll is like to white silke, which lasts long; and as the colour is naturall and not dyed, so is it perpetuall." (Page 967.)

The Guanaco, another species of llama, is described by Pigafetta in an account of the voyage of Fernando de Magalhanes, as having the head and ears like those of a mule, the body like a camel, legs like a stag, and a tail like that of a horse, which it resembled in the neighing. The natives of those parts of South America visited by Magellan wore a kind of shoe made of its skin, which caused their feet to appear like those of the animal. On this account Magellan, or as he is here called, Magalhanes, named the people Pata-gones: *Pata* signifying in the

Spanish language a hoof or paw (*Burney's Travels*, p. 34, ed. 1802). *Xaco* is a name given to the llama by another traveller.

The first llama brought to Europe was landed at Middleburgh, in 1558, and sent as a present to the German Emperor. A rude figure of this animal, engraved at Nuremberg, was copied by Gesner, the great naturalist of the time, in his work on quadrupeds (Bennett, *Menagerie of the Zoological Society*, 1830).

Of the known varieties of deer the largest was the Elk. This animal is a native of Northern Europe and Asia. It also inhabits North America, where it is usually called the Moose, from the Indian word *musu*. It is described in an account of the discovery and colonization of New England :—

<small>Elk or Moose.</small>

> "There is also a certaine beast, that the natives call a mosse, hee is as big bodies as an oxe, headed like a fallow deere, with a broad palme, which hee mues every yeare, as dothe the deere, and neck like a red deere, with a short mane running down along the ranes of his back, his haire long like an elke, but esteemed to be better then that for saddlers use, he hath likewise a great bunch hanging downe under his throat, and is of the colour of our blacker sort of fallow deere, his legs are long, and his feet as big as the feet of our oxen, his taile is longer then the single of a deere. His fleshe is excellent food, which the natives use to jerkin and keepe all the yeere to serve their turne, and so proves very serviceable for their use." (*Purchas*, vol. iv. p. 1829.)

Another traveller asserts that "the elk, that so much desired and salutiferous beast is frequently to be met with in those parts, and which for the virtue of one of his feet has obtained the name of *neoco*, signifying the excellent beast" (*Churchill's Voyages*, vol. i. p. 537). Drayton, in his poem, *Noah's Flood*, represents this animal as taking his place in the procession towards the ark :—

> "The great unwieldly elk, whose skin is of much proof,
> Throngs with the rest t' attain this wooden roof."

Shields and targets were made of the skin of the elk, which were thick enough to resist the point of the sharpest spear.

In Kennet's *History of England*, 1706, we find mention of an animal whose name is not to be found in modern dictionaries. We are told that Sir Hierom Bowes, the English ambassador to Russia, 1583, was—

"the first (if an historian may have leave to mention so trivial a matter) who brought into England the beast call'd a *machlis*, never before seen here; it is like an elk, iu Latin *alce*, having no joints in the legs and yet wonderful swift. He brought also certain fallow deer of admirable swiftness, which being yoked together, would draw a man sitting in a sled with incredible speed." (Vol. ii. p. 493.)

The machlis was in all probability the elk, and the fallow deer were no doubt reindeer.

Topsell (p. 592) gives us some information, etymological and otherwise, concerning that most valuable animal to the natives of the cold regions which it inhabits, the Reindeer.

Reindeer.

"This beast is called by the Latines *rangifer*, by the Germains *rein, reiner, raineger, reinsthier*, by the French *raingier*, and *ranglier*, and the later Latins call it *reingus*. It is a beast altogither unknowne to the auncient Græcians and Latins, except the *machlis* that Pliny speaketh of be it. This beast was first of all discovered by Olaus Magnus in this northerne part of the world, towards the Poale attique, as in Norway, Swetia, and Scandinavia, at the first sight whereof he called it raingifer, because he beareth hornes on his head like the boughes of a tree. This beast chaungeth his colour, according to the time of the yeare, and also according to the quality of the place wherein he feedeth, which appeareth by this, because some of them are found to be of the colour of asses, and shortly after to be like hartes. The King of Swetia had ten of them nourished at Lappa, which he caused every day to be driven unto the mountains into the colde ayre, for they were not able to endure the heat. The mouth of this beast is like the mouth of a cow, they many times come out of Laponia into Swetia, where they are wonderfully anoied with wolves, but they gather themselves togither in a ring, and so fight against their enimies with their hornes. They are also in their owne naturall countrey annoyed with gulons [gluttons], and generally all beastes that live upon the spoile of flesh, are enemies unto them, and desire to destroy and eate them. In their pace, both slow and speedie, the articles of their legs make a noise like' the craking of nuts. There was one of these beasts given unto the Duke of Saxony in the year of our Lord, 1561."

Olaus Magnus, the chronicler of Northern Europe referred to in the preceding passage, informs us that—

"in the northern parts of both the Bothnians, (for so are the utmost parts of the north countrey called, as if it were from the bottome of a vessel) and Great Lapland, there is a beast with three horns, that is of the kind of stags, but is far taller, stronger, and swifter: and it is called rangifer, for two reasons; one is, because it carryeth high horns on the head, like the boughs of an oke-tree; the other is, because the instruments that are put upon the horns and breast to draw their waggons withall in winter, are called in that language *rancha* and *lochai*, of these horns it hath two bigger than the rest, growing as the stags horns do; but they are with more branches, and farther out, for they augment to fifteen branches. Another stands in the middle of their head, with little small branches shorter than the other, standing round about it. These arm the head on all sides against the beasts that are enemies unto it, especially wolves; and it shews comely, and to be admired amongst strange things. The meat this beast eateth is mountain moss, that is white, chiefly in winter, that lyes on the superficies of the ground covered with snow. And though these snows be thick, yet by an instinct of nature, will it ·dig in them like a wilde horse to seek for its meat. In summer it feeds on leaves and boughs of trees, better standing and going, than stooping down the head, (because the horns are too crooked forward) and that inclining the head obliquely, and on one side. It hath a mane like a horse, and the hoofs are divided in two.

" If they be carried into other countries, especially beyond seas, they will not live long, either by reason of the climate changes, or unusual food they feed on, unless their ordinary keeper feeds them; as I remember that formerly the most illustrious Prince of Sweden, Steno Sture, the younger, sent six of these rangifers to Frederick Duke of Holsatia, and he sent two keepers with them, the man and wife that were Laplanders; these being carried out of their native countrey, and being under the government of others, because they wanted their rest, and manner of living, neither they nor the beasts, wanting a particular care for them, did live long. Likewise in the year of our Lord, 1533,

Gustavus King of Sweden sent ten pair of these beasts to some noble men in Prussia, both for sight, and for propagation, and they were all set free into the woods but there came nothing of it and changing the place did not profit for their increase." (*History of the Goths, Swedes, and Vandals*, p. 176.)

Olaus Magnus, whose work on the manners, customs, and wars of the northern nations of Europe is frequently quoted by writers of the Elizabethan era, was Archbishop of Upsal, and Metropolitan of Sweden. He died in 1568. His work was originally published in Latin. It contains much information not found elsewhere, but is uncritically written, and the author's unbounded credulity leads him occasionally to make the most absurd statements with the profoundest gravity.

The Red Deer, the most important of the wild animals of our own country, must have been at this time extremely plentiful in the forests throughout the land. Fynes Moryson, 1591, speaks of the number and extent of parks containing both red and fallow deer existing in his time:—

Red Deer.

"The kings forrests have innumerable heards of red deare, and all parts have such plenty of fallow deare, as every gentleman of five hundred or a thousand pounds rent by the yeere hath a parke for them inclosed with pales of wood for two or three miles compasse. Yet this prodigall age hath so forced gentlemen to improve their revenews, as many of these grounds are by them disparked, and converted to feed cattell. Lastly (without offence be it spoken) I will boldly say, that England (yea perhaps one county thereof) hath more fallow deare, then all Europe that I have seene." (*Itinerary*, part iii. b. 2, p. 148.)

In Ireland, however, he finds a different state of things:—

"The Earle of Ormond in Munster, and the Earle of Kildare in Lemster, had each of them a small parke inclosed for fallow deare, and I have not seene any other parke in Ireland, nor have heard that they had any other at that time, yet in many woods they have many red deare, loosely scattered, which seeme more plentifull, because the inhabitants used not to hunt them, but onely the governours and commanders had them sometimes killed with the piece." (Page 160.)

Sale of Venison. 125

Englishmen who travelled for pleasure were not very numerous at this period. Fynes Moryson was a gentleman of good position and ample means. He travelled for the space of twelve years through Germany, Bohemia, and several other countries of Europe. His *Itinerary*, which is an account of his wanderings, was first written in Latin, and then translated by himself into English. It extends over the years 1591 to 1603. This work contains many interesting details concerning early manners, both English and foreign. Moryson died about the year 1614. John Norden, in his *Description of Essex*, 1594, writes:—

"About the hundredes of Waltham, Onger, Becontré, and muche of the Libertie of Havering are for the most part woods and woodie groundes, and foreste, as the most parte of Essex in time paste hath bene. This forest is well replenished with deere, red and fallow, who seeme noe good neighbors to the foreste inhabitantes: but the kindnes which they receyve of the forest, may worke their patience towardes the game. Ther is also nere Hatfeylde Broadokes a chace called Hatfeyld Chace, a grounde well replenished with fallow deare. This shire seemeth not anie wher altogether destitute of wood, thowgh no wher well stored. It is full of parkes." (Page 9, ed. Camden Society.)

Thomas Fuller bewails the necessity which forced landlords to economize, and the consequent decrease in number of both deer and parks. He writes:—

"Deer are daily diminished in England, since the gentry are necessitated into thrift, and are forced to turn their pleasure into profit: '*jam seges est ubi parcus erat;*' and, since the sale of bucks hath become ordinary, I believe, in process of time, the best-stored park will be found in a cook's shop in London." (*Worthies of England*, vol. ii. p. 217.)

James I., who like his predecessor, Elizabeth, took great delight in hunting, has generally had the credit of introducing the dark variety of fallow deer into England. In the State Papers of his time there is more than one allusion to expenses for the transfer of deer from Denmark to this country. **Fallow Deer.**

So tenacious was James of any interference with his favourite sport, that a writer of the time declares that in his reign one man might with greater safety kill another man than cause the death of a stag.

In the *Antiquarian Repertory*, 1807 (vol. i. p. 2), a feat of agility and skill in horsemanship is reported of one John Selwyn, an under keeper of the park at Oatlands, in Surrey, in the reign of Elizabeth. A grand stag-hunt was given in Oatlands Park, on the occasion of her Majesty's visit to its owner. Selwyn attended, as was the duty of his office, and in the heat of the chase suddenly leaped from his horse upon the back of the stag, both running at that time with their utmost speed, and kept his seat gracefully in spite of every effort of the affrighted beast to dislodge him. Then drawing his sword, with it he guided the stag towards the Queen, and coming near her presence, plunged it into its throat, so that the animal fell dead at her feet. This was thought sufficiently wonderful to be chronicled on his monument, and he is accordingly there portrayed in the act of stabbing the beast. The brass which records this feat of activity was, at the beginning of the present century, preserved in the church of Walton-on-Thames, but whether it has survived the epidemic of restoration from which so many churches have suffered in late years is uncertain.

Hunting the stag was the most popular sport of the Middle Ages. The works on hunting were books without which no gentleman's library was complete, and to make a mistake in any of the technical terms employed was to show a lamentable ignorance of the ways of good society. The pages of both poets and dramatists abound in allusions to this pastime. Shakspeare's knowledge of woodcraft is frequently apparent. A spirited account of a stag-hunt, in the *Return from Parnassus*, a play written about the year

1600, is so illustrative, and contains so much of the glossary of the stag-hunters, that quotation of it may not be out of place. The passage is purposely crowded with technical expressions, in order to confuse and put to silence the scholar, *Academico* :—

> "*Amoretto*. It was my pleasure two dayes ago, to take a gallant leash of greyhounds, and into my fathers parke I went, accompanied with two or three noblemen of my neere acquaintance, desiring to shew them some of the sport: I caused the keeper to sever the rascall deere, from the bucks of the first head; now sir, a bucke the first yeere is a fawne, the second yeare a pricket, the third yeare a 'sorell, the fourth yeare a soare, the fift a buck of the first head, the sixt yeare a compleat buck: as likewise your hart is the first yeare a calfe, the second yeare a brochet, the third yeare a spade, the fourth yeare a stagge, the fift yeare a great stagge, the sixt yeare a hart: as likewise the roe-bucke is the first yeare a kid, the second yeare a girl, the third yeare a hemuse, and these are your speciall beasts for chase, or, as we huntsmen call it, for venery.... Now sir, after much travell we singled a buck, I rode that same time upon a roane gelding, and stood to intercept from the thicket: the buck broke gallantly; my great swift being disadvantaged in his slip, was at the first behinde, marry, presently coted and out-stript them, when, as the hart presently descended to the river, and being in the water, proferd, and reproferd, and proferd againe: and at last he upstarted at the other side of the water, which we call soyle of the hart, and there other huntsmen met him with an addauntreley: we followed in hard chase for the space of eight houres, thrise our hounds were at default, then we cryed *a slaine*, streight *so ho*; through good reclaiming my faulty hounds found their game againe, and so went through the woods with gallant notice of musicke, resembling so many *viols de gambo*: at last the hart laid him downe, and the hounds seized upon him, he groned, and wept, and dyed. In good faith it made me weepe too, to think of Acteon's fortune, which my Ovid speaks of." (*Dodsley's Old Plays*, vol. ix., ed. W. C. Hazlit, 1874.)

In *Love's Labour Lost* the pedant *Holofernes* plays on the words *pricket, sore*, and *sorel* (Act iv. sc. 2).

Ben Jonson has many hunting allusions. In his pretty pastoral fragment, *The Sad Shepherd* (i. 1), occurs the following :—

"A hart of ten
I trow he be, madam, or blame your men:
For by his slot, his entries, and his port,
His frayings, fewmets, he doth promise sport,
And standing 'fore the dogs: he bears a head
Large and well beamed, with all rights summed and spread."

The *slot* of a deer is the print of his feet in the ground; *entries* are places through which the deer has lately passed, which indicate his size; *frayings* are the peelings of the horns. Many other phrases are met with in plays, such as *abature*, grass trampled down by the passing deer; and *foile*, grass only slightly pressed down.

"Besides these ambiguous contigigrated phrases," writes John Taylor, the Water Poet, "the horns have many dogmatical epithets, as a hart hath the burrs, the pearls, the antlers, the surantlers, the royals, the surroyals, and the croches. A buck's horns are composed of burr, beam, branch, advancer, palm, and speller. I think Nimrod the great hunter would have been a madman or a wood-man, if he had studied half the wild and hare-brained terms that belong to this ship [wood-man-ship]." (*Works*, p. 61, ed. Hindley, 1872.)

In a note on the *Merry Wives of Windsor*, in Singer's edition of Shakspeare, we find an explanation of a passage that has been altered by several commentators. *Falstaff*, when attired in the spoils of a hart of ten, naturally uses the terms of the forest. He says:—

"Divide me like a brib'd buck, each a haunch: I will keep my sides to myself, my shoulders for the fellow of this walk, and my horns I bequeath your husbands. Am I a woodman? Ha! Speak I like Herne the hunter?" (Act v. sc. 5.)
"This," says Mr. Singer, "is the reading of the old copies, which has been unnecessarily changed to a *bribe-buck* by all recent editors. A *brib'd buck* was a *buck cut up* to be given away in portions. *Bribes* in O.F. were portions or fragments of meat which were given away. Hence *bribeur* was a beggar, and the O.E. *bribour* a petty thief."

The shoulders of the buck were the perquisites of the keeper, or *fellow of the walk*.

The order of precedence in hunting is thus given by Holinshed :—

"The stag is accounted for the most noble game, the fallow deere is the next, then the roe, whereof we have indifferent store; and last of all the hare, not the least in estimation, because the hunting of that seelie beast is mother to all the terms, blasts, and artificial devises that hunters do use." (*Chronicles*, vol i. p. 380.)

In the light of our modern civilized sport it is strange to notice that the fox is not even mentioned.

Exaggerated notions prevailed respecting the longevity of the stag. The life of a stag, according to modern authorities, does not exceed twenty years.

A "hot venison pasty" was a favourite dish at all times, but was not reckoned a very wholesome one. Andrew Boorde, better known by his nickname, "Merry Andrew," was physician to Henry VIII. He wrote a dietary, in 1542, which has been recently edited by Mr. Furnivall for the Early English Text Society. Herein the worthy doctor admits that his love of venison outweighs his discretion :—

"I have gone rownde about Crystendome, and overthwarte Crystendom, and a thousande or two and more myles out of Crystendom, yet there is not so moche pleasure for harte and hynde, bucke, and doo, and for roo bucke and doo, as is in Englande; and although the flesshe be dispraysed in physycke I pray God to sende me parte of the flesshe to oate, physycke not-withstandyng."

The pretty little Musk Deer, so valued for its perfume, was found in Thibet and Northern India. It is thus described by Marco Polo in his *Travels in the East*, in the fourteenth century :—

Musk Deer.

"In this country [Thibet] it is that the finest and most valuable musk is procured. The animal which yields it is not larger than the female goat, but in form resembles the antelope. Its coat is like that of the larger kind of deer: its feet and tail are those of the antelope, but it has not the horns. It is provided with four projecting teeth or

K

tusks, three inches in length; two in the upper jaw pointing downwards, and two in the lower jaw pointing upwards; small in proportion to their length, and white as ivory. Upon the whole it is a handsome creature." (*Travels*, p. 252, ed. Marsden, 1818.)

This account is incorrect, in so far as the long canine teeth of the musk deer exist only in the upper jaw of the animal. The scent of the musk was greatly in favour with our ancestors. *Mistress Quickly* represents the wooers of *Mistress Ford* as sending "coach after coach, letter after letter, gift after gift; smelling so sweetly, all musk" (*Merry Wives*, ii. 2, 66).

Amongst all the wonders of animal life met with by medieval travellers none could have excited more their wonder and admiration than that beautiful inhabitant of tropical Africa, the Giraffe. Probably the earliest, and certainly the quaintest, notice of this animal by an English writer occurs in Sir John Mandeville's *Travels*, written about the year 1356. In Chinese Tartary he meets with—

Giraffe.

"many bestes, that ben clept *orafles*. In Arabye, their ben clept *gerfauntz*; that is a best pomelée or spotted; that is but a lityile more highe, then is a stede: but he hathe the necke a 20 cubytes long: and his croup and his tayl is as of an hert: and he may loken over a gret highe hous." (Page 289, ed. Halliwell, 1839.)

John Sanderson, a London merchant who visited Constantinople about the year 1600, relates his impressions at the first sight of the giraffe:—

"The admirablest and fairest beast that ever I saw was a jarraff, as tame as a domesticall deere, and of a reddish deere colour, white brested and cloven footed: he was of a very great height, his fore-legs longer then the hinder, a very long necke, and headed like a camell, except two stumps of horne on his head. This fairest animall was sent out of Ethiopia, to this great Turkes father for a present; two Turkes the keepers of him, would make him kneele, but not before any Christian for any money." (*Purchas*, vol. ii. p. 1619.)

The giraffe's legs are in reality of equal length, but the

shoulder-blades are greatly elongated. The slope of the back thus caused gives the appearance of inequality.

John Leo, an African explorer of the same period, says :—

"The giraffa are so savage and wild, that it is very rare matter to see any of them: for they hide themselves among the desarts and woods, where no other beasts use to come; and so soone as one of them espieth a man, it flieth forthwith, though not very swiftly. It is headed like a camell, and eared like an oxe: neither are any taken by hunters, but while they are very young." (*Purchas*, vol. ii. p. 842.)

Fynes Moryson, in his *Itinerary*, 1597 (p. 263), also describes the giraffe :—

"Here [Constantinople] be the ruines of a pallace upon the very wals of the city, called the pallace of Constantine, wherein I did see an elephant, called *philo* by the Turkes, and another beast newly brought out of Affricke (the mother of monsters), which beast is altogether unknowne in our parts, and is called *surnapa* by the people of Asia, *astanapa* by others, and *giraffa* by the Italians, the picture whereof I remember to have seene in the mappes of Mercator; and because the beast is very rare, I will describe his forme as well as I can. His haire is red coloured, with many blacke and white spots; I could scarce reach with the points of my fingers to the hinder part of his backe, which grew higher and higher towards his foreshoulder, and his necke was thinne and some three els long. So as hee easily turned his head in a moment to any part or corner of the roome wherein he stood, putting it over the beams thereof, being built like a barne, and high for the Turkish building, not unlike the building of Italy, both which I have formerly described, by reason whereof he many times put his nose in my necke, when I thought myselfe furthest distant from him, which familiarity of his I liked not; and howsoever the keepers assured me he would not hurt me, yet I avoided these his familiar kisses as much as I could. His body was slender, not greater, but much higher then the body of a stagge or hart, and his head and face was like to that of a stagge, but the head was lesse and the face more beautifull: he had two hornes, but short and scarce halfe a foote long; and in the forehead he had two bunches of flesh, his ears and feete like an oxe, and his legges like a stagge."

There is some difficulty in identifying the different

kinds of wild cattle known at this period. Topsell (p. 51) describes an animal which he calls a Bison, and which he says has been falsely called a buffalo by earlier writers. He derives the name from Thracia, called in ancient times *Bistonia*. He says:—

Bison.

"It is generally held for a kind of wild oxe, bred in the northern parts of the world, for the most part, and never tamed; as in Scythia, Moscovia, Hercynia, Thracia, and Brussia."

He attributes extraordinary strength to the tongue of this beast:

"For by licking they grate like a file any indifferent hard substance, but specially they can therewith draw unto them any man or beast of inferiour condition, whom by licking they wound to death. The haire is red, yellow, or black, their eyes very great and terrible, they smell like a moschus or musk-cat, and their mane reacheth over their shoulders, shaking it irefully when he brayeth. Their face or forehead very broad, especially betwixt their hornes. For Sigismund, king of Polonia, having killed one of them in huuting, stood betwixt his hornes with two other men not much lesser in quantity then himselfe, who was a goodly, well proportioned, and personable prince."

This animal is apparently the European bison, sometimes called *aurochs*, *oryx*, or *bonassus*. It is still found in the forests of Lithuania and the Caucasus.

The American bison is described by Francis Lopez de Gomara in his *General History of the West Indies*, 1542 :—

"These oxen are of the bignesse and colour of our bulles, but their hornes are not so great. They have a great bunch upon their fore-shoulders, and more haire on their fore part then on their hinder part; and it is like wooll. They have as it were an horse-mane upon their backe bone, and much haire and very long from the knees downwards. They have great tuftes of haire hanging downe their fore-heads, and it seemeth that they have beardes, because of the great sorte of haire hanging downe at their chinnes and throates. The males have very long tailes, and a great knobbe or flocke at the end: so that in some respect they resemble the lion, and in some other the camell. They push with their hornes, they runne, they overtake and kill an horse when they are in their rage and anger. Finally, it is a foule and fierce beast of countenance and force of bodie. The horses fledde from them, either because of their deformed shape, or else because they had never seene them. Their masters have no other riches nor substance: of them they eat, they drinke, they apparel, they shooe themselves. And of their hides they make many things, as houses, shooes, apparell, and ropes. To bee short, they make so many things of them as they have neede of, or as many as suffice them in the use of this life." (*Hakluyt*, vol. iii. p. 455.)

Topsell (p. 57) declares that the ancient writers confused the Buffe with the elk and the rangifer (reindeer), but the picture he gives is not unlike that of the elk :—

Buffalo.

"The head of this beast," he writes, "is like the head of a hart, and his hornes branched or ragged, his body for the most part like a wild oxes, his haire deepe and harshe like a beares, his hide is so hard that the Scithians make breastplates which no dart can pierce through. His colour for the most part like an asses, but when he is hunted or feared he changeth his hue into whatever thing he seeth: as among trees he is like them; among greene boughs he seemeth greene; amongst rocks of stone he is translated into their colour also; as it is generally by most writers affirmed."

While admitting the difficulty of hair being so suddenly affected by the sensations of the animal, this author observes that, as the buffe has the face, so has he the fear of a hart, but in a higher degree.

The buffe, or losh, whether bison or buffalo, was an animal greatly valued for its hide. In a letter of the Moscovite Company in London to their Russian agents, 1560, the following instructions are given :—

"Our mind is you should provide for the next ships, five hundred losh hides, of them that be large and faire, and thickest in hand, and to be circumspect in the choosing, that you buy them that bee killed in season and well dryed and whole. If they be good we may sell them here for sixteene shillings and better the piece. We would have the whole skinnes, that is the neckes and legges withall, for these what you sent now lacke their neckes and legges. Neverthelesse for this time you must send them as you may get them. If you could find the meanes that the haire might bee clipped off them, they woulde not take so much room in the shippes as they doe." (*Hakluyt*, vol. i. p. 342.)

Dr. Giles Fletcher reports from Russia, 1588, that "the largest kinde of losh or buffe breedeth about Rostove, Wichida, Novogrod, Morum, and Perm. The lesser sort within the kingdome of Cazan" (*Hakluyt*, vol. i. p. 538).

Andrew Boorde informs us in his *Introduction to Knowledge*, a cyclopædia of miscellaneous information, that—

"the kyngdome of Boeme [Bohemia] is compassed aboute wyth great hygh mountaynes and great thyck wods, in the whyche wods be many wylde beastes; amongst al other beastes there be *bugles*, that be as bigge as an oxe; and there is a beast called a *bovy*, lyke a bugle, whyche is a vengeable beast." (Page 133, ed. Furnivall, Early English Text Society, 1870.)

Zebu. The Zebu, or Indian Ox, is noticed by Marco Polo in his observations on Armenia, Turkey, and Persia. Of the last-named country he writes:

"It hath also very great oxen, and all white, thin hayred with thicke blunt short hornes, with a camels bunch on the backe, accustomed to beare great burthens. And when the packe-saddles are set upon the bunch, they bow the knee like camels, and having received the burthen rise againe, being so taught by men." (*Purchas*, vol. iii. p. 71.)

English Cattle. The wild white cattle of Britain, at one time plentiful in the northern counties of England and in Scotland, are mentioned by Camden in his account of Scotland:—

"Caledon Forest," he tells us, "nourished in times past a number of white wild buls, with thicke manes in manner of lions, but in these daies few, and those very cruell, fierce, and so hatefull of mankind, that on a certaine time they abhorre whatsoever they had either handled or breathed upon: yea, they utterly skorne the forcible strength of dogges."

Of these cattle Topsell writes (p. 58):—

"In the woods of Scotland there are bred white oxen, maned about the necke like a lyon, but in other parts like ordinary and common oxen. This wood was once full of them, but now they are all slaine, except in that parte which is called Cummirland. This beast is so hatefull and fearful of mankind that it will not feede of that grasse or those hearbes, whereof he savoureth a man hath touched, no not for many daies together. And if by art or pollicy they happen to be taken alive, they will die with very sullen griefe. If they meete a man presently they make force at him, fearing neither dogs, speares, nor other weapons. Their flesh is very pleasant, though full of sinewes, and very acceptable to the greatest nobles, for which cause they are now growen to a small number. Their qualities being like to the former beast [bison] except their colour and beard, I will tearme them the white Caledonian, or Scotian bison."

Mr. John Storer has lately published a work, *The Wild White Cattle of Great Britain*, wherein he traces the history of this beautiful breed, and gives an account of the few herds which have been preserved to our own day. Many noblemen have attempted to restore the white cattle on account of their beauty, but their ferocity, which remains undiminished, renders them dangerous inmates of a park.

We find but little notice in the writings of the Elizabethan period of the various breeds of domestic animals. Thomas Fuller writes of the long-horned variety of Lancashire cattle :—

"The fairest in England are bred (or if you will made) in this county, with goodly heads, the tips of whose horns are sometimes distanced five feet asunder. Horns are a commodity not to be slighted, seeing I cannot call to mind any other substance so hard, that it will not break; so solid, that it will hold liquor within it; and yet so clear, that light will pass through it. No mechanick trade, but hath some utensils made thereof: and even now I recruit my pen with ink from a vessel of the same. Yea, it is useful *cap-a-pie*, from combs to shooeing-horns. What shall I say, of the many gardens made of horns, to garnish houses? I mean, artificiall flowers of all colours, and, besides what is spent in England, many thousand weight are shaven down into leaves for lanthorns and sent over daily into France. In a word, the very shavings of horn are profitable, sold by the sack, and sent many miles from London for the manuring of ground. No wonder then that the horners are an ancient corporation, though why they and the bottle-makers were formerly united into one company passeth my skill to conjecture. The best horns in all England, and freest to work without flaws, are what are brought out of this county to London, the shop-general of English industry." (*Worthies of England*, vol. i. p. 537.)

Fuller, taking a line of Drayton's *Polyolbion*,

"Set the band-dog on the bull,"

as his text, thus moralizes on the favourite amusement of bull-baiting :—

"It seems that both the gentry and country-folk in this shire [Somersetshire] are much affected with that pastime, though some scruple the lawfulness thereof. 1. Man must not be a barrater, to set the creatures at variance. 2. He can take no true delight in their antipathie, which was the effect of his sin. 3. Man's charter of dominion empowers him to be a prince, but no tyrant, over the creatures. 4. Though brute beasts are made to be destroyed, they are not made to be tormented. Others rejoyn, that God gave us the creatures as well for our pleasure as necessity; that some nice consciences, that scruple the baiting of bulls, will worry men with their vexatious cruelties. All that I dare interpose is this, that the tough flesh of bulls is not onely made more tender by baiting, but also thereby it is discoloured from ox-beef, that the buyer be not deceived." (*Worthies*, vol. ii. p. 277.)

That *neat* was a general term for oxen we learn from Shakspeare :—

"*Leontes.*   Come, captain,
We must be neat; not neat, but cleanly, captain :
And yet the steer, the heifer, and the calf
Are all call'd neat."

(*Winter's Tale*, i. 2, 123.)

A young ox or bullock was called a *stot*, a young heifer a *whie*,—names still used in Yorkshire. *Hage kye* was a term applied in the northern counties of England to cows with white faces, having white spots or streaks.

Shakspeare has no mention of the Antelope. Spenser classes this harmless creature with beasts of prey :—

Antelopes.

> "The spotted panther, and the tusked bore,
> The pardale swift, and the tigre cruell,
> The antelope and wolfe, both fiers and fell."
> (*Faerie Queene*, i. 6, 26.)

Topsell (p. 1) accounts for the supposed scarcity of antelopes in his day by the fact that Alexander and his soldiers, on their journey towards India, slew 8550. He does not inform us who kept the register of this battue. He describes the antelope as having the body of a roe, with long sharp horns made like a saw, with which it cuts asunder the branches of osiers or small trees.

Several varieties of antelopes are described by the early explorers in Africa, but generally under the native names. The accounts are not sufficiently full to make identification possible. An animal called a *lant* or *dant* is frequently mentioned, whose hide appears to have been valued in commerce. One writer tells us that the skin is red, another that it is white; according to one traveller it has long goat-like horns, another declares that it is entirely without these appendages. John Leo pays a visit to Cairo, where he finds—

> "a beast called lant or dant, in shape resembling an oxe, saving that he hath smaller legs, and comlier hornes. His haire is white, and his hoofs are as blacke as jet, and he is so exceeding swift that no beast can overtake him, but onely the Barberie horse. He is easier caught in summer then in winter, because that in regard of the extreme fretting heat of the sand his hoofs are then strained and set awry, by which meanes his swiftnesse is abated, like as the swiftnesse of stagges and roe-deere. Of the hide of this beast are made shields and targets of great defence, which will not be pierced, but onely with the forcible shot of a bullet, but they are sold at an extreme price." (*Purchas*, vol. ii. p. 846.)

Pigafetta, in his account of Congo and the surrounding country, writes :—

> "There are also to be found in this countrie certaine other fourefooted beasts, somewhat lesse then oxen, of colour red, with hornes

like goats hornes, which are very smooth and glistrin, and inclining to blacke, whereof they make divers pretie knackes, as they doe likewise of the buffes hornes. They have their heads and their haires like the heads and haires of oxen, and their skins are of great estimation; and therefore they are carried into Portugall and from thence into Germanie to be dressed, and then they are called *dantes*. The king of Congo is very desirous to have some men that had skill to cleanse them, and dresse them, and to make them fit for use, to the end he might employ them for armour of defence. There are besides these other beasts, called *empalanga* which are in bignesse and shape like oxen, saving that they hold their head and necke aloft, and have their hornes broad and crooked, three hand-breadths long, divided into knots, and sharpe at the ends, whereof they might make very faire cornets to sound withall: and although they are in the forrests, yet are they not noysome nor harmefull; the skins of their necks are used for shoo-soles, and their flesh for meate. They might likewise be brought to draw the plough, and doe good service in any other labour, and tilling of the ground." (*Purchas*, vol. ii. p. 1002.)

The eland, a large bovine antelope, seems in shape and size to correspond with these descriptions, but it cannot be called a fleet animal. Attempts have been made in recent times to introduce the eland into English parks, but without much success.

As the word chamois occurs in the authorized version of the Bible, the animal must have been known to English naturalists in the sixteenth century. Canon Tristram, however, considers that this animal is incorrectly placed in the catalogue of Arabian quadrupeds. He writes :—

"In the list of the clean animals permitted as food in Deut. xiv. 5, the *zemer* occurs, and nowhere else in Scripture. From the Arabic *zamar* we conclude that some leaping animal is intended. It cannot be the chamois, of the existence of which there is no trace in Bible lands. Nor can it be the giraffe or camelopard, an animal of Central Africa, which is the interpretation of some ancient commentators. As other words designate the rock-goats or ibex, and the various antelopes, it is probable that zemer is applied to the wild mountain sheep, called *kebsch* in Arabia, very like the mouflon of Sardinia." (*Natural History of the Bible*, 1873, p. 73.)

The translators of the Bible could not well be expected to give names to animals with which they were not themselves acquainted, but by the substitution of the names of species other than those originally intended they are responsible for many false notions respecting natural history.

There appears to have been in the time we are studying great discontent at the number of Sheep kept, to the exclusion of other farm produce. In *The Briefe Conceipt of English Policie*, by W. Stafford, a husbandman complains that—

"the sheepe is the cause of all these mischieves; for they have driven husbandry out of the countrey, by the which was increased before all kinde of victuals, and now all together sheepe, sheepe, sheepe. It was farre better when there were not onely sheepe ynough, but also oxen, kine, swyn, pig, goose, and capon, egges, butter, and cheese: yea, and breade corne, and malte corne ynough besides, reared altogether upon the same lande." (*Harleian Miscellany*, vol. ix. p. 149.)

The British farmer is somewhat given to grumbling, but that this complaint was general we may gather from Fuller's *Worthies*:—

"In Warwickshire the complaint of J. Rous continueth and increaseth, that sheep turn cannibals, eating up men, houses, and towns; their pastures make such depopulation. But, on the other side, it is pleaded for these enclosures, that they make houses the fewer in this county, and the more in the kingdom." (Vol. ii. p. 402.)

The small outlay and trouble required by this kind of stock, together with the high price of wool, induced a great number of landowners to turn their arable lands into sheep-runs. Acts passed with the object of diminishing this evil were evaded in every possible way. We learn from Mr. J. S. Brewer's introduction to Starkey's *England in the Reign of Henry VIII.* (Early English Text Society, 1871) that—

"a single furrow was driven across a field to prove that it was still under the plough; the cattle owners, to escape the statutes against sheep, held their flocks in the names of their sons or servants; the highways and the villages were covered in consequence with outcast families who were wholly reduced to beggary."

In a volume of reprints by the Percy Society is included an old ballad, anonymous, and without date. It was probably written in the reign of Henry VIII., and may well have reference to the great increase of sheep at that time, although the editor, Mr. James Goodwin, considers it a satire against the orders of friars mendicant, the number of whom had increased to so enormous an extent that England may be said to have been almost overrun by them. The power and influence of the friars was checked by the dissolution of monasteries under Henry VIII.

"The blacke shepe is a perylous beast;
   Cuius contrarium falsum est.

"The leon of lyme ys large and long;
   The beare to fyght is stowte and strong;
   But of all beastes that go or crepe,
   The mightiest ys the horned shepe.
      The blacke shepe, &c.

"The shepe ys off a monstruous myght,
   What thyng soever his hornes on lyght,
   He bearyth downe bothe castell and towre,
   None is him like in marciall powre.
      The blacke shepe, &c.

"Syx hundreth howsys with cart and plowgh
   I have earst knowen, where nowght ys now
   But grene moll-hilles, they are layde playne;
   This cruell beast over all dothe rayne.
      The blacke shepe, &c.

"This shepe he is a wycked wyght,
   Man, woman, and chylde he devowreth quite;
   No hold, no howse can him wythstande,
   He swallowth up both see and lande.
      The blacke shepe, &c.

"Men were wont ones off shepe to fede,
Shepe now eate men on dowtfull dede,
This wollwysshe shepe, this rampyng beast,
Consumeth all thorow west and est.
  The blacke shepe, &c.

"Halfe Englande ys nowght now but shepe,
In everye corner they playe boe pepe;
Lorde, them confownde by twentye and ten,
And fyll their place with Cristen men.
  The blacke shepe, &c."
            (*Percy Society*, vol. xiii., 1845.)

Topsell perhaps refers to this ballad when he writes (p. 626):—

"Till now I thought the common proverb did but jest,
That saies a blacke shepe is a biting beast."

The short-woolled breed of sheep was the most abundant, and was found in every county. According to Mr. Low the Ryeland breed, so called from their living on certain sandy tracts of country devoted to the production of rye, situated southward of the river Wye, was the breed which extended over most of the western counties. As there is no historical record of the introduction of this variety, he assumes that it was indigenous beyond all memory to the districts which it inhabited. It was admirably suited, from its endurance of scanty fare, to the commons, waste lands, and woods where it abounded. For, though that district of England is now rich and fertile, at this time it was still for the most part wild and barren, and incapable of affording rich pasture.

"The wool of the Ryeland breed," writes Mr. Low, "was long regarded as the finest that the British islands produced. The ancient city of Leominster, being surrounded by a country producing this kind of wool, and being the market-town to which it was brought for sale, gave the name to the wool of the county, which was termed Lemster wool, or Lemster ore. Camden, describing the town of Leominster, says, 'The greatest name and fame is of the wool in the territories round about it; Lemster ore they call it, which setting aside that of Apulia and Tarentum, all Europe counteth to be the verie best.'" (*Domesticated Animals.*)

The Cotswold breed, whose range extended over the hills of Gloucestershire, was also much esteemed for the quantity and quality of its wool. In the former of these it was superior, according to Drayton, to the Ryeland:—

"T' whom Sarum's Plaine gives place, though famous for her flocks,
Yet hardly doth she tythe our Cotswolde's wealthy locks:
Though Lemster him exceed in finesesse of her ore,
Yet quite he puts her downe for his abundant store."
(*Polyolbion*, song 14.)

According to Fuller, the finest sheep were bred in Buckinghamshire. The price he thought so exorbitant would hardly excite the astonishment of sheep-growers to-day:—

"The best and biggest-bodied in England are in the Vale of Ailsbury in this county, where it is nothing to give ten pound or more for a breed-ram. So that should a forrainer hear of the price thereof, he would guess that ram rather to be some Roman engine of battery, than the creature commonly so called." (*Worthies of England*, vol. i. p. 133.)

Justice Shallow inquires of his cousin, "How a score of ewes now?" To which *Silence* replies, "Thereafter as they be: a score of good ewes may be worth ten pounds" (2 *Henry IV.* iii. 2, 54).

A lamb brought up by hand was called a cosset. William Browne writes:—

"And full gladly give I wold
The best cosset in my fold,
And a mazor for a fee,
If this song thou'lt teachen me."
(*The Shepherd's Pipe*, eclogue i.)

We find this expression also in a tract called *Maroccus Extaticus*, 1595: " I have brought thee up right tenderly, as a baker's daughter would bring up a cosset by hand, and allow it bread and milke." Topsell (p. 640) gives the different names applied to a lamb:—

"The first year we call it in English a lamb, so the second year a hog, lam-hog, or teg if it be a female, the third yeare hoggrils and theaves. The common epithits expressing the nature of this beast are these: rough, yearling, weake, unripe, sucking, tender, butting, fat, milke-eater, merry, sporting, bleating, affable or gentle, field-wanderer, horne-bearer, horne-fighter, unarmed, vulgar, wooll-skinned, woollbearer, wanton, meeke, delicate, and fearefull; and all these are the epithets of a male lamb, but of the female I find these following: dumb, snow-white, neate, young, fearefull, blacke, tame, humble, and tender."

Topsell bestows epithets on most of the animals that he describes. They are for the most part taken from his classical authorities. Dodded, or hornless sheep, were considered the most profitable. To Topsell also we are indebted for the following information concerning sheep:—

"There bee many that trouble themselves about this question; namely, for what cause the sheep of England do never thirst, except they see the water, and then also seldom drink, and yet have we more sheep in England then are in any other country of the world, insomuch as we thinke it a prodigious thing that sheep should drinke; but the true cause why our English sheepe drinke not is, for there is so much dew on the grasse that they need no other water; and therefore Aristotle was deceived, who thinketh that the northern sheep had more neede of water then the southern. In Spaine those sheep bear the best fleeces of wool that drinke least." (Page 605.) "The common time whereat we sheare sheepe is in June, and lambes in July; the quantitie of wool upon our sheep is more then in any other countrey of the world, for even the least among us, such as are in hard grounds, as in Norfolke, the upper most part of Kent, Hertfort-shier, and other places, have better and weightier fleeces then the greatest in other nations. The quantitie in the least is a pound, except the sheep have lost his wooll, in the middle sort of sheepe two pounds or three pounds, as is vulgar in Buckingham, Northampton, and Leicestershieres; but the greatest of all in some of those places, and also in Rumney Marsh in Kent, foure or five pounds: and it is the manner of the shepheards and sheepe masters to wet their rams, and so to keepe their wooll two or three years together growing upon their backs, and I have credibly heard of a sheepe in Buckingham-shier in the flock of the L. P. that had shorne from it at one time, one and twentie pound of wooll. After the shearing of our sheepe, we doe not use either to annoint or wash them, as they doe in other nations, but turne them foorth without their fleeces, leaving them like meadowes new mowen, with expectation of another fleece the next yeare." (Page 624.)

Wool.

The number of sheep reared in the country rendered the employment of the wool in various manufactures a matter of national importance, and protection was resorted to in order to secure the monopoly. The introduction of felt hats interfered to a great extent with the sale of the woollen caps that had been previously worn. Accordingly, the cappers, or knit-capmakers, of England applied to Parliament for relief, and in 1571 obtained a law purporting—

" that every person above seven years of age, should wear, on Sundays and Holidays, a cap of wool, knit, made, thicked, and dressed in England, and dressed only and finished by some of the trade of cappers, on the forfeiture of three shillings and four pence for every day so neglected to be worn: excepting, however, out of this act, maids, ladies, and gentlewomen, and every lord, knight, and gentleman, of twenty marks in land, and their heirs; and also such as have born office of worship in any city, town, or shire, and also the wardens of London Companies." (Anderson, *Origin of Commerce*, p. 135.)

Notwithstanding this extreme measure, the superiority of the felt hats obtained for these articles an easy victory. They were lighter, stronger, more ornamental, and afforded greater protection against wind and rain, and in a few years knit caps were only to be seen in remote parts of the kingdom.

In consequence of the diminution of religious disputes in England, and the continuance of the like dissensions abroad, artisans of all kinds were induced to come to this country for security during the reign of Elizabeth. Hence fresh impulse was given to the woollen trade, which had languished under this queen's predecessors. Several towns near the coast, such as Norwich, Canterbury,

Colchester, and Southampton, were crowded with refugees, who brought over superior machinery as well as better taste, and contributed to the lasting prosperity of the country which gave them a new home. Towards the close of Elizabeth's reign, an event occurred which affected every branch of commerce, and which opened an almost unlimited market for English woollen goods. The East India Company came into existence on the last day of the sixteeenth century. On the 31st of December, 1600, Queen Elizabeth granted a charter to George, Earl of Cumberland, and two hundred and fifteen knights, aldermen, and merchants—

" that, at their own cost and charges, . . . they might set forth one or more voyages to the East Indians, in the country and parts of Asia and Africa, and to the Islands thereabouts, . . . divers of which countries, islands, &c., have long sithence been discovered by others of our subjects; to be one body politic and corporate, by the name of, the Governor and Company of Merchants of London trading to the East Indies."

The whole of the document, of which the above is a part, may be found in Anderson's *Origin of Commerce*, already quoted.

Sir John Mandeville professes to have discovered a tree whereon gourds containing little beasts like lambs were to be seen hanging in clusters :—

" And there [somewhere beyond Cathay] growethe a maner of fruyt, as thoughe it were gowrdes, and whan they ben rype, men kutten hem a to, and men fynden with inne a lytylle best, in flessche, in bon, and blode, as though it wer a lytylle lomb, with outen wolle and men eten bothe the frut and the best; and that is a gret marveyle. Of that frute I have eten." (*Travels*, p. 264.)

The author proceeds to crush any doubts that might arise in his reader's mind by citing the similar development of the barnacle tree into a bird.

Of Goats there is little to be said. Harrison writes, " Goats we have plentie, and of sundrie colours in the west parts of England; especiallie in

Goat.

and towards Wales, and amongst the rockie hilles, by whome the owners doo reape no small advantage (*Holinshed*, vol. i. p. 372, ed. 1807). " Not for Cadwallader and all his goats," exclaims *Pistol* (*Henry V.*, v. 1, 29).

Many accounts of hunting and training the Elephant are to be found in the travels collected by Purchas and Hakluyt, together with numerous anecdotes of the sagacity of this animal, which have become the stock in trade of all subsequent writers on natural history. The Great Mogul is described by Captain William Hawkins, in the year 1610, as having three hundred elephants royal, which are elephants whereon he himself rideth:—

Elephant.

"And when they are brought before him, they come with great jollitie, having some twentie or thirty men before them with small stremers. When hee rideth on progresse or hunting, the compasse of his tents may bee as much as the compasse of London and more, and I may say, that of all sorts of people that follow the campe, there are two hundred thousand; for hee is provided, as for a citie. This king is thought to be the greatest Emperour of the East, for wealth, land, and force of men; as also for horses, elephants, camels, and dromedaries." (*Purchas*, vol. p. 219.)

His Majesty's time must have been fully employed if he had to keep so large a number of elephants in exercise.

The elephant, or " carry-castle," according to the herald, Guillim—

"is a beast of great strength, but greater wit, and greatest ambition, insomuch, that some have written of them, that if you praise them, they will kill themselves with labour; and if you commend another above them, they will break their hearts with emulation. The beast is so proud of his strength, that he never bows himself to any, neither indeed can he; and when he is once down, as usually is the case with proud great ones he cannot rise up again." (*Display of Heraldry*, p. 146, ed. 1744.)

The popular idea that the elephant has no joints in his legs, often occurs in plays:—

The Elephant.

"*Ulysses*. The elephant hath joints, but none for courtesy:
His legs are legs for necessity, not for flexure."
(*Troilus and Cressida*, ii. 3, 113.)

"I hope you are no elephant, you have joints."
(*All Fools*, 1605.)

Sir Thomas Browne considers this absurd notion sufficiently prevalent in his time to be worthy of refutation. He also notes another fallacy regarding this animal. In consequence of its lack of joints it was necessarily unable to lie down, and as a substitute for a couch it had to lean up against a tree to sleep. Hunters came before dusk to saw the tree almost asunder, and when the tired animal sought repose the trunk gave way, and once down rising was an impossibility. Travellers, who had opportunities of watching the elephant's habits, contradict this statement as to the joints. Cada Mosto, a Venetian, writing in 1509, says:—

"Before my voyage to Africa I had been told that the elephant could not bend its knee, and slept standing; but this is an egregious falsehood, for the bending of their knees can be plainly perceived when they walk, and they certainly lie down and rise again like other animals."

This author, while correcting one error, gives credit to another not less absurd; he says, "Of the large teeth, or rather tusks, each elephant has two in the lower jaw, the points of which turn down, whereas those of the wild boar are turned up" (*Kerr's Voyages*, vol. ii. p. 233). The first elephant seen in England was a specimen brought from France in the year 1255.

Cæsar Fredericke, a Venetian merchant, giving an account of his travels in the East Indies, mentions the white elephant of Siam, an animal as rare as it is proverbially expensive. Describing the King of Siam's court at Pegu, he writes :—

"Truly it may be a king's house: withing the gate there is a faire large court, from the one side to the other, wherein there are made places for the strongest and stoutest eliphants appointed for the service of the king's person, and amongst all other eliphants, he hath foure that be white, a thing so rare that a man shall hardly finde another king that hath any such, and if this king knowe any other that hath white eliphantes, he sendeth for them as a gift." (*Hakluyt*, vol. ii. p. 363.)

CHAPTER VII.

THE only species of Rat known at this time was the black, or as it is sometimes called, the old English rat. Mr. Frank Buckland, in his *Curiosities of Natural History* (1st series, p. 57), considers that this species was introduced into England from France. The Welsh name for the rat is *Llygoden Frengig*, the French mouse. The earliest account of it is by Gesner, in his *Historia Animalium*, published at Zurich, about the year 1587. The brown species, erroneously called the Norway rat, was a native of India and Persia, and did not make its way from those distant regions till many years after the arrival in England of its black congener. The black rat, like other primitive occupiers of the soil, has been gradually expelled from its haunts by the later colonist, and is now almost extinct in this country. According to Carew, rats were rather too plentiful in Cornwall in 1602 :—

"Of all manner of vermin, Cornish houses are most pestered with rats, a brood very hurtful for devouring of meat, clothes, and writings by day; and alike cumbersome through their crying and ratling, while they dance their gallop gallyards in the roof at night." (*Survey of Cornwall*, p. 73, ed. 1811.)

The effect of poetry on Irish rats is often mentioned by dramatists. Ben Jonson writes :—

"Rhime them to death, as they do Irish rats
In drumming tunes."
(*The Poetaster*, v. apologue.)

And again, "Or the fine madrigal-man in rhyme to have run him out of the country, like an Irish rat" (*The Staple of News*, iv. 1). Shakspeare has a similar allusion. *Rosalind* says, "I never was so berhymed since Pythagoras' time, that I was an Irish rat, which I can hardly remember" (*As You Like It*, iii. 2, 187). Shakspeare also alludes to the popular notion that rats will desert a sinking vessel. *Prospero* describes to *Miranda* how both he and she were turned adrift by his usurping brother, in—

> "A rotten carcass of a boat, not rigg'd,
> Nor tackle, sail, nor mast: the very rats
> Instinctively had quit it."
>
> (*Tempest*, i. 2, 146.)

Mouse. Topsell devotes fifty folio pages to the history and literature of the "vulgar little Mouse." Among other pieces of information, he tells us that—

"the epithets of myce are these: short, small, fearful, peaceable, ridiculous, rustik, or country mouse, urbane, or citty mouse, greedy, wary, unhappy, harmefull, blacke, obscene, little, whiner, biter, and earthly mouse. Mice are sometimes blackish, sometimes white, sometimes yellow, sometimes broune and sometimes ashe colour. There are white mice amonge the people of Savoy, and Dolphin in France, called alaubroges, which the inhabitants of the country do beleev that they feede upon snow. The enemies of mice are many, not onely men, which by sundry artificiall devises kill them because of harme, but also beasts and wilde foule doe eat their flesh, and live upon them. Aud first of all cats and weasels, do principally hunt to catch mice, and have bin therefore by the late writers called murilegi [from *mus*, mouse; and *lego*, I catch], for their taking of mice. And the nature of the weasell is not onely more enclined to hunt after them, then the cat, but is more terrible also unto them, for if the braines of a weasell, the haire or rennet be sprinkled uppon cheese or any other meate whereto mice resort, they not onely forebear to eat thereof, but also to come in that place."

Batman mentions several kinds of mice: "The field mouse, the farie, with a long snout; the sleeper, that is of a dun colour and will run on the edge of a sword and sleep on the point." The dormouse from its awakening from sleep with the return of the spring was sometimes employed in ecclesiastical art as a type of the resurrection.

Stow mentions, in his *Chronicles of England*—

"a great plague of mice in the marshes of Dainsey, in Essex, which gnawed the grass, tainting the same with their venomous teeth, so that the cattle were poisoned and died."

The inhabitants of that county were in some perplexity how to deal with their small enemies, till from all the country round gathered a large number of owls, and to the great delight of the farmers soon cleared the marshes.

The odd simile, "As drunk as a mouse," dates back to the time of Chaucer. In the *Knight's Tale* (line 402) we read—

"We faren as he that drunke is as a mous."

Mr. Charles Mackay would fain save the little animal from such discredit by a suggestion that the expression is taken from the Gaelic. The word *miosa*, in this language, means the worse or worst, consequently the phrase implies simply a very advanced state of inebriation (*Notes and Queries*, 5th series, vol. v. p. 394).

Olaus Magnus was the first to notice the curious periodic migrations of the Norway Lemming. These animals sometimes make their appearance in locust-like swarms. They march steadily across the country, allowing no obstacle to stop them, destroying the crops in their route. Their numbers are thinned by foxes and ermines, but nothing daunted they pursue their way to the sea-shore and finally perish in the waves.

Lemming.

Beavers were at one time inhabitants of this country. Camden, in his description of Britain, states that the Tivey, in Cardiganshire, was in

Beaver.

times past the only British river that harboured these animals.

"This beaver," he says, "is a creature living both on land and water, footed before like a dog, and behind like a goose, with an ash-coloured skin somewhat blackish, having a long taile, broad and gristly, which in his floting he useth in lieu of a sterne. Concerning the subtile wilinesse of which creatures, Giraldus hath observed many things, but at this daie none of them are to be seene."

Drayton, in his *Polyolbion*, has a long account of the beaver, and its mode of building, but as he is indebted to some earlier writer for his information, and not to personal observation, the passage is hardly worth quoting. Mr. Frank Buckland, in his *Curiosities of Natural History*, gives it as his opinion that beavers could not have been common at any time in this country, as he has never seen a beaver's bone or tooth among ancient British or Saxon remains :—

"These former inhabitants of Great Britain used much bone in their household implements, and had beavers been common, we should probably find some bone or other converted to some useful domestic purpose." (First series, 1873, p. 90.)

Beaver hats were considered as an extravagant luxury in the time of Elizabeth. Philip Stubbes speaks of them in terms of high indignation, and says they cost twenty, thirty, and forty shillings apiece, and "were fetched from beyond the seas, from whence a great sort of other vanities do come besides."

Squirrel.
"The Squirrell," says Topsell, "is greater in compasse then a weasil, but a weasil is longer than a squirrel. The mouth of their nest is variable, sometimes at the sides, and sometimes at the top, but most commonly it is shut against the winde, and therefore I thinke that shee maketh many passages, stopping and opening them as the winde turneth. In summer time they gather together abundance of fruits and nuttes for winter, even so much as their little dray will holde and containe, which they carrie in their mouthes, and they lodge manie times two

togither, a male and a female (as I suppose). They sleep a great part of the winter like the Alpine mouse, and very soundly, for I have seen when no noise of hunters could wake them with their cries, beating their nests on the outside, and shootinge boltes and arrowes thorough it, until it were pulled asunder, wherein many times they are found killed before they be awaked. They growe exceeding tame and familiar to men if they be accustomed and taken when they are young, for they runne up to mens shoulders, and they will oftentimes sit upon their handes, creepe into their pockets for nuttes, goe out of doores, and returne home againe; but if they be taken alive, being olde, when once they get loose, they will never returne home againe. They are very harmefull, and will eat al manner of woollen garments, and if it were not for that discommodity, they were sweete-sportful-beastes, and are very pleasant playfellowes in a house." (Page 658.)

Du Bartas writes (p. 50):—

"There skips the squirrill, seeming weather-wise,
Without beholding of heav'ns twinkling eyes:
For, knowing well which way the winde will change,
He shifts the portall of his little grange."

Dr. Giles Fletcher describes the flying squirrel found in Russia:—

"They have a kinde of squirrell that hath growing on the pinion of the shoulder bone, a long tuft of haire, much like unto feathers, with a far broader tayle then have any other squirrels, which they move and shake as they leape from tree to tree, much like unto a wing. They skise a large space, and seeme for to flie withall, and therefore they call them *letach vechse*, that is, the flying squirrels. Their hares and squirrels are of the same colour with ours. In winter the hare changeth her coate into milke white, the squirrel into gray, whereof commeth the *calabar*." (*Purchas*, vol. iii. p. 417.)

In Linschoten's narrative of a voyage to Goa, in 1583, we find mention of the common grey squirrel of India:—

"There are many monkies or marmosets, that doe great hurt to the palme trees, whereon the Indian nut or cocus doth growe. In those trees you shall commonly see certaine little beasts, called *bichos de palmeyras*, that is, beasts of the palme trees: they are much like ferrets, wherewith men use to hunt and catch cunnies, and have a taile like the penner of an ink-horne, and grayish speckled haire: they are pretie beasts to keepe and to passe the time withall." (*Purchas*, vol. ii. p. 1771.)

Marmot. Topsell enlightens us as to the derivation of the word Marmot:—

"The Alpine mouse taketh her name from the Alpes wherein she is bred, and although there be many other kindes of mice bred in the Alpes, yet this being the principal thereof, receiveth denomination from the mountaines. The Italians cal it *marmota*, in Fraunce *marmote*, although marmot be a word also among them for a munkey. The Helvetians by a corrupt word, drawne from a mouse of the mountain, *murmelthier*, and *murmentle*, and some *mistbellerle*, by reason of his sharp whining voice like a little dogs." (Page 551.)

Another species of rodent, much prized for its beautiful silky grey fur, was the Chinchilla. **Chinchilla.** The earliest account of this animal is given in Joseph Acosta's *Observations on the East and West Indies*, of which a translation was published in London in 1604. He says:—

"The chinchilles is an other kinde of small beasts, like squirrels. They have a wonderfull smoothe and soft skin, which they weare as a healthfull thing to comfort the stomacke; they make coverings and rugs of the haire of these chinchilles, which are found on the Sierre of Peru." (*Purchas*, vol. iii. p. 966.)

The confusion of pronouns here is worthy of Clarendon himself.

The Viscacha of the Pampas, a strange-looking animal somewhat resembling a marmot, with **Viscacha.** a double set of whiskers, is also mentioned by Acosta, in company with another burrowing animal, the cuye:—

"There is likewise a small beast very common, which they call cuyes, and which the Indians hold for a very good meate, and they are accustomed to offer these cuyes in their sacrifices. They are like small conies, and have their burrowes in the ground, and in some places they have undermined all the land: some are grey, some white, and some speckled. There are other small animals which they call viscachas, and are like to hares, although they are bigger, they hunt them and eate the flesh. Of common hares there are great store in some parts." (*Purchas*, vol. iii. p. 966.)

A notion was prevalent among poets that the Porcupine, Porkespick, or Porkespyne could employ his quills as darts or assagais, shoot them with unerring aim, and transfix his enemies therewith. What the poor beast was to do if he was often pursued does not seem to have occurred to these writers. The porcupine uses its quills as weapons of defence; and if they penetrate deeply into its opponent, they are at times drawn from the rightful owner. Dogs and other animals have often been found with the smaller spines imbedded in their flesh. This error may have arisen from the fact that the loose quills about to be shed have been seen to drop out of the animal's skin when they were suddenly raised. The quaint writer, Du Bartas, has an amusing description of the porcupine's mode of warfare:—

Porcupine.

> "But O! what monster's this that bids me battell,
> On whose rough back an hoast of pikes doth rattle,
> Who string-less shoots so many arrowes out,
> Whose thorny sides are hedged round about
> With stiff steel-pointed quils, and all his parts
> Bristled with bodkins, arm'd with auls and darts,
> Which by fierce darting, seem still fresh to spring,
> And to his aid still new supplies to bring?
> O fortunat shaft-never-wanting bow-man!
> Who, as thou fleest, canst hit thy following foe-man,
> And never missest, or but very narrow,
> Th' intended mark of thy selfs-kindred arrow."
> (*Divine Weekes*, p. 50.)

This idea is not confined to poets, but is corroborated by John Nieuhoff in his voyage to the East Indies. He writes:—

"About Batavia and in the woods of Java are abundance of iron pigs or porcupines. When they are at rest they lay their pens or pegs close to the body, but if they are vexed they can by contracting themselves cast them forth with such strength that they kill man or beast. In the winter they retire into holes where they remain without eating or drinking, they feed upon herbs and roots and cast their pens as other creatures do their hair." (*Churchill's Voyages*, vol. ii. p. 298.)

Roger Ascham, in his *Toxophilus*, 1515, tells us that "Claudiane the poete saith, that Nature gave example of shootynge first by the porpentine, which shootes his prickes and will hitte anye thing that fightes with it."

Marlowe employs the porcupine as a simile in *Tamburlaine*, where the emperor complains that his sons are wanting in a martial appearance :—

> "Their hair as white as milk and soft as down,
> Which should be like the quills of porcupines
> As black as jet and hard as iron or steel."
>
> (2 *Tamburlaine*, i. 3.)

This comparison may have been in Shakspeare's mind when, in *Hamlet*, the ghost speaks of a tale of horror which could make—

> "Each particular hair to stand on end,
> Like quills upon the fretfull porpentine."
>
> (*Hamlet*, i. 5, 19.)

Agouti. A Portuguese writer, whose account of his residence in Brazil has been previously quoted, mentions the Agouti, an animal common in South America :—

> "The acutis are like the conies of Spaine, chiefly in their teeth : the colour is dunne, and draweth toward yellow. They are domesticall creatures, so that they goe about the house, and goe out and come in againe to it. They take with their fore-feet all that they eate, and so they carrie it to the mouth, and they eate very fast, and hide that which they leave against they be an hungrie. Of these there are many kindes, and all are eaten." (*Purchas*, vol. iv. p. 1301.)

John Lerius, a Frenchman who lived in Brazil during the years 1557 and 1558, tells us:—

"There is also among the Americans a certaine red wilde beast, which they name agouti, of the height of a weaned pig of thirty dayes old, with a cloven foot, a very short tayle, and with the nose and eares almost of an hare, most delightfull to the taste. There are also others of two or three kindes, which they call tapitis, not much unlike our hares, but somewhat of a reddish haire." (*Purchas*, vol. iv. p. 1326.)

Instead of a cloven foot, the agouti has four well-developed toes.

This author also describes the pretty little Paca, a species of cavy. Like the agouti it is easily tamed, and of lively habits. Specimens are occasionally brought over to this country. Lerius writes:— *Paca.*

"Pag, or pague (for after what manner they pronounce it, you can scarce, or not at all understand), is a wilde beast of the indifferent height of an hound, with a deformed head, the flesh comming neere the taste of veale, with a very faire skinne, distinguished with white, russet, and blacke spots, so that it would be of great price with us, if they were to be gotten."

The Guinea Pig, though now only kept as a pet in this country, was once apparently considered a palatable dish. In a list of the expenses of a dinner given by William Muigay, Mayor of Norwich, to the Duke of Norfolk and the principal knights of the county, in the year 1561, we read, among other items, two brace of partridges at two shillings, four couple rabbits at one and eightpence, and two "guiny piggs" at a shilling. *Guinea Pig.*

This little animal has been strangely misnamed. It is not a pig, but a species of cavy. It is not found in Guinea, but in Brazil and Peru.

The Hare is frequently mentioned by poets and dramatists, while allusion to its more plebeian relative, the rabbit, is rare. Drayton gives a description of the hunting of the hare, which, though *Hare.*

of some length, has an interest on account of the technical terms introduced :—

"The man whose vacant mind prepares him to the sport,
The finder sendeth out, to seek out nimble Wat,
Which crosseth in the field, each furlong, every flat,
Till he this pretty beast upon the form hath found,
Then viewing for the course, which is the fairest ground,
The greyhounds forth are brought, for coursing them in case,
And choicely in the slip, each leading forth a brace;
The finder puts her up, and gives her coursers law,
And whilst the eager dogs upon the start do draw,
She riseth from her seat, as though on earth she flew,
Forc'd by some yelping cur to give the greyhounds view,
Which are at length let slip, when gunning out they go,
As in respect of them the swiftest wind were slow,
When each man runs his horse, with fixed eyes, and notes
Which dog first turns the hare, which first the other coats,
They wrench her once or twice, ere she a turn will take,
What's offered by the first, the other good will make;
And turn for turn again with equal speed they ply,
Bestirring their swift feet with strange agility :
A harden'd ridge or way, when if the hare do win,
Then as shot from a bow, she from the dogs doth spin,
That strive to put her off, but when he cannot reach her,
This giving him a coat, about again doth fetch her
To him that comes behind, which seems the hare to bear;
But with a nimble turn she casts them both arrear :
Till oft for want of breath, to fall to ground they make her,
The greyhounds both so spent, that they want strength to take her."
(*Polyolbion*, song xxiii.)

" *To cote* is not simply to overtake, but to surpass; this being the distinctive meaning of the term; going beyond is the essential point : so *Rosencrantz* and *Guildenstern*, having coted the players on their way, reach the palace first." (*Edinburgh Review*, October, 1872.)

In Shakspeare's *Venus and Adonis* (lines 752–708) "hot scent-snuffing hounds" are spoken of as employed in a hare-hunt instead of the more usual greyhounds.

We learn from Fuller that hares were common in Cambridgeshire :—

"Though these are found in all counties, yet because lately there was in this shire an hare-park nigh Newmarket, preserved for the king's game, let them here be particularly mentioned. Some prefer their sport in hunting before their flesh for eating, as accounting it melancholicke meat, and hard to be disgested; though others think all the hardness is now to come by it." (*Worthies of England*, vol. i. p. 153.)

Burton attributes melancholy in many cases to diet, and includes this animal among the articles of food that produce it. "Hare, a black meat, melancholy, and hard of digestion; it breeds incubus, often eaten, and causeth fearful dreams; so doth all venison, and is condemned by a jury of phisicians" (*Anatomy of Melancholy*, vol. i. p. 218). The solitary habits of the hare have probably gained for it the reputation of gloominess. Drayton writes:—

"The melancholy hare form'd on brakes and briars."
(*Polyolbion*, song ii.)

Prince Henry suggests, in reply to *Falstaff*'s assertion that he is "as melancholy as a gib cat:" "What sayest thou to a hare or the melancholy of Moor-ditch?" (1 *Henry IV.*, i. 2, 86).

A hare was called a leveret the first year, a hare the second, and a great hare the third. There were several curious fancies connected with this animal. When it sleeps the hare's eyelids do not quite join, which gave rise to the notion that it slept with its eyes open:—

"That looking to my gold with such hare's eyes,
That ever open, ay, even when they sleep."
(BEN JONSON, *The Case is Altered*, v. 4.)

"Tread softly, Trollio, my father sleeps still.
Ay, fersooth: but he sleeps like a hare, with his eyes open,
An that's no good sign."
(FORD, *The Lover's Melancholy*, ii. 2.)

Topsell gives an odd explanation of the expression *hare-eyed* :—

"The eyelids comming from the brows are too short to cover their eyes, and therefore this sence is very weake in them, and besides their over much sleepe, for fear of dogs and swiftnesse causeth them to see the lesse; when they run they shut their eies, and when they sleep they open them." (Page 265.)

Lyly alludes to a very curious notion : " Hares we cannot be, because they are male one year and the next female" (*Mydas*); and Fletcher, in the *Gentle Shepherd*, writes, " Hares that yearly sexes change."

" Mad as a March hare " is an old proverb :—

> " The blast of the brymston blew away his braine
> Mased as March hare."
> (SKELTON, *The Crowne of Lawrell*.)

It was considered unlucky if a hare crossed the path :—

> " Nor did we meet
> With nimble feet,
> One little fearful lepus,
> That certaine sign, as some divine,
> Of fortune bad to keep us."
> (ELLISON, *Trip to Benwell*, lx.)

Shakspeare has many references to this creature's timidity. *Sir Toby Belch* declares that *Viola* is " a very dishonest, paltry boy, and more a coward than a hare" (*Twelfth Night*, iii. 4, 420).

In his treatise on English dogs, Dr. Caius makes mention of a performing hare :—

> " A hare (being a wilde and skippishe beast) was seene in England to the astouishment of the beholders, in the yeare of our Lorde God 1564, not onely dauncing in measure, but playing with his former feet uppon a tabbaret, and observing just number of strokes (as a practitioner in that arte) besides that nipping and pinching a dogge with his teeth and clawes, and cruelly thumping him with the force of his feete. This is no trumpery tale, (nor trifling toye) as I imagine, and therefore not unworthy to be reported, for I recken it a requitall of my travaile, not to drowne in the seas of silence any speciall thing, wherein the providence and effectuall working of nature is to be pondered."
> (*Reprint*, 1880, p. 16.)

The worthy doctor omits to inform us if the aforesaid dog

was kept in the company of the hare for the purpose of being periodically pommelled for the amusement of the spectators. If he was so retained, we may imagine without much difficulty what the reflections of the unfortunate dog may have been, both upon the providential working of nature and upon the humanity of his owner. Ben Jonson includes a similar performing animal in his list of curiosities which were exhibited at Bartholomew Fair:—

" *Waspe.* I have been at the eagle, and the black wolf, and the bull with the five legs—he was a calf at Uxbridge Fair two years agone— and at the dogs that dance the morrice, and the hare of the tabor; and mist him at all these! Sure this must needs be some fine sight that holds him so, if it have him." (*Bartholomew Fair,* v. 3.)

Mrs. Palliser (*Historic Devices,* 1870, p. 236) tells us that one of the many emblems adopted by Mary, Queen of Scots, and embroidered by her during her captivity, was a lion taken in a net, and hares wantonly passing over him, with the words, *Et lepores devicto insultant leone*— "Even hares trample on the conquered lion." Of this device Alciati gives a representation in his work on emblems. To this drawing Shakspeare possibly refers. *Philip Faulconbridge* says, tauntingly, to *Austria:*—

" You are the hare of whom the proverb goes,
Whose valour plucks dead lions by the beard."
(*King John,* ii. 1, 127.)

Rabbits were plentiful in all parts of England. William Lambarde, in his *Perambulation of Kent,* writes of that county, in 1576 :— **Rabbit.**

" Parkes of fallow deere, and games of gray conies, it maintaineth many, the one for pleasure, and the other for profit, as it may well appear by this, that within memorie almost the one halfe of the first sorte be disparked, and the number of warreyns continueth, if it do not increase daily. As for red deere, and blacke conies, it nourisheth them not, as having no forest, or great walks of waste grounde for the one,

M

and not tarying the time to raise to gaine by the other: for blacke conyes are kept partly for their skins, which have their season in winter; and Kent by the nearnesse to London, hath so quicke market of yong rabbets, that it killeth this game chiefly in summer."

Holinshed, dealing with England more generally, gives much the same account:—

"As for warrens of conies, I judge them almost innumerable and dailie like to increase, by reason that the blacke skins of those beasts are thought to countervaile the prices of their naked carcases, and this is the onelie cause whie the graie are lesse esteemed. Neere unto London their quickest merchandize is of the yong rabbets, wherefor the older conies are brought from further off, where is no such speedie utterance of rabbets and sucklings in their season, nor so great losse by their skins, sith they are suffered to grow up to their full greatnesse with their owners." (*Chronicles*, vol. i. p. 343, ed. 1807.)

In this work (p. 57) we are told that in the group of islands known as the Channel Islands—

"is also the rocky Isle of Burhoo, but now the Isle of Rats, so called of the huge plentie of rats that are found there, though otherwise it is replenished with infinit store of conies, betweene whome and the rats as I conjecture, the same which we call Turkie conies are oftentimes produced among those few houses that are to be seene in this island."

Fynes Moryson also notices the abundance of these little rodents. "England," he says, "hath infinite number of conies, whereof the skinnes especially black and silver haired are much prised, and in great quantities transported, especially into Turkey" (*Itinerary*, p. 148).

The rabbit, or cony, was considered to have but a scanty allowance of brains. The verb "to cony-catch" was often used when a simple-minded victim was deceived or entrapped. A French commentator on Du Bartas informs us that the cony is—

"a beast, which by reason of his feare, loseth all ordinarie remembrance; whence the French proverb commeth, Thou hast as much memory as a hare, or conny: thou hast lost it in running."

The name rabbet-sucker, or young cony, was sometimes given to the dupe of any imposture. Shakspeare uses the former name in its literal sense:—

"*Prince*. Dost thou speak like a king? Do thou stand for me, and I'll play my father.
"*Fal*. Depose me? If thou dost it half so gravely, so majestically, both in word and matter, hang me up by the heels for a rabbit-sucker, or a poulter's hare." (1 *Henry IV.*, ii. 4, 476.)

On account of their abundance rabbits were not held in high estimation for the table. Instructions are given in Wynkyn de Worde's *Boke of Kervynge* for *unlacing*, or cutting up, a cony. The sauce recommended is either vinegar and ginger, or mustard and sugar.

No doubt Shakspeare had often watched with amusement the antics of these merry little creatures. He may have seen, in the evening of a showery summer day, the furzy down or the woodland glade at one moment bare and deserted, and the next alive with "earth-delving conies," frisking and gambolling on the dewy grass. The servants of *Aufidius* comment on the reception which *Coriolanus* has met with from their master, and discuss the chances of a speedy attack upon Rome. One of the men declares that, although the enemies of the warlike visitor have triumphed for a time, yet *Coriolanus* has left many friends behind him. They have withdrawn from his side, and taken shelter from the storm of unpopularity that has overwhelmed him; "But when they shall see, sir, his crest up again, and the man in blood, they will out of their burrows, like conies after rain, and revel all with him" (*Coriolanus*, iv. 5, 224).

It is not easy to identify all the animals described by the early travellers, but the minute details given by Gonzalo Ferdinando de Oviedo in his account of the West Indies leaves little doubt that the subject of his discourse is the Ai, or Three-toed Sloth, a species common in Brazil.

"There is," he writes, "another strange beast, which, by a name of contrary effect, the Spaniards call *cagnuolo*, that is, the Light Dogge, whereas it is one of the slowest beasts in the world, and so heavie and dull in moving, that it can scarcely goe fiftie pases in a whole day: these beasts are in the same land, and are very strange to behold for the disproportion that they have to all other beasts: they are about two spans in length when they are growne to their full bignesse, but when they are very young, they are somewhat more grosse then long: they have foure subtill feete, and in every one of them foure clawes like unto birds, and joyned together: yet are neither their clawes or their feet able to susteine their bodies from the ground, by reason whereof, and by the heavinesse of their bodies, they draw their bellies on the ground: their neckes are high and streight, and all equal like the pestle of a morter, which is altogether equal even unto the top, without making any proportion or similitude of a head, or any difference except in the noddle, and in the tops of their neckes: they have very round faces much like unto owles, and have a marke of their own haire after the manner of a circle, which maketh their faces seeme somewhat more long then large: they have small eyes and round, and nostrils like unto monkeyes: they have little mouthes, and moove their neckes from one side to another, as though they were astonished: their chiefe desire and delight is to cleave and sticke fast unto trees, or some other thing whereby they may climbe aloft, and therefore for the most part, these beasts are found upon trees, whereunto cleaving fast, they mount up by little and little, staying themselves by their long clawes: the colour of the haire is betweene russet and white, and of the proper colour of the haire of a weasell: they have no tayles, and their voice is much differing from other beasts, for they sing onely in the night, and that continually from time to time, singing ever sixe notes one higher then another, so falling with the same, that the first note is the highest, and the other in a baser tune, as if a man should say, La, sol, fa, mi, re, ut, so this beast saith, Ha, ha, ha, ha, ha, ha. And doubtlesse, it seemeth to me that as I have said in the chapter of the beast called *bardati*, that those beasts might be the originall and document to imbarbe horses: even so the first invention of musicke might seeme by the hearing of this beast, to have the first principles of that science, rather then by any other thing in the world. But now to returne to the historie. I say that in a short space after this beast hath sung, and hath paused a while, shee returneth againe to the selfe-same song, and doth this onely in the night and not in the day. And whereas I my selfe have kept them in my house, I could never perceive other but that they live onely of aire: and of the same opinion are in like manner all men of those regions, because they have never seene them eate any thing, but ever turne their heads and mouthes toward that part where the wind bloweth most, whereby may be considered that they take most pleasure in the ayre. They bite not, nor yet can bite, having very little mouthes: they are not venemous or noyous any way, but altogether brutish, and utterly unprofitable, and without commoditie yet knowne to men." (*Purchas*, vol. iii. p. 978.)

Joseph Acosta, another traveller, is more accurate as to the number of claws that this musical animal possesses:—

"There is another strange beast, which for his great heavinesse, and slownesse in moving, they call *perico-ligero*, or the little light dogge; hee hath three nailes to every hand, and mooves both hand and feete, as it were by compasse and very heavily: it is in face like to a monkey, and hath a shrill crie; it climeth trees and eates ants." (*Purchas*, vol. iii. p. 966.)

Buffon, in his *Natural History*, gives an account of the ai. According to this naturalist every part of the unfortunate sloth is an error in nature. It is unable to walk or even to crawl; it has no weapons of offence or defence; slowness, habitual pain, and stupidity are the results of the "strange and bungling conformation of creatures to whom nature has been unkind, and who exhibit to us the picture of innate misery." More recent observers, who have studied the habits of the animal in its native haunts, tell us that its formation is in perfect harmony with its environments. The sloth's progress along the level surface of the ground is tedious and painful, but when it gains the branch of a tree, its natural habitat, the strong curved claws, which impeded its locomotion before, form so many grappling irons, by means of which it can pass from bough to bough with ease and comfort, and with fair celerity. It feeds, not upon ants, but upon young leaves and shoots.

Don Gonzalo writes further:—

Armadillo. "There is another kinde of beaste seene in the firme land [South America] which seemeth very strange and marveilous to the Christian men to behold, and much differing from all other beasts which have beene seene in other parts of the world: these beasts are called Bardati, and are foure footed, having their taile and all the rest of their bodies covered onely with a skin like to a barbed horse, or the checkered skin of a lisart or crocodile, of colour betweene white and russet, inclining somewhat more to white. And if these beasts had ever beene seene in these parts of the world where the first barbed horses had their original, no man would judge but that the forme and fashion of the coperture of horses furnished for the warres, was first devised by the sight of these beasts." (*Purchas*, vol. iii. p. 977).

Joseph Acosta, in the same work, informs us that in Peru—

"there bee little beasts which goe through the woods, called Armadillos, by reason of the defence they have, hiding themselves within their scales, and opening when they list: I have eaten of them, and doe not hold it for meate of any great worth; but the flesh of the *yguanas* is a better meate, but more horrible to the eye: for they are like to the very lizardes of Spaine, although they bee of a doubtfull kinde, for they goe to the water, and comming to land, they climbe the trees upon the bankes, and as they cast themselves from the trees into the water the boates watch underneath to receive them."

Topsell gives an account of two extraordinary animals, the latter of which corresponds to the armadillo, with the exception of the duck-like bill.

"Of the Tatus, or Guinean Beast," he writes, "this is a foure-footed strange beast, which Bellonius saith, he found in Turchia, among the mountebankes and apothicaries. It is brought for the most part out of the new-found world, and out of Guinia, and may therefore be safely conveyed into those parts, because it is naturally covered with a harde shell, devided and interlined like the fins of fishes, outwardly seeming buckled to the backe like coat-armor, with which the beast draweth up his body as a hedghog doth within his prickled skin, and therefore I take it to be a Brasilian hedghog. The merchants as I have heard and cittizens of London keepe off with these their garden wormes. . . . There is another beast that may bee compared to this, whereof Cardianus writeth, and he calleth the name of it Aiochtochth. It is a strange creature, found in Hispania Nova, neare the river Alvaradus, being not greater then a cat, having the bil or snowt of a mallard, the feet of an hedge-hog, and a very long necke. It is covered al over with a shell like the trappinges of a horse, divided as in a lobster and not continued as in an oyster; and so covered therewith, that neither the necke nor the head appeare plainely, but onely the eares; and the Spaniards for this cause call it armato and contaxto: there be some doe affirme that it hath a voice like swine, but the feet thereof are not indeed so cloven that they remaine unequal, but are like to a horses, I meane the several cloves, there are of these as I have hearde to be seene in gardens in London, which are kept to destroy the garden wormes." (Page 706.)

The former animal is possibly the Peba armadillo (*Tatusia peba*), a species of armadillo found throughout Central and South America.

A Portuguese resident in Brazil, gives a description of the Ant-eater, or Ant-bear, which, though somewhat grotesque in its wording, is fairly correct.

Ant-eater.

"The tamandua," he says, "is of notable admiration, it is of the bignesse of a great dog, more round then long, and the tayle is twice or thrice as long as the bodie, and so full of haire, that from the heate, raine, cold and winde, hee harboureth himselfe all under it, that yee can see nothing of him. The head is small, and hath a thinne snout, no greater mouth then an oyle cruze, round and not open, the tongue is of three quarters long, and with it he licketh up the ants, whereon he onely feeds; he is diligent in seeking of the ant-heapes, and with the clawes hee breaketh them, and casting out his tongue the ants stick to it, and so he drawes them in, having no more mouth then to hold his tongue full of them; it is of a great fiercenesse, and doth assault many people and beasts. The ounces doe feare them and the dogs exceedingly, and whatsoever they catch, they teare with their clawes; they are not eaten, neither are they good for any thing but to destroy the ant-heapes; and they are so many that they will never be destroyed altogether." (*Purchas*, vol. iv. p. 1301.)

The ant-eater, though provided with powerful claws, and a formidable antagonist when roused, does not attack either man or beast unprovoked. This animal is called by other travellers the *baremoe*.

Gonzalo describes, under its native name, another, and perhaps the strangest of the New-World animals, the Opossum:—

> **Opossum.** "The Churchia is as bigge as a small conie, tawnie, sharp-snowted, dogtoothed, long-tayled like a rat. They doe great harme to their hennes, killing sometimes twentie or more at once to sucke their bloud: and if they then have young, shee carrieth them with her in a bagge of skin under her belly, running alongst the same like a satchell, which shee opens and shuts at pleasure to let them in and out: and if any come with light when the damme and young are at their hen-bloud dainties, shee receives them into this bagge and runneth away with them. And if shee finde the way stopped, shee climeth up above the hen roost, and is sometimes taken alive or dead in this manner, as I have seene." (*Purchas*, vol. iii. p. 995.)

Another traveller, Girolamo Benzoni, a Milanese, writes in a work published at Venice in 1565:—

> "There exists also a monstrous animal, that has a pouch under its stomach, into which it makes the young ones get when it wants to go from one place to another; this animal has the body and the snout of a fox, with fore paws and hind feet like those of a cat, but more handy, and its ears are like those of the rat." (*History of America*, reprint, Hakluyt Society, 1857.)

From one of these descriptions Du Bartas probably derived his exaggerated notions of the formidable nature of the opossum:—

> "I fear the beast bred in the bloody coast
> Of Cannibals, which thousand times (almost)
> Re-whelps her whelps, and in her tender womb,
> Shee doth as oft her living brood_re-tomb."
> (*Divine Weekes*, p. 50.)

CHAPTER VIII.

WE must bear in mind when we pass from quadrupeds to Birds, how different was the external aspect of England in the time of Elizabeth from that which it wears to-day. Forests extended for many miles, of which now only the name and one or two patriarchal-looking trees remain. That marshes stretched far inland from the coast, even within sight of the large towns, is evident from the frequent reference to ague, low fever, and other maladies arising from malaria. Norden writes of Essex, in 1593 :—

Birds.

"This shire seemeth to me to deserve the title of the Englishe Goshen, the fattest of the lande : comparable to Palestina, that floweth with milke and hunnye. But I cannot commende the healthfulnes of it : and especiallie nere the sea coastes, Rochford, Denge, Tendering Hundreds and other lowe places about the creekes, which gave me a moste cruell quaterne fever. But the manie and sweete commodities countervayle the danger."

The same remarks would apply to many inland places. Little by little these low-lying districts have been drained, and the woods and forests have been cleared. This transition must have had more effect on the life of birds than on that of quadrupeds. The deer, though restricted in their range, had parks set aside for their preservation ; laws against their destruction made amends for their loss of freedom. Of other wild animals, the fox and hare were protected on account of the amusement their pursuit afforded, and the badger, otter, and wild cat still remained in parts of the island.

To the extensive drainage of marshy lands is to be traced the diminution and final disappearance of a great number of water and wading birds. Naturalists are indebted to the slowness with which this work of reclaiming the land proceeded for the preservation of many species to a sufficiently recent period to be recorded by the sportsman or the chronicler. "The old order changeth, yielding place to new," and though sportsmen and epicures may lament the scarcity of the heron, the curlew, and the knot, the lover of melody has full compensation in the song of the lark, the robin, and the thrush. The traveller in the Lincolnshire fens, the last resort of many species of water birds, would hardly now send his friends at home a report such as old Camden gives:—

"All this tract-over at certaine seasons, good God, what store of foules, to say nothing of fishes, is heere to be found! I meane not those vulgar birds which in other places are highly esteemed and beare a great price, as teales, quailes, woodcocks, pheasants, partridges, &c., but such, as we have no Latin names for, the very delicate dainties of service, meates for the demigods, and greatly sought for by those that love the tooth so well, I meane, puits, godwitts, knotts, that is to say, Canuts or knoutsbirds, for out of Denmark they are thought to fly hither." (*Britaine.*)

The Rev. R. Lubbock, in his work, *The Fauna of Norfolk*, published 1845, gives many interesting particulars of the feathered inhabitants of the marshy districts of that county. He writes (page 48):—

"The Norfolk fens must in days of yore have literally swarmed with different species of birds. If we glance at the position of Norfolk and Suffolk upon the map, we at once perceive that they stand out as it were offering an asylum to the storm-beaten bird coming from the ocean. If we consider the great variety of soil to be found in the marshy part of the county, and the way in which swamp and high ground are continually intermingled, it is plain that formerly the Norfolk fens must have offered the fairest retreat of water birds. It is singular how universal has been the omission of this district amongst older writers on natural history."

This author notices the preference our forefathers appear to have had for water over land birds as delicacies for the table.

"On the occasion of any festival," he says (p. 67), "the inhabitants of the marsh are found in the place of honour, and land birds are quite neglected. The same preference for fen birds, the waders especially, pervades the whole of the 'L'Estrange' housekeeping. Knotts and plovers, with the curlews, appear most prized; a redshank is about one fourth the value of a plover; teal occur only twice, and the ruff is not mentioned. Pheasants and partridges appear several times, but only two or three at the most. The sea-pye (oyster-catcher) is in the list, and another mysterious fowl called a popeler, which is inserted in company with herons."

In an account of the expenses of the Judges of Assize, going the Western and Oxford Circuits, between the years 1596 and 1601, reprinted in the fourth volume of the *Camden Miscellany*, 1857, mention is made of a variety of birds which were sent as presents to the judges by the sheriffs of the different towns. In the introduction to the reprint we find a list of the various contributions:—

"We do not now dress the bustard, one of which was given at Salisbury in 1600; or the heron; or the heronshawes, which came in at Salisbury, Dorchester, Exeter, and Launceston; the curlew, or the gull, or the puffin, which was a rarity met with in Cornwall alone; or the kite, cooked at Exeter. The peacock was once dressed at Chard; the swan at Winchester, Salisbury, Andover, Taunton, and two cygnets at Oxford. Turkeys, then a rare bird, were presented on the earliest circuit in Cornwall; the heath-poults, now seldom met with in the west, were sent as presents at Salisbury, Dorchester, and Stafford; and the heath-cock at Launceston. Pheasants, of which there were not many, and partridges, which were abundant, were killed on both Circuits in the months of June and July, and also in February. Quails, now very scarce, formed a portion of the presents in each of the western towns and at Oxford. Plovers, golden and green, arrived at Taunton and Exeter; puetts at Winchester, Salisbury, Dorchester, Exeter, Oxford, Worcester, and Stafford; and a dozen oxen and kyne, being birds, [ruffs and reeves?] appear once in July at Exeter."

Considering the difficulties of transport in the reign of Elizabeth, England appears to have been well supplied with commodities. The daily meal of even the nobles was probably simple, but on state occasions the bill of fare presented great variety. *Christmas*, one of the characters in the play by Thomas Nash, *Summer's Last Will and Testament*, printed 1600, exclaims—

"O, it were a trim thing to send, as the Romans did, round about the world for provision for one banquet. I must rig ships to Samos for peacocks; to Paphos for pigeons; to Austria for oysters; to Phasis for pheasants; to Arabia for phœnixes; to Meander for swans; to the Orcades for geese; to Phrygia for woodcocks; to Malta for cranes; to the Isle of Man for puffins; to Ambracia for chestnuts—and all for one feast.

"*Will Summer.* O sir, you need not: you may buy them at London better cheap." (*Dodsley's Old Plays*, vol. viii., ed. W. C. Hazlitt.)

Bird-fowling has from time immemorial been man's favourite pursuit, and great has been also the ingenuity displayed by him in devising methods for beguiling or destroying his feathered prey. Thomas Burton quaintly writes :—

"Fowling is more troublesome [than hawking], but al out as delightsome to some sorts of men, be it with guns, lime, nets, glades, ginnes, strings, baits, pitfalls, pipes, calls, stalking-horses, setting-dogges, coy-ducks, &c., or otherwise. Some much delight to take larks with day-nets, small birds with chaffe-net, plovers, partridges, herons, snite, &c. Henry the Third, King of Castile (as Mariana the Jesuite reports of him, lib. 3, cap. 7), was much affected with catching of quailes; and many gentlemen take a singular pleasure at morning and evening to go abroad with theyr quail-pipes, and will take any paines to satisfie their delight in that kinde." (*Anatomy of Melancholy*, vol. i. p. 528.)

Theories of Migration. 173

Among the ancients the migration of birds was made the subject of close observation. Auguries were drawn from the flight of passage birds, and agricultural operations were to some extent regulated by the early or late appearance of the different species. But however accurate may have been the knowledge which the priests and farmers of Rome possessed concerning the times and seasons of the arrival and departure of migrating birds, their conjectures, as well as those of our own early naturalists, as to the destination of the various kinds were somewhat eccentric. According to some writers, the "half-year birds," as Izaak Walton calls them, did not leave the country at all, but sought shelter from the winter's cold in mudbanks and hollow trees. Of all the different theories suggested in explanation of the annual exodus of many species of birds, the very strangest is propounded in a paper preserved in the collection of curiosities, the *Harleian Miscellany* (vol. ii. p. 583), entitled "An enquiry into the physical and literal sense of that Scripture, 'The stork in the heaven knoweth her appointed times; and the turtle and the crane, and the swallow, observe the time of their coming.' (Jeremiah viii. 7.)" The writer of this article vouchsafes to the public neither signature nor date. He argues that if the flight of storks had been in an horizontal direction flocks of migrating birds would have been frequently seen by travellers; he therefore assumes that their route must be perpendicular, and fixes upon the moon as their destination :—

"Therefore the stork, and the like may be said of other season-observing birds, till some place more fit can be assigned to them, does go unto, and remain in some one of the celestial bodies; and that must be the moon, which is most likely because nearest, and bearing most relation to this our earth, as appears in the Copernican scheme; yet is the distance great enough to denominate the passage thither an itineration or journey."

The imagination of a Jules Verne would be required to supply the details of such a passage, and of the birds' sojourn in their new habitation. Two months are allowed by this ingenious writer for the upward flight, three for the necessary repose and refreshment in the lunar world, and two more for the return journey.

Harrison, in his description of Britain, prefixed to Holinshed's *Chronicle*, gives a list of English birds; but as his knowledge of the subject is limited, the catalogue is necessarily incomplete. He writes :—

Lists of Birds.

"Order requireth that I speake somewhat of the foules also of England, which I may easilie divide into the wild and tame: but alas such is my small skill in foules, that, to say the truth, I can neither recite their numbers, nor well distinguish one kind of them from another. . . . Of such [wildfowl] therefore as are bred in our land, we have the crane, the bitter, the wild and tame swan, the bustard, the herron, curlew, snite, wildgoose, wind or dottrell, brant, larke, plover (of both sorts), lapwing, teele, wigeon, mallard, sheldrake, shoveler, pewet, seamew, barnacle, quaile (who onelie with man are subject to the falling sickenesse), the notte, the oliet or olife, the dunbird, woodcocke, partrich and feasant, besides divers other, whose names to me are utterlie unknown, and much more the taste of their flesh, wherewith I was never acquainted. . . . Our tame foule are such (for the most part) as are common both to us and to other countries, as cocks, hens, geese, duckes, peacocks of Inde, pigeons, now an hurtful evil by reason of their multitudes, and such like. I would likewise intreat of other foules which we repute uncleane, as ravens, crowes, pies, choughes, rookes, kites, jaies, ringtailes, starlings, woodspikes, woodnawes, &c. . . . It may be that some looke for a discourse also of our other foules in this place at my hand, as nightingales, thrushes, blackebirds, mavises, ruddocks, redstarts or dunocks, larkes, tivits, kingfishers, buntings, turtles, white or graie, linets, bulfinshes, goldfinshes, washtailes, cheriecrackers, yellowhammers, felfares &c. But I should then spend more time upon them than is convenient. Neither will I speake of our costlie and curious aviaries daile made for the better hearing of their melodie, and observation of their natures." (*Holinshed*, vol. i. p. 374, ed. 1807.)

The *Northumberland Household Book*, which gives

an account of the domestic economy of Percy, Earl of Northumberland, was written in the year 1512. It was reprinted by Dr. Thomas Percy, Bishop of Dromore, at the beginning of the present century. The minuteness of the details given as to the price and quantities of the articles required renders this and similar collections valuable sources of information respecting the luxuries and necessaries of the time. Bishop Percy points out, in the preface to his edition, that—

"Our nobility in the more early times lived in their castles with a gross and barbarous magnificence, surrounded with rude and warlike followers, without control and without system. As they gradually emerged from this barbarity, they found it necessary to establish very minute domestic regulations in order to keep their turbulent followers in peace and order; and from living in a state of disorderly grandeur, void of all system, would naturally enough run into the opposite extreme of reducing everything, even the most trifling disbursements, to stated formal rules. It may be considered further, that a nobleman in the Dark Ages, when retired to his castle, had neither books, nor newspapers, nor literary correspondence, nor visits, nor cards, to fill up his leisure; his only amusements were field-sports, and as these, however eagerly pursued, could not fill up all his vacant hours, the government of his household would therefore be likely enough to engage his attention."

We find from the above work that the list of birds reserved exclusively for his lordship's table includes many species which would in modern times be discarded as worthless. We see here, spelt in a variety of ways, the names of the heron, bittern, peacock, pheasant, partridge, quail, bustard, mallard, woodcock, snipe, lapwing, redshank, plover, stint, widgeon, knot, dottrell, reys (or ruffs and reeves), seagull, shoveler, curlew, seapye, and tern.

Richard Carew, in his *Survey of Cornwall*, 1602 (p. 108), gives a short list of the waterfowl on the Cornish coast:—

"Besides these floating burgesses of the ocean, there are also certain flying citizens of the air, which prescribe for a corrody [an allowance of provisions] therein; of whom some serve for food to us, and some but to feed themselves. Amongst the first sort we reckon the dipchick (so named of his diving and littleness), coots, sanderling, sea larks, oxen and kine [ruffs and reeves], seapies, puffins, pewits, meawes, murres, creysers, curlews, teals, widgeon, burranets, shags, duck and mallard, gull, wildgoose, heron, crane, and barnacle."

After the publication of Mr. Harting's learned and interesting work, *The Ornithology of Shakespeare*, it may be thought not only unnecessary but presumptuous to deal with the various kinds of birds at any length in this volume. But, on referring to his work, it will be seen that all the species of birds not mentioned by Shakspeare are omitted. The author also confines himself chiefly to Shakspeare for his illustrations. Mr. Harting's work is doubtless in the hands of every student of our great dramatist; quotations of any length will therefore not be made from *The Ornithology*, nor will the birds described in its pages be treated of in detail. The hope may be entertained that the following account of the different varieties of birds mentioned by Elizabethan writers generally may serve as an appendix to Mr. Harting's admirable work.

Mr. Harting on Birds.

It accords well with the idea that the reign of force is no longer paramount, that in modern scientific classification birds of song have usurped the place once filled by birds of prey. The Song Thrush, or Throstle, placed by Mr. Wallace first on the list of the feathered race, is the compeer of the nightingale in volume of song, though not in variety or in sweetness. Drayton writes of this chorister—

Thrush.

" The throstel, with shrill sharps; as purposely he sang
T' awake the lustless sun; or chiding that so long
He was in coming forth, that should the thickets thrill."
(*Polyolbion*, song xiii.)

The mavis is considered by Yarrell to be another name

for the thrush; but a distinction between the two is made by Spenser as well as by Harrison:—

"The thrush replyes; the mavis descant playes."
(*Epithalamion*, line 80.)

And Skelton, in his poem, *Philip Sparow*, writes:—

"The threstill with her warblynge,
The mavis with her whistell."

In a poem by Gascoigne, *The Complaint of Phylomena*, a distinction is made between the mavis and the thrush. The "darling of the summer's pride" thus betrays all the jealousy of a neglected opera-singer in decrying her rivals:—

"These thriftles birds (quoth she) which spend the day
In needlesse notes, and chaunt withouten skil,
Are costly kept, and finely fedde alway
With daintie foode, whereof they feede their fil.
* * * * *
"The throstle, she which makes the wood to ring
With shryching loude, that lothsome is to heare,
Is costly kept, in cage: O wondrous thing!
The mavis eke, whose notes are nothing cleare."

The Missel-thrush, or Storm-cock, sometimes called the Holm-thrush from its fondness for holly-berries, though now one of the best known of our British birds, was apparently much scarcer in earlier times. Thomas Muffett, in his *Healths Improvement* (p. 101), says, "Thrushes and mavisses feed most upon hawes, sloes, misle-berries, and privot-berries. Feldefares," he adds, "are of the like feed, and give (almost) as good nourishment, yea better, when juniper-berries be ripe, for then all their flesh is perfumed with the scent thereof."

<small>Missel-thrush.</small>

The Redwing is mentioned in the article on migration already noticed: "Such are the winter-birds that breed not here, as the woodcock, and wind-thrush (or the redwing, wheenerd, whindle; for so

<small>Redwing.</small>

many names it has in divers countries), field-fare, snipe, &c."

Blackbird. The Blackbird, Ouzel, Woozel, or Merle is occasionally referred to by poets. Drayton writes:—

> "The woosel near at hand, that hath a golden bill;
> As nature him had markt of purpose t' let us see
> That from all other birds his tunes should different be:
> For, with their vocal sounds, they sing to pleasant May;
> Upon his dulcet pipe the merle doth only play,
> When in the lower brake, the nightingale hard by
> In such lamenting strains the joyful hours doth ply,
> As though the other birds she to her tunes would draw."
> (*Polyolbion*, song xiii.)

When *Shallow* meets his neighbour and fellow-justice, he inquires after *William* and *Ellen*: "And how doth my cousin, your bedfellow? and your fairest daughter and mine, my god-daughter Ellen?" *Silence* answers, "Alas, a black ousel, cousin Shallow" (2 *Henry IV.*, iii. 2, 6). The ambiguity of the reply has caused some discussion among commentators. Mr. Harting, who takes for granted that it refers to the young collegian, considers the expression "a black ousell" equivalent to the phrase "a black sheep." Mr. Guy, a writer in *Notes and Queries* (5th series, vol. i. p. 19), assumes the reply to have reference to the lady, and suggests that, as the blackbird is a solitary warbler, *Silence* means to say that his daughter is still unmarried. Another interpretation is that *Ellen* is a comely brunette, and that her father uses the expression to deprecate her godfather's too partial commendation of her charms.

Nightingale. The range of the far-famed Nightingale in England is limited to certain counties. According to Mr. Garner (*History of Stafford*, 1844), most parts of the county of Stafford are without the nightingale, and the bird is unknown in the rich valley of the Trent north of Lichfield. Its song is heard in Yorkshire and occasionally in the more northern counties, but not in Scotland. Fynes Moryson records that it was unknown in Ireland.

Mr. Harting has noticed at some length the fable that the nightingale leans against a thorn for fear she should be overtaken by sleep, so often referred to by poets. Of all epithets applied to this songster none is more poetical and appropriate than that used by Ben Jonson, in his pastoral poem, *The Sad Shepherd* (ii. 3)—

> "I grant the linnet, lark, and bullfinch sing,
> But best the dear good angel of the spring,
> The nightingale."

Though, as Mr. Gifford points out, this expression is a literal translation from the Greek of Sappho, *angel* is used in the original signification of a messenger or harbinger. Spenser writes:—

> "Like as the darling of the summer's pryde
> Faire Philomele."
>
> (*The Tears of the Muses*, l. 235.)

Giles Fletcher calls the nightingale "the bird of sorrow," and Drayton, "that charmer of the night." In the *Mirror for Magistrates* (vol. ii. p. 468) we find a different epithet:—

> "Sweete are the songs that merry night crow singes,
> For many parts are in those charming notes.
> * * * * *
> "It is a sport to heare the fine night crow
> Chaunt in the queere upon a pricke-song plaine:
> No musicke more may please a prince's vaine
> Than descant strange, and voice of faurets breest,
> In quiet bower when birds be all at rest."

Of all the small birds that seek the neighbourhood of dwelling-houses, the Robin Redbreast, or Ruddock, has ever held first place in the affections of man; and the robin has been associated in

Robin.

the minds of children with kind actions, through the medium of the various ballads on the doleful story of "the Babes in the Wood." Drayton probably refers to that tragic history when he writes :—

"Covering with moss the dead unclosed eye,
The little redbreast teacheth charity."

(*The Owl.*)

The robin is introduced with a double meaning in a poem on Robert Earl of Essex, which is supposed to have been written by one of the friends of that nobleman while he was in possession of the queen's favour.

"The goose but gaggelith in her gate,
The cock he can but crowe,
A thousand birdes do not but prate,
And gangell wheare they goo :
The lark and lynnett singith well,
The thrisell dothe his best ;
The robbyn beares away ye bell,
And passeth all the rest.
He is famyllyer with a lorde,
And dreames wheare ladies are ;
He can in howse singe and recorde,
When busshe and bryer is bare."

(*Camden Miscellany*, vol. ii.)

Thomas Fuller, writing of Sussex, tells us that—

Wheat-ear. "the Wheat-ear is a bird peculiar to this county, hardly found out of it. It is so called because fattest when wheat is ripe, whereon it feeds ; being no bigger than a lark, which it equalleth in the fineness of the flesh, far exceedeth in the fatness thereof. The worst is, that being only seasonable in the heat of summer, and then naturally larded with lumps of fat, it is soon subject to corrupt. That palate-man shall pass in silence, who being seriously demanded his judgment concerning the abilities of a great lord, concluded him a man of very weak parts, 'because once he saw him, at a feast, feed on chickens when there were wheat-ears on the table.'" (*Worthies of England*, vol. ii. p. 382.)

This etymology is not quite correct. Notwithstanding the

name given to the bird, the wheat-ear is an insect-feeder. Fuller was probably also mistaken when he confined the range of this much-prized bird to one English county. In modern times the wheat-ear, œnanthe, or stone-smatch, is found in some abundance in the North of England and in Scotland. In the northern counties a superstition prevails that its note gives warning of approaching death.

John Taylor, "the Water Poet," also includes the wheat-ear among the commodities of Sussex, in the following doggrel rhymes:—

> "There were rare birds I never saw before,
> The like of them I think to see no more :
> Th' are called wheat-ears, less than lark or sparrow,
> Well roasted, in the mouth they taste like marrow.
> When once 'tis in the teeth it is involv'd,
> Bones, flesh, and all, is lusciously dissolv'd.
> The name of wheat-ears, on them is ycleped
> Because they come when wheat is yearly reap'd,
> Six weeks, or thereabouts, they are catch'd there,
> And are wellnigh 11 months, God knows where."
> (*Works*, ed. Hindley, 1872.)

The little Wren, by its habit of frequenting the neighbourhood of human habitations, its bright lively movements, and its peculiar shape, has always been a favourite with country folk :—

> "The hedge-sparrow and her compeer the wren,
> Which simple people call our lady's hen."
> (DRAYTON, *The Owl*.)

Wren.

Chester speaks of "the little wren that many young ones brings." *Sir Toby Belch*, on the entrance of *Maria*, exclaims, "Look where the youngest wren of nine comes !" (*Twelfth Night*, iii. 2.) It is hardly safe to assume from these words that Shakspeare had at any time counted the number of wren's eggs, yet this expression has been quoted by commentators in proof of the dramatist's accuracy in ornithological details.

The Archangel is the name given by Chaucer to
the Titmouse. In Gascoigne's *Complaint of
Phylomena* the nightingale laments over the
popularity of her diminutive rival:—

Titmouse.

> "Now in good sooth, quoth she, sometimes I wepe
> To see tom tyttimouse so much set by."

The patience must have been great and the appetite
small of any one who could make a meal on these tiny
songsters, and the caution contained in Andrew Boorde's
Dyetary cannot often have been required:—

> "All maner of smale byrdes be good and lyght of dygestyon,
> excepte sparowes, whiche be harde of digestyon. Tytmoses, colmoses,
> and wrens, the whiche doth eate spyders and poyson, be not com-
> mendable. Of all smale byrdes the larke is the beste: then is praysed
> the blacke byrde and the thrusshe." (Early English Text Society,
> ed. Furnivall, 1870, p. 133.)

The Golden Oriole, or Golden Ouzel, a brilliantly
coloured species of thrush, is an occasional
visitant to Great Britain. Giraldus Cambrensis
reports that on one occasion Baldwin, Archbishop of
Canterbury, made a progress through Wales. Travelling
through a valley near Bangor, Baldwin and his attendants
sat down under some trees to rest. Cambrensis, who
accompanied the archbishop in his tour, describes the
scene, and writes:—

Oriole.

> "The sweet notes are heard, in an adjoining wood, of a bird, which
> some said was a wood-pecker, and others more correctly, an aureolus.
> The wood-pecker is called in French, *spec*, and, with its strong bill,
> perforates oak trees; the other bird is called *aureolus*, from the golden
> tint of its feathers, and at certain seasons utters a sweet whistling note,
> instead of a song." (*Itinerary through Wales*, 1187, p. 442, ed. Wright,
> 1863.)

The note of the oriole is loud and flute-like, and may
well be called a whistle.

The Golden Oriole.

Woodwele, the name of a bird, occurs occasionally in medieval poetry. Chaucer writes:—

> "In many places were nyghtyngales,
> Alpes, fynches, and wodewales,
> That in her swete song deliten
> In thilke places as they habiten."
> (*The Romaunt of the Rose*, ed. Bell.)

The woodwele is explained by Percy, in his *Reliques of English Poetry*, to be the oriole. We find the name again in the ballad of Robin Hood and Guy of Gisborne:—

> "The woodweele sang and wolde not cease,
> Sitting upon the spray,
> So lowde he wakened Robin Hood,
> In the greenwood where he lay."

The oriole is said to prefer fruit when it can be procured, but failing this it is not above eating insects. Thomas Muffett, in his *Healths Improvement* (p. 100), informs us that "witwols are of excellent good nourishment, feeding upon bees, flies, snails, cherries, plums, and all manner of good fruit." It may be that this beautiful bird was less rare in former times than it is at present.

Mr. Harting gives the derivation of Magpie from *magotpie*; another explanation of the name of this bird is that *magot* is the French for a hoard of secreted money, and may have been bestowed in consequence of the magpie's hiding propensities. Another is that *mag*, a contraction of Margaret, is a nickname corresponding to robin redbreast, or tom titmouse. Skelton speaks of "the flecked pye."

Magpie.

Next we have—

Crow.

> "The caryon crowe, that lothsome beast,
> Which cries against the rayne,
> Both for hir hewe and for ther rest,
> The devil resembleth playne."
> (GASCOIGNE, *Good-morrow*.)

This evil-disposed bird was much commoner than the raven. It closely resembled that bird in its habits and in appearance, and, like the raven, was regarded with superstitious awe by the country people. In his list of the birds of Norfolk, Sir Thomas Brown includes "rooks, crows, as every where also the pied crow, with dun and black interchangeable." Moryson, in his *History of Ireland*, 1600, says that "Ireland hath neither singing nightingale nor chattering pie, nor undermining mole, nor black crow, but only crows of mingled colour, such as we call royston crows" (vol. i. p. 368). Derrick, in his *Image of Irelande*, makes a similar observation:—

> "No pies to plucke the thatch from house
> Are bred in Irishe grounde;
> But worse then pies the same to burne
> A thousand maie be founde."

Rook. The rook is seldom mentioned by early writers, which may be accounted for by the fact that the terms crow and rook were often used indiscriminately. When Shakspeare makes *Troilus* announce that—

> "The busy day,
> Waked by the lark, hath roused the ribald crows,"

he is probably recalling the effect of sunrise on the rookery near the village green at Stratford.

According to Harrison, crows, or more probably rooks, met with but little protection or encouragement at the hands of the country people:—

"Neither are our crowes and choughs cherished of purpose to catch up the woormes that breed in our soiles (as Polydor supposeth) sith there are no uplandish townes but have (or should have) nets of their owne in store to catch them withall. Sundrie Acts of Parlement are likewise made for their utter destruction, as also the spoile of other ravenous foules hurtful to pultrie, conies, lambs, and kids, whose valuation of reward to him that killeth them is after the head: a devise brought from the Goths, who had the like ordinance for the destruction of their white crowes, and tale made by the becko, which killed both lambs and pigs. The like order is taken with us for our vermines, as with them also for the rootage out of their wild beasts, saving that they spared their greatest beares, especiallie the white, whose skins are by custome and privilege reserved to cover those planchers wher upon their priests doo stand at masse, least he should take some unkind cold in such a long peece of worke : and happie is the man that may provide them for him, for he shall have pardon inough for that so religious an act, to last if he will till doomes day doo approach: and manie thousands after." (*Holinshed*, vol. i. p. 375.) *

Whether meant seriously or not, the reference to Olaus Magnus in the latter part of this passage shows how well the Northern chroniclers' work was known in England.

One of the chief features of East Indian life, the impudent, intruding crow, is mentioned, and some of its freaks described, by Linschoten, an early explorer :—

"There [Goa] is a most wonderfull number of blacke crowes, which doe much hurt, and are so bold that oftentimes they come flying in at their windowes, and take the meat out of the dish, as it standeth upon the table, before them that are downe to eat: and as I my selfe sate writing above in a chamber of the house, the windowes being open, one of those crows flew in at the window, and picked the cotton out of my inke-horne, and blotted all the paper that lay on my table, doe what I could to let him. They sit commonly upon the buffles and pecke off their haire, so that you shall find very few buffles that have any haires upon their backes, and therefore to avoyd the crowes they get themselves into marishes, and watrie places, where they stand in the water up to their neckes, otherwise they could never be rid of them." (*Voyage to Goa*, 1588, *Purchas*, vol. ii. p. 1770.)

The water buffaloes of India have probably other objects in view in seeking the marshes than merely to rid themselves of the depredations of the crows, however pertinacious these may be.

The "Raven called Rolfe" performs the same office in cold countries that the vulture does in warmer regions, and, like the latter bird, pays the penalty of unpopularity on account of his un-

Raven.

* See page 84.

savoury diet. The raven's croak, like many other rural sounds, was thought to forebode illness and death:—

> "The om'nous raven with a dismal chear,
> Through his hoarse beak of following horror tells,
> Begetting strange imaginary fear,
> With heavy echoes like to passing bells."
> (POOLE, *English Parnassus*.)

Shakspeare and most of his brother dramatists have effectively introduced the belief in the prophetic powers of this bird. Thus Peele writes:—

> "Like as the fatal raven, that in his voice
> Carries the dreadful summons of our deaths,
> Flies by the fair Arabian spiceries,
> Her pleasant gardens, and delightsome parks,
> Seeming to curse them with his coarse exclaims,
> And yet doth stoop with hungry violence
> Upon a piece of hateful carrion."
> (*David and Bethsabe.*)

Du Bartas has a very similar passage:—

> "Ev'n as the rav'ns with windy wings o'er-fly
> The weeping woods of happy Araby,
> Despise sweet gardens and delicious bowrs
> Perfuming heav'n with odoriferous flowres,
> And greedy, light upon the loathsom quarters
> Of some late *Lopez*, or such Romish martyrs."
> (*Divine Weekes*, p. 118.)

The voice of this bird is certainly sufficiently gruff to afford some excuse for the dismay which it caused, especially when heard at night, in a lonely wood, by the belated traveller.

Guillim, in his *Display of Heraldry*, refers to the extraordinary belief handed down from antiquity that the parent birds, not approving of the colour of their newly hatched offspring, forsake the nest for a time. He says:—

"It has been an ancient receiv'd opinion, and the same also grounded upon the warrant of the sacred Scriptures, if I mistake not, that such is the property of the raven that from the time his young ones are hatched or disclosed, until he seeth what colour they will be of, he never taketh care of them, nor ministreth any food unto them; therefore it is thought that they are in the mean space nourished with the heavenly dew. And so much also doth the kingly prophet David affirm, *which giveth fodder unto the cattle, and feedeth the young ravens that call upon him. Psal.* 147, 9. The raven, when he perceiveth his young ones to be penfeather'd and black like himself, then doth he labour by all means to foster and cherish them from thenceforward." (Page 222.)

Why the raven should be so deficient both in common sense and in parental affection the worthy herald does not attempt to explain.

By the Scandinavians the raven was consecrated to Odin. By the early Christians it was tranferred from him to St. Martin, who inherited Odin's reputation for prophetic knowledge. Hence its name, "St. Martin's bird."

It is not quite clear what bird was meant by the night raven. Spenser writes :—

"And after him owles and night ravens flew,
The hateful messengers of heavy tidings."
(*Faerie Queene*, ii. 7, 23.)

Lyly also classes these two birds together : "The owle hath not shrikt at the window, or the night raven croked, both being fatal" (*Sappho and Phaon*). These passages would seem to have reference to the raven itself, but it has been suggested that the bittern, from the weird drum-like sound of its cry, is meant. Harrison perhaps speaks of the latter, when he says :—

"There is no cause why I should describe the cormorant amongse hawkes, of which some be blacke and manie pied chiefelie about the Ile of Elie, where they are taken for the night raven, except I should call him a water hawke." (*Holinshed*, vol. i. p. 382.)

The night-crow, or gor-crow, was probably the same bird as Lyly's night raven:—

"Raven and gorcrow, all my birds of prey,
That think me turning carcase, now they come."
(BEN JONSON, *The Fox*, i. 1.)

Ben Jonson makes the augurs—

"Shew all the birds of food or prey,
But pass by the unlucky jay,
The night-crow, swallow, or the kite."
(*The Masque of Augurs.*)

Jackdaw. The Jackdaw, or *monedula*, seldom obtains honourable mention. Drayton calls him "the thievish daw." In the *Interlude of the Four Elements*, 1510, we read:—

"But he that for a commyn welth bysyly
Studieth and laboryth, and lyveth by Goddes law,
Except he wax rich, men count hym but a daw."
(*Rep. Percy Soc.*, 1848, vol. xxii.)

Warwick, the king-maker, declares that, in nice legal questions, he is "no wiser than a daw." These insinuations that jackdaws are inferior to their feathered comrades in intelligence will be treated as calumnies by all who have been fortunate enough to possess one of these birds as a pet.

Chough. Closely allied to the jackdaw is the Cornish Chough, Cornyshe-daw, or Red-legged Crow, a slighter made bird, and more elegant in shape, chiefly frequenting the coasts in the west of England. It is mentioned by Camden in his description of Cornwall:—

"The rocks underneath [St. Michael's Mount] as also along the shore everywhere breedeth the Pyrrhocorax, a kind of crow with bill and feet red, and not, as Plinie thought, proper to the Alpes onely. This bird the inhabitants have found to be an incendiarie, and theevish besides: for oftentimes it secretly convcieth fire sticks setting their houses a fire, and as closely filcheth and hideth little pieces of money." (*Britain*, p. 189.)

Carew, in his *Survey of Cornwall*, published 1602, gives an account of the various sea-fowl found in that country:—

"Amongst which, jackdaw (the second slander of our country) shall pass for company, as frequenting their haunts, though not their diet. I mean not the common daw, but one peculiar to Cornwall, and there-through termed a Cornish chough: his bill is sharp, long, and red, his legs of the same colour, his feathers black, his conditions, when he is kept tame, ungracious, in filching and hiding of money, and such short ends, and somewhat dangerous in carrying sticks of fire." (Page 110, ed. Tonkin, 1811.)

Such an incendiary proceeding as these historians refer to might have occasionally happened, but it could not have been of frequent occurrence.

One of the earliest descriptions of the Bird of Paradise is given in the voyage of Magalhanes, or Magellan, the celebrated explorer, in 1521:— *Bird of Paradise.*

"The king of Bachian, one of the Molucca Islands, sent two dead birds preserved, which were of extraordinary beauty. In size, they were not larger than the thrush: the head was small, with a long bill; the legs were of the thickness of a common quill, and a span in length; the tail resembled that of the thrush; they had no wings, but in the place where wings usually are, they had tufts of long feathers, of different colours; all the other feathers were dark. The inhabitants of the Moluccas had a tradition that this bird came from Paradise, and they called it *bolondinata*, which signifies the 'bird of God.' Gomara relates some marvellous things concerning this bird and that it was called *mamucos*." (*Burney's Travels*, p. 105.)

If the law of compensation is not universally carried out in the animal kingdom, it certainly appears to be in the case of the Bird of Paradise. The existence of this bird, according to all accounts, must be most unhappy; but perhaps the consciousness of its surpassing beauty consoles it for the want of personal comfort.

The writer quoted above mentions the Bird of Paradise as possessing legs, but in later times they were supposed to be destitute of these appendages. Navarette, a missionary to China, about 1670, writes :—

"The bird of paradise has neither feet nor wings; I have often viewed them carefully, but could never find any sign of feet, that they have not wings is more visible to every body. The beak is somewhat thick and large, fit to catch gnats, which is their food. They never light nor can they rest upon the ground, as may be easily conceived as they have no feet. Their fixed abode is the region of the air, for which reason they are called birds of paradise. They alight upon trees and by the help of the wind they fly from one to another, making use of their sightly tail. If the wind fails they presently fall, and their bill being heavy it is the first which lights upon the sand, where it sticks so that they cannot stir but are taken with ease." (*Churchill's Voyages*, vol. i. p. 41.)

Wonders like these lose nothing when transmitted by poets. Accordingly we find, in that storehouse of natural-history marvels, Du Bartas's *Divine Weekes and Works* (p. 45), a still more astonishing account of the habits of the Bird of Paradise :—

"But note we nowe, towards the rich Moluques,
Those passing strange and wondrous birds mamuques:
Wondrous, indeed, if sea, or earth, or sky,
Saw ever wonder swim, or go, or fly,
None knowes their nest, none knowes the dam that breeds them:
Food-less they live; for th' aire alonely feeds them:
Wing-less they fly; and yet their flight extends,
Till with their flight, their unknow'n lives-date ends."

The belief in the absence of wings and legs is easily explained by the fact that the natives, when they prepared the birds for exportation, removed these members as likely to interfere with the beauty of the specimens. These early writers surmounted the difficulty as to the nests and parentage of these birds by the suggestion that the female laid her eggs on the back of the male, and hatched them as they floated through the air in their endless flight. This explanation is met with in an account of the Bird of Paradise given by the learned author of the *Summary on the Poem of Du Bartas*—a commentary which was published in England in 1637:—

"There is found (saith Cardan) in the Moluques, both upon the sea, and on the land, a dead bird, which the ilanders call manucodiata, and never was he seene living, because he hath no feete. I have seene such a dead bird three times, and I suppose the cause why he hath no feete, is for that he liveth very high in the ayre, and far severed from the sight of men. He hath a body and beake almost like a swallow: his wings, and taile containe more widenesse then those of the hawke, and almost equall those of the eagle. His plumes are very soft, and very much resemble the feathers of a pea-hen. The backe of the male manucodiata is hollow, and within the same the female hatcheth and layeth her egges, which by this meanes are kept as it were in a box. The male hath in his tayle a long thred, more then three hands breadth in length, blacke; neither square, nor round, nor thicke: but small, and resembling a coblers grosse thred: which seemeth to serve to tye and joyne the male with the female when she sitteth, to the end to defend her from the winds and other accidents. So likewise it seemeth to serve them for a grapple, or counterpoize, according to the changes of the aire. It is not to be wondred at that this bird remaineth alwaies in the aire: for his tayle and wings are spred so properly in a round that this maketh an equal counterpoize, which sustaineth the bird perpetually. I suppose that he liveth on no other thing but on dew.",

This explanation is all the more ingenious as the writer admits that he had no opportunity of studying a living specimen. He must be, therefore, indebted to his own imagination or to a careful anatomical examination of the bird's structure.

A distinction seems early to have been made between the Swallow and the Martin. Lyly rather confuses the two: "But thou, *Euphues*, dost rather resemble the swallow, who in the summer creepeth under the eaves of every house, and in the winter leaveth nothing but dirt behind hir" (*Euphues*, 91).

Swallow.

Chester describes:—

"The artificiall nest-composing swallow,
That eates his meate flying along the way,
Whose swiftnesse in our eyesight doth allow,
That no imperial bird makes her his pray:

> His yong ones being hurt within the eies,
> He helpes them with the herbe calcedonies."
> (*Love's Martyr*, p. 122.)

Drayton, in reference to the habit of feeding during flight, in his account of the effect produced upon various creatures by the approaching Deluge, writes :—

> "The swift-wing'd swallow feeding as it flies,
> With the fleet martlet thrilling thro' the skies,
> Feeling th' unusual moisture of the air,
> Their feathers flag, into the ark they come,
> As to the some rock or building, their own home."
> (*Noah's Flood*.)

In connexion with the herb-cure referred to in the last two lines of the quotation from Chester, it may be said that Reginald Scot, in his book on witchcraft, 1584, repeats with some caution statements as to the restorative effect of certain herbs:—

> "And for that you shall not say that hearbs have no vertue, for that in this place I cite none, I am content to discover two or three small qualities and vertues, which are affirmed to be in hearbes; marry as simple as they be James and Jambres might have done much with them if they had had them. If you prick out a young swallowes eies, the old swallow restoreth again their sight, with the application, they say, of a little celandine. Zanthus, the author of Histories, reporteth, that a young dragon being dead, was revived by her dam, with an hearb called balim." (*Discovery of Witchcraft*, p. 213, ed. 1654.)

Martin. The heraldic Martin is always blazoned without legs. It was frequently borne as a charge by those who took part in the Crusades, as indicating the sacrifice of personal ease and comfort they were prepared to make. Guillim observes that—

> "the martlet hath legs so exceeding short, that they can by no means go. And if perchance they fall upon the ground, they cannot raise themselves upon their feet, as others do, and so prepare themselves to flight. For this cause they are accustomed to make their nests upon rocks, and other high places, from whence they may easily take their

flight, from the support of the air. Hereupon it came, that this bird is painted in arms without feet: and for this cause it is also given for a difference of younger brethren, to put them in mind to trust to their wings of vertue and merit, to raise themselves, and not in their legs, having no land to put their foot on." (*Display of Heraldry*, p. 231.)

Of the Finch tribe only one or two kinds seem to have been distinguished. Harrison mentions "bulfinshes and goldfinshes."

Finches.

Gascoigne writes:—

"The finche which singeth never a note but peepe."
(*Complaint of Phylomena.*)

The Bullfinch was known by a variety of names. In Chaucer he appears as the *Alp*:—

"In many places were nyghtyngales,
Alpes, fynches, and wodewales."
(*The Romaunt of the Rose.*)

He was also called bulspink, hoop, monk, pope, and in Scotland coallyhood.

In the same poem by Chaucer we find mention of the chalaundre, which is interpreted by commentators to mean the Goldfinch:—

"Chalaundres fele saw I there,
That very nigh forsongen were."

Drayton writes:—

"And of these chaunting fowles the goldfinch not behind,
That hath so many sorts descending from her kind."
(*Polyolbion*, song xiii.)

In a poem by Alexander Montgomery, a Scotch poet, about 1570, we read:—

"About a bank with balmy bewis,
Quhair nychtingales thair notis renewis,
With gallant goldspinks gay;
The mavis, merle, and progne proud,
The lintquhyt, lark, and lavrock loud,
Salutit mirthful May."
(*The Cherrie and the Slae.*)

The learned commentator on Du Bartas, who has been previously quoted, gives the etymology of goldfinch :—

"The Greekes call this bird *pœkilis*, that is to say, painted, by reason of the pleasant varietie of his feathers. The Latines call him *carduelis*; the French, *chardoueret*; the English, *gold-finch*; and therefore it is called chardoueret, because, saith Belon in his seventh booke, and thirteenth chapter, he liveth upon the grain of the thistle [carduus]."

Of the Spinke, a finch of some kind, probably the Chaffinch, the same writer adds :—

"He is described by Belon in the seventh booke, chapter 28, and is so called, because hee pincheth and holdeth very strongly with his neb, as Belon saith. The Latines call him *fringilla*, and he useth a pleasant warbling note." (*Summary on Du Bartas*, p. 235.)

The chaffinch was also known as the pink, or wet bird, from a notion that its song indicated rain.

Thomas Muffett, in his *Healths Improvement*, informs us that "finches for the most part live upon seeds, especially the goldfinch, which refuses to eat of anything else" (p. 101). "So also," he says, "doth the canary finch or siskin." The siskin is well named by this author the canary finch. It much resembles that bird in shape and movements, though it is not so brilliant in colour. The siskin is called in the southern counties the barley-bird, being seen about the time when barley is ripe ; in other parts of the country it is called the aberdavine.

Several of the finch tribe seem to have been taught small accomplishments. Sir Thomas Browne mentions—

"a kind of anthus, goldfinch, or fool's coat, commonly called a draw-water, finely marked with red and yellow, and a white bill, which they take with trap-cages, in Norwich gardens, and, fastening a chain about them, tied to a box of water, it makes a shift, with bill and leg, to draw up the water in to it from the little pot, hanging by the chain about a foot below." (Vol. iv. p. 323, ed. Wilkins.)

In Whitney's *Emblems*, printed in 1585, there is a

drawing of a small bird in a cage; the bird is busily employed in drawing up water in the manner above described.

While on the subject of performing birds, it may not be uninteresting to note another kind of bird-training practised in Egypt, and described by John Leo, in an account of his visit to that country.

"There is," he writes, "also another kind of charmers or juglers, which keep certaine little birds in cages after the fashion of cupboords, which birds will reach unto any man with their beaks certaine skroules, containing either his good or evill successe in time to come. And whosoever desireth to know his fortune, must give the bird an half-penny; which shee taking in her bill, carrieth into a little boxe, and then comming forth againe, bringeth the said skroule in her beake. I my selfe had once a skroule of ill fortune given me, which although I little regarded, yet had I more unfortunate successe then was contained therein." (*Purchas*, vol. ii. p. 837.)

A precisely similar exhibition to that by which the itinerant mountebank of Cairo beguiled John Leo of his coin may be seen at the present day in the London streets.

The precise date of the introduction of the Canary into Europe is not known. Gesner, who wrote in 1585, makes mention of this bird, and Aldrovandus, in his *Ornithology*, printed at Frankfort, in 1610, gives the first good description of it. Bolton, in his *British Song Birds*, says that probably the canary was not known in England till after the time of Aldrovandus, though Willoughby, in his *History of Birds*, tells us that they were common in his time. Some uncertainty also prevails as to what colour they were when first imported from their native country. Writers of the sixteenth century seem to concur in supposing them to be green and yellow, and to bear a near resemblance to our siskin.

Canary.

In a description of the Azores, by Linschoten, we read:—

"The principal iland of them all, is that of Tercera, . . the iland hath not any wild beasts or fowles, but very few, having onely canary birds, which are there by thousands, where many birders take them, and thereof make a daily living, by carrying them into divers places." (*Purchas*, vol. iv. p. 1669.)

In an account by Laurence Aldersey, merchant of London, of his journey to Jerusalem and Tripolis, in 1581, he relates that he stopped at Augusta, in Germany, where a resident, to whom he had an introduction, took him through the town to show him the sights:—

"He shewed me first the State House, which is very faire, and beautifull. Then he brought mee to the finest garden, and orchard, that ever I sawe in my life: for there was in it a place for canarie birdes, as large as a faire chamber, trimmed with wier both above and beneath, with fine little branches of trees for them to sit in, which was full of those canaries birdes." (*Hakluyt*, vol. ii. p. 268.)

Gascoigne, who died in 1577, tells us that—

"Canara byrds come in to beare the bell."
(*Complaint of Phylomena*.)

Belon, who wrote about the year 1555, does not mention the canary. It was sometimes called the *sugar-bird*, from a supposed fondness for the sugar-cane.

Linnet. Drayton places the Linnet second only to the nightingale in his list of songsters, and Gascoigne writes :—

"The lennet and the larke, they sing alofte,
And coumpted are as lordes in high degree."
(*Complaint of Phylomena*.)

Crossbill. Sir Thomas Browne in his catalogue of Norfolk birds includes the Crossbill; he states that it was at times kept as a cage bird, but that it never survived its captivity throughout the winter. In Carew's *Survey of Cornwall*, published 1602 (p. 73), occurs mention of the crossbill, though not actually by name :—

"Not long since, there came a flock of birds into Cornwall, about harvest season, in bigness not much exceeding a sparrow, which made a foul spoil of the apples: their bills were thwarted crosswise at the end, and with these they would cut an apple in two at one snap, eating only the kernels. It was taken at first for a foreboden token, and much admired [wondered at], but soon after, notice grew that Gloucestershire, and other apple countries, have from them an over-familiar harm."

These birds are called by Willoughby, the ornithologist, shell-apples or crossbills. The statement that this bird divides an apple at a bite must be received with caution, as the crossbill hardly exceeds the bullfinch in size. Moreover, the mandibles of the beak, instead of being opposed, are curved right and left and cross each other. The apple that would admit of being divided at a single snap must have been a very small one.

John Locke, in an account of a voyage to Jerusalem, 1553, mentions a little bird which is possibly the highly prized Ortolan, still a favourite with epicures.

? Ortolan.

"They have also in this island [Cyprus] a certaine small bird much like unto a wagtaile in fethers and making, these are so extreme fat that you can perceive nothing els in all their bodies: these birds are now in season. They take a great quantitie of them, and they use to pickle them with vinegar, and salt, and to put them in pots and send them to Venice and other places of Italy for presents of great estimation. They say they send almost 1200 jarres or pots to Venice, besides those which are consumed in the island, which are a great number. These are so plentiful that when there is no shipping, you may buy them for 10 carchies, which coine are 4 to a Venetian soldo, which is peny farthing the dozen, and when there is store of shipping, 2 pence the dozen, after that rate of their money." (*Hakluyt*, vol. ii. p. 223.)

The Starling, or Stare, was probably as common and as widely distributed in early times as it is now. At certain periods of the year starlings congregate in great numbers, and fly from one part of the country to another in large flocks. We are told by Walter Yonge, in his *Diary*, that in September, 1621—

Starling.

"there were an infinite company of birds, like unto stares, which câme flying over Corke, a town in Ireland, which fought in so terrible a manner, as many thousands fell down dead into the town." (*Rep. Camden Soc.*, 1877.)

This battle of starlings, which is mentioned by other historians, may have been the result of a chance meeting of two migrating bodies of birds.

The talking powers of the starling are referred to by Shakspeare:—

> "I'll have a starling shall be taught to speak
> Nothing but 'Mortimer,' and give it him,
> To keep his anger still in motion."
> (1 *Henry IV.*, i. 3, 224.)

So much has been written in praise of Larks by poets of all ages, that there is little to note respecting this particular period of the bird's history, except that it was probably less common than at present, owing to the increase, in modern times, in the number of well-drained fields and meadows. To the quotations from Shakspeare given by Mr. Harting, a few from other writers may be added. William Browne writes:—

Lark.

> "The mounting larke, daies herauld, got on wing,
> Bidding each bird chuse out his bough and sing."
> (*Britannia's Pastorals*, b. i. song 3.)

Drayton:—

> "The lark that holds observance to the sun,
> Quavered her clear notes in the quiet air."
> (*The Legend of Robert Duke of Normandy.*)

The beautiful lines of Lyly, to which Shakspeare may have been indebted:—

> "Who is 't now we heare?
> None but the larke so shrill and cleare;
> Now at heaven's gate she claps her wings,
> The morne not waking till shee sings."
> (*Campaspe*, act v. song.)

And lastly, Marlowe's poetical simile:—

"Now Phœbus ope the eyelids of the day,
And for the raven wake the morning lark,
That I may hover with her in the air,
Singing o'er these as she does o'er her young."
(*Jew of Malta*, ii. 1.)

Without quoting any other passages at length, mention may be made of the appropriate epithets, the "crested lark" (Ben Jonson, *The Vision of Delight*); "the airy lark" (Drayton, *Noah's Flood*); and "the lark with the long toe" (Skelton, *Boke of Philip Sparow*).

Larks were plentiful in Fuller's time. We read in the *Worthies of England*, that—

"The most and best of these are caught and well dressed about Dunstable in this shire [Bedfordshire]. A harmless bird whilst living, not trespassing on grain; and wholesome when dead, then filling the stomack with meat, as formerly the ear with musick. In winter they fly in flocks, probably the reason why *alauda* signifieth in Latine both a lark and a legion of souldiers; except any will say a legion is so called because helmetted on their heads, and crested like a lark, therefore also called in Latine *galerita*. If men would imitate the early rising of this bird it would conduce much unto their healthfulness." (Vol. i. p. 133.)

Drayton gives the woodlark the third place in his list of English songsters:—

"To Philomel the next the linet we prefer,
And by that warbling bird the wood-lark place we then."
(*Polyolbion*, song xiii.)

The little Wagtail, or Washtaile, was once made the theme of a lively jest:— **Wagtail.**

"A certayn artificer in London there was, whyche was sore seke, and coulde not well dysgest his meat. To whom a physician cam to give hym councell, and sayd that he must use to ete metis that be light of digestyon and small byrdys, as sparowes, swalowes, and specyally that byrd which is called a wagtayle, whose flessh is merveleuse lyght of dygestyon, bycause that byrd is ever moving and styryng. The sekeman, herynge the phesicion say so, answered him and seyd: Sir, if that be the cause that those byrdes be lyght of dygestyon, than I know a mete moch lyghter of dygestyon than other sparow, swallow, or wagtaile, and that is my wyves tong, for it is never in rest, but ever meuying and sterryng." (*A. C. Mery Tales*, ed. W. C. Hazlitt, p. 21.)

This jest is repeated, with slight variation, in *An Interlude of Four Elements*, which was written about the year 1510.

Sparrow. The Sparrow, the commonest of our small birds, especially in the neighbourhood of houses, is frequently mentioned by Shakspeare, and is utilized as a simile by Ben Jonson:—

> "The use of things is all, and not the store:
> Surfeit and fulness have killed more than famine:
> The sparrow with her little plumage flies,
> While the proud peacock overcharged with pens,
> Is fain to sweep the ground with his grown train
> And load of feathers."
> (*The Staple of News*, vol. ii.)

According to Chester this little bird was gifted with prophetic power:—

> "The unsatiate sparrow doth prognosticate,
> And is held good for divination,
> For flying here and there, from gate to gate,
> Foretels true things by animadvertion;
> A flight of sparrowes flying in the day,
> Did prophesie the fall and sacke of Troy."
> (*Love's Martyr*, p. 122.)

Bishop Stanley, in his *Familiar History of Birds* (p. 89), considers the range of the sparrow to be co-extensive with the tillage of the soil. He writes:—

"From certain entries in the *Hunstanton Household Book*, from 1519 to 1578, in which sparrows, or, as they are there written, *spowes* or *sparrouse*, are frequently recorded, it would appear that these birds took their place in the larders of the nobility as delicacies with other game, from which we may infer that they were at that time as rare in Norfolk as they are still in some parts of Russia, owing probably to the same cause, viz. the limited state of tillage and growth of corn."

On this passage, Mr. Stevenson (*Birds of Norfolk*, 1866, vol. i. p. 213) has the following comment:—

"That the sparrow was scarce in that part of Norfolk in those days is most probable, and for the cause alleged, but at the same time the bishop was in error in supposing that the term 'spowes,' so frequently met with in the L'Estrange *Accounts*, referred to our *passer domesticus*. The term invariably occurs in connection with knots, ring-dotterels, redshanks, and other grallatorial species, common enough then, as indeed they still are, upon the Hunstanton beach, and under this name the whimbrell was invariably designated in these old records. Once only, in the same *Accounts*, is the word sparrouse used, as 'Item xij sparrouse of gyste,' articles given in lieu of rent, and these, thus entered alone, were in all probability real sparrows, brought as a delicacy by some poor retainer."

Drayton includes the red-sparrow in his list of song-birds. Skelton, in his satirical poem, *The Boke of Philip Sparow*, arranges that—

"Robyn red breaste
He shal be the priest
The requiem mass to syng
Lofty warbeling
With help of the red-sparow."

By both these authors the reference is perhaps to the reed-sparrow.

The Yellow Bunting, Yellow-hammer, or, as Harrison spells it, Yellow-hamer, is not often mentioned. Drayton, however, calls attention to its song:—

<small>Yellow-hammer.</small>

"The yellow-pate, which though she hurt the blooming tree,
Yet scarce hath any bird a finer pipe than she."

(*Polyolbion*, song xiii.)

Dr. Percival Wright (*Animal Life*, p. 263) says that the song of the yellow-hammer is not equal to its beauty, and attracts no human ear; whereas the note of this little bird, by its very monotony and constant repetition, inforces attention, and is one of the most familiar of country sounds. Almost any day in summer, in the roadside copse, the overgrown chalkpit, or even on the cottage roof, may be heard the tuneful call of the yellow-hammer, generally echoed back by some distant rival.

CHAPTER IX.

SHAKSPEARE has no mention of the Woodpecker, or Laughing-hecco. Drayton, in his poem, *The Owl*, describes the persecution which the unfortunate bird of night undergoes from the woodpecker and the rest of his feathered comrades:—

Woodpecker.

> "The wood-pecker, whose hardened beak hath broke,
> And pierc'd the heart of many a solid oak;
> That where the kingly eagle wont to pray,
> In the calm shade in heat of summer's day,
> Of thousands of fair trees there stands not one
> For him to perch or set his foot upon;
> Upon the sudden all these murderous fowl,
> Fallen together on the harmless owl,
> * * * * * *
> The crow is digging at his breast amain;
> And sharp-neb'd hecco stabbing at his brain."

The woodpecker is called in some countries the yaffle, and rainbird, as his cry was held to foretell rain. Other names were specke, woodspecke, and woodspike; in *The Parlyament of Byrdes*—a poem, without date, reprinted in the *Harleian Miscellany* (vol. v. p. 507)—two of these names occur:—

> " *The Specke.* Then in his hole, sayd the wood-specke,
> 'I wolde the hawk had broke his necke,
> Or brought into mischevous dale,
> For of every byrde he makyth a tale.'"

Sir Thomas Browne records that in Norfolk are found—

"*picus martius*, or woodspeck, many kinds. The green, the red, the leucomelanus, or neatly marked black and white, and the cinereus or dun-colored little bird, called a nuthack. They make holes in the trees without any consideration of the winds or quarters of heaven; but as the rotteness thereof best affordeth convenience." (Vol. iv. p. 319.)

The Toucan, one of the most peculiar of the feathered race, an inhabitant of America, is described by John Lerius, a Frenchman, who lived in Brazil about the year 1557.

Toucan.

"Among the rest of the American birds," he writes, "the first place shall be given to a certaiue bird named toucan, whereof we made mention before. It is of the bignesse of a pigeon, of a blacke colour like a crow, except the brest, which is of a yellow colour, compassed from the lower part with a ring of red feathers, which being taken away, the Barbarians use it for ornament. And it is highly esteemed with them, because they use it when they intend to dance. From this it hath taken the name of *toucan-tabourace*, yet notwithstanding, they have such store of them they refuse not to exchange them for our merchandizes. The bill of this bird exceeds the whole body in length, wherewith a crane's beak is not to be compared, and therefore it is to be accompted the most monstrous bill of the whole world." (*Purchas*, vol. iv. p. 1330.)

Gonzalo Ferdinando de Oviedo mentions these birds, but under a different name :—

"There is another kind of bird in the Firme Land, which the Christians call *picuti* because they have very great beakes, in respect of the littlenesse of their bodies, for their beakes are very heavie, and weigh more than their bodies: their feathers are very faire, and of many variable colours. Their beakes are a quarter of a yard in length or more, and bending downe toward the earth, and three fingers broad neere unto the head. Their tougues are very quils, wherewith they make a great hissing." (*Purchas*, vol. iii. p. 980.)

The tongue of this bird differs from that of every other species in being feathered.

Chester writes of one of the most familiar of our English birds, the Cuckoo:—

Cuckoo.

> "The spring-delighting bird we call the cuckow,
> Which comes to tell of wonders in this age,
> Her pretie one note to the world doth show
>   Some men their destinie.
>
> "The winters envious blast she never tasteth,
> Yet in all countries doth the cuckoe sing,
> And oftentimes to peopled townes she hasteth,
> Therfor to tell the pleasures of the spring:
>   Great courtiers heare her voyce, but let her flye,
>   Knowing that she presageth destinie.
>
> "She scornes to labour or make up a nest,
> But creepes by stealth into some others roome,
> And with the larkes deare yong, her yong-ones rest,
> Being by subtile dealing overcome:
>   The yong birds are restorative to eate,
>   And held amongst us as a princes meate."
>   (*Love's Martyr*, p. 118.)

Shakspeare is more correct in giving the hedge-sparrow as the foster-mother whose nest is usually selected by the parent bird.

> "The hedge-sparrow fed the cuckoo so long,
> That it had its head bit off by its young."
>   (*Lear*, i. 4, 235.)

And again:—

> "And, being fed by us, you used us so
> As that ungentle gull, the cuckoo's bird,
> Useth the sparrow: did oppress our nest;
> Grew by our feeding to so great a bulk,
> That even our love durst not come near your sight,
> For fear of swallowing."
>   (1 *Henry IV.*, v. i. 59.)

Mr. Singer, in a note on this passage, remarks:—

"Shakespeare seems to speak from his own observation, and to have been the first to notice how the hedge-sparrow was used by the young cuckoo—a curious fact, now well known and established by the observations of ornithologists. Something of the same kind is related of the cuckoo and the titlark by Pliny, but Holland's translation was not published before 1602. 'The titling, therefore, that sitteth, being thus deceived, hatcheth the egge, and bringeth up the chicke of another bird:—and this she doth so long, untill the young cuckow being once fledge and readie to flie abroad, is so bold as to seize upon the old titling, and eat up her that hatched her' (Pliny, *Nat. Hist.*, by Holland, b. x. ch. 9)."

For the credit of bird nature, it is to be hoped that such highly reprehensible conduct on the part of the young cuckoo is of rare occurrence.

The cuckoo was sometimes called "the Welch Ambassador." This name arose, perhaps, from the fact that Welsh labourers came into the neighbouring counties about spring time, in search of employment. In Middleton's play, *A Trick to catch an Old One*, we read, " Why, thou rogue of universality, do I not know thee? Thy sound is like the cuckoo, the Welch Ambassador" (iv. 5).

The change in this bird's note as summer advances is observed by Ben Jonson:—

" From a fiddle out of tune
As the cuckow is in June."
(*The Gipsies Metamorphosed.*)

Also by John Heywood, 1587 :—

" In April the Coocoo can sing her song by rote.
In June oft time she cannot sing a note.
At first, koo, koo ; koo, koo ; sings till can she do
At last, kooke, kooke, kooke ; six kookes to one koo."
(*Epigrams.*)

Richard II. had, by too frequent appearance and by his unseemly familiarity with the common people, "disgraced his kingly glory:"—

" So when he had occasion to be seen,
He was but as the cuckoo is in June,
Heard, not regarded."
(1 *Henry IV.*, iii. 2, 75.)

The attempt of the "wise men of Gotham" to keep perpetual spring by setting a hedge round a cuckoo is often referred to by poets and dramatists. It may not be out of place to give the origin of the allusion, though it can hardly be said to come under the title of natural history. The story, as given in T. Blount's *Ancient Tenures of Land*, runs thus :—

"King John, passing through the village of Gotham towards Nottingham, intending to go over the meadows, was prevented by the villagers, they apprehending that the ground over which a king passed was for ever after to become a public road. The king, incensed at their proceedings, sent from his court soon after some of his servants, to inquire of them the reason of their incivility and ill-treatment, that he might punish them by way of fine, or some other way he might judge most proper. The villagers, hearing of the approach of the king's servants, thought of an expedient to turn away his majesty's displeasure from them : when the messengers arrived at Gotham, they found some of the inhabitants engaged in endeavouring to drown an eel in a pool of water; some were employed in dragging carts upon a large barn, to shade the wood from the sun; others were tumbling their cheeses down a hill, that they might find their way to Nottingham for sale ; and some were employed in hedging in a cuckoo which had perched upon an old bush which stood where the present one now stands ; which convinced the king's servants that it was a village of fools; whence arose the old adage 'the wise men' or 'the fools of Gotham.'" (Page 133, ed. W. C. Hazlitt, 1874.)

Michael Drayton was a close observer of nature, and better acquainted with the habits of birds than most of his contemporaries. In one of the picturesque descriptions of the marshy district in which he delighted, this poet paints the commotion that results from the rapid swimming of a swan through the water :—

Kingfisher.

> "The jealous swan, there swimming in his pride,
> With his arch'd breast the waters did divide,
> His saily wings him forward strongly pushing,
> Against the billows with such fury rushing,
> As from the same, a foam so white arose,
> As seem'd to mock the breast that them oppose :

And here and there the wand'ring eye to feed,
Of scatter'd tufts of bulrushes and reed,
Segges, longleaved willow, on whose bending spray,
The py'd King-fisher, having got his prey,
Sate with the small breath of the water shaken,
Till he devour'd the fish that he had taken."
(*The Man in the Moon.*)

Mr. Harting has referred to the wide-spread belief in the Halcyon days. William Browne in his pastoral poems speaks of—

"The mevy and the halcyon famosed
For colours rare, and for the peaceful seas,
Round the Sicilian coast, her brooding days."
(*Britannia's Pastorals*, b. ii. song 1.)

Montaigne (essay liv.) gives a full account from Plutarch of the structure of the kingfisher's nest, and of the habits of the bird.

Giraldus Cambrensis calls the kingfisher the martinet. The French name of this bird is the *martinet-pêcheur*. This author never allows any marvel to shake his faith by "supposing it a thing impossible." He has preserved some curious folk-lore about the kingfisher:—

"It is remarkable in these little birds that, if they are preserved in a dry place, when dead, they never decay; and if they are put among clothes and other articles, they preserve them from the moth and give them a pleasant odour. What is still more wonderful, if, when dead, they are hung up by their beaks in a dry situation, they change their plumage every year, as if they were restored to life, as though the vital spark still survived and vegetated through some mysterious remains of its energy." (*Topography of Ireland*, 1187, ed. Wright, 1813, p. 39.)

The students of folk-lore are much beholden to their ancestors for this sublime credulity. Had they discarded such stories as absurd they would not have cared to record them, and the occupation of the students would have been largely gone.

The range of the beautiful bird, the Hoopoe, is very extensive. It was known to the Greeks as well as to the Egyptians. Sir Thomas Browne tells us that this bird is seen in Norfolk—

Hoopoe.

"Yet we often meet with it in this county. From the proper note it is called an hoopebird with us; we apprehend not the hieroglyphical considerations which the Egyptians made of this observable bird; who, considering the order and variety of colors, the 26 or 28 feathers in its crest, and mewing this handsome outside in the winter, they made it an emblem of the varieties of the world, the succession of times and seasons and signal mutations in them. And therefore, Orus, the hieroglyphic of the world, had the head of an hoopebird upon the top of his staff." (Vol. iv. p. 184.)

Muffett, in his *Healths Improvement* (p. 100), writes:—

"Houpes were not thought by Dr. Torner to be found in England, yet I saw Mr. Serjeant Goodrons kill one of them in Charingdon Park, when he did very skilfully and happily cure my Lord of Pembroke at Ivy Church; they feed upon hurthe-berries, and worms, but delight to feed most upon graves."

The Goat-sucker or Night-jar, sometimes called a Nighthawk, must have been sufficiently common to attract notice by its noiseless, owl-like flight, and its weird monotonous cry. Its habits, however, are so retiring that there was little chance afforded to our forefathers of making observations that would be correct.

Goat-sucker.

Sir Thomas Browne, writing to Dr. Merritt, inquires, "Have you a caprimulgus, or dorhawk: a bird as a pigeon, with a wide throat, as little as a titmouse, white feathers in the tail, and paned like a hawk?" (vol. i. p. 399). Gilbert White, of Selborne, a naturalist who paid especial attention to the habits of this bird, writing still later, gives it the various names of churn-owl, fern-owl, eve-jarr, and puckridge. He ridicules the popular belief that existed in his day, and that still lingers in our own, that the night-jar is injurious to cattle, and explains that what the bird really seeks as he wheels round the sleeping kine is not a milk, but an insect diet.

Skelton probably refers to the night-jar in the following lines:—

"The wodhacke, that singeth churre,
Horsly as hee had the mutre."
(*Philip Sparow.*)

That this bird was classed among the foreboders of evil will not surprise any one who has listened to the curious sound it utters, on still summer evenings, whilst itself hidden from view.

"Night-jars and ravens, with wide stretched throats,
From yews and hollies send their baleful notes."
(POOLE, *English Parnassus.*)

Humming-bird. With a somewhat abrupt transition we turn from the hoarse-voiced night-jar of our own country, with its gloomy associations of darkness and ill omen, to the glittering fragments of sunshine that enliven the forests of America. Joseph Acosta mentions the jewel-plumaged Humming-birds, the feathered fairies of the western world :—

"In Peru there are birds which they call *tomineios*, so small, that oftentimes I have doubted, seeing them flie, whether they were bees or butter-flies; but in truth they are birds." (*Purchas*, vol. iii. p. 965.)

Gonzalo Ferdinando de Oviedo, in his description of these beautiful little creatures, pays them but a poor compliment when he compares them to the fanciful representations of birds in the illuminated missals painted by cloistered artists. He writes:—

"There are found in the Firme Land [South America] certaine birds, so little that the whole bodie of one of them is no bigger then the top of the biggest finger of a mans hand, and yet is the bare body without feathers not halfe so bigge; this bird, beside her littlenesse, is of such velocitie and swiftnesse in flying, that whoso seeth her flying in the aire, cannot see her flap or beate her wings after any other sorte then doe the dorres, or humble bees, or beetels: so that there is no man that seeth her flye, that would thinke her to be any other than a dorre: they make their nests according to the proportion of their bignesse, and I have seene that one of these birds with her nest put into a paire of gold weights altogether, hath waide no more then a *tomini,* which are in poise 24 graines, with the feathers, without the which she would have waied somewhat less; and doubtlesse, when I consider the finenesse of the clawes and feete of these birds, I know not whereunto I may better liken them then to the little birds which the lymners of bookes are accustomed to paint on the margent of church bookes, and other bookes of divine service. Their feathers are of manie faire colours, as golden, yellow, and greene, beside other variable colours: their beake is verie long for the proportion of their bodies, and as fine and subtile as a sowing needle: they are verie hardy, so that when they see a man clime the tree where they have their nests, they flye at his face, and strike him in the eyes, comming, going, and returning with such swiftnesse, that no man should lightly beleeve it that had not seene it, and certainly these birds are so little, that I durst not have made mention hereof, if it were not that divers others which have seene them as well as I can beare witnesse of my saying. They make their nests of flocks and cotten, whereof there is great plentie in these regions, and serveth well for their purpose." (*Purchas,* vol. iii. p. 977.)

We find these small birds mentioned elsewhere under another name. Antonio Galvano, of New Spain, writes:—

"There be certaine small birds named *vicmalim,* their bil is small and long. They live of the dew, and the juyce of flowers and roses. Their feathers bee small and of divers colours. They be greatly esteemed to worke gold with. They die or sleepe every yeere in the moneth of October, sitting upon a little bough in a warme and close place: they revive or wake againe in the moneth of Aprill after that the flowers be sprung, and therefore they call them the revived birds." (*Purchas,* vol. ii. p. 1693.)

The Portuguese naturalist, whose observations during his residence in Brazil have been frequently quoted, also describes the humming-bird, and adds some curious information respecting its mode of reproduction :—

"Of all the small birds called *guaimimbique,* there are sundrie kindes, as, fruit of the sunne; by another name, that is, the covering of the sunne; or the haire of the sunne; in the Autilles they call it the risen or awaken bird, and they say it sleepeth sixe moneths, and liveth other sixe moneths. It is the finest bird that can bee imagined; it hath a cap on his head, to which no proper colour can be given, for on whatsoever side yee looke on it, it sheweth red, greene, blacke, and more colours, all very fine, and shining; and yellow more fine then gold. The bodie is grey; it hath a very long bill, and the tongue twice the length of the bill; they are very swift in flight, and in their flight they make a noise like the bee, and they rather seeme bees in their swiftnesse then birds, for they alwaies feed flying without sitting on a tree, even as the bees doe flie sucking the honnie from the flowers. They have two beginnings of their generation, some are hatched of egges like other birds, others of little bubbles, and it is a thing to bee noted, a little bubble to beginne to convert itselfe into this little bird, for at one instant it is a bubble and a bird, and so it converts itselfe into this most faire bird, a wonderful thing, and unknowne to the philosophers, seeing one living creature without corruption is converted into another." (*Purchas*, vol. iv. p. 1305.)

It is matter for regret that Shakspeare had no chance of seeing these flying jewels. *Puck* might have exchanged his bat courser for one of these tiny steeds, " Swifter than arrow from the Tartar's bow." But alas, had they been permitted to grace the revels of *Titania's* court, prosaic critics would have pointed out that fairies carefully avoid the sunshine that these tropic gems delight in; so perhaps it is well that humming-birds were unknown to the poet.

The Parrot, in consequence of its amusing ways, and the ease with which it may be taught to talk and imitate various sounds, has been in all times a favourite domestic pet. The rose-ringed parrakeet is described with minuteness by Skelton in his singular poem, *Speak Parrot* :—

Parrot.

> "My name is parrot, a bird of Paradise,
> By nature devised, of a wondrous kynd
> Dienteli dieted, with divers delicate spice
> Tyl Euphrates that floud, driveth me into Inde
> Where men of that countrey by fortune me find
> And send me, to great ladyes of estate,
> Then parrot must have an almond or a date.

> "With my becke bent, my little wantou eye,
> My feders fresh, as is the emrawde grene,
> About my necke a circulet, lyke the ryche rubye,
> My little legges, my fete both nete and cleane.
>
> * * * * *
>
> For parrot is no churlish chough, nor no fleked py,
> Parrot is no pendugum, that men call a carlyng,
> Parrot is no woodcocke, nor no butterfly,
> Parrot is no stamring stare, that men call a starling,
> But parrot is mine own dere harte, and my darling."

The phrase "An almond for parrot" seems to have been proverbial. Shakspeare uses it, and Ben Jonson writes:—

> "How do you, ladybird? so hard at work still!
> What's that you say; so you bid me walk, sweet bird,
> And tell our knight? I will. How! Walk, knave, walk!
> I think you are angry with me, Pol. Fine Pol!
> Pol is a fine bird! O, fine lady Pol!
> Almond for parrot. Parrot's a brave bird."
>
> (*The Magnetic Lady*, v. 5.)

The phrase occurs again in Haughton:—

> "Ah, sirrah, now we'll brag with Mistress Moore,
> To have as fine a parrot as she hath.
> Look, sisters, what a pretty fool it is!
> What a green greasy shining coat he hath,
> An almond for parrot: a rope for parrot."
>
> (*English-Men for my Money: or a Woman will have her Will*, v. 2.)

There has been some discussion as to the meaning of the word Popinjay, so often used by old writers. In some cases a parrot is evidently intended; but Mr. Bell, in a note in his edition of Chaucer, points out that this name occurs in almost all Chaucer's descriptions of spring. He considers it most unlikely that a poet so accurate in portraying nature should introduce the parrot in pictures of European scenery, and that the jay is more probably the bird intended. In Skelton's *Philip Sparow*, however, both the jay and the popinjay are included. Phineas

Fletcher, in one of his poetical miscellanies, classes the parrot with the "fatal belman of the night":—

> "Cousin, day-birds are silenc't, and those fowl
> Yet only sing which hate warme Phœbus' light:
> Th' unlucky parrot, and death-boding owl."

Mr. Grosart in a note suggests that parrot may here be the local name for some English bird.

Parrots were found in almost all the hot regions of the globe, and were brought over in considerable numbers by sailors; they are often mentioned by travellers in their descriptions of foreign parts. Sir John Mandeville indulges in his usual exaggeration, and tells of some parrots in the land of Prester John, which rival the Irishman's echo, and speaks of "their propre nature, and salven men that go throughe the desertes, and speken to them appropriately as if they were human" (*Travels*, ed. Halliwell, p. 274). These talking parrots, he goes on to say, have a large tongue, and have five toes on each foot, but those that only scream have but three toes.

Dr. Percival Wright, in his *Animal Life* (p. 289), makes mention of a parrot supposed to be of the grey species, the property of a cardinal in Rome, in the year 1500. This bird was bought for the high price of a hundred pieces of gold, on account of its ability to repeat, clearly and without hesitation, the Apostle's Creed.

Navarette, a missionary to China, reports that "at Marassa there are a great number of a sort of bird they call *cacatua*. They are all white, their beak like a parrot. They are easily made tame, and talk" (*Churchill's Voyages*, vol. i.). From this word cacatua is derived the English name Cockatoo.

Macaws are mentioned by one of Purchas's pilgrims, a Portuguese, who had lived for some time in Brazil:—

"The Arara parots are those that by another name are called

The Green Parokeet. 215

Macaos; it is a great bird, and are very rare, and by the east coast they are not found, it is a faire bird in colours; their breasts are red as scarlet; from the middle of the bodie to the taile some are yellow, others greene, others blue, and through all the bodie they have scattering some greene, some yellow and blue feathers, and ordinarily every feather hath three or foure colours, and the taile is very long. The Indians esteeme them very much, and of their feathers they make very fine things, and their hangings for their swords. It is a very pleasant bird, they become very tame and domesticall, and speake very well if they be taught." (*Purchas*, vol. iv. p. 1804.)

It is uncertain whether the confusion of pronouns in the foregoing passage is the fault of the translator, or whether it must be ascribed to the long exile of the writer from civilization and books of grammar. These macaws evidently made a *very* strong impression on the traveller.

A Dutch traveller, whose description of the Gold Coast of Guinea is also included in Purchas's collection of travels, mentions the little Parokeets, now so common in drawing-room aviaries:—

"The birds that are found there," he writes, "are of divers colours, and are little birds like unto ours; first, there are blewe parrots, whereof are great store, which being young, and taken out of their nests, and made tame, having not flowne abroad, they are better to teach, and to learne to speake; but they will not prate so much as the greene Brasilian parrots doe. They have also another kind of greene birds as big as sparrows, like the catalinkins of West India, but they cannot speake. These birds are called *asuront*, and by our Netherlanders, called *parokites*. They are taken with nets, as you use to take sparrowes. They keepe much in low land, where much corne or millet groweth, for they eate much thereof. Those birds are alwaies very kind one to the other; for when you put a male and a female in a cage, they will alwaies sit together without making any noyse. The female is of such a nature, that when she is coupled with the male, she respecteth him much, and letteth him sit on the right hand, setting her selfe on the left hand; and when he goes to eate, shee followeth him, and so they live together quietly, being almost of the nature of the turtle-doves. They are of a very faire greene colour, with a spot of orange-tawnie upon their noses. Thére are another kind of parokiten, which are much like them, being of the same nature, and condition, but are of colour as red as bloud, with a spot of blacke upon their noses, and a blacke taile, being somewhat greater than the parokites." (*Purchas*, vol. 2, p. 956.)

Another bird of the parrot tribe is described by Linschoten, a Portuguese, in his account of a voyage to Goa, 1583:—

"There commeth in India, out of the iland of Molucas, beyond Malacca, a kind of birds, called *noyras*: they are very faire to looke on, and speake sweetly: there could never yet be any of them brought living into Portugall, although they have sought and used all the meanes they could to bring them for a present to the king, which he greatly desireth: but they die upon the way, for they are very delicate, and will hardly be brought up." (*Purchas*, vol. ii. p. 1771.)

The Purple-capped Lory is probably here intended. This bird is a native of the Moluccas, and is arrayed in gorgeous scarlet plumage. The difficulty of transit has been overcome by modern collectors, and the ease with which the lory is tamed, no less than its brillant colouring, makes it a favourite cage-bird.

Pigeon. It seems almost unnecessary to suggest that Shakspeare must in his youth have had the charge of Pigeons, as few boys living in the country have not; but only those who are well acquainted with the habits of these birds can realize the almost photographic accuracy with which the poet has observed them. The references to their "golden couplets" (*Hamlet*, v. 1), their method of feeding their young (*As You Like It*, ii. 27), their gentleness (*Midsummer Night's Dream*, i. 2), courage (2 *Henry IV.*, iii. 2), and jealousy (*As You Like It*, ii. 2),—all show how closely he had watched them. Mr. Harting has given a full description of pigeons, and numerous illustrative quotations from Shakspeare's works.

The Dove, from its association with certain scriptural legends, has in Christian art ever been held as a type of love, simplicity, innocence, fidelity, gentleness, and peace. The possession of all these amiable qualities has not, however, procured for the bird any exemption from ill-treatment at the hand of man. In early times, among the Hebrews, doves were carefully reared in order to be slain by thousands as sacrifices; in the medieval period their chief mission was to provide food and exercise for their unrelenting foe, the hawk; and in our own day they are selected as the favourite victims for shooting matches.

The cruel custom of fastening or sewing up the eyes of pigeons is referred to by Sir Philip Sidney :—

> "Like as the dove, which seeled up, doth fly;
> Is neither freed, nor yet to service bound;
> But hopes to get some help by mounting high,
> Till want of force do force her to the ground."
> (Vol. iii. p. 146, ed. 1726.)

And again, by Ford :—

> "Ambition, like a seeled dove, mounts upward,
> Higher and higher still, to perch on clouds,
> But tumbles headlong down with heavier ruin."
> (*The Broken Heart*, ii. 2.)

Thomas Fuller gives us some information with respect to the number of pigeons that were kept, and the complaints that consequently arose.

"Pigeons," he writes, "against their wills, keep one Lent for seaven weeks in the year, betwixt the going out of the old and growing up of the new grain. Probably, our English would be found as docile and ingenious as the Turkish pigeons, which carry letters from Aleppo to Babilon, if trained up accordingly. But such practices, by these wing-posts would spoil many a foot-post, living honestly by that painful vocation."

What would the worthy doctor have said had any one told him that messages would one day be carried by a means far outstripping in speed the swiftest pigeon! He adds:—

"I find a grievous indictment drawn up against the poor pigeons for felony, as the grand plunderers of grain in this land; my author, computing six and twenty thousand dovehouses in England and Wales, and allowing five hundred pair in each house, four bushels yearly for each pair, hath mounted the annual wast they make to an incredible sum; and, if the moiety of his proportions hold true, doves may be accounted the causers of death, and justly answer their etymology in Hebrew, *Jonah*, which is deduced from a root signifying to spoil or destroy." (*Worthies of England*, vol. ii. p. 158.)

Though pigeon-breeding was doubtless practised as an amusement, we find no mention by name of any fancy varieties. In a poem by Barnfield, published about 1590, we meet with a suggestion of a feathered-toed pigeon :—

> " And when th' art wearie of thy keeping sheepe,
> Upon a lovely downe, to please thy minde,
> Ile give thee fine ruffe-footed doves to keepe,
> And pretty pigeons of another kind."

Later on, we are informed that—

> "House-doves are white, and oozels blacke-birds bee."
> (*The Affectinate Shepheard*.)

Thomas Muffett tells us that " wild doves be especially four; rock-doves, stock-doves, ring-doves, and turtle doves " (*Healths Improvement*, p. 100).

The wood-pigeon was called the wood-quist, or wood-queest. Lyly writes:—

> " Me thought I saw a stock-dove, or wood-quist, I know not how to tearme it, that brought short strawes to build his nest on a tall cedar." (*Sappho and Phaon*, iv. 3.)

Dodo. Sir Thomas Herbert, in his lively narrative of the travels on which he set out in 1626, gives some interesting particulars of the long extinct Dodo, a species of bird closely allied to the pigeon. He is describing the island of Mauritius, and writes :—

> "This noble isle, as it is prodigal in her water and wood, so she corresponds in what else a fruitful parent labours in: not onely boasting in that variety, but in feathered creatures also; yea, in the rareness of that variety : I will name but some, and first the dodo; a

bird the Dutch call *walgh-vogel* or *dod eersen* : her body is round and fat, which occasions the slow pace or that her corpulencie; and so great as few of them weigh less than fifty pound : meat it is with some, but better to the eye than stomach ; such as only a strong appetite can vanquish: but otherwise, through its oyliness it cannot chuse but quickly cloy and nauseate the stomach, being indeed more pleasurable to look than feed upon. It is of melancholy visage, as sensible of natures injury in framing so massie a body to be directed by complemental wings, such indeed as are unable to hoise her from the ground, serving only to rank her amongst birds : her head is variously drest; for one half is hooded with down of a dark colour, the other half, naked and of a white hue, as if lawn were drawn over it; her bill hooks and bends downwards, the thrill or breathing place is in the midst; from which part to the end, the colour is of a light green mixt with a pale yellow: her eyes are round and bright, and instead of feathers has a most fine down; her train (like to a Chyna [Chinaman's] beard) is no more than three or four short feathers : her leggs are thick and black; her tallons great; her stomach fiery, so she can easily digest stones ; in that and shape not a little resembling the ostrich." (*Travels*, p. 383, 4th ed.)

With regard to the culinary properties of the dodo it must be borne in mind that Sir Thomas Herbert was somewhat hard to please, and scarcely ever condescended to approve of the different dishes that necessity compelled him to investigate.

The Rev. R. Lubbock writes of the Capercaillie, or cock of the wood :—

Capercaillie.

"By reclaiming waste lands and draining marshes we gradually lose certain species ; but by cultivating and planting we either encourage or gain others. The greatest achievement is the one lately carried through in the Highlands, the complete restoration of the cappercaillie. This noble bird was annihilated with the pine forests which sheltered him. The mountains were again clothed with wood, and, without much trouble, he was reinstated in his former possessions." (*Fauna of Norfolk*, 1845, p. 41.)

According to Sir Thomas Browne, Grouse were unknown in Norfolk, as was also the Health-poult, by which he meant, in all probability, the black grouse.

"The corn-land loving Quail, the daintiest of our bits"
    (DRAYTON, *Polyolbion*, song xxv.),

Quail. was in the time of Elizabeth considered a delicacy. This bird was plentiful in Lancashire and several other counties, and Sir Thomas Browne mentions it as common in Norfolk. Quails, however, had one peculiarity, which gave the ancients a dislike to their flesh; Harrison writes, "They onelie with man are subject to the falling sicknesse." Against the assertion that quails were unwholesome, Muffett brings forward the fact that these birds were sent to the Israelites in the wilderness, when they wearied of manna, as the best and daintiest meat that could be provided (*Healths Improvement*, p. 98).

Lyly gives the quail credit for peculiar taste in the way of food. He compares some one to "the quaile that forsaketh the malowes to eat hemlock" (*Euphues*, p. 240).

Partridge. Partridges were chiefly valued as quarry for the smaller kinds of hawks. The French commentator on Du Bartas writes of the partridge:—

"The reason why she is called delicate hath relation to their taste who eat therof; although Martiall hath sometimes said, *Charior est perdrix, sic sapit illa magis.* As if he had said, as they say in French, *The coust fait le goust*: the cost makes the taste." (*Summary on Du Bartas*, p. 235.)

Peacock. The "Peacock of Inde," mentioned by Harrison, is noticed by Navarette, in his account of China: "They carry this bird from Siam, for they do not breed in China, but abundance of them do in some parts of India" (*Churchill's Voyages*, vol. i. p. 40).

Chester refers to the admiration expressed by Alexander the Great and his soldiers at the sight of these beautiful birds:—

"The proud sun-braving peacocke with his feathers,
 Walkes all along, thinking himselfe a king,

And with his voyce prognosticates all weathers,
Although God knows but badly he doth sing;
But when he lookes downe to his base blacke feete,
He droopes, and is asham'd of things unmeete.

"The mighty Macedonian Alexander,
Marching in lovely triumph to his foes,
Being accounted the worlds conquerour,
In Indie spies a peacocke as he goes,
And marvelling to see so rich a sight
Charg'd all men not to kill his sweet delight."
(*Love's Martyr*, p. 121.)

Du Bartas writes:—

"There the fair peacock, beautifully brave,
Proud, portly-strouting, stalking, stately-grave,
Wheeling his starry trayn, in pomp displayes
His glorious eyes to Phœbus golden rayes."
(Page 46.)

Peacocks' plumes have in all ages been prized for their beauty, but it is somewhat curious to find that these birds were reared in the northern countries of Europe expressly for their æsthetic value. Olaus Magnus tells us that—

"in Ostrogothia, and Vestrogothia, and Sweden, many peacocks breed, and they are bred up very carefully: so that at first they are fed with pellets made of barley meal; after that with new-milk cheese, pressed from the milk, for the whey hurts them, then when 35 days are past they are fed with whole barley; and next in the open fields, where, by instinct of nature, they can feed themselves more freely, especially where foxes cannot come at them. The reason why they are fostered more than other birds is, the profit they make, and their fine feathers, which painters and weavers imitate in the north, to make distinction of colours, because the pictures of great artists are seldome brought hither from far countries, because the way is so long." (Page 203.)

Lyly mentions another use to which peacocks' feathers may be put: "They that feare the stinging of waspes make fannes of peacock tailes, whose spots are like eyes" (*Prologue to Campaspe*).

An attempt was apparently made to utilize these feathers in archery. Roger Ascham, in his *Toxophilus* (p. 152), 1551, writes :—

> "Truly, at a short butt, which some men doth use, the peacock feather doth seldom keep up the shaft either right or level, it is so rough and heavy; so that many men, which have taken them up for gayness, have laid them down again for profit : thus, for our purpose, the goose is the best feather for the best shooter."

The peacock, probably more on account of the ornament which its gorgeous plumage added to the banquet than from any tenderness of its flesh, was a standard dish on every great occasion. This royal bird was usually "eten with gynger," and was served up amidst considerable pomp and ceremony. If we may trust the poet, the city feasts of this period were sometimes the occasion of lavish expenditure. Thus Massinger writes :—

> "Men may talk of country-Christmasses, and court-gluttony,
> Their thirty-pound butter'd eggs, their pies of carp's tongues,
> Their pheasants, drench'd with ambergris, the carcasses
> Of three fat wethers bruised for gravy, to
> Make sauce for a single peacock; yet their feasts
> Were fasts, compared with the city's."
>   (*The City Madam*, ii. 1.)

Montaigne refers to the extravagant luxury of these banquets :—

> "I could have been glad, the better to judge of it, to have tasted the culinary art of those cooks, who had so rare a way of seasoning exotick odours with the relish of meats; as it was particularly observed in the service of the King of Tunis, who in our days landed at Naples, to have an interview with Charles the Emperour, where his dishes were forc'd with odoriferous drugs, to that degree of expence, that the cookery of one peacock and two pheasants amounted to a hundred ducats, to dress them after their fashion. And when the carver came to break them up, not only the dining-room, but all apartments of his palace and the adjoining streets were fill'd with an aromatick vapour, which did not presently vanish." (*Essay* xlii.)

The custom frequently adopted by knights, of taking

a solemn vow on the pheasant to perform some deed of prowess, is ascribed by Dr. Brinsley Nicholson to a Pagan source, though at the same time he identifies it with the token of the covenant of the rainbow, mentioned in Genesis :—

"The mediæval knights," he writes, "seem to have kuown nothing of the origin or meaning of the oath by the peacock or pheasant, there is therefore the more reason for believing it to have been traditional and imported. Its incongruous combination also with vows to God and the Virgin seems to show that it was a Pagan oath Christianized in outward form by the adspersion of holy words. From it as an example, and when birds were divided into noble and common, and taken as heraldic devices, other similar oaths would follow. But these were the oaths of particular persons, and, as in the case of the swan, oaths by one's ancestral honour, that by the peacock was universal among the nobly born. I conjecture then, and believe, that the oath by the peacock, and that by the pheasant, were variants of one and the same oath, the irid-coloured pheasant being the representative of the peacock where peacocks were scarce or unknown, and both of them the emblems or representatives of the covenant bow in the clouds. The bringing of the bird alive, or dressed in its feathers, the great solemnity of the oath, the fidelity to it that was meant to be thus ensured, and perhaps the taking of it by many or with many, as though entering into a compact or covenant, are all further circumstances tending to corroborate this view." (*Notes and Queries*, 4th series, vol. iii. p. 565.)

Dr. Nicholson explains the connexion between Iris and the peacock as arising from the fact that Iris was the attendant on Juno. When the peacock became known, her place was taken by that bird. Be this as it may, the oath thus taken was considered most binding. In 1458, Philip le Bon, Duke of Burgundy, vowed, "Sur le faisan," to go to the deliverance of Constantinople, which had recently fallen into the hands of the Turks.

The Pheasant was apparently plentiful in England. Though not preserved in the modern sense of the word, it was the quarry pursued by the goshawk, and was protected accordingly.

Pheasant.

The Pheasant is repeatedly mentioned in the old

"accounts." The instructions for serving it, given in Wynkyn de Worde's *Boke of Kervynge*, are that the legs and wings are to be lifted the same as those of hens, and that no sauce is to be used with it, but only salt and powder of ginger.

According to Andrewe (*Noble Lyfe*, part ii. m. 4), the pheasant was sometimes taken by the simple yet ingenious device of painting a representation of the bird on a cloth, and holding it in view of the quarry. This proceeding so attracted the attention of the bird, that another fowler was able to approach from the rear and throw a net over it. Considering the great want of likeness prevalent in portraits of this period, it is more than probable that if the pheasant was attracted at all it was by curiosity, to discover what new species of fowl had come into the neighbourhood. This same writer informs us that—

"thys byrde morneth sore in fowle weder, and hideth hym from the rayne under the bushes. Towarde the morning and towardes night, than commeth he out of the busshe, and is oftentimes so taken, and he putteth his hede in the ground, and he weneth that all his boddy is hyden and his flessh is very light and good to disjest." (*Babees Book*, ed. Furnivall, p. 101.)

Ben Jonson, in his enumeration of the various luxuries which Penshurst afforded for its owner's entertainment, writes:—

"The tops
Fertile of wood, Ashore and Sydneys copp's,
To crown thy open table, doth provide
The purpled pheasant with the speckled side:
The painted partridge lies in ev'ry field,
And for thy mess is willing to be killed."

(*The Forest.*)

The Argus Pheasant is a native of Sumatra. A variety of the pheasant mentioned by Marco Polo may possibly be this argus: "Pheasants are found in it [Thibet] that are twice the size of ours, but something smaller than the peacock. The tail-feathers are eight or ten palms in length" (*Travels*, p. 225, ed. Marsden, 1813).

"The princely Cock distinguished the hours," writes Drayton; and Du Bartas, in his poem on the Creation, thus describes the "Harbinger of Morn:"—

Cock.

> "Close by his side stands the courageous cock,
> Crest-peoples king, the peasants trusty clock,
> True morning watch, Aurora's trumpeter,
> The lyons terror, true astronomer,
> Who daily riseth when the sun doth rise;
> And when Sol setteth then to roost he hies."
> (Fifth Day, p. 46.)

The notion to which reference is here made, that the lion had a strong antipathy to the crowing of a cock, is mentioned by Reginald Scot, 1584, in a passage which recalls *Shylock's* answer to the *Duke's* appeal for clemency:—

"It is almost incredible, that the grunting, or rather the wheeking of a little pig, or the sight of a simple sheep should terrify a mighty elephant; and yet by that means the Romans did put to flight Pyrrhus and all his hoast. A man would hardly beleeve, that a cocks combe or his crowing should abash a puissant lion; but that the experience hereof hath satisfied the whole world. Who would think that a serpent should abandon the shadow of an ash, etc.? But it seemeth not strange because it is common, that some man otherwise hardy and stout enough should not dare to abide or endure the sight of a cat." (*Discovery of Witchcraft*, p. 70, ed. 1654.)

According to Hakewill (*Apologie*, p. 13) King James I. made trial of the lion's courage, and found that it was quite proof against the crowing of a cock.

The porter in *Macbeth* replies to the accusation of keeping late hours, "Faith, sir, we were carousing till the second cock,"—a time identical with that referred to by *Lady Macbeth* after the banquet, "Almost at odds with morning, which is which."

Spenser refers to the several periods of crowing :—

> "What time the native belman of the night,
> The bird that warned Peter of his fall,
> First rings his silver bell t' each sleepy wight,
> That should their mindes up to devotion call."
> (*Faerie Queene*, V. vi. 36.)

Tusser, more precise, gives the exact hours in the night when the cock goes through his performance :—

> "Cock croweth at midnight, few times above six,
> With pause to his neighbour, to answer betwix:
> At three a clock thicker; and then as ye know,
> Like al in to mattins, near day they do crow.
>
> "At midnight, at three, and an hour ere day,
> They utter their language, as well as they may;
> Which who so regardeth, what counsel they give,
> Will better love crowing, as long as they live."
> (*Five Hundred Points of Good Husbandrie.*)

Mr. Harting illustrates from *Hamlet* the popular notion that ghosts vanished at the sound of cock-crowing, and that consequently no spirit dare stir abroad at Christmas time, since at that period of the year chanticleer clamors the livelong night. It has been suggested that as the cock wakes readily, and crows lustily if roused by any artificial light, the prolonged labours of the housewife consequent upon the approaching Christmas festivities, and the extension of hours of the lights of the household at this season, keep him in constant activity.

The process of hatching eggs by artificial heat is not by any means a recent invention. The plan adopted in Cairo is minutely described by George Sandys, in his account of a journey into Africa, in 1610 (*Purchas*, vol. ii. p. 906). According to this author, as many as six thousand eggs were laid on mats in a single oven. The floor of the oven was grated, and a slow, smouldering fire was kindled underneath. After eight days of moderate heat the eggs were carefully sorted over, and the bad were distinguished from the good by holding them in front of a lamp. The oven was shut up for ten days longer, at the end of which time the eggs were "disclosed," or hatched simultaneously. A similar method of hatching eggs was employed in China, about the same date.

Sir John Mandeville relates that in China he found hens without feathers, but with white wool like sheep. Whether the worthy knight was indulging in romance, or whether he mistook the furry appearance of the Cochin China fowl for wool, is uncertain.

According to Mr. Bennett (*Gardens of the Zoological Society*, 1830), much uncertainty prevails as to the date of the introduction of the Turkey into England. This author writes:— **Turkey.**

"It is a singular fact that the origin of this, the most important addition to our domestic poultry that has been made in modern times, should have been involved in such obscurity, as to remain for more than two centuries out of the three that the bird has been known to us, doubtful and undetermined. . . . In 1541 we find it mentioned in a Constitution of Archbishop Cranmer, published in Leland's *Collectanea*, by which it was ordered that of such large fowls as cranes, swans, and turkey-cocks, there should be but one in a dish. In 1566 a present of twelve turkeys was thought not unworthy of being offered by the municipality of Amiens to the king; at whose marriage, in 1570, it is said, they were first eaten in France."

Daines Barrington, in his amusing *Miscellanies*, 1781, tells us that "four young turkies, and consequently bred in England, were dressed at a serjeant's feast in 1555," and claims to find a still earlier mention of this fowl in the statement that—

"capons of grease (Greece, probably) made part of an entertainment in the sixth year of Edward IV., 1467; it being highly probable that this bird was common to two countries lying so near to each other as Greece and Asia Minor. Turkies had so increased in England that Caius, in his account of our rarer animals, printed in 1570, omits mention of them, though he is very particular in the description of a guinea hen, stiling it *meleagris*."

In the *Book of Carving*, printed by Wynkyn de Worde, in 1513, instructions are given for cutting up a capon, or "henne of grece," by which is simply meant a fat hen; and in John Russell's *Book of Nurture*, the expression "hen of hawt grese" occurs, which, being interpreted, means plump, well fed, so that Mr. Barrington's ingenious theory must be given up.

Mr. Harting (*Ornithology*, p. 179), referring to Shakspeare's anachronism in introducing the domestic turkey in the reign of Henry IV., gives full particulars of the various names by which the bird has been known.

According to Mr. Henry Green—

"a general knowledge of the bird was at any rate spread abroad in Europe soon after the middle of the sixteenth century, for we find it figured in the emblem-books; 'one of which, Freitag's *Mythologia Ethica*, in 1579 (p. 237), furnishes a most lively and exact representation to illustrate the violated rights of hospitality." (*Shakspeare and the Emblem Writers*, 1870, p. 356.)

In the accompanying picture a stately turkey-cock is depicted advancing with spreading plumes. He is met by a fine specimen of the domestic cock, who, with lifted spur and threatening aspect, prepares to attack the intruder. Beneath the drawing is the text, "And if a stranger sojourn with thee in your land ye shall not vex him" (Lev. xix. 33).

Early travellers often confuse the Guinea-fowl with the turkey. The former is a native of Africa, and the latter of America, which difference of habitation should save them from being mistaken for each other. Francis Pretty, in his account of a voyage undertaken by Thomas Candish between the years 1585 and 1588, says:—

<small>Guinea-fowl.</small>

"We found in this place [Saint Helena] great store of guinie-cocks, which we call turkies, of colour black and white, with red heads: they are much about the same bignesse which ours be of in England: their egges be white, and as bigge as a turkies egge." (*Purchas*, vol. i. p. 70.)

This author is quite incorrect in his statement respecting the eggs of the guinea-fowl. They are not white, but light red, with small dark spots, and they are not larger than those laid by the domestic hen.

A traveller in Sierra Leone, in 1607, also mentions this bird :—

"On land are great numbers of gray parrots, as also store of guiny hennes, which are very hurtfull to their rice. This is a beautiful fowle, about the bignesse of a phesant, with parti-coloured feathers. (*Purchas*, vol. i. p. 416.)

CHAPTER X.

As if to give importance to the most prominent representative of a class which is often endowed
Vulture. with virtues beyond its merits, the second in
rank is sometimes unfairly depreciated. Thus, while the
lion is ennobled the tiger is debased. The eagle is held
up for admiration, while the vulture, its rival in size and
really its superior in usefulness, has in all ages been
regarded with dislike. Mr. Bennett observes (*Gardens of
the Zoological Society*, 1830) that, ignoring the fact that
both birds are acting alike in accordance with their
peculiar instincts, and both fulfilling a part in the
economy of nature—

"man has chosen to fix upon the one a character for bravery and
generosity, and to brand the other with the epithets of base, cowardly,
and obscene. The vulture, perhaps the most useful and certainly the
most inoffensive of birds, has been consigned to perpetual infamy,
while the eagle, in the true cant of that military romance which has
ever borne so great a sway over the passions of mankind, has been
exalted, in common with the warrior that desolates the world, as an
object of admiration, and selected as the type of military glory."

The Vulture is one of the most valuable scavengers of
the East. The repulsive nature of its food, together with
its ungainly appearance and great voracity, are some
excuse for the disgust it has inspired. From a passage
in Ben Jonson, it would appear that vultures were once

seen on our shores, unless, as Gifford suggests, the Spanish troops, which poured into the Netherlands, under D'Alva, are thus complimented :—

"That ruff of pride
About thy neck, betrays thee; and is the same
With that which the unclean birds, in seventy-seven,
Were seen to prank it with on divers coasts."
(*The Alchemist*, iv. 4.)

The ancients were by no means precise in distinguishing the species of either birds or quadrupeds. In the English translation of the Bible, the word eagle is probably substituted for the vulture in some instances. Spenser speaks of a vulture striking at a heron on the wing, not a very likely occurrence.

The vulture in Egypt and Southern Europe is not much larger than a rook. John Leo, who was probably familiar with the sight of this useful bird in the cities of Italy, was surprised to find one of the larger African species called by the same name. He says :—

"The nesir is the greatest fowl in all Africa, and exceedeth a crane in bignesse, though the bil, necke, and legs are somewhat shorter. In flying, this bird mounteth up so high into the aire, that it cannot be discerned: but at the sight of a dead carcasse it will immediately descend. This bird liveth a long time, and I myselfe have seene many of them unfeathered by reason of extreme old age : wherefore, having cast all their feathers, they returne into their nest, as if they were newly hatched, and are there nourished by the younger birds of the same kind. The Italians call it by the name of a vulture; but I thinke it to be of another kind. They nestle upon high rocks, and upon the tops of wilde and desart mountains, especially upon Mount Atlas."
(*Purchas*, vol. ii. p. 849.)

The Condor, the largest of the American vultures, derives its name from a Mexican word expressive of a keen sense of smell. It is mentioned by Joseph Acosta in his *Travels* :—

"In Peru there are birds which they call *condores*, of an exceeding greatnesse, and of such a force, that not only they will open a sheep and eate it but also a whole calfe." (*Purchas*, vol. iii. p. 965.)

Though denied by modern scientific classification the honour of heading the list of the feathered tribes, the Eagle held in earlier and more poetic times the same position among birds that the lion occupied among beasts, and was in consequence the chosen emblem of royalty in many countries.

Eagle.

The lofty flight of the eagle, beyond the range of any but the most practised archer, and quite out of the reach of the clumsy guns of this period, together with the inaccessible crags which it frequented, gave it comparative immunity from disturbance. The eagle must have therefore been far more common than at present. Sir Thomas Browne says that the great eagle was not met with in Norfolk, though several of the fen eagles were found there. Derricke, in his *Image of Irelande*, describes—

"A mighty fowle, a goodlie birde,
 Whom men doe eagle call,
This builds her nest in highest toppe
 Of all the oken tree ;
Or in the craftiest place, whereof
 In Irelande manie be."

Leland, in his *Itinerary*, tells us that an eagle built its nest every year on the side of the rock on which the Castle of Dinas Brane, near Chester, was built. This castle was, at the time he wrote, in ruins. Robert Chester speaks of—

"The princely eagle of all birds the king,
 For none but she can gaze against the sunne,
 Her eye-sight is so cleare, that in her flying
 She spies the smallest beast that ever runne,
  As swift as gun-shot using no delay,
  So swiftly doth she flie to catch her pray.

> "She brings her birds being yong into the aire,
> And sets them for to looke on Phœbus light,
> But if their eyes with gazing chance to water,
> Those she accounteth bastards, leaves them quight,
> But those that have true perfect constant eyes,
> She cherisheth, the rest she doth despise."
>
> (*Love's Martyr*, p. 118.)

Prince Edward, in 3 *Henry VI.* (ii. 1, 91), is appealed to by his brother *Richard* to prove in like fashion his royalty:—

> "Nay, if thou be that princely eagle's bird,
> Show thy descent by gazing 'gainst the sun."

Spenser refers to the notion that the eagle by bathing could renew its youth:—

> "An eagle, fresh out of the ocean wave,
> Where he hath left his plumes all hory gray,
> And deckt himselfe with fethers youthful gay,
> Like eyas-hauke up mounts unto the skies,
> His newly-budded pineons to assay,
> And marveiles at himselfe, stil as he flies."
>
> (*Faerie Queene*, I. xi. 35.)

In the English translation of the Bible a similar expression occurs: "Thy youth is renewed like the eagle's" (Psalm ciii. 5).

The eagle was evidently a favourite with Lyly, the Euphuist, who has perpetuated some curious classical lore concerning its habits. He writes, "The princely eagle, who fearing to surfet on spices, stoopeth to bite on wormwood" (*Sappho and Phaon*). "The eagle is never stricken with thunder, nor the olive with lightning" (*Galathea*). "The eagles feathers consume the feathers of all others," and "every feather of the eagle is of force to consume the beetle" (*Euphues*, p. 214). Lastly, he mentions "the precious stone, ætites, which is found in the filthy neastes of the eagle" (*Euphues*, p. 240). This stone, ætites, or eagle-stone, is a flint, which rattles on being shaken, and contains a nucleus. The story goes that the female eagle takes up this stone into her nest, while she is sitting, to prevent her eggs from becoming addled. The corrosive quality of the eagle's feathers is mentioned by other writers. Du Bartas writes:—

> "And so the princely eagles ravening plumes
> The feathers of all other fowls consumes."
>
> (Page 96.)

In heraldry the eagle ranks next in popularity to the lion as a charge. It is portrayed in different attitudes, and with a varying number of heads. It is occasionally blazoned without either beak or legs; then it is termed an allerion. According to the chroniclers, Godfrey of Boulogne, Duke of Lorraine, during the siege of Jerusalem shot three of these footless birds with an arrow. In honour of that exploit three allerions upon a bend are borne in commemoration by the Dukes of Lorraine to the present day. "It is perfectly evident," observes Mr. Planché, in commenting on this legend, "that the narrator was the party who drew the long bow, and not the noble Godfrey." The similarity of the two names, Lorraine and Allerion, probably gave rise to the story.

Ben Jonson does not often mention the eagle. He says, in one play:—

> "Every stoop he made
> Was like an eagle's at a flight of cranes:
> As I have read somewhere."
>
> (*The New Inn*, iv. 3.)

Shakspeare, on the contrary, though probably like Jonson he drew his knowledge of this "royal bird" from description, or from some tame specimens in the "costly aviaries" mentioned by Harrison, has frequent references to its power of flight, strength of vision, longevity, and other qualities, all which may be found noticed in Mr. Harting's volume.

As to synonyms for this bird, according to Harrison the eagle was frequently called the erne. He says:—

"I was once of the opinion that there was a diversitie of kind between the eagle and the erne till I perceived that our nation used the word erne in most places for the eagle." (*Holinshed*, vol. i. p. 381.)

Ben Jonson probably means the eagle when he represents the augurs watching—

"Which hand the crow cried on, how high
The vulture or the erne did fly."
(*The Masque of Augurs.*)

And again, *Godolphin* was the ancient Cornish name for the white sea-eagle, now sometimes called the erne.

Olaus Magnus thus describes the varieties of eagles found in Scandinavia:—

"There are six kinds of eagles: the first is *Herodius*, called also a gir-faulcon, the most noble bird of all, of a blew colour, tending to white, except the breast and wings, where it more evidently represents a celestial colour: she is so strong, that she will carry an eagle, and so full of animosity that if she be let fly in the ayr after four or five cranes, she will never forsake the prey, till she strike them all down to the ground one after another, and a dog bred for the sport takes them away. Nor will this gir-faulcon come down for indignation, till he takes away what is fallen. She never breeds more than one young one.

"The second noble kind after this, is that, which when she hath young ones, flyes at geese, swans, coneys, and hares chiefly. This is lesse than the gir-faulcon, of divers colours, her feathers are white, and ash-colour mingled, and she hath white feathers in her short tail.

The third, which sits on the bodies of trees, whose tops are cut off, whence it hath its name; and it is of an ash-colour; she flyes at geese and ducks, and is less in body and courage than the former two.

"The fourth, which catcheth fishes, is of divers colours under the belly, white and black on the back, and upon the bunch it hath black spots: it hath one foot like a duck, to swim with; another like the hawk, to catch the prey: she sits on trees over rivers, lying in wait for fish; and there are great multitudes of them in the northern waters.

"The fifth kind is small, and various in colour, but notable cunning, for she will carry bones into the ayr, and let them fall down upon a stone, that she may break them, and so come at the marrow.

"The sixth kind is white, and lives by flying at hares, coneys, hogs, whelpes, foxes, and such like: yet the eagle so loves her young, that she will put her self like a buckler, between her young ones and the arrow shot.

"But all the kinds of them have this property, that they wrap their eggs in fox or hare skins to be hatched, which they find by chance or else flea them themselves, and these they leave in their nests to come to maturity by heat of the sun. For they cannot always sit and stay in their nests, because their talons would grow so crooked that they would not be able to catch their prey." (*History of the Goths*, etc., p. 196.)

Kite. The Kite is sometimes called the glead; though in the English translation of Deuteronomy xiv. 13, glede and kite are mentioned separately. According to Belon, who wrote about the year 1560, an amazing number of kites used to collect in the streets of London for the sake of the refuse which was thrown into the gutters. People were forbidden to kill them, and the birds were so tame that they took their prey in the midst of the greatest crowds, after the manner of pigeons in our time. Their familiarity, however, was not quite so harmless, for they occasionally invaded the butchers' stalls, and helped themselves to what they fancied.

Gascoigne, in his *Councell to Duglasse Dive*, has the following defence of the kite:—

"The kight can weede the worme from corne and costly seedes,
 The kight can kill the mowldiwarpe, in pleasant meads that breedes,
 Out of the stately streets the kight can clense the filth,
 As men can clense the worthlesse weedes, from fruitfull fallowed tilth;
 And onely set aside the hennes poor progenie,
 I cannot see who can accuse the kight for felonie.
 The falcon, she must feede on partridge, and on quayle,
 On pigeon, plover, ducke and drake, hearne, lapwing, teale, and raile."
 (*English Poets*, vol. ii., ed. Chalmers.)

The puttock was another name for this bird. In the same poem we find:—

"A puttocke set on pearch, fast by a falcons side,
Will quickly shew it selfe a kight, as time hath often tried."

Du Bartas, in his poem on the Creation (p. 66), translated by Sylvester, mentions—

"The ravening kite, whose train doth well supply
A rudders place."

Drayton has the same idea :—

"The kite his train him guiding in the air,
Prescribes the helm, instructing how to steer."
(*The Owl.*)

In the time of Elizabeth no amusement was more universally popular than falconry. Every class could partake of it; and as the quarry pursued included almost all the wild birds, herons, wild duck, partridges, blackbirds, as well as hares, there was no difficulty in finding game. In Ben Jonson's *Every Man in his Humour* (act i. sc. 1), *Master Stephen*, a young man coming from the country to begin his career as a fashionable town gentleman, inquires immediately at his cousin's house in London—

"Uncle, afore I go in, can you tell me, an he have e'er a book of the sciences of hawking and hunting; I would fain borrow it.

Knowell. Why, I hope you will not a hawking now, will you?

Stephen. No, wusse; but I'll practise against next year, uncle. I have bought me a hawk, and a hood, and bells, and all; I lack nothing but a book to keep it by.

Knowell. O, most ridiculous!

Stephen. Nay, look you now, you are angry, uncle:—why, you know an a man have not skill in the hawking and hunting languages now-a-days, I'll not give a rush for him: they are more studied than the Greek, or the Latin."

Mr. Harting, himself an enthusiastic lover of this sport, and an advocate for its revival in our own time, has so fully described the different kinds of falcons and hawks employed, together with the terms and appliances

connected with falconry, that there is nothing to be
added so far as Shakspeare himself is concerned. The
writings of most of the poets and dramatists of the time
abound with allusions to this pastime. It is somewhat
curious that the works of Shakspeare's immediate fore-
runners, Peele, Greene, and Marlowe, should furnish
exceptions to this statement. We do not find a single
important allusion to hawks or falcons in their plays.
A highly poetical description of hawking is given by
Massinger. The terms employed, though obscure to us
from their technicality, were at that time perfectly
familiar to the audience :—

> "*Durazzo.* In the afternoon,
> For we will have variety of delights,
> We'll to the field again ; no game shall rise,
> But we'll be ready for it : if a hare, my greyhounds
> Shall make a course ; for the pie or jay, a sparhawk
> Flies from the fist; the crow so near pursued,
> Shall be compelled to seek protection under
> Our horses' bellies ; a hern put from her siege,
> And a pistol shot in her breech, shall mount
> So high that, to your view, she'll seem to soar
> Above the middle region of the air :
> A cast of haggard falcons, by me mann'd
> Eying the prey at first, appear as if
> They did turn tail ; but with their labouring wings
> Getting above her, with a thought their pinions
> Cleaving the purer element, make in,
> And by turns binds with her; the frightened fowl,
> Lying at her defence upon her back,
> With her dreadful beak awhile defers her death,
> But, by degrees forced down, we part the fray,
> And feast upon her.
> *Caldoro.* This cannot be, I grant,
> But pretty pastime.
> *Durazzo.* Pretty pastime, nephew !
> 'Tis royal sport. Then for an evening flight,
> A tiercel gentle, which I call, my masters,
> As he were sent a messenger to the moon,
> In such a place flies, as he seems to say,

See me, or see me not! The partridge sprung,
He makes his stoop; but wanting breath is forced
To cancelier; then with such speed as if
He carried lightning in his wings, he strikes
The trembling bird, who even in death appears
Proud to be made his quarry."
         (*The Guardian*, i. 1.)

To *bind with* is to seize. A hawk was said to *cancelier* when she circled once or twice in the air before she swooped down on her prey.

In the play by Thomas Heywood, *A Woman Killed with Kindness*, 1607, a quarrel during a hawking expedition forms the groundwork of the plot. In the following extract we have evidence of the care that was bestowed on details so minute as the tone of the bells attached to the falcon's legs :—

"*Charles.* So, well cast off; aloft, aloft, well flowne:
O now she takes her at the sowse, and strikes her
Downe to the earth, like a swift thunder-clap.
 Wendoll. She hath stroke ten angels out of my way.
 Francis. A hundred pound from me.
 Charles. What, faulc'ner?
 Paul. At hand, sir.
 Charles. Now she hath seis'd the fowle, and gins to plume her,
Rebecke her not; rather stand still and checke her.
So: seise her gets, her jesses, and her bels:
Away.
 Francis. My hawke kill'd too.
 Char. I, but 'twas at the querre,
Not at the mount, like mine.
 Fran. Judgement, my masters.
 Cran. Yours mist her at the ferre.
 Wend. I, but our merlin first had plum'd the fowle,
And twice renew'd her from the river too ;
Her bels, Sir Francis, had not both one waight,
Nor was one semi-tune above the other:
Mee thinkes these millaine bels do sound too full,
And spoile the mounting of your hawke.
 Char. 'Tis lost.
 Fran. I grant it not. Mine likewise seised a fowle

> Within her talents; and yeu saw her pawes
> Full of the feathers: both her petty singles,
> And her long singles, grip'd her more than other;
> The terrials of her legges were stain'd with blood:
> Not of the fowle onely she did discomfite
> Some of her feathers, but she brake away.
> Come, come, your hawke is but a rifler.
> *Char.* How?"

The dispute waxes warm, and ends in a fight between the rival sportsmen and their retainers, in which *Sir Francis* is slain.

Any bells were thought good enough for sparrow-hawks, but for goshawks those made at Milan were most highly prized. They were made partly of silver, and hence were sufficiently expensive.

Shakspeare notices these musical appendages to the falcon:—

> "Harmless Lucretia, marking what he tells,
> With trembling fear, as fowl hears falcon's bells."
>
> (*Lucrece,* line 510.)

And in a similar passage, Du Bartas writes:—

> "Eveu as a duck, that nigh some crystal brook
> Hath twice or thrice by the same hawk been strook,
> Hearing aloft her gingling silver bels,
> Quivers for fear, and looks for nothing else
> But when the falcon, stooping thunder-like,
> With sudden souse her to the ground shall strike;
> And with the stroak, make on the senseless ground
> The gutless quar, once, twice, or thrice, rebound."
>
> (Page 170.)

To return to the extract from Heywood. An explanation of some of the technical terms there used may be found in Gervase Markham's edition of *The Book of St. Albans,* 1595. The writer describes the finding of the quarry in a river or pit, and says:—

> "If shee [the hawk] *nyme,* or take, the further side of the river or pit, from you, then she slaieth the foule at *fere juttie:* but if she kill it on

that side that you are yourselfe, as many times it chanceth, then you shall say shee killed the foule at the *jutty ferry*, if your hawke nyme the foule aloft, you shall say she tooke it at *the mount*. If you see store of mallards separate from the river and feeding in the fielde, if your hawke flee covertly under hedges, or close by the ground, by which means she nymeth one of them before they can rise, you shall say, that foule was killed *at the querre*."

Guillim, in his work on heraldry, gives some of the phrases employed by falconers. This list, as the terms so constantly recur in Shakspeare and elsewhere, it may be well to quote :—

" A hawk is said to *bate*, when she striveth to fly from the fist. She is said to *rebate*, when by the motion of the bearer's hand she recovereth the fist.

" You must say, '*Feed* your hawk,' and not 'Give her meat.'

" A hawk is said, after she hath fed she *smiteth* or *sweepeth* her beak, and not wipeth her beak or bill.

" By the *beak* of an hawk is understood the upper part which is hooked; the neather part of the beak is called the hawk's *clap*. The holes in the hawk's beak are called her *nares*. The yellow between the beak and the eyes is called the *sere*. Hawks of long, small beakfeathers like hairs about the sere, are properly called *crinites*.

" You must say your hawk *jouketh*, and not sleepeth. She *mantleth*, (and not stretcheth), when she extendeth one of her wings along her legs, and so the other. After she hath thus mantled herself, she crosseth her wings together over her back, which action you shall term the *warbling* of her wings, and say, she warbleth her wings.

" You shall *cast* your hawk to the perch, and not set your hawk upon the perch." (*Display of Heraldry*, p. 218, 6th ed., 1724.)

Marco Polo, a traveller passionately fond of hawking, loses no opportunity of mentioning the falcons and hawks of the countries he explores. According to him the Tartars were most enthusiastic sportsmen, and carried on this amusement with true Eastern magnificence. In one portion of his work he describes the Khan of Tartary setting out on a hunting expedition, attended by—

" full ten thousand followers, who carry with them a vast number of gerfalcons, peregrine falcons, and sakers, as well as many vultures, in order to pursue the game along the banks of the river. It must be understood that he does not keep all this body of men together in one place, but divides them into several parties of one or two hundred or more, who follow the sport in various directions, and the greater part of what they take is brought to his majesty." (*Travels*, p. 342, ed. Marsden, 1817.)

The falconers were provided with calls and hoods, in orthodox fashion, and each hawk belonging to his Majesty, or to his nobles, had a silver label attached to its leg, by which, if lost, it could be readily identified—a refinement only occasionally adopted in Europe. Supposing the author was not exaggerating, we can easily imagine that, conducted on such a grand scale, hawking in Chinese Tartary was "unrivalled by any other amusement in the whole world."

In such honour was falconry held in old times, that in Wales the Master of the Hawks was the fourth officer in rank and dignity, and sat in the fourth place from his sovereign at the royal table. This promotion had, however, one drawback—the falconer was only permitted to drink three times lest he should neglect his birds. When he was more than usually successful in his sports the prince was obliged, by law and custom, to rise up to receive him as he entered the hall, and sometimes to hold his stirrup as he alighted from his horse.

Robert Burton tells us (*Anatomy of Melancholy*, vol. i. p. 528) that at the time in which he writes, about the year 1617—

"the ordinary sports which are used abroad, are hawking, hunting. . . . Paulus Jovius (*Descr. Brit.*) doth in some sort tax our English nobility for it, for living in the country so much, and too frequent use of it, as if they had no other means but hawking and hunting to approve themselves gentlemen with. Hawking comes neer to hunting, the one in the aire, as the other on the earth, a sport as much affected as the other, by some preferred. It was never heard of amongst the Romans, invented some 1200 years since, and first mentioned by Firmicus (lib. 5, cap. 8). The Greek emperours began it, and now nothing so frequent : he is nobody, that in the season hath not a hawke on his fist: a great art, and many books written on it. It is a wonder to hear what is related of the Turkes officers in this behalf, how many thousand men are employed about it, how many hawks of all sorts, how much is spent at Adrianople alone every year to that purpose. The Persian kings hawk after butterflies with sparrows, made to that purpose, and stares; lesser hawks for lesser games they have, and bigger for the rest, that they may produce their sport to all seasons. The Muscovian emperours reclaime eagles to fly at hindes, foxes, etc., and such a one was sent for a present to Queen Elizabeth : some reclaime ravens, castrils, pies, etc., and man them for their pleasure."

There was, however, a darker side to this amusement, which is suggested by Gifford, in a note in his edition of Massinger.

"Humanity," he writes, "has seldom obtained a greater triumph than in the abolition of this most execrable pursuit, compared to which cock-fighting and bull-baiting are innocent amusements : and this not so much on account of the game killed in the open field, as the immense number of domestic animals sacrificed to the instruction of the hawk. The blood runs cold while we peruse the calm instructions of the brutal falconer, to impale, tie down, fasten by the beak, break the legs and wings of living pigeons, hens, and sometimes herons, for the hourly exercise of the hawk, who was thus enabled to pull them to pieces without resistance." (Note to *The Picture*, vol. ii.)

Probably, with the increase of consideration for animal suffering, many of the practices Gifford condemns have been abandoned by modern falconers.

The excess to which love of hawking was occasionally carried provoked some opposition from the less extravagant portion of the community. A correspondent in *Notes and Queries* (5th series, vol. viii. p. 133) quotes a passage from a volume of sermons by a nephew of Bishop Jewell, printed at Oxford in 1633, after the death of the author :—

"Hunting, hawking are almost become essential to a gentleman, so that perhaps he defined not much amisse who said, a gentleman was a beast riding upon a beast, with a beast on his fist, having beasts following him, and himselfe following beasts."

Sir Philip Sidney is reported to have said, "Next to hunting I like hawking worst," and certainly there are few allusions to the latter sport to be met with in his poems.

The Rev. R. Lubbock (*Fauna of Norfolk*, 1845, p. 12) draws attention to the way in which, in many instances, the very nature of birds has been affected by the alteration in the manners and customs of man. This is more especially the case in the larger birds of prey :—

"The forgotten sport of falconry has left behind it abundant record of the immunity which in days of yore clung to every feathered thing which called itself a hawk; not only were the generous kinds protected, but kites and buzzards marauded in security, hiding their misdeeds under the shadow of the nobler species. In those days might fairly be seen the nature of the bird as it really was, and that in many instances appears to have been to cling to man. The wild hawks, we are told in old treatises, often paused in their flight to observe the sportsman and his dogs, and gain for themselves some of the booty which had escaped the trained bird. But amongst ourselves, a hawk when seen has the air of a convicted felon; he skulks along, conscious that every man's hand is against him; the nature of the bird is in some degree changed by the untoward circumstances in which he is placed."

One result of the indiscriminate slaughter of the hawk tribe in modern times has been, that diseased birds of the species pursued by hawks, which would otherwise have fallen easy victims in the struggle for existence, continue to exist, and so tend to deteriorate their kind.

The passage in *Hamlet*, ii. 2, 396, "I am but mad north-north-west: when the wind is southerly I know a hawk from a hernshaw," noticed by Mr. Harting (p. 75), is still further elucidated by Mr. Aldis Wright. He points out that, as the morning used to be the favourite time for the sport of hawking, when the wind blew from the northwest the birds would probably fly so that any person watching them had the sun in his eyes, and could not easily distinguish the quarry from its pursuer, but that

when the wind was southerly, the birds flew from the sun, and one could easily "know a hawk from a hernshaw."
An expression in the First Part of *Henry VI.* (i. 3, 36) has led to some discussion. Gloucester, indignant at the opposition of the turbulent prelate, Bishop of Winchester, exclaims:—

> "I'll canvass thee in thy broad cardinal's hat,
> If thou proceed in this thy insolence."

According to a writer in the *Edinburgh Review*, October, 1872—

"*canvass* was a technical name for the peculiarly constructed net with which wild hawks were snared by the falconer, in order to be manned for the fist, the flight, and the lure. At least, it was a term technically applied to catching wild hawks in this way, and to be canvassed in this sense was to be taken, trapped, or netted.

> 'That restlesse I, much like the hunted hare,
> Or as the canvist kite doth fear the snare.'
> (*Mirror for Magistrates*)."

Wild hawks were trapped by means of a net attached to a bow of iron or wood. Strings fastened to the sides of the net were held by the falconer:—

"Now," writes the reviewer, "the circular sweep of the cardinal's hat, with its knotted strings, has a not unapt resemblance to the hawk-net machinery; and Gloucester, in saying, ' I'll canvass thee in thy broad cardinal's hat,' expressed his determination to trap and seize the arrogant Churchman, if he persisted in his violent course."

For much information concerning hawking and hunting in medieval times, as well as for every subject connected with Shakspeare, the reader is referred to Dr. Drake's learned work, *Shakspeare and his Times*, published 1817, 4to.

Harrison enumerates the various kinds of hawks known in his time:— **Varieties of Hawks.**

" We have also the lanner and the lanneret: the tersell and the gosehawk: the musket and the sparhawke: the jack and the hobbie: and finally some (though very few) marlions. And these are all the hawkes that I do heare (as yet) to be bred within this iland." (*Holinshed*, vol. i. p. 381.)

Derricke, in the *Image of Ireland*, published 1581 gives the varieties of hawks found in that island:—

> "The goshauke, first of all the crewe
>   Deserves to have the name;
> The faucon next for high attemptes,
>   In glorie, and in fame.
> The tarsell then ensueth on,
>   Good reason 'tis that he,
> For flying haukes in Ireland next
>   The faucon plaste should bee.
> The tarsell gentle's course is nexte,
>   The fourthe peer of the lande,
> Combined to the faucon with
>   A lovers friendly bande.
> The pretie marlion is the fifth,
>   To her the sparhauke nexte,
> And then the jacke and musket laste,
>   By whom the birds are vexte.
> These are the haukes which cheefly breed
>   In fertile Irish grounde;
> Whose marche for flight and speedie wyng,
>   Elsewhere be hardly founde."

The peregrine was the largest of the true falcons, or long-winged hawks, found in Britain. The Ger-falcon of Iceland and Scandinavia was occasionally imported, but, owing to its great strength and fierceness, the time required for training this species rendered it so expensive that it was usually reserved for royalty. Hakluyt mentions that among the presents sent by the Czar Ivan Basiliewitz, by his ambassador, to Queen Mary, 1556, was "a large and fair white jer-fawcon, for the wild swan, crane, goose, and other great fowls."

Of Peregrines, Camden writes:—

"A noble kind of falcons have their airies here [Pembrokeshire] and breed in the rocks, which King Henry the Second, as the same Giraldus writeth, was wont to prefer before all others. For of that kind are those, if the inhabitants doe not deceive mee, which the skilful faulconers call peregrines; for they have, that I may use no other wordes than the verses of Augustus Thuanus Esmerius, that most excellent poet of our age, in that golden booke entituled *Hieracasophioy*:—

> "Head flat and low, the plume in rewes along
> The body laid: legges pale and wan are found.
> With sclender clawes and talons there among
> And those wide spred: the bill is hooked round."

Peregrine.

Marco Polo mentions peregrines as numerous in Siberia:—

"When the Grand Khan is desirous of having a brood of peregrine falcons he sends to capture them at this place; and in an island lying off the coast, gerfalcons are found in such numbers that his majesty may be supplied with as many of them as he pleases." (*Travels*, p. 221.)

The female peregrine alone was dignified with the name of falcon, the male being known as the tiercel, or tassel. The falcon was flown at herons and rooks, and the tiercel at partridges or magpies. Izaak Walton begins the first chapter of his *Complete Angler* by a conference between an angler, a falconer, and a hunter, each commending his own recreation. The falconer, after dwelling on the advantages of hawking as an amusement, proceeds to enumerate the various species of hawks, which he divides into noble and ignoble birds. He says:—

"You are to note that they are usually distinguished into two kinds; namely, the long-winged, and the short-winged hawks: of the first kind; there be chiefly in use amongst us in this nation—

> The gerfalcon and jerkin,
> The falcon and tassel gentle,

The laner and laneret,
The hockerel and bockeret,
The saker and sacaret,
The merlin and jack merlin,
The hobby and jack:
There is the stelletto of Spain,
The blood-red rook from Turkey,
The waskite from Virginia:
And there is of short-winged hawks,
The eagle and iron [erne],
The goshawk and tercel,
The sparhawk and musket,
The French pye of two sorts:

These are reckoned hawks of note and worth; but we have also of an inferior rank—

The stanyel, the ringtail,
The raven, the buzzard,
The forked kite, the bald buzzard,
The hen-driver, and others that I forbear to name."

Some confusion seems to have prevailed in the names given to the different kinds of hawks here and elsewhere. By the ringtail and hen-driver are probably meant the hen-harrier of modern times. According to Yarrell (*British Birds*, vol. i. p. 133)—

"The old male, from his almost uniform ash-grey colour, is often called provincially the dove-hawk, blue hawk, or miller, and by the general name of hen-harrier. The female, or ring-tail, is entirely different. Though it has been previously supposed by many naturalists that the hen-harrier were the male and female of the same species, others held the opinion that they were distinct, and Montagu seems to have been the first who actually and clearly proved that the remarkable difference between these two birds was but a sexual peculiarity."

The same authority informs us that *eyas*, or *nyas*, was the name of the young peregrine taken from the nest, as distinguished from the *peregrine* or *passage* hawk, a young bird caught during the period of migration; while *haggard* was used for a bird caught after the first moult was completed, and reclaimed. If kept over a moult they were then called *intermewed* hawks. The term *gentil falcon* seems to have had a general rather than a particular meaning. The bird so called by Pennant is certainly a goshawk, while the lanner of this author is a young female of the same species. When young the peregrine bears some resemblance to the lanner, which probably has never been caught in this country. The young of the year were called respectively a red falcon, and a red tiercel, on account of the ruddy tinge of their plumage. The heroner, a name sometimes met with, was probably also the peregrine. This hawk is explained by Francis Thynne, 1559, as—

"an especiall hawke of the kyndes of longe winged hawkes, of more accompte then other hawkes are, because the flighte of the herone is more dangerous then of other foules." (*Animadversions of Francis Thynne*, p. 39, ed. Furnivall.)

The true Lanner was imported from the continent, and was trained to fly at the kite. The male was called the lanneret.

Lanner.

Marco Polo frequently speaks of the lanner and the saker in his *Travels*. Of Tartary, he writes:—

"In the mountains there are falcons of the species called saker, *falco sacer*, which are excellent birds and of strong flight; as well as of that called lanner, *falco lanarius*. There are also goshawks of a perfect kind, *falco astus*, or *palumbarius*, and sparrow-hawks, *falco nisus*."

Of these two birds, the lanner and the saker, the Rev. R. Lubbock writes:—

"Two species of falcon, formerly prized, have been involved in much obscurity; the saker, which in size and courage rivalled or excelled the gyrfalcon, and the lanner, which came from Sicily, Malta, and the South and East. Temminck makes no mention of this last species in the edition of 1815. The name lanner seems to have been sometimes given to the young of the peregrine falcon, and consequently confusion arose from believing the lanner to be a British bird. After dividing the peregrine in different plumage into two or three kinds, the old treatises on hawking always add that the birds are alike in feeding, habits, and flight. But the lanner stood alone in its peculiarities: rather inferior to the peregrine in swiftness and boldness, it was noted for docility and perseverance; it hung long upon wing without fatigue, remembered the lessons taught faithfully, would make repeated flights in the same morning, and was far less nice in its food than the other; it was the hawk recommended to young and eager falconers, as being the most difficult to spoil in flight or injure in feeding." (*Fauna of Norfolk*, 1845, p. 26.)

Hobby. The Hobby was very common. It was small but beautifully shaped, docile, and easily trained. It was flown at quails, snipe, and other small birds, but chiefly at skylarks. It was also employed in taking larks alive, by the method called *daring* them. If the hobby were thrown up in a field, the larks rose and thus betrayed their nests. According to Lyly, it could "o'ermount the lark." He writes, "No bird can looke against the sunne but those that be bredde of the eagle, neither any hawks soare so high as the broode of the hobby."

Merlin. The "pretie Marlion," or Merlin, was the favourite falcon of the ladies, and of beginners in the art of hawking. One of the smallest, it was at the same time one of the handsomest species, and readily became attached to its owner. It was flown at quails, snipe, and lark, and in its mode of flight resembled the goshawk, not swooping, but closely following its prey in the rear, darting along near the surface of the ground with great rapidity.

Kestrel. The Kestrel, called also Standgale, Stannel, and Windhover, is not often mentioned. It was the hawk allotted to persons of inferior rank. The name is derived by some from *coystril*, a knave or peasant, a word which was spelt in a variety of ways. Drayton informs us that—

> "The soaring kite there scantled his large wings,
> And to the ark the hovering castril brings."
>
> (*Noah's Flood.*)

Another name by which the kestrel was known was the wind-sucker. Nashe, in his *Lenten Stuffe*, describing the expedition of the birds against the fishes, says that the former chose "the kistrilles or windsuckers, that filling themselves with winde, fly against the wind evermore, for their ful-sailed standerd bearer" (*Harleian Miscellany*, vol. vi. p. 170).

The kestrel was easily tamed, and was affectionate in captivity. It was trained to fly at small birds, though in its wild state mice were its usual food. It is not impossible that when kept in a farm-yard the kestrel might strike up an acquaintance with the pigeons that it saw daily, otherwise Reginald Scot's theory of their alliance is difficult to accept. Scot writes (*Discovery of Witchcraft*, p. 213, ed. 1634) :—

"The friendly society betwixt a fox and a serpent is almost incredible: how loving the lizzard is to a man, we may read though we cannot see. Yet some affirm that our newt is not only like to the lizzard in shape, but also in condition. From the which afection towards a man, a spaniell doth not much differ, whereof I could cite incredible stories. The amity betwixt a castrell and a pigeon is much noted among writers; and specially how the castrell defendeth her from her enemie the sparrow-hawke; whereof they say the dove is not ignorant."

Another species, the Slightfalcon, is mentioned by Dr. Giles Fletcher, in his treatise on Russia, 1588, in which he reports that in that country "they have great store of hawkes; the eagle, the gerfaulcon, the slightfaulcon, the goshawke, the tassell, the sparhawke," etc. (*Purchas*, vol. iii. p. 417).

Slightfalcon.

The Goshawk is the largest of the short-winged hawks. The male was sometimes called the tercel. It was flown at quadrupeds more frequently than at birds, chiefly hares and rabbits, and in its wild state it is quite possible that it might attempt still larger game:—

Goshawk.

"Ha, sweet Nature! What goshauk would prey upon such a lamb?"
(BEN JONSON, *Bartholomew Fair*, ii. 1.)

Though equal in size it was inferior in power to the largest of the falcons. It was not common, and was probably confounded with the peregrine. Unlike the last-named species, the goshawk does not swoop down upon its prey, but glides along the surface of the ground in pursuit of it; this mode of attack was called *raking*.

The Sparrow-hawk, now the species most commonly encountered, was then held in low estimation.

Sparrow-hawk.

It is one of the most uniformly distributed of the hawk tribe, and according to Linschoten, an early traveller, was found in the Azores:—

"The Iles of Acores, or the Flemish Ilands, are seven. They are called Acores, that is to say, Sparhawks or Hawkes, because that in their first discovery they found many sparhawks in them, whereof they hold the name, although at this day there is not any there to be found." (*Purchas*, vol. iv. p. 1667.)

This hawk was used for taking land-rails, partridges, blackbirds, and other small birds.

The Buzzard was considered too ignoble a bird to be reckoned among the hawks. Not unlike the owl in its stealthy noiseless flight, not far from the ground as a rule, it was capable of soaring to a considerable height, and of prolonged exertion. Sir Thomas Browne, in his list of Norfolk birds, gives the grey and bald buzzard.

Buzzard.

The Osprey, or Fishing-hawk, was not an uncommon bird at the mouth and along the banks of large rivers. Harrison, in his description of England, tells us that the fishing propensity of the osprey was often taken advantage of by the country people.

Osprey.

"We have," he writes, " ospraies which breed with us in parks and woods, whereby the keepers of the same doo reape in breeding time no small commoditie; for so soone almost as the yoong are hatched, they tie them to the but ends or ground ends of sundrie trees, where the old ones finding them, doo never cease to bring fish unto them which the keepers take and eat from them, and commonlie is such as is well fed, not of the worst sort. It hath not beene my hap hitherto to see anie of these foules, and partlie through mine owne negligence: but I heare that it hath one foot like an hawke to catch hold withall, and another resembling a goose wherewith to swim; but whether it be so, or not so, I refer the further search and trial thereof to some other." (*Holinshed*, vol. i. p. 382.)

The notion alluded to in the last paragraph was a laudable but unscientific attempt to explain how this bird performed the difficult feat of holding in a firm grasp such a slippery object as a live fish. Giraldus Cambrensis, 1187, is perhaps the first English authority for this assertion—that one foot of the osprey is spread open and armed with talons, while the other is close, harmless, and only fit for swimming. The worthy ecclesiastic, who never loses an opportunity of improving the occasion, and can "make a moral of the devil himself," utilizes thus ingeniously the osprey's mode of fishing:—

"In like manner, the old enemy of mankind fixes his keen eyes on us, however we may try to conceal ourselves in the troublesome waves of this present world; and ingratiating himself with us by temporal prosperity, which may be compared to the peaceable foot, the cruel spoiler then puts forth his ravenous claws to clutch miserable souls and drag them to perdition." (*Topography of Ireland*, p. 38, ed. Wright, 1863.)

> "Amongst the thickest of these several fowl
> With open eyes still sat the broad fac'd Owl." **Owl.**
> (DRAYTON, *Noah's Flood*.)

If to "give a dog a bad name and you may as well hang him" were literally true, the poor owl would have long ago ceased to exist, for never was any bird so maligned.

Mr. Harting has given many illustrations from Shakspeare, and has written fully of the various traditions which refer to the owl; little, therefore, is left to add. In the beautiful lament of *Eglamour* for his lost *Earine*, the lover bewails, in his "deep hurt phant'sie," that there was—

> "Not a voice or souud to ring her bell,
> But of that dismal pair, the scritching owl
> And buzzing hornet! hark! hark! hark! the foul
> Bird ! how she flutters with her wicker wings!
> Peace! you shall hear her scritch."
> (BEN JONSON, *The Sad Shepherd*, i. 1.)

The expression "wicker wings" probably refers to the straw colour of the owl's feathers. Daniel alludes to the rough reception which the little birds accord to their enemy if he makes his appearance in the daytime:—

> "Look how the day-hater, Minerva's bird,
> Whilst privileg'd with darkness and the night,
> Doth live secure t' himself of others fear'd :
> If but by chance discover'd in the light,
> How doth each little fowl, with envy stirr'd,
> Call him to justice, urge him with despite ;
> Summon the feathered flocks of all the wood,
> To come and scorn the tyrant of their blood."
> (*Hist. of the Civil Wars*, book ii.)

No distinction appears to have been made between the different varieties of owls. However, a passage bearing upon this point occurs in Dr. Giles Fletcher's account of Russia. He reports that in that country they have "an owle of very great bignesse, more ugly even then the owles of this countrey, with a broad face, and eares much like unto a man " (*Purchas*, vol. iii. p. 417).

CHAPTER XI.

"The Raile, which seldom comes but upon rich men's spits"—
(DRAYTON, *Polyolbion*, song xxv.)

this was probably the Water Rail, which is still a common bird. Sir Thomas Browne, writing in the seventeenth century, mentions among the land birds of Norfolk, the ralla, or rail, which he counts a dainty dish; and Leigh, somewhat later, describing the birds of Lancashire, says :—

Rail.

"The rale is a bird about the bigness of a partridge and is common in these parts, it hides it self in the grass, and is discovered by the snarling noise that it continually makes; it is very excellent food and doubtless of extraordinary nutriment." (*Nat. Hist. of Lancashire*, p. 126.)

This latter bird is the land-rail or corncrake, whose familiar cry is heard in corn lands and rich meadows, in most parts of the country.

Of the various Water Fowl frequenting the Lincolnshire fens, Drayton writes :—

"The gossander with them, my goodly fens do show
His head as ebon black, the rest as white as snow,
With whom the widgeon goes, the golden-eye, the smeath,
And in odd scatterd pits, the flags and reeds beneath;
The coot, bald, else clean black, that whiteness it doth bear
Upon her forehead star'd, the water-hen doth wear
Upon her little tail, in one small feather set.

> "The water-woosell next, all over black as jet,
> With various colours, black, green, blue, red, russet, white,
> Do yield the gazing eyes as variable delight,
> As do those sundry fowls, whose several plumes they be."
>
> (*Polyolbion*, song xxv.)

Leigh (p. 149) tells us that "the water-hen is common in ponds and meers, but not much regarded, because esteemed unpleasant food." The last bird on Drayton's list must not be mistaken for the dipper, or water-ouzel. This is a small bird allied to the thrush, that frequents the banks of streams, but is not found in marshy districts. By the water-woosell, or black bird, the little moor-hen may be meant.

Of waders, Drayton writes :—

> "And under them again (that water never take,
> But by some ditches side, or little shallow lake
> Lie dabbling night and day) the pallat-pleasing snite,
> The bidcock, and like them the redshank, that delight
> Together still to be, in some small reedy bed,
> In which these little fowls in summer's time were bred."

Snipe. Thomas Muffett (*Healths Improvement*, p. 96) mentions the Snipe, or Snite—

"a kind of wood-snite in Devonshire, greater then the common snite, which never comes into shallows nor springs of water: and in Holland I remember snites never living out of springs, as great almost as our woodcocks, called *heeren-schneffs*, because they are in comparison the lords or chief of snites, or that they are onely fit for lords tables."

Woodcock. The habits of the Woodcock are somewhat eccentric. These birds may be found in great plenty one day and the next not one can be seen. This peculiarity is noticed in an article in the *Harleian Miscellany* (vol. ii. p. 583) :—

"In woodcocks especially it is remarkable that upon a change of the wind to the east, about Alhallows-tide, they will seem to have come all in a night; for though the former day none are to be found, yet the next morning they will be in every bush. I speak of the west of England, where they are most plentiful."

Though not valued now as an article of food, the name of the Redshank appears in the early lists of provisions. Sir Thomas Browne says this bird was plentiful in his day in the marshes, and "of common food, but no dainty dish." At the end of the seventeenth century redshanks were reported to be common in Lancashire, but the depredations committed on their nests during the breeding season have greatly diminished their numbers.

Redshank.

> "The long neck'd hern, there watching by the brim,
> And in a gutter near again to him
> The bidling snite, the plover on the moor,
> The curlew, scratching in the ouse and ore."
> (DRAYTON, *The Man in the Moon.*)

Our ancestors seem to have been chiefly indebted for the delicacies of the table to the various species of fowl supplied by the marshy parts of this island, which were then of much greater extent than they are to-day. In the L'Estrange *Accounts* we find curlews ranking first in importance. Pheasants and partridges were apparently less prized, as they were probably more easily procured.

The Rev. R. Lubbock (*Fauna of Norfolk*) points out that from the position Norfolk occupies, jutting out as it does as a refuge from storms for the weary flights of passage birds, and also from the variety of soil which that county presents, it must have literally swarmed with different species of water fowl. He notices also the curious omission of any account of this district amongst older writers on natural history. Sir Thomas Browne's careful list of the birds found there was not written until the middle of the seventeenth century.

Leigh, in his *Natural History of Lancashire*, 1700, speaks of two sorts of Curlews, "the curlew and the curlew-hilp, these are the larger, and not very unlike the woodcock; they frequent the sea-coasts, and are very good meat."

Curlew.

Shakspeare has no mention of the curlew, but, as he was a dweller in a midland county, this omission is easily explained.

Any peculiarity of bird or animal was sure to lead to the investment of its possessor with some supernatural qualities, and the curlew was no exception to this rule. Sir J. Emerson Tennent remarks that—

"the prayer for protection against 'witches and warlocks, and langnebbed things,' is familiar amongst the peasantry of Scotland, by whom it has also been implanted in the folk-lore of Ulster. The word whaap, which is the popular name of the curlew, a bird notorious for the length of its bill, is also the term used to signify a hobgoblin; which, as Jamieson says in his Scottish Dictionary, is believed to have a long beak, and to haunt the eaves of houses after nightfall. Wright, in his *History of Caricature and Grotesque*, has given numerous examples from the 16th to the 18th century, in which the artists have always combined a prolonged beak with the other attributes of demons." (*Notes and Queries*, 3rd series, vol. vii. p. 334.)

Another correspondent in this periodical, quoting Waring, mentions a different mode by which the curlew inspired dread among the benighted peasantry:—

"Mr. William Weston Young describes the nocturnal cry of a flight of curlews as not unlike the cry of hounds and huntsmen in full chase. This sound, heard at night, and in desolate places, might well cause terror. The *cwn wybr*, dogs of the sky, otherwise called *cwn annwn*, dogs of hell, are imaginary spirits of the same family as the diabolical sky hunts of German demonology." (Page 404.)

"The whistler shrill that whoso hears doth die," referred to by Spenser, may be either the curlew, or the green or golden plover, whose shrill cry sounds more like a human note than that of a bird, and may well startle the belated traveller.

In the early works on diet and housekeeping, a bird called a brew, or brewe, frequently appears, generally in close proximity to the curlew. **Whimbrel.** The word Brew has by some writers been explained to mean the Whimbrel, a bird sometimes called, from its resemblance to the last-named species, the Half-curlew or Jack-curlew.

According to Mr. Stevenson (*Birds of Norfolk*), the word *spowe*, which frequently occurs in the early lists of birds for the table, was also a name given to the whimbrel. In the L'Estrange *Accounts* spowes are nearly always mentioned in connexion with other shore birds, such as knots, ring-dotterels, and redshanks. By Bishop Stanley the word *spowe* is considered to mean sparrow.*

The name given to the whimbrel in the Shetland Islands is the tang-whaap, or small curlew.

The Ruff and Reeve were sometimes called Oxen and Kine. The male is during the spring months adorned with a handsome ruff of feathers **Ruff and Reeve.** round its neck, which it can erect or depress at pleasure. Sir Thomas Browne notices another peculiarity of this bird, which is that no two specimens are taken exactly similar in colour:—

"*Ruffe*, a marsh bird of the greatest variety of colour; every one therein somewhat varying from other. The female is called a *reeve*, without any ruff about the neck, lesser than the other, and hardly to be got. They abound mostly in Marshland." (Vol. iv. p. 319.)

The Knot, Gnat-snap, or Canute's bird, was esteemed a great delicacy. It was found in large numbers at the mouth of tidal rivers. Sir Thomas **Knot.** Browne writes:—

"The gnat, or knot, a small bird, which, taken with nets, grow excessively fat, being mewed and fed with corn. A candle

---

* See page 201.

lighted in the room, they feed night and day, and when they are at their height of fatness they begin to grow lame, and are then killed, as at their prime and apt to decline." (Vol. iv. p. 140).

The knot is mentioned by Drayton :—

> "The knot, that called was Canutus' bird of old,
> Of that great king of Danes, his name that still doth hold,
> His appetite to please, that far and near was sought,
> For him, as some have said, from Denmark hither brought."
> (*Polyolbion*, song xxv.)

Du Bartas (p. 45) speaks of—

> "The little gnat-snap, worthy princes' boords."

And his commentator adds, "This is the fig-pecker, which the Latines call *ficedula*, and *scalis*, very delicious" (*Learned Summary on Du Bartas*, p. 235).

> "The puet, Godwit, stint, the palate that allure
> The miser, and do make the wasteful epicure."
> (*Polyolbion*, song xxv.)

Godwit. Sir Thomas Browne accounts the godwit the daintiest bird taken in England, and, for its size, the biggest price. According to this author the stint was found plentifully in Marshland, in Norfolk; also the shurr, or purre, a bird "somewhat larger than stints, and taken among them." The purre, or perr, was another name for the dunlin, the commonest of the shore-frequenting sandpipers.

Plover. In the palmy days of water-loving birds, and those species that delighted in heathy open country, Plovers must have been found in great abundance. Drayton tells us that in the marshy lands about Axholme, in Lincolnshire, plovers were plentiful:—

> "For neare this batning isle in me is to be seen
> More than on any earth, the plover, gray, and green."
> (*Polyolbion*, song xxv.)

A Delicacy.

Spenser introduces this bird as denoting loneliness and desolation :—

> "Where my high steeples whilom used to stand,
> On which the lordly falcon wont to towre,
> There now is but a heap of lyme and sand
> For the scriche-owle to build her baleful bowre :
> And where the nightingale wont forth to powre
> Her restless plaints to comfort wakeful lovers,
> There now haunt yelling mewes and whining plovers."
> (*The Ruines of Time*, 1. 127.)

Harrison mentions "plovers of both sorts, lapwings and pewets;" but Skelton classes these last two varieties together "with puwytt the lapwing." Sir Thomas Browne distinguishes between the plover and the lapwing or vanellus; the former, he says, are plentiful in Norfolk, both the green and grey varieties, but "they do not breed in that county but in some parts of Scotland and plentifully in Iceland." Mr. Stevenson (*Birds of Norfolk*, vol. ii. p. 70) considers that by Iceland Ireland is here intended, but gives no reason for this supposition.

The ringed plover, mentioned by Sir Thomas Browne under the name of ringlestone, was "common about Yarmouth sands, laying its eggs, about June, in the sand and shingle" (vol. iv. p. 319). The name Sea-dotterel was also applied to this plover, and occurs in two instances in the Hunstanton *Accounts*. The white plover which is also mentioned in these *Accounts* was probably the grey plover in its winter plumage.

The proverb quoted by Muffett, in his *Healths Improvement*, as applied to a discontented person, "A gray plover cannot please him," shows that this bird was held in high estimation as an article of food.

"There is also," writes Sir Thomas Browne, "a handsome, tall bird, remarkable eyed, and with a bill not above two inches long, commonly called a stone curlew, breeds about Thetford, about the stone and shingle of the rivers."

Other names for this bird are the Norfolk plover or thick-kneed bustard.

The green plover, lapwing, tyrwhit, or peewit is often referred to, chiefly on account of its peculiar appearance, monotonous wail, and from its habit of attempting to divert the attention of passers-by from its nest by plaintive cries. Mr. Harting has given several quotations illustrating this peculiarity, to which may be added an extract from Chester :—

> " The lapwing hath a piteous mournefull cry,
> And sings a sorrowfull and heavy song,
> But yet shee's full of craft and subtility,
> And weepeth most being farthest from her yong :
> In elder age she serv'd for soothsayers,
> And was a prophetesse to the augurers."
>
> (*Love's Martyr*, p. 119.)

Olaus Magnus writes an account of this plover, to which he also gives the name of the whonp :—

" Lapwings, when at a set-time they come to the northern countries from other parts, they fore-shew the nearnesse of the spring coming on. It is a bird that is full of crying and lamenting to preserve her eggs, or young. By importunate crying she shews that foxes lye hid in the grasse ; and so she cries out in all places, to drive away dogs, and other beasts. Made tame, she will cleanse a house of flyes, and catch mice. She foreshows rain when she cries." (Page 205.)

As a delicacy for the table, the peewit seems to have been highly prized, and its name often occurs in the household accounts of this period.

The note of every variety of plover is a shrill, human-like whistle. In his *English Folk-lore*, 1878 (p. 95), Mr. Dyer informs us that—

" there is a Lancashire superstition which identifies the plover with the transmuted soul of a Jew. When seven of them are seen together, they are called the ' seven whistlers,' and their sound, it is said, foretells misfortune to those who hear it. A correspondent of *Notes and Queries* thus alludes to this odd piece of superstition : ' One evening a few years ago, when crossing one of our Lancashire moors, in company with an intelligent old man, we were suddenly startled by the whistling overhead of a covey of plovers. My companion remarked that, when a boy, the old people considered such a circumstance a bad omen, "as the person who heard the wandering Jews," as he called the plovers, "was sure to be overtaken with some ill-luck."'"

Closely allied to the plover is "the Dotterell, that foolish peck" (Skelton, *Boke of Philip Sparow*):— **Dotterel.**

"which being a kind of bird as it were of an apish kind, ready to imitate what they see done, are caught according to foulers gesture: if he put forth an arme, they also stretch out a wing: sets he forward his legge, or holdeth up his head, they likewise doe theirs; in briefe, whatever the fouler doth, the same also doth this foolish bird untill it be hidden within the net." (*Camden*, on Lincolnshire.)

There is a passage in Drayton's *Polyolbion*, so similar to the above as to suggest plagiarism on the part of one author:—

"The dotterel, which we think a very dainty dish,
Whose taking makes such sport, as man no more can wish;
For as you creep, or cowr, or lie, or stoop, or go,
So marking you with care the apish bird doth go,
And acting everything, doth never mark the net,
Till he be in the snare, which men for him have set."
(*Polyolbion*, song xxv.)

Ben Jonson writes:—

"Bid him put off his hopes of straw, and leave
To spread his nets in view thus. Though they take
Master Fitzdottrel, I am no such foul,
Nor, fair one, tell him, will be had with stalking."
(*The Devil is an Ass*, ii. 1.)

The Oyster-catcher, or Sea-pye, was apparently an abundant species. Leigh, in his *Natural History of Lancashire*, writes: "The sea-pyes are very common, they are birds of the colour and about the size of a magpie, and are a very agreeable food" (p. 163). That this was the prevailing opinion is **Oyster-catcher.**

evident from sea-pyes being included in the bill of fare on state occasions. An entry occurs in the *Northumberland Household Book*, " Item, see-pyes for my lorde at princypall feastes and none other tyme."

Mr. Stevenson considers the name oyster-catcher a misnomer for this bird, as it chiefly lives on limpets, mussels, and whelks, which it strikes off the rock with its " blunt-pointed, flat-sided beak, hammer and chisel in one " (*Birds of Norfolk*, 1866, vol. ii. p. 124). William Browne gives a quaint description of the mode in which a shore bird obtains its prey. He does not mention any name, but his description can hardly apply to any other species than the oyster-catcher:—

" On the sand she spyes,
A busie bird, that to and fro still flyes,
Till pitching where a hatefull oyster lay,
Opening his close jawes, closer none than they
Unlesse the griping fist, or cherry lips
Of happy lovers in their melting sips.
Since the decreasing waves had left him there,
He gapes for thirst, yet meetes with nought but ayre,
And that so hote, ere the returning tyde
He in his shell is likely to be fride;
The wary bird, a prittie pibble takes,
And claps it 'twixt the two pearle-hiding flakes
Of the broad-yawning oyster, and she then
Securely pickes the fish out, as some men
A tricke of policie thrust 'tweene two friends,
Sever their powres, and his intention ends."
(*Britannia's Pastorals*, book ii. song iii.)

" The big-bon'd Bustard then, whose body bears that size,
That he against the wind must run, e'er he can rise "
(DRAYTON, *Polyolbion*, song xxv.),

Bustard. must have been the most conspicuous inhabitant of corn and pasture lands. As late as Sir Thomas Browne's time (1660), it was " not unfrequent in the champian and fieldy part of the country."

The large dimensions of the bustard, its habit of

making a nest in young corn, and the small number of the eggs, the hen only laying two at a time, all contributed to its extinction. Its protection lay chiefly in the choice which it made for its abode of open country. As long as the crossbow was the principal weapon of the sportsman, the wide expanse of country over which this bird could look must have enabled it to see and escape danger; but the practice of making small plantations at intervals as screens against the force of the wind, which was adopted for many years in Norfolk, afforded opportunities for approach by the hunter, which no amount of watchfulness on the part of the unfortunate bird could contend against. Mr. Stevenson, in his *Birds of Norfolk* (1866), has an interesting chapter on the bustard, and the gradual process of its extermination.

Shakspeare has no mention of this bird. Coming from a part of the country so well wooded as Warwickshire, he probably had no opportunity of seeing it in his early days.

Thomas Muffett tells us that bustards were called by the Scots *gusestards*, that is to say, "slow geese;" that they fed upon flesh and young lambs out of sowing time, and in harvest time on the ripe corn. He says he has seen as many as six lying in a wheat-field in the summer (*Healths Improvement*, p. 91, ed. 1655).

The Crane, now only an occasional visitor to our coasts, was once indigenous, frequenting the fens of Lancashire and Cambridgeshire in large flocks. Drayton, describing the marshes of the former county, writes:—

Crane.

"There stalks the stately crane, as though he merch'd in war."
(*Polyolbion*, song xxv.)

By an Act of Parliament (25 Henry VIII., 1533), a fine of twenty pence was imposed on every person who should "withdraw, purloin, take, destroy, or convey," any egg of this species.

In Sir Thomas Browne's time, cranes seem to have grown scarce. He says:—

"Cranes are often seen here in hard winters, especially about the champian and fieldy parts, but it seems they have been more plentiful, for in a bill of fare, when the mayor entertained the Duke of Norfolk I meet with cranes in a dish." (Vol. iv. p. 314.)

The crane was a customary dish at great entertainments in the reign of Henry VIII., though it is not improbable that cranes were often confounded in the records with herons.

The crowned African crane was first brought into Europe by the Portuguese in the fifteenth century. It is a native of Africa, particularly of the coast of Guinea, the Gold Coast, and as far as Cape Verd.

Marco Polo, one of the earliest travellers, whose works were much read in the Middle Ages, writing of Tartary at the close of the thirteenth century, describes some birds of gorgeous hues, that he calls cranes:—

"The first sort are entirely black as crows, and have long wings. The second sort have wings still longer than the first, but are white and the feathers of the wings are full of eyes, round like those of the peacock, but of a gold colour and very bright; the head is red and black and well-formed, the neck is black and white, and the general appearance of the bird is extremely handsome. The third sort are of the size of ours in Italy, the fourth are small cranes, having the feathers prettily streaked with red and azure. The fifth are of a grey colour, with the head red and black, and are of a large size." (*Travels*, p. 248, ed. Marsden.)

The Portuguese Friar, whose travels in Africa in 1586 are recorded in Purchas's *Collection*, probably describes the crowned crane in the following passage:—

"They have one kinde of fowles, called *curvanes*, as bigge as cranes, but more beautiful, the back like black sattin, exceeding white on the belly and breast: the neck two spannes and a halfe long, covered with fine white feathers like silke, which are excellent for plumes: upon the head it hath a cap of black feathers, very faire (as our gold finches have red), and in the midst thereof a crest or plume almost a span long, of white, fine, straight feathers, equall on the top, and there spreading themselves into a round forme, like a very white mushroom with a white stalke, and resembling a *sombrero de sol* (or Indian canopie) to keepe off the sunne. The Cafars call this the king of birds, because their kings have such a sombreiro, and for the greatnesse and beauty of them." (*Purchas*, vol. ii. p. 1545.)

There was a notion, derived from antiquity, that cranes during their migrations carried stones in their beaks to keep them quiet. According to Pliny, the stone acted as ballast and maintained the steadiness of their flight. Lyly alludes to this notion : " Having alwayes the stone in their mouths which the cranes use when they flye over mountaines least they make a noise" (*Euphues,* p. 416).

Du Bartas gives a description of the passage of a herd of cranes, more remarkable for its minuteness than for its poetry:—

"I hear the crane, if I mistake not, cry
Who in the clouds forming the forked Y,
By the brave orders practiz'd under her,
Instructeth souldiers in the art of war.
For when her troops of wandring cranes forsake
Frost-firmed Strymon, and (in autumn) take
Truce with the northern dwarfs, to seek adventure
In southern climates for a milder winter;
A front each band a forward captain flies,
Whose pointed bill cuts passage through the skies;
Two skilful sergeants keep the ranks aright,
And with their voyce hasten their tardy flight;
And when the honey of care-charming sleep
Sweetly begins through all their veines to creep
One keeps the watch, and ever carefull-most,
Walks many a round about the sleeping hoast,
Still holding in his claw a stony clod,
Whose fall may wake him if he hap to nod.
Another doth as much, a third, a fourth,
Untill, by turns the night be turned forth."

(Page 46.)

Shakspeare has no mention of the crane.

Mr. Harting gives a long and animated description, from Freeman and Salvin's work on falconry, of the sport of Heron-hawking. It is somewhat curious that Shakspeare, notwithstanding his evident love of hawking, and his intimate knowledge of the terms employed in this sport, should not once make mention of the heron by name, except in the disputed "handsaw" passage.

Heron.

Bearing somewhat the same relation to the recreation of the nobles of the Tudor period as the fox does to the hunting squires of our own times, "the heron so gaunt" was of course carefully preserved, and with about the same amount of consideration for its personal feelings. A law was passed forbidding the capture of herons except by means of hawking, or with the long bow.

There is much variety in the spelling of the name of this bird—harnsey, heronsewe, hornseu, hernshaw, hern, and heyronsewe, all being met with.

The heron was esteemed a great delicacy, and stood at the head of the game course at every state banquet. The price of an egret, or dwarf heron, in the time of Edward I., was eighteen pence, the very highest assessed price of water fowl in those days.

In the accounts of the great feasts of the Tudor period the word *egret* or *egritte* sometimes appears, and in the time of Henry IV. it is said that a thousand egrets were served up at a single entertainment. It has been suggested that lapwings were here intended, this name being given to them from the aigrette, or tuft of feathers forming the crest, which this bird possesses. This is possible as far as this particular entry is considered, but in John Russell's *Boke of Nurture*, 1450, among the instructions as to how various dishes are served and seasoned, we find:—

"Sauce gamelyn to heyron-sewe, egret, crane and plover,
Also brewe, curlew, sugre and salt, with watere of the ryvere,

Gamelyn Sauce.

Also for bustard, betowre and shovelere, gamelyu is iu sesoun;
Wodcok, lapewynk, mertenet, larke and venysoun,
Sparows, thrusches, all these seven with salt and synamon."
(*Babees Book*, p. 36, ed. Furnivall, 1868.)

Gamelyn, or *cameline*, we are told, was a dainty Italian sauce, composed of nuts, bread-crumbs, ginger, cinnamon and vinegar. From the egret being placed between heron and crane a large bird is evidently meant, and as mention of plover and lapwing occurs later on, the name cannot be used in mistake for the name of one of these. In a work on carving the different joints, printed by Wynkyn de Worde, 1413, the egret has its place after the heron and bittern.

Muffett, in his *Healths Improvement*, p. 93, speaks of four kinds of herons or heronshaws—the black, white, criel-heronshaw, and the mire-dromble. Sir John Hawkins, in his account of the fowls frequenting the waters of Florida, mentions—

"an egript, which is all white as the swanne, with legs like to an hearnshaw, and of bignesse accordingly, but it hath in her taile feathers of so fine a plume, that it passeth the estridge his feather."
(*Hakluyt*, vol. iii. p. 616.)

Ben Jonson gives the heron as an attendant upon the goddess of wisdom, on the authority of Homer :—

"Minerva's hernshaw, and her owl,
 Do both proclaim thou shalt control
 The course of things."
(*The Masque of Augurs.*)

Vows were often made on the heron, as well as upon the peacock, swan, and pheasant.

Another favourite quarry in hawking was the Bitter, Bittour, Betowre, or Bittern, then abundant, but now only occasionally seen. Sir Thomas Browne states that it was common in his time. It was esteemed a choicer dish than the heron. The booming

Bittern.

cry which the bittern gives out was imagined to be due to the bird burying its beak in the mud, or inserting it in a hollow reed; but modern observers have borne witness to the fact that the bittern, when it utters its note, raises its bill perpendicularly.

Drayton describes how—

" The buzzing bitter sits, which through his hollow bill
A sudden bellowing sends, which many times doth fill
The neighbouring marsh with noise, as though a bull did roar."
(*Polyolbion*, song xxv.)

Shoveler.
" The Shovelar with his brode beck.'
(SKELTON, *Philip Sparow*.)

" The shouler, which so shakes the air with saily wings,
That ever as he flies, you still would think he sings."
(DRAYTON, *Polyolbion*, song xxv.)

The word *shovellewre*, or *shovelar*, has been interpreted by some authors as designating a variety of duck, and by others as denoting the white spoonbill, a bird now only an occasional visitor to our shores. Sir Thomas Browne, in his account of the birds of Norfolk, mentions—

" the platea, or shovelard, which build upon the tops of high trees. They formerly built in the hernery at Clayton and Reedham, now at Trimley, in Suffolk. They come in March, and are shot by fowlers, not for their meat, but for the handsomeness of the same; remarkable in their white colour, copped crown, and spoon or spatule-like bill." (Vol. iv.)

Olaus Magnus, in his work on Norway and Sweden (p. 200), writes:—

" There is a bird called a shevelar that is in the Northern waters, that is a cruel enemy to birds that dive in the sea to catch fish: wherefore she lyes in wait for them thus: she flyes upon them, and bites their heads, and rends them till she hath got the prey for herself; and they, thus tormented, soon let it go."

As he does not describe the bird, it is impossible to identify the species. The work was originally written in

Latin, and the name here given to it may have been invented by the translator.

The name of the shovelard, variously spelt, appears frequently in the lists of birds served up at banquets. It has often been observed that our ancestors seem to have eaten with relish many birds that in our time would be considered as tough and worthless. It may be that their outdoor life gave an edge to their teeth as well as to their appetite. In Wynkyn de Worde's *Boke of Kervynge*, 1413, the following instructions are given:—" Pecocke, storke, bustarde, and shovyllarde, unlace them as a crane, and let the feet be on styll " (*Babees Book*, p. 159, ed. Furnivall, 1868).

Robert Laneham, writing of the preparations made for the entertainment of Queen Elizabeth at Kenilworth, describes with some exactness a couple of aviaries, which, if they held all the varieties named, must have been rather crowded. He says:—

"Upon the first pair of posts [of the bridge] were set two comely square wire cages, three feet long and two feet wide, and high in them live bitterns, curlews, shovelers, hernshaws, godwits, and such like dainty birds of the presents of Sylvanus the god of fowl."

The White Stork, never at any time a resident in this country, was an occasional visitor, and was probably driven to our shores by stress of weather. From the earliest times the stork has been regarded with respect as the emblem of temperance, fidelity, and filial affection. The ancient Egyptians reverenced the stork on account of the great services it performed in acting as scavenger, and among the Hebrews also it received respect. Drayton writes:—

Stork.

> "The careful stork, since Adam wondered at
> For thankfulness to those where he doth breed,
> That his ag'd parents naturally doth feed,
> In filial duty as instructing man."
>
> (*Noah's Flood*.)

The Dutch held the belief that the stork, in leaving a house where she had been encouraged to build, left one of her young ones behind for the owner. If this were the case, the mother made but a poor return for her offspring's affection. The kindness with which the bird is treated in Holland is repaid by confidence and familiarity—a pair of birds returning year after year to the same nest.

Spenser makes the curious mistake of giving the stork a voice:—

> "Let not the skriech-owle nor the storke be heard,
> Nor the night-raven, that still deadly yells."
>
> (*Epithalamion*, l. 435.)

The only sound it utters is the sharp snap of its beak, a noise not unlike the rattle of a pair of castanets.

CHAPTER XII.

WILD Geese were very abundant in several counties, and, according to Camden, were the source of much profit to the native population. In his description of the country near Haddington, in Scotland, Camden exclaims:—

Goose.

"What a multitude of sea foules, and especially of those geese which they call scoutes and soland geese flocke hither at their times, for, by report, their number is such, that in a cleere day they take away the sunnes light; what a sort of fishes they bring, for, as the speech goeth, a hundred garison souldiours that here lay for the defense of the place fed upon no other meat but the fresh fish that they brought in; what a quantity of little twigges they get together for the building of their nests, so that by their means the inhabitants are abundantly provided of fewell for their fire; what a mighty gaine groweth by their fethers and oyle: the report thereof is so incredible, that no man scarcely would beleeve it, but he that had seene it."

The same authority relates the strange effect which certain portions of ground had on these birds, more especially in the neighbourhood of the Abbey of St. Hilda, near Whitby, in Yorkshire. To the influence of the abbess, he writes—

"they ascribe, that those wilde geese, which in wintertime flie by flockes unto pooles and rivers that are not frozen over, in the south partes; whiles they flie over certaine fields neere adjoyning, soudainely fall downe to the ground, to the exceeding great admiration of all men: a thing that I would not have related, had I not heard it from very many persons of right good credit. But such as are not given to superstitious credulity, attribute this unto a secret property of the ground, and to a hidden dissent betweene this soile and those geese, such as is betweene wolves and squilla root."

Drayton gives a similar report, in verse, as to the multitude of geese which frequented the fens of Lincolnshire:—

> "And with my wondrous flocks of wildgeese come I then,
> Which look as though alone they peopled all the fen,
> Which here in winter time, when all is overflow'd
> And want of solid sward inforceth them abroad,
> Th' abundance then is seen, that my full fens do yield,
> That almost through the isle, do pester every field.
> The barnacles with them, which wheresoe'er they breed,
> On trees, or rotten ships, yet to my fens for feed
> Continually they come, and chief abode do make,
> And very hardly forc'd my plenty to forsake."
>
> (*Polyolbion*, song xxv.)

John Taylor, "the Water Poet," in his *Penniless Pilgrimage*, or account of a tour through Scotland, makes mention of the Solan goose, a variety which still breeds in great numbers on the Bass Rock, in the Frith of Forth:—

> "It is very good flesh, but it is eaten in the form as we eat oysters, standing at a sideboard, a little before dinner, unsanctified without grace; and after it is eaten, it must be well liquored with two or three good rouses of sherry or canary sack. The lord or owner of the Bass Rock doth profit at the least two hundred pounds yearly by those geese; the Bass itself being of a great height and near three quarters of a mile in compass, all fully replenished with wild fowl, having but one small entrance into it, with a house, a garden, and a chapel in it; and on the top of it a well of pure water." (*Works*, p. 60, ed. Hindley, 1872.)

The tame goose was considered to act as a guard against thieves, being a light sleeper and very clamorous if disturbed.

The origin of the custom of having goose for dinner

on Michaelmas Day is still involved in obscurity, notwithstanding much learned discussion on the subject. It certainly dates as far back in English history as the reign of Edward IV. The tradition which assigns the choice of this dish on the 29th of September to the delight of Queen Elizabeth on hearing the news of the destruction of the Spanish Armada is still pertinaciously believed, despite the well-known fact that the date of the victory was the 21st of July. It is more likely that the habit of eating goose on Michaelmas Day arose from the fact that the 29th of September was a great festival. Geese were then plentiful and in full season, and would therefore be chosen as the chief article of diet.

Mr. Harting has referred at some length to the strange notion, so often alluded to by writers of this period, that the Barnacle Goose was produced, according to some authors, from trees, according to others from rotten wood. Camden, it would appear, was too enlightened to adopt either of these theories, though he was not quite prepared with a satisfactory solution of the curious resemblance between the bird and the marine production. In his work on Britain he writes:—

Barnacle.

"Concerning these claike geese, which some with much admiration have believed to grow out of trees, both upon this shore and else where, and when they be ripe to fall downe into the sea, it is scarce worth the labour to mention them. That there be little birds engendered of old and rotten keeles of ships, they can beare witnesse who saw that ship wherein Francis Drake sailed about the world, standing in a docke neere the Tavish, to the outside of the keele whereof a number of such little birds without life and fethers sticke close. Yet would I gladly thinke that the generation of these birds was not out of those logges of wood; but from the very ocean, which the poets termed the father of all things."

The barnacle or brent goose was often seen in great numbers in the north of England and Scotland, but its breeding-place was unknown. Gerat de Veer, in the description of a voyage to Cathay and China, 1596, takes credit to himself for giving the first account of its haunts. Speaking of the barnacles, he writes:—

"Those geese were of a perfit red colour, such as come into Holland about Weiringen, and every yeere are there taken in abundance, but till this time it was never knowne where they hatcht their egges, so that some men have taken upon them to write, that they sit upon trees in Scotland that hang over the water, and such egges as fall from them downe into the water become young geese, and swim there out of the water; but those that fall upon the land burst asunder and are lost : but this is now found to be contrary, and it is not to be wondered at, that no man could tell where they breed their egges, for that no man that ever wee knew, had ever beene under 80 degrees : nor that land under 80 degrees was never set downe in any card, much lesse the red geese that breed therein." (*Purchas*, vol. iii. p. 484.)

The pains that Harrison took to fathom the great barnacle mystery entitles him to be quoted, at the risk of exhausting the reader's patience. He writes, in his description of England prefixed to *Holinshed's Chronicles*:—

"For my part I have been verie desirous to understand the uttermost of the breeding of barnacles, and questioned with divers persons about the same. I have read also whatsoever is written by forren authors touching the generation of that foule, and sought out some places where I have beene assured to see great numbers of them: but in vaine. Wherefore I utterlie despaired to obteine my purpose, till this present yeare of grace 1584, and moneth of Maie, wherein going to the Court at Greenewich from London by bote, I saw sundrie ships lieng in the Thames newlie come home, either from Barbarie or the Canarie Iles (for I doo not well remember now from which of these places) on whose sides I perceived an infinit sort of shells to hang so thicke as could be one by another. Drawing neere also, I tooke off ten or twelve of the greatest of them, and afterward having opened them, I saw the proportion of a foule in one of them more perfectlie than in all the rest, saving that the head was not yet formed, bicause the fresh water had killed them all (as I take it) and thereby hindered their perfection. Certeinlie the feathers of the taile hoong out of the shell at least two inches, the wings almost perfect touching forme were garded with two shels or sheeldes proportioned like the selfe wings, and likewise the brestbone had hir coverture also of like shellie substance, and altogither resembling the figure which Lobell and Pena doo give foorth in their description of this foule: so that I am now fullie persuaded that it is either the barnacle that is ingendred after one maner in these shels, or some other sea-foule to us as yet unknowen. For by the feathers appearing and forme so apparent, it cannot be denied, but that some bird or other must proceed of this substance, which by falling from the sides of the ships in long voiages, may come to some perfection." (*Holinshed*, vol. i. p. 67.)

Du Bartas puts into verse the theory of the various transformations of this bird:—

> " So, slowe Boôtes underneath him sees,
> In th' ycie iles, those goslings hatcht of trees;
> Whose fruitfull leaves, falling into the water,
> Are turn'd (they say) to living fowls soon after.
> So, rotten sides of broken ships do change
> To barnacles; O transformation strange!
> 'Twas first a green tree, then a gallant hull,
> Lately a mushroom, now a flying gull."
>
> (Page 58.)

Before we find fault with our ancestors for their credulity in regard to matters now clearly understood by us, it will be well to consider if we ourselves are not daily making mistakes almost as ridiculous, mistakes which the enlightenment of after ages will have to correct.

Mr. Harting inquires, " When men of education are so credulous, how can we wonder at the superstitions of the illiterate ? " Surely the resemblance of a barnacle to a young bird was strong enough to justify the idea, in the absence of any other suggestion, that there was some connexion between them. Nor must we forget that only within quite recent times have our men of science made the discovery that the infant cirripedia are very different in appearance from their parents. Instead of being affixed to rocks or ships, they possess and use organs for locomotion, and move rapidly through the water. A strange similarity caused our ancestors to confuse the barnacle with the bird; a curious difference has till recently prevented our contemporaries from recognizing the relationship between the barnacle and its young. One error is hardly worse than the other.

An early mention of the Booby, a bird closely allied to the Gannet or Solan goose, occurs in Sir Thomas Herbert's *Travels*, 1626 (p. 9). The author, who was at that time cruising off the south coast of Africa, mentions that some boobies perched upon the yardarm of his ship, and suffered his men to capture them. He adds that the simplicity of this bird has become a proverb, and this statement proves that the booby was known to previous travellers.

Booby.

There was a strong tendency among early writers to give a generic name to all animals of a somewhat similar nature. Thus many large-horned beasts were called oxen, and many small close-furred animals, mice. The ichneumon was Pharaoh's mouse; the beaver was the Pontic dog; the ostrich was called by classical writers the Libyan sparrow. In the following passage from Oviedo's account of the West Indies, the name *sparrow* is given to a bird which was in all probability the booby:—

"There are other fowles called *passere sempie*—that is, simple sparrowes: these are somewhat lesse then scamewes, and have their feet like unto great malards, and stand in the water sometimes, and when the ships saile fiftie or a hundred leagues about the ilands, these fowles beholding the ships coming toward them, breake their flight and fall down upon the saile yards, masts, and cables thereof, and are so simple and foolish, that they tarrie untill they may easily bee taken with mens hands, and were therefore called simple sparrows: they are blacke, and have upon their head and shoulders feathers of a darke russet colour, they are not good to bee eaten, although the mariners have sometimes been forced to eate them." (*Purchas*, vol. iii. p. 980.)

Swans were, from all accounts, most abundant at this period. Paul Hentzner, in his account of a journey to England in 1598, writes of the Thames:—

Swan.

"This river abounds in swans swimming in flocks, the sight of them and their noise is vastly agréeable to the fleets that meet them in their course." (*Dodsley's Fugitive Pieces*, vol. ii. p. 244.)

The swan was called a royal bird, and any stray swan was appropriated by the sovereign wherever it might be found, unless its owner could establish a prior claim by means of certain marks. The frequent enforcement of the royal prerogative gave rise to a system of marking all swans on the beak. The ceremony of "upping," or taking up the swans once a year for the purpose of marking them, was conducted according to the strictest regulations. The various marks assigned to the owners of swans in the different rivers or waters were duly registered in a roll, or standard book. The chief inspector or master was called the gamester, and seems to have had a somewhat onerous post. The penalty for stealing a swan's egg from the nest was imprisonment for a year and a day, with a fine at the will of the king.

The cock bird was called the cobbe, and the hen the penne. A full account of the customs connected with swan-marking, or, as it is now called, "swan-hopping," is given in Yarrell's *British Birds*, 1837 (vol. iii.).

The Dyers' and Vintners' Companies of the City of London obtained the consent of the Crown to keep swans on the Thames at any part of the river between London and Windsor.

The wild swan was not uncommon in England at this time, though probably only as a visitor. Drayton, describing the Lincolnshire fens, writes:—

"But wherefore should I stand upon such toys as these,
That have so goodly fowls, the wandering eye to please?
Here in my vaster pools, as white as snow or milk,
In water black as Stix, swims the wild swan, the ilke,
Of Hollanders so termed, no niggard of his breath
(As poets say of swans who only sing in death),
But as other birds, is heard his tunes to roat,
Which like a trumpet comes, from his long arched throat."
(*Polyolbion*, song xxv.)

Sir Thomas Browne also mentions the "elk, a kind of wild swan," as plentiful in Norfolk in his time.

Aldrovandus, who wrote about the year 1580, was the first to observe the singular bendings of the windpipe in the wild swan. He was, however, not aware of the difference between the wild and the tame varieties of swan, and regarded this structure as a confirmation of the old opinion that the swan possessed a melodious voice, with which, on the approach of death, it sounded its own funeral dirge. This fabulous power of singing before death, so often noticed by poets, has been dwelt on at some length by Mr. Harting. He says (*Ornithology*, p. 202), "Although the swan has no *song*, properly so called, it has a soft and rather plaintive note, monotonous, but not disagreeable."

Allusions are sometimes made to a black variety. "Hee is gone to seeke a hayre in a hennes nest, a needle in a bottle of haye, which is as sildome seene as a blacke swan" (*The Two Angrie Women of Abington*). "It is as rare to see a rich surety, as a black swan" (Lyly, *Euphues*, p. 229). Little did these writers imagine that this proverbial rarity would one day be found in as great abundance as the common wild swan upon the lakes of Europe. "Such," writes Mr. Bennett, "has been one of the many results of the discovery of the continent of New Holland'" (*Gardens of the Zoological Society*).

Duck. Wild Ducks, or Mallards, were so common that no description of them is met with. They were evidently, as one author expresses it, "ordained for the purpose" of hawking. Of Lincolnshire, Drayton writes:—

> "My various fleets for fowl, O who is he can tell
> The species that in me for multitudes excel?
> The duck and mallard first, the falconer's only sport,
> Of river-flights the chief, so that all other sort,

> They only green-fowl term, in every mere abound,
> That you would think they sate upon the very ground,
> Their numbers being so great, the waters covering quite,
> That rais'd, the spacious air is darken'd with their flight;
> Yet still the dangerous dykes, from shot do them secure,
> Where they from flash to flash, like the full epicure
> Waft, as they love to change their diet every meal.
> And near to them you see the lesser dibbling teale
> In bunches, with the first that fly from mere to mere,
> As they above the rest were lords of earth and air."
>
> (*Polyolbion*, song xxv.)

Teal. The Teal does not appear to have been valued as an article of food. In the regulations of the *Northumberland Household Book*, 1512, teals are ordered to be brought only when no other wild fowl can be procured.

Sheldrake. The Sheldrake, or Shieldrake, included by Harrison in his list of English birds, was common in many parts of England. This handsome bird was called also the Burrow Duck, from its habit of breeding in rabbit burrows, in sandy soil in the neighbourhood of the sea. Sir Thomas Browne speaks of the "Bargander, a noble-coloured fowl, which herd in coney-burrows." This name, suggests Mr. Wilkins, may be a corruption of burrow-gander or burrow-duck. Drayton writes:—

> "The greedy sea-maw, fishing for the fry;
> The hungry *shell-fowl*, from whose rape doth fly
> Th' unnumber'd sholes; the mallard there did feed;
> The teale and morecoot raking in the weed."
>
> (*The Man in the Moon.*)

Loon. The Loon is described by Sir Thomas Browne, as—

"a handsome and specious fowl, cristated, and with divided fin feet placed very backward, and after the manner of all such which the Dutch call *arsvoote*. They come about April, and breed in the broad waters; so making their nest on the water, that their eggs are seldom dry while they are set on." (Vol. iv. p. 314.)

The great crested grebe is probably here meant by the loon. When *Macbeth* exclaims to the terrified soldier—

"The Devil damn thee black, thou cream-faced loon!"
(Act v. 3, 11),

he probably used the word as a synonym for a coward, but the epithet "cream-faced" was well chosen, as the white cheeks of the grebe form a noticeable contrast to the darker portions of its head.

It is probable that the larger kinds of birds frequenting the rocks of the sea-coast were vaguely classed as Gulls without any attempt to discriminate between the different varieties. The word *gull* was frequently employed to denote a dupe or a simpleton, and Sir John Davis well defines the meaning of the name as used by old writers in its metaphorical sense :—

Gull.

"Oft in my laughing rimes I name a gull,
But this new terme will many questions breede,
Therefore at first I will express at full
Who is a true and perfect gull indeede :
A gull is he which fears a velvet gowne,
And when a wench is brave, dares not speak to her :
A gull is he which traverses the towne,
And is for marriage known a common wooer.
A gull is he which while he proudly weares
A silver hilted rapier by his side,
Indures the lyes, and knocks about the eares,
While in his sheath his sleeping sword doth bide :
A gull is he which weares good hansome cloathes,
And stands in presence stroaking up his hayre,
And fills up his imperfect speech with oathes,
But speaks not one wise word throughout the yeare,
But, to define a gull in termes precise,
A gull is he which seems, and is not, wise."

(*Epigrams*, ii.)

The word *gull* was also used for a nestling, or unfledged bird of any kind. So *Worcester* speaks of "that ungentle gull, the cuckoo's bird" (1 *Henry IV.*, v. 1, 59), and the Athenian senator thus prognosticates *Timon's* downfall :—

"I do fear,
When every feather sticks in his own wing,
Lord Timon will be left a naked gull,
Which flashes now a phœnix."
(*Timon of Athens*, ii. 1, 29.)

Mr. Harting is, for once, somewhat misleading when he writes :—

"It is amid such scenes [of the sea-coast] that we naturally look for and find the next of Shakespeare's birds, the gull, or, as he sometimes calls it, *the sea-mell.*" (*Ornithology*, p. 266.)

With the single exception of "scamells from the rock," dainties that *Caliban* offers to procure for his patrons, this most beautiful frequenter of our coasts is not once mentioned by name by Shakspeare. Even in the description of the cliff in *Lear*, where we might naturally expect to find it, the more familiar choughs and crows rise to his mind. This is but one indication among many that Shakspeare was an inland naturalist. There is scarcely an allusion throughout his plays to those species of birds or to those various phenomena of the sea which, in a month's voyage or a week's sojourn on the coast, would have attracted his attention.

For the word *scamell*, Mr. Harting reads sea-mell, or young sea-gull. Doubtless *Caliban* was well acquainted with the haunts of every bird that frequented his rocky isle; *Miranda* loved to rear the downy fledglings, brought to her from the nests: to the strange men, therefore, they might be an acceptable present. A less poetical explanation of the word is that *scamell* is a common name for the limpet, both in Cornwall and Ireland.

Thomas Muffett (*Healths Improvement*, p. 108) mentions "white gulls, gray-gulls, and black-gulls (commonly termed by the name of plungers and water-crows.)"

Petrel. The Stormy Petrel, or Mother Cary's Chicken, is mentioned by one of Purchas's pilgrims under the appropriate name of sea-stamper. We read:—

> "The calcamar are as bigge as turtle-doves, or pigeons; the men of the countrie say, that they lay their egges in the sea, and there they hatch, and breed their young; they flie not, but with their wings and feet they swimme very swiftly, and they foreshow great calmes and showres, and in calme weather they are so many along the shippes that the mariners cannot tell what to doe, they are even the very spite it selfe, and melancholy." (*Purchas*, vol. iv. p. 1317.)

This bird, so dreaded by superstitious sailors, flies close to the surface of the waves, and assists itself in its progress by means of its webbed feet. This manner of skimming along gives it the appearance of treading on the water, whence the bird has obtained the name of petrel, in allusion to Saint Peter.

Cormorant. The Cormorant was found in the fens, as well as on the coast of Britain, if we may credit Drayton, who mentions it in that part of his work which relates to Lincolnshire:—

> "The cormorant then comes, by his devouring kind,
> Which flying o'er the fen, immediately doth find
> The fleet best stor'd of fish, when from his wings at full,
> As though he shot himself into the thicken'd skull,
> He under water goes, and so the shoal pursues,
> Which into creeks do fly, when quickly he doth chose
> The fin that likes him best, and rising, flying feeds."
>
> (*Polyolbion*, song xxv.)

This bird was often trained to catch fish to afford amusement, and Mr. Harting has given full particulars of the fondness of James I. for this sport.

Olaus Magnus gives an account, in his work on Scandinavia (p. 199), of sea-crows or cormorants:—

> "There is a kind of water-crows, or called eel-rooks. These birds are extreme black, except their breasts and bellies; for they are all ash-

coloured, and they will eat exceedingly. They hunt for fishes, they fly slowly, and they stay long under water when they dive, their bills are made tooth-ways, as mower's sickles, and with those they hold fast slippery fish, chiefly eels."

Shakspeare's references to the cormorant are only as an emblem of insatiable appetite.

The Pelican might almost be ranked among the fabulous birds, so strange and unnatural were the qualities attributed to it by the older writers. *Pelican.* The principal myth concerning the pelican was that the parent bird, if unable to procure food for her offspring, pierced her flesh, and thus provided an impromptu repast for the little ones. This bird was therefore chosen by artists as an emblem of charity, and a pelican, "in her piety," was a favourite heraldic emblazonment. There are several modern explanations of this theory; unlike most myths, the fable is not derived from classical authority, but in all probability owes its origin to the passages referring to the pelican in the Scriptures, and to the notes of the commentators thereon. Chester quotes one of these learned authorities in his account of the bird:—

> "The pellican, the wonder of our age,
> As Jerome saith, revives her tender yong,
> And with her purest blood she doth asswage
> Her yong ones thirst, with poisonous adder stung.
>   And those that were supposed three dayes dead,
>   She gives them life once more being nourished."
>   (*Love's Martyr*, p. 122.)

Shakspeare has been accused of maligning the character of the juvenile members of the pelican family, when he calls *Regan* and *Goneril* "pelican daughters." If it be true that the parent bird, when provisions ran short, supplied temporary nourishment by giving herself, Portia-like, a voluntary wound, it would be hard to blame the young birds for accepting the sacrifice. The more usual form of the fable was that the "kind, life-rendering pelican" adopted this means of feeding the young ones when urged by necessity; but still a notion seems to have been current that the young birds in some cases acted as aggressors, instead of being grateful recipients of their parent's bounty. Shakspeare evidently has this idea in his mind in *Richard II. Gaunt* retorts:—

> "O, spare me not, my brother Edward's son,
> For that I was his father Edward's son;
> That blood already, like the pelican,
> Hast thou tapp'd out, and drunkenly caroused."
> (*Richard II.*, ii. 1, 124.)

In the *Mirror for Magistrates* we read that a like bitter complaint was made by Henry II. against the ill-treatment and ingratitude he had received from his sons:—

> "Whereof to leave a long memoriall
> In minde of man evermore to rest,
> A picture hee made and hung it in his hall
> Of a pellicane sitting on his nest,
> With four youg byrdes, three pecking at his brest,
>   With bloudy beakes, and furder did devise,
>   The youngest byrde to pecke the father's eyes."
> (Vol. ii. p. 132, ed. Haslewood, 1815.)

The amiable qualities of the pelican could not, however, compensate, in the eyes of Sir John Hawkins, for her want of personal attraction. In the account of his second voyage made to the coast of Guinea, 1564, he tells us:—

"Of the sea-fowle above all other not common in England, I noted the pellicane, which is fained to be the lovingst bird that is; but for all this lovingnesse she is very deformed to beholde; for she is of colour russet; notwithstanding in Guinea I have seene of them as white as a swan, having legs like the same, and a body like a hearne, with a long nocke, and a thick long beake, from the nether jaw whereof downe to the breast passeth a skinne of such a bignesse, as is able to receive a fish as big as one's thigh, and this her big throat and long bill both make her seem so ougly!" (*Hakluyt*, vol. iii. p. 616.)

Other travellers mention the pelican, though not always by that name. The pelican was generally found in company with the flamingo, and there could have hardly been a more striking spectacle than flocks of these two species of birds, the snowy white of the one contrasting with the brilliant red of the other, and attracting and riveting attention even in those lands where strange and beautiful sights abounded. Francois Pyrard de Laval, who gives an account of a journey to the East, writes:—

"When I was on the Maldives, there was found a bird which landed in an iland, of prodigious shape and greatnesse. It was three foot high, the body exceeding greate, more than a man could fathom: the feathers all white as a swan, the feet broad like fowles that swim, the necke halfe a fathom long, the beake halfe an ell; on the upper part at the end a kinde of crooked claw, underneath larger then above, whence hung a very great and capable bagge of a yellow-gilded colour resembling parchment. The king was much astonished whence this creature should come, and what was the nature of it: and enquiring of all men which came from other regions, at the last hee happened on certaine strangers, who told him that this creature was particular to China, and that it was bred no where else, and the Chinois use them to take fish." (*Purchas*, vol. ii. p. 1653.)

Gonzalo Ferdinando de Oviedo, again, in his report of the Indies, addressed to Charles V., the Emperor of Germany, writes:—

" In these regions there are likewise found certaine fowles or birds, which the Indians call *alcatraz*: these are much bigger than geese, the greatest part of their feathers are of russet colour, and in some parts yellow, their bils or beakes are of two spannes in length, and very large neere to the head, and growing small toward the point, they have great and large throates, and are much like to a fowle which I saw in Flanders, in Brussels, in your majesties palace, which the Flemmings call *haina*: and I remember that when your majestie dined one day in your great hall, there was brought to your majesties presence a caldron of water, with certain fishes alive, which the said fowle did eat up whole, and I think verily that that fowle was a fowle of the sea, because she had feet like fowles of the water, as have also these alcatrazi, which are likewise fowles of the sea, and of such greatnesse, that

I have seene a whole coate of a man put into the throate of one of them in Panama, in the yeere 1521. (*Purchas,* vol. iii. p. 979.)

The court favourite referred to by Gonzalo was probably identical with the bird noticed thirty years later by Roger Ascham, in a letter to Mr. Edward Raven, Fellow of St. John's College, Cambridge, 1551. He writes:—

"At Mechlin we saw a strange bird. The emperor doth allow it 8*d.* a day. It is milk-white, greater than a swan, with a bill somewhat like a shovel, and having a throat well able to swallow, without touch of crest, a white penny loaf of England, except your bread be bigger than your bread-master of St. Johns is wont willingly to make it. The eyes are as red as fire, and as they say, it is an hundred years old. It was wont in Maximilian's days to fly with him whithersoever he went." (*Ascham's Works,* p. 854, ed. 1815.)

Mr. Harting tells us (*Ornithology,* p. 288) that Mr. Bartlett, the superintendent of the Zoological Gardens, whose practical knowledge of animals is almost unrivalled, is of opinion that the word *pelican* in the English translation of the Bible should be *flamingo,* as this latter bird could exist in desert places, where the pelican, a lover of fish, would starve. Mr. Bartlett also asserts, from personal observation, that the flamingo has the power of secreting a red fluid, which it mixes with the food for its young, in the same way that the pigeon does, and that this may have given rise to the idea of the bird feeding her young with her own blood. That some confusion existed as to the name of this bird is evident from a passage in a narrative included in Purchas's collection of Travels. An Englishman was taken prisoner by the Portuguese and sent to Angola, in Africa, where he lived for nearly eighteen years. Describing that part of the country, he writes:—

"Here is a kind of fowle that lives in the laud bigger then a swan, and they are like a heron, with long legges, and long neckes, and it is white and blacke, and hath in her breast a bare place without feathers, where she striketh with her bill. This is the right pelican, and not those sea-birds which the Portugalls call pelicans, which are white, and as bigge as geese, and those abound in this country also." (*Purchas*, vol. ii. p. 983.)

In the second voyage to the West Indies made by Mr., afterwards Sir, John Hawkins, 1564, mention is made of the flamingo:—

" For the fowle of the fresh rivers [in Florida] these two I noted to be the chiefe : whereof the flemengo is one, having all red feathers, and long red legs like a herne, a necke according to the bill, red, whereof the upper neb hangeth an inch over the nether." (*Hakluyt*, vol. iii. p. 617.)

As an instance of how long the fabulous element in natural history lingers, in a treatise on animals, published so lately as the end of the last century, this extraordinary statement deserves notice :—

"Wild animals come to the pelican's nest to drink the water which the parent bird brings in a sufficient quantity to last for many days. She carries the water in her pouch, and pours it into the nest to refresh her young ones, and to teach them to swim."

The name alcatrazi, sometimes given by the Spaniards to the pelican, is bestowed by Sir Richard Hawkins, in his account of a voyage to the South Seas in 1593, on an allied species, the tropic bird. He writes:—

"The alcatrace is a sea-fowle, different to all that I have seene, either on the land, or in the sea. His head like unto the head of a gull, but his bill like unto a snites bill, somewhat shorter, and in all places alike. He is almost like to a heronshaw, his legs a good spanne long, his wings very long, and sharpe towards the points, with a long taile like to a pheasant, but with three or foure feathers onely, and these narrower. He is all blacke, of the colour of a crow, and of little flesh ; for hee is almost all skinne and bones, hee soareth the highest of any fowle that I have seene, and I have not heard of any, that have seene them rest in the sea." (*Purchas*, vol. iv. p. 1376.)

The tropic bird, well known to travellers, is about the size of the common gull. The long tail feathers, here noticed, equal in length the rest of the bird. It is unrivalled for strength of wing, and for power of endurance; it is called by sailors the boatswain, from its peculiar cry, which is shrill, harsh, and perpetually repeated, night and day. Captain John Smith, 1622, notes:—

"The tropike bird hath his name of the places where he is most seene. Another bird of her cry is called *pemblico*, seldome seene by day, an unwelcome prophet of tempests by her clamorous crying." (*Purchas*, vol. iv. p. 1801.)

Penguins, from their abundance and the ease with which they were captured, must have been of great value to the early explorers in distant seas. After the privations of a long voyage and a compulsory fish diet, sailors would not be disposed to be critical, but from all accounts the flesh of the penguin would under other circumstances scarcely be appreciated. Anthonie Parkhurst, in a letter dated 1578, and addressed to Richard Hakluyt of the Middle Temple, gives a report of the commodities of Newfoundland. After describing some novelties, he writes:—

Penguin.

"There are sea-guls, murres, duckes, wild geese, and many other kind of birdes store, too long to write, especially at one island named Penguin, where we may drive them on a planke into our ship as many as shall lade her. These birds are also called penguins, and cannot flie, there is more meate in one of these then in a goose: the Frenchmen that fish neare the Grand Baie, doe bring small store of flesh with them, but victuall themselves alwayes with these birdes." (*Hakluyt*, vol. iii. p. 123.)

Either Mr. Parkhurst confused the penguin with the puffin, or the wholesale slaughter led to the extinction of the species in northern latitudes. The penguin is now almost entirely confined to the southern seas. John Jane, "a man of good observation," describes the appearance of this bird in an account of a voyage to South America:—

"This penguin hath the shape of a bird, but hath no wings, only two stumps in the place of wings, by which he swimmeth under water with as great swiftnes as any fish. They live upon smelts, whereof there is great abundance upon this coast: in eating they be neither fish nor flesh: they lay great eges, and the birde is of a reasonable bignes, very neere twise so big as a ducke. . . . We stayed in this harbor [Penguin Isle, in the Straits of Magellan] until the 22 of December, in which time we had dried 200,000 penguins." (*Hakluyt*, vol. iv. p. 370.)

Sir Thomas Herbert, describing a different part of the world, writes, in 1626 :—

"We dropt our anchor 14 leagues short of Souldania Bay afore a small isle call'd Coney Isle through corruption of speech : the proper name of that isle being *Cain-yne* in Welch. The isle is three miles about, in which we saw abundance of pen-gwins, in Welch whiteheads, agreeable to their colour; a bird that of all other goes most erect in motion, the wings or fins hanging down like sleeves, covered with down instead of feathers, their legs serving them better than their wings; they feed on fish at sea and grass ashore, and have holes to live in like conies; a degenerate duck, for using both sea and shore, it feeds in the one, breeds in the other; is very fat and oily, and some adventure to eat them; for curiosity may invite." (*Travels*, p. 12.)

Souldania Bay, we are informed, is on the south-east coast of Africa, twelve leagues from the Cape of Good Hope. The worthy knight loses no opportunity of proving by etymology his favourite theory, that Welshmen were the earliest explorers, both in South Africa and in America. In this opinion he is supported both by Purchas and Hakluyt, and also by the lawyer and statesman, John Selden. In a note on Drayton's ninth book of the *Polyolbion*, Selden confirms an assertion of that poet in the following words :—

"About the year 1170, Madoc, brother to David ap Owen, Prince of Wales, made this sea voyage; and by probability, those names of Capo de Briton in Norumbeg, and Pengwin in part of Northern America, for a white rock, and a white headed bird, according to the British, were relicks of this discovery, so that the Welsh may challenge priority of finding that new world, before the Spaniards, Genoese, and all other mentioned in Lopez, Ninæus, Cortez, and the rest of that kind." (*Works*, vol. iii. part 2, p. 1802, ed. 1725.)

Another traveller, Sir Thomas Roe, 1613, also describes the islands in Souldania Bay :—

"Soldania is," he writes, "as I suppose, an iland, in the south end whereof is the Cape of Good Hope, divided from the maine land by a deepe bay on the south-east side, and due east by a river, which wee discerne upon the table. There is on the iland, buls, cowes, antelops, baboones, moules of great bignesse, feasants, passerflannugos, and many others. On Pengwin [Island] there is a fowle so called, that goes upright, his wings without feathers, hanging down like sleeves faced with white: they fly not, but walke in pathes and keep their divisions and quarters orderly; they are a strange fowle, or rather a miscellaneous creature of beast, bird, and fish, but most of bird, confuting that definition to be *animal bipes implume*, which is nearer to a description of this creature." (*Purchas*, vol. i. p. 536.)

The great auk, now extinct, was probably abundant. Pennant, in his *Zoology*, says that the great auk is a bird observed by seamen never to wander beyond soundings; and according to its appearance they direct their measures, being then assured that land is not very remote. Describing the wonders of the East Riding of Yorkshire, Drayton writes :—

> "The mullet, and the awke (my fowlers there do find,)
> Of all Great Britain brood, birds of the strangest kind,
> That building in the rocks, being taken with the hand,
> And cast beyond the cliff, that pointeth to the land,
> Fall instantly to ground, as though it were a stone,
> But put out to the sea, they instantly are gone,
> As only by that air they on their wings were borne,
> And fly a league or two before they do return."
>
> (*Polyolbion*, song xxviii.)

Dabchick. The Dabchick, or Little Grebe, has acquired a variety of names from the peculiarity of its movements. Shakspeare applies to it the appropriate name of dive-dapper :—

The Dive-dapper. 293

"Like a dive-dapper peering through a wave,
Who, being look'd on, ducks as quickly in."
(*Venus and Adonis*, l. 86.)

Drayton uses the same name, with a difference of one letter:—

"And in a creek where waters least did stir,
Set from the rest the nimble divedopper,
That comes and goes so quickly and so oft,
As seems at once both under and aloft."
(*The Man in the Moon.*)

Drayton elsewhere gives this little bird another title:—

"The diving dob-chick, here amongst the rest you see,
Now up, now down again, that hard it is to prove,
Whether under water most it liveth, or above."
(*Polyolbion*, song xxv.)

In his allegorical poem, *The Boke of Philip Sparow*, Skelton has a different name again:—

"The divendop to cleep,
The water hen to weep."

Du Bartas writes (p. 46):—

"But (gentle muse) tell me what fowls are those
That but even-now from flaggy fenns arose?
'Tis th' hungry hern, the greedy cormorant,
The coot and curlew, which the moors doe haunt,
The nimble teale, the mallard strong in flight,
The di-dapper, the plover and the snight."

The common shore bird, "the Puffin that is halfe fish, halfe flesh (a John Indifferent, and an ambo-dexter betwixt either)" (Nashe, *Lenten Stuffe*), is mentioned by Carew in company with the burranet:—

Puffin.

"The puffin hatcheth in holes of the cliff, whose young ones are thence ferretted out, being exceeding fat, kept salted, and reputed for fish, as coming nearest thereto in their taste. The burranet hath like breeding, and after her young ones are hatched, she leadeth them sometimes over-land, the space of a mile or better into the haven, where such as have leisure to take their pastime, chace them one by one with a boat and stones, to often diving, until through weariness, they are taken up at the boat's side by hand, carried home, and kept tame with ducks. The eggs of divers of these fowls are good to be eaten." (*Survey of Cornwall*, 1602, p. 109.)

Ostrich.

The Ostrich was considered by the ancients to be partly bird and partly beast. As a compromise they gave it the name of *camel-bird*. Its range extends over the whole of Africa and even as far as the deserts of Arabia. John Leo, the African traveller, after a correct description of the ostrich, relates that—

"this fowle liveth in drie desarts and layeth to the number of ten or twelve egges in the sands, which being about the bignesse of great bullets weigh fifteen pounds a piece; but the ostrich is of so weak a memorie, that she presently forgetteth the place where her egges were laid, and afterwards the same or some other ostrich hen finding the said eggs by chance hatched and fostereth them as if they were certainely her owne. The chickens are no sooner crept out of the shell but they prowle up and downe the desarts for their food, and before theyr feathers be growne they are so swift that a man shall hardly overtake them. The ostrich is a silly and deafe creature, feeding upon any thing which it findeth, be it as hard and indigestable as yron." (*Purchas*, vol. ii. p. 849.)

Jack Cade thus threatens *Iden*: "I'll make thee eat iron like an ostrich, and swallow my sword like a great pin, ere thou and I part" (2 *Henry VI.*, iv. 10, 30). This fondness for metals has obtained for the bird the name of the "iron eating-ostrich." Lyly tells us that "the estrich digesteth hard yron to preserve his health" (*Euphues*, p. 110). The statements as to the fancied property of the bird of digesting iron, assigned to it by popular credulity, Sir Thomas elaborately refutes, in his work on popular errors. He mentions the arrival of two ostriches, brought from Tangier, and says, "I sawe one in the latter end of King James his dayes, at Greenwich, when I was a schoolboy."

The female ostrich was supposed by some to hatch her eggs by the steadfast gaze of maternal affection. In consequence of this imaginary exploit the ostrich has been employed as an emblem of faith.

Shakspeare has several references to the ostrich. *Harry Hotspur* asks, Where are—

> "The nimble-footed madcap Prince of Wales
> And his comrades, that daff'd the world aside
> And bid it pass?"

He is answered :—

> "All furnish'd, all in arms;
> All plumed, like estridges that with the wind,
> Baited like eagles having lately bathed."
> (1 *Henry IV.*, iv. 1, 97.)

This is the reading of the *Globe* edition. Mr. Harting reads :—

> "All plum'd like estridges that with the wind
> Bated; like eagles having lately bath'd."

In reference to this passage, Mr. Douce says it is by no means certain that the ostrich is meant. This critic considers that a line is probably lost from the passage, which, if supplied, would only the more clearly show that the falcon was here intended; "estrich," in the old books on falconry, denoted that bird, or rather, the goshawk. It is clear that in this latter sense the word *estrich* is used in the lines in *Antony and Cleopatra* :—

> "To be furious
> Is to be frighted out of fear; and in that mood
> The dove will peck the estridge."
> (*Antony and Cleopatra*, iii. 13, 195.)

Mr. Dyce, on the other hand, explains *estridge* to mean ostrich. In support of this reading, a passage from Drayton's *Polyolbion* may be quoted :—

> "Prince Edward all in gold, as he great Jove had been:
> The Mountfords all in plumes, like estriges were seen,

To beard him to his teeth, to th' work of death they go;
The crowds like to a sea seem'd waving to and fro."
(Song xxii.)

Cassawary. The near relatives of the ostrich, the Cassawary, and the Emeu, are described by various travellers. In an account of the first voyage of the Dutch to the East Indies, the narrator informs us that—

"on the third day of December they came to Tuban and Cydaia [Java], where they bought nutmegs and cloves, and the Sabander gave them a great fowle called *eme*, about foure foot in height, somewhat like an ostrich, saving that the foote were not cloven." (*Purchas*, vol. i. p. 708.)

In the same collection of travels a Portuguese traveller describes the coast of Zanzibar, and writes:—

"From Magadoxo to Sacotora one hundred and fiftie leagues is a desart coast, and dishabited without rivers. In which desarts breed the great birds, called *emas*, which breed on the sands, and have but two young ones, as pigeons. Their stomacks will consume iron and stones, and they flye not but touch the ground with their feet, running with their wings spread, as lightly as other birds flye. They are white, ash-coloured; their egges white, holding almost three pints." (*Purchas*, vol. ii. p. 1556.)

In an account of Sumatra written by John Nieuhoff, a Dutch traveller, published in Harris's collection of travels, the writer asserts that "the bird is called *emeu*, or *eme*, by the natives, and *casuaris* by the Duch." After a very correct description of the emeu, the narrator evidently considers himself entitled to draw on his imagination as a relief, and informs us that it is exceeding greedy, "devouring everything it meets with, even to iron and burning coals."

The first emeu was seen in Europe in 1597, when the Dutch travellers brought one home on their return from their first voyage to the East Indies. This specimen was given them as a great curiosity by one of the Javanese princes, as a token of friendship.

CHAPTER XIII.

OF English Reptiles, Harrison writes, in his description of Britain, prefixed to *Holinshed's Chronicle*:— Reptiles.

"First of all we have the adder, in our old Saxon toong called an atter, which some men doo not rashlie take to be the viper. We have also efts, both of the land and water, and likewise the noisome swifts, whereof to saie anie more it should be but losse of time, sith they are well knowne and no region to my knowledge found to be void of them." (*Holinshed*, vol. i. p. 383.)

Harrison has no further mention of the snake than in the following passage: "And as we have great store of todes where adders commonlie are found, so doo frogs abound where snakes doo keepe their residence."

Drayton describes the gathering of representatives of the reptile clans at Noah's bidding. From the commendation bestowed on the considerate conduct of the asp and little slow-worm, it is probable that the writer had some idea that the tooth of a venomous snake could be rendered innocuous at will:—

> "The salamander to the ark retires,
> To fly the floods it doth forsake the fires;
> The strange camelion comes to augment the crew,
> Yet in the ark doth never change her hue;
>
> * * * * *
>
> The watchful dragon comes the ark to keep,
> But lull'd with murmur, gently falls to sleep:

> The cruel scorpion comes to climb the pile,
> And meeting with the greedy crocodile,
> Into the ark together meekly go,
> And like kind mates themselves they there bestow;
> The dart and dipsas, to th' ark coming in,
> Infold each other as they were a twin;
> The cockatrice there kills not with his sight,
> But in his object joys, and in the light
> The deadly killing aspick when he seeth
> This world of creatures sheaths his poyson'd teeth,
> And with the adder and the speckled snake,
> Them to a corner harmlessly betake;
> The lizard shuts up his sharp-sighted eyes,
> Among these serpents, and there sadly lies;
> The small-eyed slow-worm held of many blind,
> Yet this great ark it quickly out could find,
> And as the ark it was about to climb,
> Out of its teeth shoots the invenom'd slime.
>
> * * * * *
>
> All these base, grovelling, and ground-licking sute,
> From the large boas, to the little newte;
> As well as birds, or the four footed beasts,
> Came to the ark their hostry as Noah's guests."
>
> (*Noah's Flood.*)

The statement made by Giraldus Cambrensis, that Ireland possessed an immunity from every kind of poisonous creature, has been repeated by almost all subsequent writers on that country. This notion can be traced back as early as the "venerable Bede," who writes, in his *Ecclesiastical History* (book i., c. i.) :—

> "No reptile is found there; no serpent can live there; for, though often carried thither out of Britain, as soon as the ship draws near the land, and the scent of the air from off the shore reaches them, they die. On the contrary almost all things produced in the island have virtues against poison."

Cambrensis, who quotes this passage, confirms the statement, and declares that, though some authors have attributed this absence of noxious creatures to St. Patrick and other saints—

"history asserts, with more probability, that from the earliest ages, and long before the island was favoured with the light of revealed truth, this was one of the things which never existed here, from some natural deficiency in the produce of the island." (*Typography of Ireland*, 1187, p. 48, ed. Wright, 1863.)

To the notion that nothing venomous could exist in Ireland, England is, according to Cambrensis, indebted for the possession of the Isle of Man. This island is situate midway between Britain and Ireland:—

" Which country it rightly belonged to was a matter of great doubt among the ancients : but the controversy was settled in this way ; since the island allowed venomous reptiles, brought over for the sake of experiment, to exist in it, it was agreed by common consent that it belonged to Britain." (Page 70.)

Much time and bloodshed might have been saved if such a delightfully simple method of proving the right of possession had been elsewhere adopted.

Even the soil of Ireland was supposed to be antagonistic to snakes. Andrew Boorde, in his *Introduction of Knowledge*, written 1542, tells us that " marchauntes of England do fetch of the erth of Irlonde to caste in their gardens, to kepe out and to kyll venimous wormes " (p. 133, Early English Text Society, 1870). More recently this antipathy of serpents to everything Irish was turned to good account ; Paul Hentzner, in his account of a journey to England, 1598, describes a visit to the Houses of Parliament at Westminster, and records :—

" In the chamber where the Parliament is usually held, the seats and wainscot are made of wood, *the growth of Ireland* ; said to have had that occult quality, that all poisonous animals are driven away by it: and it is affirmed for certain, that in Ireland there are neither serpents, toads, nor any other venomous creature to be found." (*Dodsley's Fugitive Pieces*, vol. ii. p. 244.)

Allusions to this expulsion of reptiles from Ireland

abound in the writings of the Elizabethan era. Shakspeare only echoes the popular sentiment when he makes *Richard II.* speak so uncivilly of the Irish kerns—

"Which live like venom where no venom else
But only they have privilege to live."
(*Richard II.*, ii. 1, 156.)

John Trundle, the narrator of some exploits of a Sussex dragon, writes, in 1614:—

"The Irish ground is most happie, and it seemeth lesse sinfull, since it is free from contagion of these venomous creatures: but, *non omnis fert omnia tellus*, 'every ground brings not forth all kind of fruites.' This land were happie if it were less fertile in these contagious kinds of serpents, which I ascribe not to the nature of the earth, but to the sinfull nature of men." (*Harleian Miscellany*, vol. iii. p. 109.)

The herb origanum, or marjoram, appears to have been esteemed the cure for all diseases. In *Euphues* (p. 61), Lyly writes: "The torteyse having tasted the viper sucketh origanum and is quickly revived." Montaigne, in his *Essays*, has an expression so similar, that had not these two works been published in the same year, one of the authors would have been accused of plagiarism. They were probably both equally indebted to Pliny for their information. The learned seigneur inquires:—

"Why should we say, that it is only for man by knowledge improv'd by art and meditation, to distinguish the things commodious for his being, and proper for the cure of diseases, to know the virtues of rhubarb, and polypody: and when we see the goats of Candie, wounded with an arrow, amongst a million of plants, choose out dittanie for their cure; and the tortoise, when she has eaten of a viper, immediately go to look out for origanum to purge her, the dragon to rub, and clear his eyes with fennel,—why do we not say the same, that this is knowledge and prudence?"

Drayton, describing the universal stampede of living creatures towards the ark, classes the snail-paced Tortoise with the lively little hedgehog, as if their movements were similar:—

Tortoise.

> "The tortoise and the hedgehog both so slow,
> As in their motion scarce designed to go,
> Good footmen grown, contrary to their kind,
> Lest from the rest they should be left behind."
>
> (*Noah's Flood.*)

In our own time we adopt Drayton's arrangement, but with a difference. We give the tortoise credit for equal speed with the hedgehog. Quite recently a considerable traffic has been carried on in the London streets. Small African tortoises have been taken about on barrows, and passers-by have been beguiled into becoming purchasers of these little reptiles, by the assurance that one of them will soon clear a kitchen of black beetles. The wish is, no doubt, father to the thought, and any information as to the purely vegetable diet of the new purchase, volunteered by a presumptuous naturalist, is slighted. We smile at the absurd notions of our forefathers in matters of natural history, but anything more comic than the picture presented to the imagination by a tortoise in wild pursuit of a cockroach would be difficult to find.

A traveller in Eastern Tartary tells of "tortoises as big as an oven" (*Hakluyt*, vol. ii. p. 163). This simile is rivalled in exactness by one made use of by a farmer who appeared as a witness in a court of law. In reply to a question of counsel as to the size of some article, he said it was "about as big as a bit of chalk." The tortoises referred to were, no doubt, turtles. An early mention of the turtle, or sea tortoise, occurs in an account of Sir John Hawkins's second voyage to the West Indies. The writer, one of the ship's company, chronicles as follows:—

> The 5th of July [1565] we had sight of certain islands of sand, called the Tortugas, which is low land [in the Gulf of Mexico] where the captain went in, with his pinnace; and found such a number of birds that, in half an hour, he laded her with them; and, if there had been ten boats more, they might have done the like. These islands bear the name of Tortles, because of the number of them which there do breed: whose nature is to live both in the water and also upon land,

but breed only upon the shore, by making a great pit, wherein they lay eggs, to the number of three or four hundred, and covering them with sand, they are hatched by the heat of the sun; and by this means, cometh the great increase. Of these, we took very great ones, which have both back and belly all of bone of the thickness of an inch; the fish whereof we proved, eating much like veal: and finding a number of eggs in them tasted also of them, but they did eat very sweetly." (*Hakluyt*, Arber's *English Garner*, vol. v. p. 121.)

Another notice of these reptiles may be quoted, chiefly interesting as showing how opinions may vary in the matter of articles of food. Sir Thomas Herbert writes, in the year 1626:—

"Suffer me (whiles in memory) to tell you of a fish or two which, in these seas [round Madagascar] were obvious. The sea tortoise is one, a fish not differing from those at land, her shell only being something flatter; by overturning they are easily taken; some we took, for pastime more than food, and upon trial found that they taste waterish; they have neither tongue nor teeth, superabound in eggs, in those we took some having near 2000, pale and round, and not easily made hard though extreamly boiled: they cover their eggs with sand, and are hatched by the heat of the sun, as some affirm; such as have strong appetites eat them and the flesh (or fish as you please to call it), but by the Levitical law it was forbidden; and though our religion consists not in ceremonies (ending in the prototype) yet except famine or noveltie invite, with such cates my pallat craves not to be refreshed." (*Travels*, p. 26, ed. 1677.)

The bad taste manifested in this long-winded sentence may be due to the want of culinary skill on the part of the ship's cook; we must remember also that the worthy knight was a most fastidious traveller, and seldom expressed approval of any novelty. The city magnates had perhaps learned in the time of Muffett, about 1646, that the turtle by judicious manipulation might be rendered palatable, for in that author's work we read that—

"tortoises are likewise no usuall meat amongst us: yet I see no reason but that riot may bring them in, and make them as familiar unto us as turkies are; their flesh nourishes plentifully, and recovers men out of consumption." (*Healths Improvement*, p. 190.)

"*Lepidus.* What manner o' thing is your Crocodile? Crocodile.
Antony. It is shaped, sir, like itself; and it is as
broad as it hath breadth: it is just so high as it is, and moves with its
own organs: it lives by that which nourisheth it; and the elements
once out of it, it transmigrates.
Lep. What colour is it of?
Ant. Of its own colour too.
Lep. 'Tis a strange serpent.
Ant. 'Tis so. And the tears of it are wet."
(*Antony and Cleopatra*, ii. 7, 46.)

Little more explicit are some of the descriptions of the crocodile by early writers. As a rule no distinction seems to have been made between the crocodile and the alligator, but *Romeo's* mention of—

"An alligator stuff'd, and other skins
Of ill-shaped fishes".
(*Romeo and Juliet*, v. 1, 42),

shows that the name *alligator* was in use at least, though the word *crocodile* would here probably be more correct. The amphibious habits of these animals seem to have puzzled our ancestors how to classify them; sometimes, as by *Lepidus*, it is called a serpent. Chester writes:—

"The crocadile a saffron coloured snake,
Sometimes upon the earth is conversant,
And other times lives in a filthy lake,
Being oppressed with foule needy want:
The skinn upon his backe as hard as stone,
Resisteth violent strokes of steele or iron."
(*Love's Martyr*, p. 116.)

Marlowe had a somewhat exaggerated idea of its power of resistance to attacks from without:—

"Lie slumbering on the flowery banks of Nile,
As crocodiles that unaffrighted rest,
While thundering cannons rattle on their skins."
(1 *Tamburlaine*, iv. 1.)

The crocodile, " Nile's fell rover," is sometimes ranked as

a fish. It is strange that, as this reptile was an inhabitant of a country so well known as Egypt, its manners and customs are not more correctly described. Probably the terror it inspired, added to the difficulty which the natives must have had in its destruction, may have given rise to the fanciful accounts that have been handed down from antiquity. The explorers of Elizabeth's time, however, brought back more accurate descriptions and probably several specimens. Job Hortop, a sailor in the crew of Sir John Hawkins, 1591, thus describes the capture and attempted preservation of a legarto, or alligator :—

"He was twenty three feet by the rule, headed like a hog, in body like a serpent, full of scales as broad as a saucer, his tail long and full of knots as big as a 'falcon shot.' He had four legs; his feet had long nails like unto a dragon; we opened him, flayed him, dried his skin, and stuffed it with straw, meaning to have brought it home, had not the ship been cast away." (*Hakluyt's Voyages.*)

But for the mischance of the wreck this specimen might have graced the shop of some needy apothecary in Fleet Street.

A Portuguese traveller, in his account of the southern coast of Africa, says:—

"The crocodile is five and twentie spans long, and thicker then a man; they are cowardly on land, cruell in the water, greene with darke yellow spots, and gray, and blacke; they have many rowes of teeth, no tongue. The Caffres call them *goma*." (*Purchas*, vol. ii. p. 1547.)

Marco Polo's description of the crocodile is too grotesque to be omitted. In his travels in the East, towards the end of the thirteenth century, he tells us:—

"Here are seen huge serpents, ten paces in length, and ten spans in the girt of the body. At the fore-part, near the head they have two short legs, having three claws like those of a tiger, with eyes larger than a fourpenny loaf, and very glaring. The jaws are wide enough to swallow a man, the teeth are large and sharp, and their whole appearance is so formidable, that neither man, nor any kind of animal, can approach them without terror."

An Indigestible Meal. 305

The impression left on the mind of the reader is, that the crocodile has no hind legs at all. Perhaps the illustrious traveller's courage did not hold out long enough to enable him to wait till the animal had emerged sufficiently out of the water to ascertain the proper number of its limbs.

The American crocodile, or alligator, is mentioned by Sir Walter Raleigh, in his account of Guiana, under its native name, *el lagarto*, the big lizard :—

"Upon this river [the Great Aman] there were great store of fowl, and of many sorts: we saw in it divers sorts of strange fishes, and of marvellous bigness; but for lagartos it exceeded; for there were thousands of those ugly serpents, and the people call it for the abundance of them the river of Lagartos, in their language. I had a negro, a very proper young fellow, that, leaping out of the galley to swim in the mouth of this river, was in all our sights taken and devoured with one of these legartos." (*Sir W. Raleigh's Works*, vol. viii. p. 42.)

Lopes, a Portuguese traveller, in Africa, gives the crocodile another name: " In this river Jaire (in Congo), there are divers kinds of creatures, and namely, mightie great crocodiles, which the country people there call *caiman*" (*Purchas*, vol. ii. p. 990). Andrew Battell, a traveller in Angola, records an astonishing feat of rapacity, and its consequence :—

"One crocodile was so huge and greedy, that he devoured an *alibamba*, that is, a chained company of eight or nine slaves: but the indigestible iron paid him his wage, and murthered the murtherer, found after in his belly." (*Purchas*, vol. ii. p. 985.)

Tom Coryat, the celebrated pedestrian traveller, gives an account of a visit paid by him to the church and monastery of some rich Benedictine monks at Padua, about the year 1608. He describes the monastery as very extensive, occupying, with its gardens, the space of a mile in compass. His account of the dispensary attached to the building recalls the humbler dwelling of the poor Mantuan vendor of drugs :—

" Also I saw two goodly faire rooms within the monastery

abundantly furnished with passing variety of pleasant fine waters and apothecary drugges that serve onely for the monkes. In the first of these roomes I saw the skin of a great crocodile hanged up at the roofe, and another skinne of a crocodile in the inner roome. This crocodile is a beast of a most terrible shape, fashioned like a dragon, with wonderfull hard scales upon his backe; I observed that he hath no tongue at all; his eyes are very little, and his teeth long and sharp." (*Coryat's Crudities*, vol. i. p. 181, ed. 1776.)

Reference is often made to the notion, handed down from antiquity, that the crocodile attracted its victims by affected weeping. Spenser writes:—

> " As when a wearie traveller, that strayes
> By muddy shore of broad seven-mouthed Nile,
> Unweeting of the perilous wandring wayes,
> Doth meete a cruell craftie crocodile,
> Which, in false griefe hyding his harmefull guile,
> Doth weepe full sore, and sheddeth tender teares;
> The foolish man, that pities all this while
> His mournfull plight, is swallowed up unwares;
> Forgetfull of his owne, that mindes another's cares."
>
> (*Faerie Queene*, I. v. 18.)

Othello exclaims, when *Desdemona* weeps:—

> "O devil, devil!
> If that the earth could teem with woman's tears,
> Each drop she falls would prove a crocodile."
>
> (*Othello*, iv. 1, 256.)

Dr. Andrew Wilson has recently explained the belief in *crocodile's tears* as originating from the loud and singularly plaintive cries the creature emits, not unlike the mournful howling of a dog :—

"The earlier travellers would very naturally associate tears with these cries, and once begun, the supposition would be readily propagated, for error and myth are ever plants of quick growth. The belief in the movement of the upper jaw rests on an apparent basis of fact. The lower jaw is joined to the skull very far back on the latter, and the mouth-opening thus comes to be singularly wide; whilst, when the mouth opens, the skull and upper jaw are apparently observed to move. This is not the case, however; the apparent movement arising from the manner in which the lower jaw and the skull are joined together. The belief in the absence of the tongue is even more readily explained. When the mouth is widely opened, no tongue is to be seen. This organ is not only present, but is, moreover, of large size; it is, however, firmly attached to the floor of the mouth, and it is specially adapted, from its peculiar form and structure, to assist these animals in the capture and swallowing of their prey." (*Leisure Time Studies*, p. 75, 1879.)

The tongue of the crocodile acts as a flood-gate to prevent water passing down the throat when the jaws are opened.

John Leo, an African traveller, tells the story of the crocodile's feathered attendant, that has been for a long time considered a myth. His version differs from the account given by Herodotus, and repeated by Aristotle, of this strange partnership, only in the termination. In the ancient tale the crocodile moves its neck as a signal that it is about to shut its mouth, so as to warn the trochilus to avoid the danger. Leo says:—

"As we sayled further we saw great numbers of crocodiles upon the bankes of the ilands in the midst of Nilus lye baking them in the sunne with their jawes wide open, whereinto certaine little birds about the bignesse of a thrush entering, came flying forth againe presently after. The occasion whereof was told me to be this: the crocodiles by reason of their continuall devouring beasts and fishes have certaine pieces of flesh sticking fast betweene their forked teeth, which flesh being putrified breedeth a kind of worme, wherewith they are cruelly tormented; wherefor the said birds flying about and seeing the wormes enter into the crocodiles jaws to satisfie their hunger thereon, but the crocodile perceiving himselfe freed from the wormes of his teeth offereth to shut his mouth, and to devour the little bird that did him so good a turne, but being hindred from his ungratefull attempt by a pricke which groweth upon the birds head, hee is constrayned to open his jawes and to let her depart." (*Purchas*, vol. ii. p. 847.)

Webster makes use of this story as an illustration, and follows it so closely, except in the size of the bird, that it is not unlikely he had the passage before him at the time of writing:—

"*Flamineo.* Stay, my Lord; I'll tell you a tale. The crocodile which

lives in the river Nilus, hath a worm breeds i' th' teeth of it, which puts
it to extream anguish: a little bird, no bigger than a wren, is barber
surgeon to this crocodile; flies into the jaws of it, pieks out the worm,
and brings present remedy. The fish, glad of ease, but ungrateful to
her that did it, that the bird may not talk largely abroad of her for non-
payment, closeth her chaps, intending to swallow her, and so put her
to perpetual silence. But nature, loathing such ingratitude, hath
arm'd this bird with a quill or prick on the head top, which wound the
crocodile i' th' mouth, forceth her to open her bloody prison, and away
flies the pretty took-picker from her cruel patient." (*Vittoria
Corombona*, act iv. ed. Dyce.)

This bird, which was called the trochilus by the
ancients, is referred to by Lyly: "The birde trochilus
liveth by the mouth of the crocodile and is not spoyled"
(*Euphues*, p. 45). In modern times this little bird, which
in any case must have had a somewhat precarious existence, has been identified by M. Geoffroy St. Hilaire, as a
species of plover, which enters the crocodile's mouth in
search of gnats. By the prick on its head, mentioned by
Leo, the slender crest peculiar to this species of bird is
probably meant.

The crocodile, secured by his armour against violence,
was not proof against cunning, and Du Bartas, in his poem
on the Creation, describes the joint attack of the ichneumon and this same little bird upon the unwieldy
reptile:—

> "Thou mak'st th' ichneumon whom the Memphs adore
> To rid of poysons Nile's manured shore;
> Although indeed he doth not conquer them
> So much by strength as subtle stratagem.
> * * * *
> So Pharoahs rat, yer he begin the fray
> 'Gainst the blinde aspick, with a cleaving clay
> Upon his coat he wraps au earthen cake,
> Which, afterward, the sun's hot beams doe bake:
> Arm'd with this plaister, th' aspick he approcheth,
> And in his throat his crooketh tooth he brocheth;
> While th' other boot-less strives to pierce and prick
> Through the hard temper of his armour thick:

Yet, knowing himself too-weak, for all his wile,
Alone to match the scaly crocodile;
Hee, with the wren, his ruine doth conspire.
The wren, who seeing, prest with sleeps desire
Nile's poys'ny pirate press the slimy shore,
Suddenly comes, and hopping him before,
Into his mouth he skips; his teeth he pickles,
Cleanseth his palate, and his throat so tickles,
That, charm'd with pleasure, the dull serpent gapes
Wider and wider with his ugly chaps:
Then, like a shaft, th' ichneumon instantly
Into the tyrants greedy gorge doth flie,
And feeds upon that glutton, for whose riot
All Nile's fat margents scarce could furnish diet."
(*Divine Weekes*, p. 51.)

Lyly gives the crocodile credit for an elasticity which, to judge by some of the old pictures, was possessed by St. George's Dragon, but assuredly by no other animal:—

"The crocodile, who, when one approcheth neere unto him, gathereth up himselfe into the roundnesse of a ball, but running from him, strotcheth him-self into the length of a tree." (*Euphues*, p. 364.)

Thomas Fuller adds poison to the crocodile's other weapons of destruction:—

"The sovereign power of genuine saffron is plainly proved by the antipathy of the crocodile thereunto: for the crocodile's tears are never true, save when he is forced where saffron groweth (whence he hath his name of χροχό-δειλος, or the saffron-fearer, knowing himself to be all poison, and it all antidote." (*Worthies of England*, vol. i. p. 336.)

Tom Coryat also notices the dread which the crocodile was supposed to have of saffron:—

"For which cause those amongst the ancient Egyptians that had the charge to looke to their bees in their gardens, were wont to smear their bee hives with saffron, which as soone as the crocodile perceived, he would presently run away." (*Crudities*, p. 182.)

Unless crocodiles were armed with scales internally as well as externally, a hive full of bees must have been even more trying a meal than cold iron.

We read, in the early travels, that the Moors anticipated the recent fashion of having purses made of crocodile skin, and no doubt they turned the scaly coat of the destructive reptile to good account in many ways.

In a pageant on the occasion of Lord Mayor Garway's procession, about 1600, a crocodile made what was probably its first appearance in public, and formed a part of the show, heralded by a black man, who represented the river Nile. We have no record as to whether this particular crocodile was alive or stuffed.

Lizard.
"The Lizard is a kind of loving creature,
Especially to man he is a friend:
This property is given him by nature,
From dangerous beasts poore man he doth defend:
For being sleepy he all sence forsaketh,
The lizard bites him till the man awaketh."
(CHESTER, *Love's Martyr*, p. 114.)

This friendly relation between the lizard and man has been noticed by Reginald Scot.*

In *Henry VI.* we find two references to the venomous properties of the poor little lizard, but as the play is doubtful they cannot be quoted as proving Shakspeare's ignorance on this point. The lizard is, however, in other places classed with noxious creatures. *Thersites* exclaims:—

"To be a dog, a mule, a cat, a fitchew, a toad, a lizard, an owl, a puttock, or a herring without a roe, I would not care; but to be Menelaus! I would conspire against destiny." (*Troilus and Cressida*, v. 1, 67.)

Chameleon.
It is somewhat curious that an animal of such retiring habits, and living in regions so remote, as the Chameleon, should have had so much attention bestowed upon it. Accounts of the chameleon are in the main fabulous, and derived in great measure from Pliny. Du Bartas (p. 50) declares that—

* See page 251.

> "Th' eye of Heav'n beholdeth nought more strange
> Then the chameleon, who with various change
> Receives the colour that each object gives,
> And food-less else of th' aire alonely lives."

Drayton has a similar passage, and Shakspeare refers several times to this creature's atmospheric diet. *Hamlet* replies to inquiries as to his health, "Excellent well, i' faith; of the cameleon's dish: I eat the air, promise crammed: you cannot feed capons so" (*Hamlet*, iii. 2, 98).

The power of changing colour which this animal possessed was well known:—

> "I can add colours to the cameleon."
> (3 *Henry VI.*, iii. 2, 191.)
> "A true cameleon, I can colour for it."
> (BEN JONSON, *The Staple of News*, iii. 1.)

But the cause of the alteration was not clearly understood. The change of hue is explained by modern naturalists as due to the contraction and dilatation of elastic colour-bags in the animal's skin. Sir Francis Bacon says that—

> "the chameleon feedeth not only upon air, though that be his principal substance, for sometimes he taketh flies as was said, yet some that have kept chameleons whole years together, could never perceive that they fed upon anything else but air."

He gives a fairly accurate description of the creature itself. George Sandys, in his *Relations of Africa*, 1610, does not confirm the stories of this extreme abstemiousness, though he alludes to them. This traveller describes the chameleon as—

> "a creature about the bignesse of an ordinary lizard; his head unproportionably bigge, his eyes great and moving without the writhing of his necke, which is inflexible; his backe crooked, his skinne spotted with little tumors, his tayle slender and long, on each foot he hath five fingers, three on the outside, and two on the inside, slow of pace, but swiftly expanding his tongue of a manner marvellous for the proportion

of his body, wherewith he preyes upon flyes, the top thereof being hollowed by nature for that purpose, so that deceived they be who thinke that they eate nothing but live upon aire; though surely aire is their principal sustenance." (*Purchas*, vol. ii. p. 904.)

Another traveller writes:—

"There [Malay Archipelago] are store of lizards, and chamelions, which agree to Plinies description; onely it is airie, that they live of aire without other meat; for having kept one aboord but a day, we might perceive him to hunt for flies, in a very strange manner. Having espied her setting, he suddenly shootes a thing forth of his mouth, perhaps his tongue, lothsome to behold, the fashion almost like a birdbolt, wherewith he takes and eates them, with such speed, that a man can scarsly discern what he doth; even in the twinkling of an eie." (*Purchas*, vol. i. p. 417.)

A still earlier description of the chameleon is given by Sir John Mandeville, 1356, in an account of a visit to some islands off the coast of China.

"Ther ben also in that contree manye camles, that is a lytille best as a goot, that is wylde, and he lyvethe by the eyr, and etethe nought ne drynkethe nought at no tyme. And he chaungethe his colour often tyme: for men seen him often scithes, now in a colour and now in another colour: and he may chaunge him in to alle mauer of couloures that him list, saf only in to red and white." (*Travels*, p. 289, ed. Halliwell, 1839.)

Blind-worm. The "gray-headed error," to use Sir Thomas Browne's expression, of the venomous qualities possessed by the harmless little Blind-worm, or Slow-worm, still lingers in country districts, and has caused the death of many an innocent victim. In his account of English reptiles, Harrison tells us:—

"We have also the sloworme, which is blacke and graiesh of colour, and somewhat shorter than an adder. I was at the killing once of one of them, and thereby perceived that she was not so called of anie want of nimble motion, but rather of the contrarie. Neverthelesse we have a blind worme to be found under logs in woods, and timber that hath lien long in a place, which some also doo call (and upon better ground) by the name of slow-worms, and they are known by their more or lesse varietie of striped colours, drawen long waies from their heads, their whole bodies little exceeding a foot in length, and yet is their venem deadlie."

Timon appeals to the earth to yield him out of her vast storehouse simple sustenance. He adjures the common mother—

"Whose self-same mettle,
Engenders the black toad and adder blue,
The gilded newt and eyeless venom'd worm,
With all the abhorred births below crisp heaven
Whereon Hyperion's quickening fire doth shine;
Yield him, who all thy human sons doth hate,
From thy plenteous bosom, one poor root!"
(*Timon of Athens*, i. 2, 179.)

Among night's black agents employed by the witches are the—

"Adder's fork, and blind-worm's sting."
(*Macbeth*, iv. 1, 16.)

Captain Dampier, one of the early travellers, bestows the classical name of Amphisbena on what was probably the worm-like reptile found in South America. He writes of Brazil:— *Amphisbena.*

"They have here also the amphisbæna, or two-headed snake, of a grey colour, with black streaks, its bite is reckoned incurable: the best is, that it seldom wounds. Having two specks in the head, instead of eyes, some say it is altogether blind, and lives underground like a mole. Its length is about fourteen inches, with an head at each end; whence the Portuguese call it *cobra de dos cabasees*, *i.e.* the snake with two heads; but I never saw one of these." (*Harris's Voyages*, p. 116.)

Lyly mentions "the serpent amphisbena, which, having at each ende a sting, hurteth both ways" (*Euphues* p. 286). Sir Thomas Browne, in his *Inquiry into Vulgar Errors*, doubts the possibility of such a creature. Modern science has retained the name *amphisbæna* for a species of footless lizard.

In the oak woods of Warwickshire Shakspeare may
Adder. often have found that—

"It is the bright day that brings forth the Adder;
And that craves wary walking."
(*Julius Cæsar*, ii. 1, 14.)

Shakspeare uses both the names adder and viper, but applies the latter word chiefly in a metaphorical, and the former in a literal sense.

The popular notion of the adder's deafness was derived from a passage in the Bible; and in a sermon by Dr. Montague, 1602, the worthy preacher ingeniously improves on his original, and describes the process by which the reptile contrived to escape:—

"The Scripture telleth us that of all beasts the serpent is the most subtill, and his subtility is observed in three points: first, when those nations in Syria and other hott countries found themselves often endangered by the stinging of venomous beasts, amongst other remedies they invented charming, which the serpent percevinge, to avoyd their cunning and effect his malice, he would stop both his eares, the one by laying it close to the earth, the other by stopping it with his tayle." (*Diary of John Manningham*, 1602, p. 26, *Camden Soc. Rep.*)

In this extract the adder is supposed to possess the sense of hearing, but from natural depravity to refuse to listen to the voice of the charmer. The more generally received opinion was that the adder was in reality deaf. The absence of external ears probably led to this idea.

The question whether or not the old adder swallows her young, to protect them from danger, is hardly decided even at the present time. At the period of which we write, this maternal device was generally believed to be resorted to when occasion required. Ben Jonson says:—

"Or, till we speak, must all run in, to one,
Like the young adders to the old one's mouth."
(*The Devil is an Ass*, prologue.)

Our forefathers had rather hazy notions as to the exact

position of this little reptile's weapon of defence. *Richard II.* conjures his native earth to defend his kingdom from the usurper's tread :—

> "And when they from thy bosom pluck a flower,
> Guard it, I pray thee, with a lurking adder
> Whose double tongue may with a mortal touch
> Throw death upon thy sovereign's enemies."
> (*Richard II.*, iii. 1, 29.)

Webster writes :—

> "Repentance then will follow like the sting
> Placed in the adder's tail."
> (*Vittoria Corombona*, act 2.)

Another dramatist, John Kirke, says :—

> "So thinks the adder when his sting is gone,
> His hissing has the power to venom too."
> (*The Seven Champions of Christendom*, iii. 1.)

Andrew Boorde, in his *Dyetary*, 1542, probably refers to some larger species of snake than the adder, if indeed any meaning at all can be attached to the following passage. Jews, he says—

"lovyth not porke nor swynes flesshe, but doth vituperat and abhorre it; yet for all this they wyll eate adders, which is a kynd of serpentes, as well as any other Crysten man dwellyng in Rome, and other hyghe countries; for adders flesshe there is called 'fysshe of the mountayn.' This notwithstandynge, physycke doth approbat adders flesshe good to be eaten, sayinge it doth make an olde man yonge, as it apperyth, by a harte eatyng an adder, maketh hym yonge agayne." (Early English Text Society, 1870.)

> "The Aspis is a kind of deadly snake. **Asp.**
> He hurts most perillous with venom'd sting
> And in pursute doth neare his foe forsake,
> But slaies a man with poysonous venoming:
> Betweene the male and female is such love,
> As is betwixt the most kind turtle dove.

> "This is the snake that Cleopatra used,
> The Egyptian queene belov'd of Anthony,
> That with her breasts deare bloud was nourished,
> Making her die (faire soule) most patiently,
> Rather than Cæsar's great victorious hand,
> Should triumph ore the queene of such a land."
> (CHESTER, *Love's Martyr*, p. 114.)

"The pretty worm of Nilus," the supposed cause of Cleopatra's death, is thought by modern writers to have been the horned snake (*Vipera cerastes*). This serpent, according to Dr. Wright, was well known to the ancients, and is found abundantly in Egypt.

Snake. Shakspeare is not inclined to trust the harmlessness of the common English Snake. Perhaps in some passages he may have the credit of referring to a foreign species. Macbeth exclaims :—

> "We have scotch'd the snake, not kill'd it:
> She'll close and be herself, whilst our poor malice
> Remains in danger of her former tooth."
> (*Macbeth*, iii. 2, 13.)

The expression often used, "a tame snake," meant a mean-spirited creature, from whom no danger was to be apprehended.

A circumstantial account of a serpent nine feet long, found in a wood called St. Leonard's Forest, near Horsham, in Sussex, written by John Trundle, 1614, is recorded in that repertory of curiosities, the *Harleian Miscellany* (vol. iii. p. 109). Unfortunately the writer's caution did not allow him to approach near enough to ascertain the exact size of the creature, or to describe its anatomy with scientific accuracy.

"This serpent," he writes, "or dragon, as some call it, is reputed to be nine feete, or rather more, in length, and shaped almost in the forme of an axletree of a cart; a quantitie of thickness in the middest, and somewhat smaller at both endes. The former part, which he shoots forth as a necke, is supposed to be an elle long; with a white ring, as it were, of scales about it. The scales along his backe seem to be blackish, and so much as is discovered under his bellie, appeareth to be red; for I speak of no nearer description than of a reasonable ocular distance, for coming too neare it, hath already beene too dearely payd for, as you shall heare hereafter. It is likewise discovered to have large feete, but the eye may be there deceived; for some suppose that serpents have no feete, but glide upon certain ribbes and scales. . . . He is of countenance very proud, and at the sight or hearing of men or cattel will raise his necke upright, and seem to listen and looke about, with great arrogancy. There are likewise on either side of him discovered two great bunches so big as a large footeball, and as some thinke will in time grow to wings; but God, I hope, will so defend the poor people in the neighbourhood that he shall be destroyed before he grow so fledge.

"He will cast his venome about four rodde from him, as by woefull experience it was proved on the bodies of a man and a woman coming that way, who afterwards were found dead, being poysoned and very much swelled, but not prayed upon. Likewise a man going to chase it, and as he imagined, to destroy it with two mastive dogs, as yet not knowing the great danger of it, his dogs were both killed, and he himselfe glad to returne with hast to preserve his own life. Yet this is to be noted, that the dogs were not prayed upon, but slaine and left whole: for his food is thought to be, for the most part, in a conicwarren, which he much frequents; and it is found much scanted and impaired in the encrease it had woont to afford. Three persons, whose names are hereunder printed, have scene this serpent, beside divers others, as the carrier of Horsam, who lieth at the White Horse in Southwarke, and who can certifie the truth of all that has been here related.

"JOHN STEELE,
"CHRISTOPHER HOLDER;
"And a widow woman dwelling nere Faygate."

The names snake, serpent, adder, and worm were used indiscriminately, and little attempt was made to identify the various species. Batman includes as worms, adders, serpents, all creeping beasts that pass from place to place by stretching of the body and drawing together again. He uses the word *adder* as the generic name for all kinds of serpents. Quoting Pliny, he states that in India " be so great adders that they swallow up both harts and bulls all whole" (*Batman upon Bartholome*, 1582).

Don John Bermudez, ambassador from Presbyter John, sovereign of the northern parts of India, to John III. of Portugal, in the year 1565, describes several snakes under their native names. One of these seems to correspond to the *cobra di capello*, a species found in abundance in India and the neighbouring countries.

"There be other," he writes, "which they call, Of the shadow, or Canopie, because it hath a skinne on the head, wherewith it covereth a very precious stone, which they say it hath in her head." (*Purchas*, vol. ii. p. 1169.)

Among the adventures of Antoine Knivet, who accompanied Thomas Candish in his second voyage to the South Seas, in 1591, an encounter with a *sorocucu*, a species of snake, is related:—

"The serpent that I killed was thirteene span long, it had foure and twentie teeth, as sharpe as any naile, about the necke it has greater shels then the other parts of her body; the shels were blacke and russet like a coller, and on her body they were russet and darke greene; under her belly all speckled with black and white. It had foure sharpe feet, no longer than a mans finger, it had a tongue like a harping iron, her taile was like a straight bull horne, all black and white, listed. (*Purchas*, vol. iv. p. 1230.)

Champlain, in his account of a voyage to the West Indies and Mexico in the years 1599–1602, mentions the rattlesnake. He, however, confuses this species with the horned snake, and makes an obvious mistake as to the venomous property of the creature's tail. He writes:—

"Throughout New Spain, there is a kind of snake, which is of the length of a pike, and as thick as the arm; the head as large as a hen's egg, on which they have two plumes; at the end of the tail they have a rattle, which makes a noise as they glide along. They are very dangerous with their teeth, and with their tail; nevertheless the Indians eat them, after having taken away the two extremities." (Page 3, ed. Hakluyt Soc., 1859.)

The Salamander. 319

Modern works on natural history tell us that the rattlesnake is only found in America. We find it mentioned as occurring in Congo, in Africa, by one of Purchas's pilgrims, Lopes, a Portuguese :—

"Other serpents there are that are venemous, that carrie upon the tippe of their tayle, a certaine little roundell like a bell, which ringeth as they goe, so as it may be heard." (*Purchas*, vol. ii. p. 1003.)

A description of the Boa Constrictor occurs in the natural history notes of the Portuguese resident in Brazil, so frequently quoted in this volume :—

Boa.

"The giboya is a snake of the greatest that are in this countrie, and there are some found of twentie foot in length. They are very faire, but more wonderfull they are in swallowing a whole deere; they have no poison, neither are their teeth great according to the bodie. To take their prey whereon they feed, they use this sleight. It layeth it selfe along by the highwayes, and when the prey passeth it leapeth upon it, and windes it selfe in such order, and crusheth it so that it breaketh all his bones, and afterward licketh it, and his licking hath such vertues that it bruiseth or suppleth it all, and then it swallowes it up whole." (*Purchas*, vol. iv. p. 1303.)

The Salamander was supposed, by reason of the intense cold of its body, to be able to exist in the hottest flames, and even to put out the fire. Sir Thomas Herbert writes, in 1626 :—

Salamander.

"Salamanders here [Madagascar] be also, a sort of lizard extreme cold by nature, whence (like ice) for some time they endure the fire, yea (if little) extinguish it as Aristotle affirms; yet by tryal we find that they will quickly be burnt if the fire be powerful. . . . Commonly they obscure themselves in moist and umbragious places, so as when they appear they are sure presages of a storm approaching; their teeth and tongues are venemous, but the other parts may be eaten without danger." (*Travels*, p. 23.)

A modern author, Mr. Frank Buckland, considers it possible that the power possessed by these reptiles of exuding a fluid has given rise to the fable of their incombustibility.

Falstaff, after many uncomplimentary remarks on *Bardolph's* personal appearance, exclaims, "I have maintained that salamander of yours with fire any time this two and thirty years; God reward me for it!" (1 *Henry IV.*, iii. 3, 52).

A lizard in the midst of flames was adopted by Francis I. as his badge, with the legend, *Nutrisco et extinguo*, "I nourish and extinguish."

> "You spotted snakes with double tongue,
> Thorny hedgehogs, be not seen;
> Newts and blind-worms, do no wrong;
> Come not near our fairy queen."
> (*Midsummer Night's Dream*, ii. 2, 9.)

Newt. "All things that breede in the mudde are not evets," writes Lyly, either quoting or originating a proverb; but it was quite sufficient that the harmless Newt or Eft was found in damp, cold places that it should have gained the reputation of being spiteful and poisonous. *Timon of Athens* classes "the gilded newt" with "all the abhorred births below crisp heaven" (iv. 2, 182). "The wall-newt and the water" formed part of *Poor Tom's* unsavoury diet.

Frog. Frogs as well as toads were banished from Ireland, though upon what pretext it is hard to say. Giraldus Cambrensis reports that a solitary frog was found in his time in a meadow, near Waterford, and brought as a curiosity to court. It was pronounced by the best authorities to be an omen of an invasion of the English. As it was quite impossible that this frog could have been born and bred on Irish soil, the learned writer accounts for its appearance by the suggestion that it must have been wafted across the channel on a cloud; or a ship might have brought it over from some neighbouring port. Dr. Perceval Wright, in his recent work, *Animal Life* (p. 410), tells us that the introduction of frogs into Ireland is due to Dr. Gwythers, physician, and a Fellow of Trinity College, Dublin, who imported a supply of these creatures from England, in the year 1700, and turned them out into the ditches of the college park. Their surroundings were apparently uncongenial, and in a short time they all perished. Not discouraged by his failure, the doctor sent for a fresh supply, not of frogs, but of frog-spawn, which he threw into the same ditches. The second experiment was more successful, and in the course of some years the frog family had increased sufficiently to spread itself over the whole island.

Both frogs and toads were supposed to have this natural property, that when they sit erect they hold their heads steady and without motion. This stately action Spenser, in his *Shepherd's Calendar*, calls the "lording" of frogs.

Topsell quotes from Albertus Magnus the statement that the mouth of the frog closes about the end of August and remains shut throughout the winter. This remarkable assertion is repeated and confirmed by Izaak Walton.

The frog as an article of diet seems never to have found favour in England, but it was early appreciated by our continental neighbours. Andrew Boorde tells us that—

"in Flaunders, and Braban, and other provinces anexed to the same the people wil eate the hynder loynes of frogges, and wyll eate todstooles." (*Introduction of Knowledge*, 1542, ed. Early English Text Society, 1870.)

Edgar, in his assumed madness, replies to *Gloucester's* query as to his name, " Poor Tom, that eats the swimming frog, the toad, the tadpole, the wall-newt and the water" (*King Lear*, iii. 4, 134). The connexion between frogs and tadpoles was noticed, though probably not rightly understood. Du Bartas refers to the common

Y

notion that frogs came down in showers of rain. He writes :—

> "Earths green bed
> "With stinking frogs is sometimes covered :
> Eyther becanse the floating cloud doth fold
> Within it self both moist, dry, hot, and cold,
> Whence all things heer are made : or else for that
> The active windes, sweeping this dusty flat,
> Sometimes in th' aire som fruitfull dust doo heap :
> Whence these new-formed ugly creatnres leap :
> As on the edges of some standing lake
> Which neighbour mountains with their gutters make,
> The foamy slime, it selfe transformeth oft
> To green half-tadpoles, playing there aloft,
> Half-made, half-unmade; round about the flood
> Half-dead, half-living; half a frog, half-mud."
>
> (Page 13.)

And again :—

> "Why! Think ye (fond) those people fell from heav'n
> All-ready-made; as in a summer ev'n
> After a sweltring day, som sultry showr
> Doth in the marshes heaps of tadpals pour,
> Which in the ditches (chapt with parching weather)
> Lie crusht and croaking in the mud together?"
>
> (Page 130.)

Topsell gives a somewhat confused account of the transformations of the young frog, but leans also to the theory that some kinds of frog are bred from slime. He refers to the plague of frogs in Egypt in support of the popular belief in frog showers.

> "Sweet are the uses of adversity ;
> Which, like the Toad, ugly and venomous,
> Wears yet a precious jewel in his head."
>
> (*As You Like It*, ii. 1, 12.)

Toad. "The foule Toad has a faire stone in his heade," writes Lyly (*Euphues*, p. 53) ; and again, " The fayrer the stone is in the toades head the more pestilent the poyson is in hir bowelles" (p. 326). Many quotations might be given from early writers setting forth the medicinal qualities of the toad-stone. When set in a ring, it was a sure preservative of the wearer against poison. Fenton, writing in 1569, says, "There is to be found in the heads of old and great toads a stone they call borax or stelon, which being used as rings gives forwarning against venom." In these "good old times" the study of chemistry seems to have been chiefly pursued with the object of gaining possession of the deadliest weapon in nature's armory. That this knowledge was practical as well as theoretical, we gather from the precautions against poison that were universally adopted, and from the anxiety that was felt to secure some unfailing antidote.

The toad so common in English gardens is not found in Ireland, but a species of toad, called the Natter Jack, is met with in that country. Gonzalo Ferdinando de Oviedo, in his history of the West Indies, mentions some species of South American toads possessed of considerable vocal powers. These toads, he says—

"sing after three or foure sort, for some of them sing pleasantly, other like ours of Spaine, some also whistle, and other some make another manner of noise: they are likewise of divers colours, as some greene, some russet or gray, and some almost blacke, but of all sorts they are great and filthie, and noious by reason of their great multitude, yet are they not venemous, as I have said." (*Purchas*, vol. ii. p. 976.)

In his quaint treatise on gardening, published 1593, Thomas Hyll recommends, on the authority of the Greek writer Apuleius, that when the earth is dug preparatory to seed sowing, a speckled toad should be first drawn round the garden, then put into an earthen pot, buried in the centre of the bed and left there until sowing time. The toad is then to be dug up and cast a great way off, lest the plants growing in the neighbourhood should acquire a bitter taste; after this precaution no creeping thing will presume to disquiet or grieve the owner (*Art of Gardening*, 1593, p. 22).

Lyly explains the origin of the toadstool, a fungus that springs up in what are called fairy rings :—

"I am of this minde with Homer, that as the snayle that crept out of hir shell was turned eftsoones into a toad, and therby was forced to make a stoole to sit on, disdaining her own house : so the travailler that stragleth from his own countrey, is in short tyme transformed into so monstrous a shape, that hee is faine to alter his mansion with his manners, and to live where he canne, not where he would." (*Euphues*, p. 240.)

CHAPTER XIV.

THE large Catholic population, and the great strictness with which fast-days were observed in medieval England, rendered a constant supply of fish most important. Even after the Reformation, abstinence was still enjoined on all Fridays and Saturdays, as well as on other days denominated fish-days. Queen Elizabeth, it is said, who continued to enforce this change of diet, expressly stated that her object in thus adopting a Catholic custom was to encourage "fishermen, the chiefest nurse for mariners," and to diminish the consumption of mutton. This was a measure of protection, not of religious observance, but at the same time it was politic on the queen's part to maintain a ceremonial abstinence which was harmless and had certain advantages. In the fifth year of her Majesty's reign it was ordained that a penalty of £3 should be inflicted on any one eating flesh on fish-days, or the alternative of three months' imprisonment. This punishment was considered excessive, and on the 10th of March, 1594, an order of Privy Council reduced the penalty to £1. This order is given in full in Mr. Arber's *English Garner*, 1877 (vol. i. p. 299). In this document it is estimated that the number of oxen killed weekly in the city of London amounted to 67,000; the fish-days in the year, including Lent, amounted to 153.

Thomas Fuller not only urges the necessity of continuing fast-days for the maintenance of fishermen, but he points out the appropriateness of the days originally selected :—

"Our English fishermen, in Kent, Sussex, Hantshire, &c. set forth on Monday and catch their fish, which on Tuesday they send up to London, where on Wednesday it is sold and eaten. Such therefore, who have lately propounded to antidate fish-eating, and to remove it from Wednesday to Tuesday, must thereby occasion the encroaching the Lord's day to furnish the markets with that commodity." (*Worthies of England*, vol. i. p. 24.)

Harrison, in his description of England, gives a tolerably complete list of the fresh and salt water fish used as articles of commerce in his time :—

"Besides the salmon therefore, we have the trout, barbell, graile, powt, chevin, pike, goodgeon, smelt, perch, menan, shrimpes, creveses, lampreies, and such like, whose preservation is provided for by verie sharpe lawes, not onelie in our rivers, but also in plashes or lakes, and ponds, which otherwise would bring small profit to the owners. In December and Januarie we commonlie abound in herring and red fish, as rochet and gurnard. In Februarie and March we feed on plaice, trowts, turbut, muskles, &c. In Aprill and Maie, with makrell, and cockles. In June and Julie, with conger. In August and September, with haddocke and herring: and the two moneths insuing with the same, as also thornbacke and reigh of all sorts; all which are the most usuall, and wherewith our common sort are best of all refreshed. Of fishes therefore as I find five sorts, the flat, the round, the long, the legged, and shelled: so the flat are divided into the smooth, scaled, and tailed. Of the first are the plaice, the but, the turbut, birt, floke or sea flounder, dorreie, dab, &c. Of the second the soles, &c. Of the third are chaits, maidens, kingsons, flath and thornebacke, whereof the greater be for the most part either dried and carried into other countries, or sodden, sowsed, and eaten here at home, whilest the lesser be fried or buttered. Under the round kinds are commonlie comprehended lumps, an ugly fish to sight, and yet verie delicat in eating, if it be kindlie dressed: the whiting, an old waiter or servitor in the Court, the rochet, sea breame, pirle, hake, sea trowt, gurnard, haddocke, cod, herring, pilchard, sprat, and such like. And these are they whereof I have best knowledge, and be commonlie to be had in their times upon our coasts. Under this kind also are all the great fish con-

teined as the scale, the dolphin, the porpoise, the thirlepoole, whale, and whatsoever is round of bodie be it never so great and huge. Of the long sort are congers, eeles, garefish, and such other of that forme. Finallie, of the legged kind we have not manie, neither have I seene anie more of this sort than the polypus called in English the lobstar, crayfish, or crevis, and the crab. ... We have in like sort no small store of great whelkes, scalops and perewinkles, and each of them are brought farre into the land from the sea coast in their several seasons."
(*Holinshed*, vol. i. p. 377.)

The word *polypus* is here used according to its literal significance of "many feet."

Du Bartas (p. 40) quaintly notices the difference in structure of various species of what he chooses to call fish:—

"Some have their heads groveling betwixt their féet,
As th' inky cuttles, and the many-feet:
Some in their breast (as crabs), some head-less are,
Foot-less, and finnless (as the banefull hare,
And heatfull oyster), in a heap confus'd,
Their parts unparted, in themselves diffus'd."

Richard Carew gives the following short list of fish taken in the havens of Cornwall:—

"They may be divided into three kinds, shell, flat, and round fish. Of shell fish, there are winkles, limpets, cockles, muscles, shrimps, crabs, lobsters, and oysters.

"Of flat fish, rays, thornbacks, soles, flowks, dabs, plaice.

"Of round fish, brit, sprat, barn, smelts, whiting, scad, chad, sharks, cuddles, eels, conger, basse, millet, whirlpool, and porpoise.

"Of eels there are two sorts: the one valsen, of best tasté, coming from the fresh rivers, when the great rain floods after September do break their beds, and carry them into the sea: the other, bred in the salt water, and called a conger eel, which afterwards, as his higness increaseth, ventureth out into the main ocean, and is enfranchised a burgess of that vast commonwealth."

Of the different species found on the coast he writes:—

"The coast is plentifully stored, both with those fore-remembered, enlarged to a bigger size, and divers other, as, namely, of shell-fish, sea-hedgehogs, scallops and sheath-fish: or flat, brets, turbots, dories, holybut: round, pilcherd; herring, pollock, mackrell, gurnard, illek, tub, bream, old-wife, hake, dog-fish, lounp, cunner, rockling, cod, wrothe, becket, haddock, gilt-head, rough-hound, squar-scad, seal, tunny, and many other.

"The sheath, or razor-fish, resembleth in length and bigness a man's finger, and in taste the lobster, but reputed of greater restorative. The sea-hedgehog, of like or more goodness, is enclosed in a round shell, fashioned as a loaf of bread, handsomely wrought and pincked, and guarded by an outer skin full of prickles, as the land urchin." (*Survey of Cornwall*, 1602, p. 97, ed. Tonkin, 1811.)

We may form some idea of the variety of fish considered appropriate for the table from the contributions which were sent as presents to the Judges on the Western and Oxford Circuits during the years 1596–1601.

"Of the sturgeon, pieces were sent at Taunton, Dorchester, and Exeter. The salmon was usual in February and in July in all the western counties. Salmon peale were also general in the west and at Gloucester. The shewings, or sea-trout, appear at Hereford. The dolphin appears once at Dorchester in February; a piece of porpoise, to be roasted or cooked like the sturgeon, once at Launceston; and the dory at Oakhampton and Taunton. The conger was eaten at Taunton, Oakhampton, and Exeter. The cod was used fresh, and also salted and dried, and a cod's head is not unfrequent; whilst the milwell, a fish allied to the cod, appears in Dorsetshire, Devonshire, and Cornwall; turbot were not very frequent, but are mentioned at Taunton, Dorchester, and Exeter. Braymes were used at Exeter and Gloucester; basse, or sea-perch, at Exeter, Salisbury, and Dorchester, and also at Reading; mulletts were not unfrequent; and soles, plaice, haddock, herrings, whiting, the thornback or scate, and sprats were common. The other dried fish were the buckthorn, or whiting, split and dried; the haberdine, or salt cod; ling of various sorts, viz. the London, Devonshire, Organ, and green salt ling; herrings; and the dried and salted hake, once called in the *account* 'a drie fish called Poor John,' and most contemptuously treated by Shakspeare. The shell-fish included oysters of two sorts, one called at Salisbury and Chard the 'long oyster;' lobsters, crabs, shrimps, cockles, mussels whelks, the razor-fish once, and craw-fish plentiful. The fresh-water fish were the Thames trout, at Reading, and trout frequently elsewhere; the pike, carp, tench, perch, roach, flounders, barbel, lampreys in February, eels generally, and Holland eels, at Winchester, and flounders at Exeter."

This extract is taken from an account of the expenses of the Judges of Assize riding the Western and Oxford Circuits, in the time of Elizabeth, contributed to the *Camden Miscellany* (vol. iv., 1857).

A long poem on the secrets of angling, written by John Dennys, and published before the year 1613, has lately been reprinted by Mr. Arber, in his *English Garner*, 1877 (vol. i. p. 143). This author professes to teach "the choicest tools, baits, and seasons for the taking of any fish, in pond or river: practised and familiarly opened in three books." The whole poem will well repay perusal, but three verses must serve here for a sample :—

"The crocodile that weeps when he doth wrong,
The halibut that hurts the appetite,
The turbot broad, the seal, the sturgeon strong,
The cod and cozze that greedy are to bite,
The hake, the haddock, and conger long,
The yellow ling, the milwell fair and white,
　　The spreading ray, the thornback thin and flat,
　　The boisterous base, the hoggish tunny fat.

"These kinds of fish that are so large of size,
And many more that here I leave untold,
Shall go for me, and all the rest likewise
That are the flock of Proteus' wat'ry fold;
For well I think my hooks would not suffice,
Nor slender lines, the least of these to hold.
I leave them therefore to the surging seas:
In that huge depth, to wander at their ease.

"And speak of such as in the fresh are found,
The little roach, the menise biting fast,
The slimy tench, the slender smelt and round,
The umber sweet, the grayling good of taste,
The wholesome ruff, the barbel not so sound,
The perch and pike that all the rest do waste,
　　The bream, the carp, the chub and chavender,
　　And many more that in fresh waters are."

Burton, in his *Anatomie of Melancholy* (vol. i. p. 528),

weighs the advantages of the sport of fishing with other amusements, but he is too cautious to pronounce any decided opinion on the matter.

" Fishing," he writes, " is a kinde of hunting by water, be it with nets, weeles, baits, angling or otherwise, and yeelds all out as much pleasure to some men, as dogs, or hawks. . . . James Dubravius, that Moravian, in his book *De Pisc.* telleth, how travelling by the highway side in Silesia, he found a nobleman booted up to the groines, wading himself, pulling the nets, and labouring as much as any fisherman of them all: and when some belike objected to him the baseness of his office, he excused himself, 'that if other men might hunt hares, why should not he hunt carpes?' Many gentlemen in like sort, with us, will wade up to the arm-holes, upon such occasions, and voluntarily undertake that to satisfie their pleasure, which a poor man for a good stipend would scarce be hired to undergo. . . . But he that shall consider the variety of baits, for all seasons, and pretty devices which our anglers have invented, peculiar lines, false flies, severall sleights, etc., will say, that it deserves like commendation, requires as much study and perspicacity as the rest, and is to be preferred before many of them: because hawking and hunting are very laborious, much riding, and many dangers accompany them: but this is still and quiet: and if so be the angler catch no fish, yet he hath a wholesome walk to the brook side, pleasant shade, by the sweet silver streams; he hath good aire and sweet smels of fine fresh meadow flowers; he hears the melodious harmony of birds; he sees the swans, herns, ducks, water-hens, cootes and many other fowle, with their brood, which he thinketh better than the noise of hounds, or blast of hornes, and all the sport that they can make."

With regard to the wholesomeness of fish as an article of diet, Burton writes :—

" Gomesius doth immoderately extol sea-fish, which others as much vilifie, and, above the rest, dryed, sowced, indurate fish, as ling, fumados, red-herrings, sprats, stock-fish, aberdine, poor-john, all shell-fish. Tim. Bright excepts lobster and crab. Messarius commends salmon, which Bruerinus contradicts. Magninus rejects congre, sturgeon, turbot, mackerel, skate." (Vol. i. p. 218.)

Although the number of fish known at this time nearly equals that of birds and quadrupeds, the habits of the finny tribes were so little studied that they are rarely mentioned by poets. The list of fish mentioned in Shakspeare's plays is a short one; the references to freshwater fish are scanty, and those to salt-water inhabitants are more suggestive of a fishmonger's counter than of their natural element. Even Mr. Russel, in his enthusiastic defence of the "gentle craft," while he claims to find angling fondly mentioned by almost every English poet, has to admit that Shakspeare had apparently little acquaintance with the sport. The oft-quoted speech of Ursula tells us that—

"The pleasantest angling is to see the fish
Cut with her golden oars the silver stream,
And greedily devour the treacherous bait.
(*Much Ado*, iii. 1, 26.)

This is, Mr. Russel, in his recent work, *The Salmon* (p. 26), declares, so far from being "pleasant, not possible, angling, for if you see the fish, the fish sees you, and that's an end of it;" but some allowance may be made for the fact that this was written in an age when British fish were in a comparatively primitive state of mind.

Shakspeare refers more than once to the avidity with which English people crowd to see any rarity. *Trinculo* exclaims, at the sight of *Caliban*:—

"A strange fish! were I in England now, as once I was, and had but this fish painted, not a holiday fool there but would give a piece of silver: there would this monster make a man; any strange beast there makes a man." (*Tempest*, ii. 2, 28.)

This passion for novelty was abundantly supplied by the curiosity-mongers of the period. Peacham, in his *Complete Gentleman*, records the wondrous sights of London in his time, each to be seen for a penny. Amongst others we have—

"That horne of Windsor, of an unicorne very likely,
The cave of Merlin, the skirts of old Tom a Lincolne;
* * * * *
Saint James his ginney hens, his cassawarway moreover,

The beaver i' the parke, strange beast as er'e any man saw,
Downe-shearing willowes with teeth as sharpe as a hand-saw,
  * * * * *
Drakes ship at Detford, King Richards bed-sted i' Leyster,
The Whitehall whale-bones, the silver bason i' Chester,
The live caught dog-fish, the wolfe and Harry the lyon,
Hunks of the beare-garden, to be feared, if he be nigh ou."

In Sir Henry Herbert's *Office Book*, which contains a register of all the shows of London from 1623 to 1642, occurs "a licence to Francis Sherret to show a straunge fish for a yeare, from the 10th of March, 1635."

In Mayne's *City Match* (iii. 1) allusion is made to this custom of exhibiting monsters, though the particular subject under discussion is an imposture :—

"*Roseclap.*   Some
Say 'tis an o'ergrown porpoise ; others say
'Tis the fish caught in Cheshire ; one to whom
The rest agree, said 'twas a mermaid.
 Plot.   'Slight !
Roseclap shall have a patent of him. The birds,
Brought from Peru, the hairy wench, the camel,
The elephant, dromedaries, or Windsor Castle,
The woman with dead flesh, or she that washes,
Threads needles, writes, dresses her children, plays
O' th' virginals with her feet, could never draw
People like this."
     (*Dodsley's Old Plays*, vol. xiii. p. 248.)

Stickleback. The tiny Stickleback, Stickle-bag, Hackle, Sharplin, Bansticle, probably owes its proud position at the head of the great fish class to the fact that it is a good representative of the spiny-finned fishes, which according to modern naturalists form the first order. It was doubtless as common in early times as it is at present. It had probably also the same fascination for juvenile anglers. It was found both in salt and fresh water. No doubt Izaak Walton first learned to love his craft by sitting by the pond side with hook fashioned from a bent pin, and with a bottle by his side ready to receive the tiny prey. Afterwards, become "his craft's master," he writes:—

"There is also a little fish called a sticklebag, a fish without scales, but hath his body fenced with several prickles. I know not where he dwells in winter; nor what he is good for in summer, but only to make sport for boys and women-anglers, and to feed other fish that be fish of prey." (Part i. ch. 18.)

"The Pearch with prickling fins against the pike prepared,
 As nature had thereon bestow'd this stronger guard,
 His daintiness to keep (each curious palate's proof)   **Perch.**
 From his vile ravenous foe: next him I name the ruffe,
 His very near ally and both for scale and fin,
 In taste, and for his bait (indeed) his next of kin."
                          (DRAYTON, *Polyolbion*, song xxvi.)

Leland speaks of Perches in great number in a Welsh lake near Brecknock. The perch was considered a very wholesome fish, and was recommended for invalids. Perch in jelly seems to have been a fashionable dish. The perch was found in all lakes and rivers, with few exceptions, throughout England. Sir Thomas Browne includes among the fishes of Norfolk—

"*perca* or perch, great and small; whereof such as are taken in Breydon, on this side Yarmouth, in the mixed water, make a dish very dainty; and I think, scarce to be bettered in England."

He next mentions its "next of kin," the Ruffe, or Pope—

"the *aspredo perca minor*, and probably the *cernua* of Cardan, commonly called a ruff; in great plenty in Norwich river, and even in the stream of the city; which though   **Ruffe.**
Camden appropriated unto this city yet they are also
found in the rivers of Oxford and Cambridge." (Vol. iv. p. 335.)

The ruffe, or pope, says Cuvier, was first noticed by Dr. Caius, who sent a drawing of a specimen found by him in the river Yare, near Norwich, to Gesner, the Swiss naturalist. The name *aspredo*, from *asper*, rough, was bestowed on this fish on account of the harshness of its scales. The title *cernua* given by Cardan has been explained by some to signify the downward position of its head. Thomas Muffett writes (*Healths Improvement*, p. 187) :—

"Ruffs or ruggels are not much unlike to perches, for the goodness of their flesh though their skin be rougher: the best live in sandy places where they wax exceeding fat and sweet."

Izaak Walton endorses this opinion of the fine flavour of this little fish.

Drayton, singing the praises of the German Ocean, thus enumerates the fish taken on the east coast of England :—

"What fish can any shore, or British sea-town show
That's eatable to us, that it doth not bestow
Abundantly thereon? The herring king of sea,
The faster feeding cod, the mackarel brought by May,
The dainty sole, and plaice, the dab, as of their blood;
The conger finely sous'd, hot summer's coolest food;
The whiting known to all, a general wholesome dish;
The gurnet, rochet, mayd, and mullet, dainty fish;
The haddock, turbet, bert, fish nourishing and strong;
The thornback, and the scate, provocative among;
The weaver, which althoug his prickles venom be;
The fishers cut away, which buyers seldom see :
Yet for the fish he bears, 'tis not accounted bad;
The sea-flounder is here as common as the shad;
The sturgeon cut to keggs, too big to handle whole,
Gives many a dainty bit, out of his lusty jole."

(*Polyolbion*, song xxv.)

Mullet. The finest Mullets were taken off the coast near Arundel in Sussex. Of the mullet Mr. Couch writes :—

"The charge of imbecility brought against this fish by Pliny, as shown by the fact that it hides its head for concealment, and then acts as if persuaded that its whole body was concealed, is, as Cuvier has remarked, the opposite to what we know of the character of these fishes, of which the vigilance when exposed to observation is very great, although this is accompanied with little appearance that would lead us to suspect its existence." (*British Fishes*, 1877, vol. iii. p. 8.)

Montaigne (*Essay* liv.) bears witness to the amiable character of this little fish.

" Mullets," he writes, " when one of their companions is engaged cross the line over their back and with a fin they have there indented like a saw, cut and saw it asunder."

Thomas Muffett (*Healths Improvement*, p. 158) tells us that—

" sea-mullets differ little or nothing in shape from barbels, saving that they are very little or nothing bearded, and those that have beards, have them onely on the nether lip."

Gurnets, or Gurnards, according to Muffett (p. 152), " are of two sorts, swart or reddish ; either of them are of a white, firm, dry, and wholesome substance." By the dark variety the piper is perhaps meant. It was less common than the red gurnet. When soused, or pickled, the gurnet was held in low estimation. *Falstaff* exclaims, " If I be not ashamed of my soldiers, I am a soused gurnet " (1 *Henry IV.*, i. 2, 12).

Gurnet.

" Currs," writes Muffett, " are supposed by Dr. Cajus to be all one with our gurnard; but it somewhat differeth, being of a very firm, whitish, dry sound and wholesome flesh."

The Miller's Thumb, or Bullhead, is mentioned by William Browne in one of his pastoral poems :—

Miller's Thumb.

> " The trout, the dace, the pike, the breame,
> The eele, that loves the troubled streame,
> The millers thombe, the hiding loach,
> The perch, the ever nibbling roach,
> The shoats with whom is Tavie fraught,
> The foolish gudgeon, quickly caught,
> And last the little minnow-fish,
> Whose chiefe delight in gravell is."
> (*Britannia's Pastorals*, book i, song ii.)

Yarrell gives an explanation of the name :—

"The hand of the miller is constantly under the meal-spout, to ascertain by actual contact the character and qualities of the meal produced. By a peculiar movement the thumb spreads the sample over the fingers, and is, therefore, employed with tact, the gauge of the value of the produce. Hence the proverb, 'An honest miller hath a golden thumb,' in reference to the amount of profit that is the reward of his skill. By incessant use in this way, the miller's thumb acquires a form which is said to resemble exactly the shape of the head of the little fish so constantly found in the mill-stream." (*British Fishes*, vol. i. p. 57.)

Thomas Nashe, in his *Lenten Stuffe*, alludes to the voracity of this small creature, which is out of all proportion to its size :—

"In my exile, and irkesome discontented abandonment, the silliest miller's thombe, or contemptible stickle-back of my enemies, is as busie nibbling about my fame, as if I were a dead man throwne amongst them to feede upon." (*Harleian Miscellany*, vol. vi. p. 146.)

Mackerel. The Mackerel used to be included in the list of migratory fishes, but, according to Yarrell, this was a mistake. It only retires a short distance from the shore, returning to the shallow waters to spawn.

Warwickshire now boasts that, although an inland county, it is the best supplied with fish. But this was not the case in the Middle Ages, and there may be some connexion between the condition of the fish which reached the market town of Stratford-on-Avon, and Shakspeare's frequent reference to its unsavoury state. He has but one allusion to mackerel, not of the freshest, and in the case of this fish the tediousness of transport must have been peculiarly unfortunate.

Tunny. The Tunny, a fish of considerable size, was well known to the ancients, and has in all times been highly prized. It was eaten both fresh and salted, though from Muffett's directions some skill seems to have been required in this preparation.

> "As porpesses must be baked while they are new, so tunny is never good till it have been long pouldred [pickled] with salt, vinegar, coriander, and hot spices." (Page 173.)

According to Pliny a vast shoal of tunnies arrayed themselves against Alexander the Great, and were more formidable to his army than Tyrians, Indians, or Persians. Du Bartas refers to this incident, but omits to describe their mode of warfare:—

> "Shall I omit the tunnies, that durst meet
> Th' Eoan monarchs never daunted fleet,
> And beard more bravely his victorious powrs
> Than the defendants of the Tyrian towrs;
> Or Porus, conquered on the Indian coast;
> Or great Darius, that three battels lost?"
>
> (Page 40.)

Montaigne attributes mathematical knowledge to this fish:—

> "In the manner of living of the tunnies, we observe a singular knowledge of the three parts of mathematicks. As to astrology, they teach it men, for they stay in the place where they are surpriz'd by the Brumal solstice, and never stir from thence till the next equinox: for which reason, Aristotle himself attributes to them this science. As to geometry and arithmetick, they always form their body in the figure of a cube, every way square, and make up the body of a battalion, solid, close and environed round with six equal sides, so that swimming in this square order, as large behind as before; whoever in seeing them can count one rank, may easily number the whole troop, by reason that the depth is equal to the breadth, and the breadth to the length." (*Essay* liv.)

The Bonito, or Striped-bellied Tunny, is similar to the tunny in form, but inferior in size, being only thirty inches long. Sir Richard Hawkins, in his description of a voyage to the South Sea, speaks of three fish which accompany ships in the

Bonito.

tropics; one of these is "the bonito, or Spanish makerill, altogether like unto a mackerell, but that it is somewhat more growne; he is reasonable food, but dryer than a mackerell" (*Purchas*, vol. iv. p. 1375). The name Spanish mackerel is given by Yarrell to another species of fish. The name Bonito, according to this author, belongs properly to a species of tunny, which is very common in the tropical seas, and which is especially noticed by sailors for its inveterate pursuit of the flying-fish. In a second voyage, Sir Richard Hawkins gives an account of the persecution of the unfortunate flying-fish by its numerous enemies:—

"There be also of sea-fishes, which we saw coming along the coast flying, which are of the bignesse of a smelt, the biggest sort whereof have foure wings, but the other have but two: of these wee sawe comming out of Guinea a hundred in a company, which being chased by the gilt-heads, otherwise called the bonitos, do to avoid them the better, take their flight out of the water, but yet are they not able to flie farre, because of the drying of their wings, which serve them not to flie but when they are moist, and therefore, when they can flie no further, they fall into the water, and having wet their wings, take a new flight againe. These be of bignesse like a carpe, and in colour like a makarell, but it is the swiftest fish in swimming that is, and followeth her prey very fiercely, not only in the water, but also out of the water, for as the flying fish taketh her flight, so doth this bonito leape after them, and taketh them sometimes above the water. There were some of these bonitos, which being galled by a fisgig, did follow our shippe comming out of Guinea 500 leagues. There is a sea-fowle also that chaseth this flying fish as well as the bonito: for as the flying fish taketh her flight, so doth this fowle pursue to take her, which is a greater pleasure then hawking, for both the flights are as pleasant, and also more often then an hundred times: for the fowle can flie no way, but one or other lighteth in her pawes, the number of them are so abundant. There is an innumerable yoong frie of these flying fishes, which commonly keepe about the ship, and are not so big as butter-flies, and yet by flying do avoid the unsatiablenesse of the bonito." (*Hakluyt*, vol. iii. p. 616.)

It is perhaps scarcely necessary to point out an error in the above account. The fish whose existence is thus embittered by double persecution, has no power of flight in the proper sense of the word. According to modern observers, the length of time which it can remain in the air is determined by the power of the spring which it makes on leaving the water. The motion is more that of a leap than of a flight, and cannot be prolonged after the original impetus has diminished.

The Sword-fish, or Xiphias of Spenser, is thus described by Sir Thomas Browne, from a specimen taken in his neighbourhood:— Sword-fish.

"A sword-fish, entangled in the herring-nets at Yarmouth, agreeable unto the Icon [picture] in Johnstonus, with a smooth sword, not unlike the *gladius* of Rondeletius, about a yard and a half long; no teeth; eyes very remarkable; enclosed in a hard cartilaginous covercle, about the bignesse of a good apple." (Vol. iv. p. 326.)

Olaus Magnus, on the contrary, has drawn on his own imagination, for with the exception of a pointed snout, the account he gives of this fish is wrong in every particular. The mouth of the sword-fish is a mere slit, and the projection of the upper jaw would effectually baffle any attempt on the part of the inquisitive mariner to look into it.

"The sword-fish," he writes, "is like no other, but in something it is like a whale. He hath as ugly a head as an owl: his mouth is wondrous deep, as a vast pit, whereby he terrifies and drives away those that look into it. His eyes are horrible, his back wedge-fashion, or elevated like a sword; his snout is pointed." (Page 228.)

This fish is said to pursue the whale, and to pierce it with its beak-like weapon, but no motive has been discovered for this wanton attack. It also dashes against the sides of ships, probably mistaking them for whales, piercing the timbers for some inches.

The Yellow Skulpin is one of the most beautiful little fishes to be seen on our coasts, and not very uncommon. It is yellow, with delicate Uranoscopus.

blue and purple markings, and is called in Sussex the lizard fish. Modern names for it are yellow gurnard, gemmeous dragonet, gowdie, and golden skulpin.

"This fish," writes Mr. Couch, "is common in the Mediterranean, and must therefore have been known to the ancients, but from their want of precision on subjects of natural history, it is not easy to pronounce whether it be the same with the species known to them by the name of *callionymus*, which is the term adopted by Linnæus as the designation of the genus in which the yellow skulpin is arranged. Some fish which bore this name is referred to by Aristophanes, as sufficiently known for popular allusion by the supposed property of possessing a large abundance of gall. It is also mentioned by Aristotle, and in later times by Ælian. Pliny further tells us that with the Romans, in addition to the name of callionymus, it was known as the *uranoscopus*, or sky-gazer, because its eyes were on the top of the head, with their vision directed upward. This latter circumstance, in connection with the former name, which recognises the beauty of its appearance, may be supposed to point to the yellow skulpin, which answers to both the particulars." (*British Fishes*, vol. ii. p. 174.)

Du Bartas, who no doubt drew most of his descriptions from classical sources, makes still clearer the identity of this fish by taking notice of its lengthened fin; though if we interpret the word *admire*, to wonder at, his lines would apply equally well to the ugly sea-angler.

"O! who can here sufficiently admire
That gaping-fish whose glistening eyes aspire
Still toward heav'n; as if beneath the skies
He found no object worthy of his eyes.
As the woodpecker, his long tongue doth lill
Out of the clov'n pipe of his horny bill,
To catch the emets; when, beguil'd with-all,
The busie swarms about it creep and crawl:
Th' urano-scope, so, hid in mud, doth put
Out of his gullet a long limber gut,
Most like unto a little worm (at sight)
Where-at, oft-soons, many small fishes bite:
Which ther-withall this angler swallows straight,
Alwaies self-armed with hook, line, and bait."

(Page 41.)

Muffett calls the Cod a great sea-whiting. This fish was called, at different stages of its growth, a whitling, codling, and cod. In the north of Britain it was called a keeling, in the south a cod, and in the west a melwell.

Cod.

Mr. Daniel writes (*Rural Sports*, vol. ii. p. 29):—

"The greater fisheries of cod were on the coast of Iceland, and of our western isles, before the discovery of Newfoundland. That discovery took place by Cabot, about the year 1500; and although the English began settling there twenty years afterwards, the fishery did not flourish until 1577, when England had the least share of it. Mr. Anderson, in his *History of Commerce*, says the French began to fish there, and, it is somewhere asserted, that their first pretence for fishing for cod in these seas, was only to supply an English convent with that article. Notwithstanding this intrusion, about 1625, Devonshire alone employed one hundred and fifty ships, and 8000 persons at Newfoundland for six months in the year."

Iago's reference to this fish—

"She that in wisdom never was so frail
 To change the cod's head for the salmon's tail"
 (*Othello*, ii. 1, 155),

has been quoted by some writers to prove that the distance from which the cod was brought rendered it a delicacy superior even to salmon. Mr. Couch, on the contrary, interprets the passage to mean that—

"in the reign of Elizabeth, a salmon at table was accounted a matter of fashion, in which a person of ordinary rank might be tempted to ape the rich and the great." (*British Fishes*, vol. iv. p. 194.)

He objects, however, to the incongruity of placing the reference in the mouth of one to whom the cod could scarcely have been known. The great abundance of salmon at this period makes it probable that the former view is correct. In Queen Elizabeth's *Household Book* for the forty-third year of her reign, we find an entry, "Item, the master cookes have to fee all the salmons' tailes."

"Here swimmes the pearch, the cuttle and the stocke-fish,
That with a wooden staffe is often beaten."

(CHESTER, *Love's Martyr*, p. 99.)

Stockfish is here spoken of as a distinct fish, but no such species is found in the works of modern naturalists. Cotgrave says it was a small kind of cod, called a melwell, or keeling, which was dried for winter use, but the name was not confined to dried cod. Stow, in his *Survey of London* (p. 32), quotes from a book of household accounts, in the time of Edward II. : "For six thousand eight hundred stockfishes, so called for dried fishes of all sorts, as lings, habardines, and other, £41 6s. 7d." Stockfish was evidently uncommonly tough eating, and had to be pummelled on a stone before it could be penetrated by human teeth. *Stephano* thus threatens *Trinculo*, who has irritated *Caliban* past endurance :—

"Trinculo, run into no further danger: interrupt the monster one word further, and, by this hand, I'll turn my mercy out o' doors, and make a stockfish of thee." (*Tempest*, iii. 2, 78.)

Thomas Muffett, in his *Healths Improvement* (p. 170), informs us that—

"Stockfish whilst it is unbeaten is called buckhorne, because it is so tough; when it is beaten upon the stock, it is termed stockfish. Erasmus thinketh it to be called stockfish, because it nourisheth no more than a dryed stock : wherefore howsoever it be sod, buttered, fried, or baked, and made both toothsomer and delectable by good and chargeable cookery ; yet a stone will be a stone, and an ape an ape, howsoever the one be set up for a saint, and the other apparelled like a judge."

The Latin name given to this commodity, *asellus aridus*, also denotes the treatment to which it was subjected.

Stockfish was considered inferior even to salt fish. An account is given by Mr. C. W. Shepherd, in his work on *The North-West Peninsula of Iceland*, 1867 (p. 11), of the mode in which this uninviting article of diet is prepared in that island in recent times. A very similar process was probably adopted by our medieval ancestors:—

"Dried fish is the most extensively used article of food; and ling and cod are the most desired sorts. When caught, they are split open and hung upon lines or exposed on the shore to the cold winds and the hot sun; this renders them perfectly hard, and they keep good for years. In this dried state it is pummelled on a stone anvil, with a sort of sledge hammer, formed by a round stone with a hole drilled through it for the handle to pass through; but, even after this severe ordeal, it requires Icelandic teeth and skill to eat it. Butter and stock-fish form the ordinary Icelandic dinner. After the pummelling, the fish is cut up, or torn into strips of a convenient width to go into the mouth. The butter is not spread on the fish, but the two are consumed in alternate mouthfuls."

The stockfish, or cod, was borne as a charge by the King of Denmark.

The Haddock, as well as the dory, was dignified with the title of the Peter-fish, from the legend that money was found in its mouth by the saint who left the impress of his finger and thumb on the fish's sides. It has been pointed out that the choice of this fish to perpetuate this incident was somewhat unfortunate, as it does not exist in the seas of the country where the miracle was performed. It is, moreover, a saltwater inhabitant. *Haddock.*

The haddock was plentiful all round the coast of Britain, and was valuable as an article of food, though not considered a delicacy. It was dressed with a sauce compounded of vinegar, powder of cinnamon, and ginger. Thomas Heywood writes:—

" We'll make the sea their graves, and themselves food
For the sea worme call'd haddock."
(*If You know not Me, You know Nobody.*)

The Whiting was served with garlic, or mustard, vinegar, and pepper. Young whitings were called whiting mops. Beaumont and Fletcher write, " They will swim their measure like whiting mops, *Whiting.*

as if their feet were fins" (*Love's Cure*, ii. 2). The word *mop* was used, says Nares, as a diminutive, and term of endearment, as is shown by the following, from Puttenham's *Arte of English Poesie*:—

"Understanding by this word *moppe* a litle prety lady, or tender young thing. For so we call little fishes, that be not come to their full growth *moppes*, as whiting moppes, gurnard moppes."

The whiting appears in company with other fish in some verses uncomplimentary to ladies, included in a Collection of songs and carols, published about the year 1490 :—

"When whytynges do walke forestes to chase hertys;
And herynges ther hornnys in forestes boldly blow;
And marmsattes [marmosets] morn in mores and lakys;
And gurnardes schot rokes owt of a crose bow;
And goslynges hunt the wolfe to overthrow;
And sprates ber sperys in armys of defens;
Than put women in trust and confydens."
(Ed. Percy Soc., vol. xxiii. p. 67.)

Hake. The Hake was a very abundant fish. It was the cheapest fare that could be procured, and was valued accordingly. When dried and salted it was called Poor-John. At the sight of *Caliban* crouching in fear on the sands, *Trinculo* exclaims :—

"What have we here? a man or a fish? Dead or alive? A fish; he smells like a fish; a very ancient and fish-like smell; a kind of not of the newest Poor-John." (*Tempest*, ii. 2, 26.)

A servant in Massinger's play, *The Renegado* (i. 1.), replies to his master's query as to his religion :—

"Troth, to answer truly,
I would not be of one that should command me
To feed upon Poor-John, when I see pheasants
And partridges on the table."

Another name for this fish was the Sea-pike or Merluce.

The Ling.

The hake frequently pursued the shoals of herrings and drove them away from the coast; hence the proverb, "What we gain in hake we lose in herring." The Ling was another very useful fish. In appearance it was not unlike a small cod. An oil, says Yarrell, was extracted from the liver of this fish, as well as from the cod, which was used as a remedy for rheumatism. This oil was used also by poor people to supply their lamps.

Muffett writes:—

"Ling perhaps looks for great extolling, being counted the beefe of the sea, and standing every fish day (as a cold supporter) at my Lord Maiors table; yet is it nothing but a long cod; whereof the greater sised is called *organe ling*, and the other *codling*, because it is no longer than a cod, and yet hath the taste of ling: whilst it is new it is called greenfish, when it is salted it is called ling, perhaps of lyinge, because the longer it lyeth (being conveniently turned, and the peace-straw often shifted wherein it lyeth), the better it is, waxing in the end as yellow as the gold noble, at which time they are worth a noble a piece. They are taken only in the far Northern Seas, where the biggest and sweetest live; but codlings are taken in great plenty neer to Bedwell in Northumberlandshire." (*Healths Improvement*, p. 155.)

"In the *Rutland Papers*, printed for the Camden Society, we are told," writes Mr. Couch (*British Fishes*, vol. iii. p. 90), "That on the visit of the Emperor Charles V. to London, in the reign of Henry VIII., salted ling was among the principal matters provided for the entertainment of the guests. . . . Although the taste appears to have declined in the reign of the first James, the practice seems to have maintained its ground; for, among the pieces of merriment of this king, he is said to have professed that if his royal brother of the lower regions should be pleased to visit him, his dinner should consist of a pole of ling and mustard, with another equal favourite of his, a pipe of tobacco for digestion. According to Fuller (*Worthies of England*), the extent of the adventure was equal to the value set on the fish. Referring to the mischief wrought by the civil war, he says, 'We are sensible of the decay of so many towns on our north-east sea, Hartlepool, Whitebay, Bridlington, Scarborough, and generall all from Newcastle to Harewich, which formerly set out yearly, as I am informed, two hundred ships and upwards, imployed in the fisheries, but chiefly for the taking of ling, that noble fish.'"

The Plaice was found everywhere in great abundance.
The peculiar countenance of this fish early attracted notice. "His mouth shrinks sideways like a scornful plaice," writes Hall (*Satires*, b. iv. sat. i.). Muffett writes, "Plaise (called the sea-sparrows, because they are brown above and white beneath) are of good, wholesome, and fine nourishment" (p. 164).

Plaice.

Taste seems to have changed regarding the proper season for eating this fish. Yarrell says the plaice is considered to be in finest condition for the table at the end of May, but Harrison gives as its season February and March. It was generally served with wine sauce.

The opinion was once held that the plaice was produced from a small crustacean animal of the shrimp kind. Modern discoverers, writes Mr. Couch, have explained this notion, from the fact that the ova is deposited in places frequented by shrimps; it frequently adheres to the under portion of these shrimps, at times when the parent plaice is seeking to devour them.

The Flounder was taken in both salt and fresh water, and was one of the commonest of the flat fish. It was called the butt at Yarmouth, and the flook, or fleuk, in other parts. It was caught all round the coast, and in the mouth of large rivers, which it also ascended for some distance.

Flounder.

Drayton, writing of the Severn, says:—

> "The flounder smooth and flat, in other rivers caught,
> Perhaps in greater store, yet better are not thought."
> (*Polyolbion*, song xxvi.)

Dame Juliana Berners observes that the flounder, like the plaice, is a ground feeder:—

> "The flounder is an holsom fysshe and a free, and a subtyll byter in his manere: for comynly whan he soukyth his meete he fedyth at grounde, and therfore ye must angle to hym wyth a grounde lyne lyenge."

Enumerating the commodities of Newfoundland, one of Purchas's pilgrims writes:—

"As touching the kindes of fish beside cod, there are herring, salmons, thornebacke, plase, or rather wee should call them flounders, dog-fish, and another most excellent of taste called of us a cat."

The flounder and the plaice had their odd-shaped mouths bestowed upon them, according to Nashe (*Lenten Stuffe*, Harl. Misc., vol. vi. p. 170), for sneering at the elevation of the herring to the sovereignty of the finny tribes:—

"None wonne the day in this but the herring; whom al their clamorous suffrages saluted with *Vive le Roy*, 'God save the King, God save the King;' save only the playse and the butte, that made wry mouthes at him, and, for their mocking, have wry mouthes ever since; and the herring ever since wears a coronet on his head, in token that hee is, as he is."

The dab, mentioned by Drayton, was distinguished from the flounder chiefly by the roughness of its skin.

The Holibut, or Halybut, was a fish taken in the northern seas, chiefly valuable for its large size. On grand occasions this fish was cooked whole, and set up as an ornamental dish. As specimens have been occasionally taken weighing three hundred pounds, it must have formed a striking feature at a banquet.

Holibut.

"Turbuts, which some call the Sea-pheasant," Muffett informs us (p. 172), "were in old times accounted so good aud delicate that this proverb grew upon them, *Nihil ad rhombum*; that is to say, what is all this in comparison of a turbutt. Verily, whilst they be young (at which time they are called butts), their flesh is moist, tender, white, and pleasant."

Turbot.

"Soles, or Tongue Fishes, are counted the partridges of the sea, and the fittest meat of all other for sick folks" (*Muffett*, p. 168).

Sole.

Brill. The Brill was generally known by the names Bert, Bret, or Burt Fish. It was found in the same localities as the turbot, but was more common, and consequently not so much esteemed.

Dory. The Dory, as well as the haddock, claimed the name of St. Peter's Fish, and for the same reason. This is probably the fish referred to by Sir Thomas Browne, though he does not give the English name :—

"The *faber marinus*, sometimes found very large, answering the figure of Rondeletius, which though he mentioneth it as a rare fish, and to be found in the Atlantic and Gaditane Ocean, yet we often meet with it in these seas, commonly called a Peter-fish, having one black spot on either side the body; conceived the perpetual signature, from the impression of St. Peter's fingers, or to resemble the two pieces of money which St. Peter took out of this fish; remarkable also from its disproportionable mouth, and many hard prickles about other parts." (Vol. iv. p. 330.)

The probable derivation of the name of this fish is from the French *dorée*, on account of its golden tinge. Harrison spells it dorreie, and other authors dorray, dorrey, doree, and dorn. The name John is said to have been bestowed on this fish by Quin, the actor and epicure, as a mark of his esteem for its good qualities. We meet with this name, however, in the sketch of the character of the poor fiddler, in Bishop Earle's *Microcosmography*, the first edition of which was published in 1628 : "Hunger is the greatest pain he takes, except a broken head sometimes, and the labouring John Dory" (p. 170, ed. Philip Bliss, 1811). Mr. Bliss explains the name to mean a tune.

CHAPTER XV.

FLUELLEN speaks "but by guess" when he volunteers the information that—

Salmon.

"there is a river in Macedon; and there is also moreover a river at Monmouth: it is called Wye, at Monmouth; but it is out of my prains what is the name of the other river; but 'tis all one, 'tis alike as my fingers is to my fingers, and there is Salmons in both." (*Henry V.*, iv. 7, 27.)

Mr. John Booth, speaking of the myth, as he calls it, of the salmon being at one time so plentiful in our English rivers that parents stipulated that their children, when bound apprentices, should not be dieted on this fish more than twice in the week, asks if the stipulation, if ever made, may not have been against fish generally, and not against salmon in particular. Herrings, eels, cod, plaice, and other kinds of white fish were common enough, and were much cheaper food than meat, fresh or salt. Salmon, he contends, always fetched a good price compared with other articles of food (*Notes and Queries*, vol. vi., 3rd series, p. 13).

Fynes Moryson, in his European tour, 1591, finds salmon so plentiful in Hamburg that a stipulation was there made by the servants that they should not be expected to eat this fish more than twice a week. Perhaps the fish may have been dried and imported, or the like contract may have been made by German servants in

England. In Sir Thomas Browne's time, at least, the salmon was no longer common, though " many," he writes, " are taken in the Ouse; in the Bure or North River; in the Waveney or South River; in the Norwich River but seldom " (vol. iv. p. 334). Captain Frauck, a Cromwellian trooper, writing in 1658, states that the price of a salmon formerly did not exceed the value of sixpence sterling, and he repeats the tradition regarding apprentices. Defoe also corroborates the statement that servants declined to eat this fish oftener than twice a week. These stories, if true, only indicate the abundance of salmon in particular localities: the difficulty of transport would necessarily make this fish cheap when taken in great numbers. Mr. Alexander Russel, the salmon's biographer, observes, however, that there is no confirmation for this tradition, so often repeated, and that the Royal Commissioners of Inquiry into the Salmon Fisheries of England and Wales, 1860, endeavoured in vain to obtain a sight of these indentures of apprentices, though they met with persons who declared they had seen such documents. He tells a story of a Highland laird of the last century, who, going to a London hotel with his gilly, ordered, from motives of economy, a beef-steak for himself, and " salmon for the laddie." On reckoning with his host, he discovered to his annoyance that he had to pay a shilling for his own dinner, and a guinea for " the laddie's " (*The Salmon*, p. 96, 1874).

Thomas Fuller writes that the salmon is—

"a daintie and wholesome fish, and a double riddle in nature: first, for its invisible feeding, no man alive ever found any meat in the maw thereof. Secondly, for its strange leaping (or flying rather), so that some will have them termed salmons, à saliendo. Being both bow and arrow, it will shoot it selfe out of the water an incredible heighth and length." (*Worthies of England*, vol. i. p. 446.)

Drayton has an account of the method by which the salmon ascends mountain streams:—

"When as the salmon seeks a fresher stream to find,
Which from the sea comes yearly by his kind,
As he in season grows, and stems the watry tract,
Where Tivy falling down doth make a cataract,
Forc'd by the rising rocks that there her course oppose,
As though within their bounds they meant her to inclose;
Here, when the labouring fish doth at the foot arrive,
And finds that by his strength but vainly he doth strive,
His tail takes in his mouth, and bending like a bow,
That's to the compass drawn, aloft himself doth throw;
Then springing at his height, as doth a little wand,
That, bended end to end, and flirted from the hand,
Far off it self doth cast; so doth the salmon vault,
And if at first he fail, his second summersaut
He instantly assays; and from his nimble ring,
Still yerking, never leaves, until himself he fling
Above the streamful top of the surrounded heap."
                              (*Polyolbion*, song iii.)

Harrison gives the different names by which the salmon was known at the successive stages of its existence: "The first year a gravelin, and commonlie so big as an herring, the second a salmon peale, the third a pug, and the fourth a salmon." This fish has received a variety of names in the different localities in which it is taken. According to Yarrell (*British Fishes*, vol. ii. p. 155)—

"the smolt or young salmon is by the fishermen of some rivers called a laspring, and various couplets refer to the fish as well as to the time and circumstances under which the descent is made:—

'The last spring floods that happen in May,
Carry the salmon fry down to the sea.'

Under three pounds weight, they are called salmon peal. The laspring of some rivers is the young of the true salmon, but in others it is only a parr. A grilse is a young salmon that has not spawned."

In John Dennys's poem on angling, published before 1613, several names of fish occur, some of which are now considered to belong to the salmon at different ages:—

> "And with this bait hath often taken bin
> The salmon fair, of river fish the best;
> The shad that in the springtime cometh in;
> The *suant* swift, that is not set by least;
> The *bocher* sweet, the pleasant flounder thin;
> The *peel*, the tweat, the botling, and the rest,
> With many more, that in the deep doth lie
> Of Avon, Usk, of Severn and of Wye."
> (ARBER'S *English Garner*, vol. i. p. 175.)

Of the suant, sewant, or shuin, Muffett writes:—

"Shuins seem unto me a kind of salmon, whereof plenty is taken in the river running by Cardiffe Castle: but it far surpasseth the salmon as much in goodness, as it is surpassed by him in length and greatness." (*Healths Improvement*, p. 187.)

The name *sewin* is given by modern authors to the bull or grey trout. The bocher, or botcher, is a salmon over a year old, which has accomplished a journey to the sea. The botcher is smaller and more delicate in shape than the salmon, and weighs from three to twelve pounds. The peel is also a two-year-old salmon. Izaak Walton writes (part i. ch. 8):—

"I might here, before I take my leave of the salmon, tell you that there is more than one sort of them, as, namely, a *tecon*, and another called in some places a *samlet*, or by some a *skegger*; but these, and others which I forbear to name, may be fish of another kind, and differ as we know a herring and a pilchard do, which, I think, are as different as the rivers in which they breed, and must, by me, be left to the disquisitions of men of more leisure, and of greater abilities than I profess myself to have."

Trout. "The wary Trout that thrives against the stream" was sufficiently common. According to Izaak Walton—

"Gesner says, his name is of German offspring; and he says he is a fish that feeds clean and purely, in the swiftest streams, and on the hardest gravel; and that he may justly contend with all fresh-water fish; as the mullett may with all sea-fish, for precedency and daintiness of taste; and that being in right season, the most dainty palates have allowed precedency to him." (Part 1, ch. 4.)

Drayton also gives the trout the first place among fish :—

> "The trout by nature mark'd with many a crimson spot,
> As though she curious were in him above the rest,
> And of fresh-water fish, did note him for the best."
> (*Polyolbion*, song xxvi.)

Muffett writes :—

"Trouts are so great in Northumberland, that they seem thicker then salmons, and are therefore called bull-trouts; there are especially two sorts of them, red trouts resembling little fresh-water salmon, and therefore termed salmon-trouts; and gray trouts or skurffs, which keep not in the chanel of bournes or rivers, but lurk like the alderlings under the roots of great alders." (Page 188.)

Alderlings, this author explains—

"are a kind of fish betwixt a trout and a grayling, scaled (as the trout is not) but not so great scaled as the grailing is; it lyeth ever in a deep water, under some old and great alder." (Page 175.)

The device of tickling trout was not unknown to Shakspeare : " Here comes the trout that must be caught with tickling," cries *Maria* (*Twelfth Night*, ii. 5, 24). Also to Beaumont and Fletcher—

> "He is mine own, I have him;
> I told thee I would tickle him like a trout."
> (*Rule a Wife and have a Wife*, act ii.)

The Char was a very local fish. According to Camden it was only taken in one of the English lakes :—

Char.

" For, among these mountaines the greatest standing water in all England, now called Winander-mere, lieth streatched out for the space of tenne miles or there about with crooked bankes, and is all paved, as it were, with stone in the bottom: in some places of wonderfull depth, and breeding a peculiar kind of fish found no where else, which the inhabitants there by call a chare."

The range of the char is not quite so limited as Camden imagined. It is found in Scotland and in Wales. The Welsh charr, or torgoch, was formerly taken in Llanberis Lake, on Snowdon.

Gwiniad. The Gwiniad, another local species, was found, according to Pennant, in one of the lakes of Ireland, Lough Neagh, where it was called the pollen; in Loch Mabon, in Scotland, where it was known as the vangis. The old British name, gwiniad, or whiting, was given to it from the whiteness of its scales. It is sometimes called the fresh-water herring, as like that fish it dies very soon after being taken from the water, and will not keep long. On account of the large size of the scales it was also called the schelly. Camden asserts that—

"the river Dee, in Merionethshire, abounds with salmon, and Pemble Mere in that county with the gwiniad, yet is the salmon never taken in the mere, nor the gwiniad in the river."

Grayling. "The Grayllynge, by another name called Umbre, is a delycyous fysshe to mannys mouthe," writes Dame Juliana (*Treatise on Fishing*, p. 27, ed. 1841). The name Thymallus was bestowed on the grayling, on account of the peculiar odour which it emits when fresh, similar to that of water thyme. Umbra comes from its rapid swimming, which causes it to disappear like a passing shadow. The dusky lines along the body give it the third name, grayling, and the epithet of "the flower of fishes," or "flower-fish," was given to it by Ambrose, Bishop of Milan.

Drayton mentions—

"The greyling, whose great spawn is as big as any pease."
(*Polyolbion*, song xxvi.)

A distinction was sometimes made between the grayling and the umber, the latter name being generally given to the fish when advanced in years.

" Aldrovandus says," writes Walton (part i. ch. vi.), " The salmon, the grayling, and trout, and all fish that live in clear and sharp streams, are made by their mother Nature of such exact shape, and pleasant colours, purposely to invite us to a joy and contentedness in feasting with her. Whether this is true or not, it is not my purpose to dispute: but it is certain, all that write of the umber, declare him to be very medicinable. And Gesner says that the fat of an umber, or grayling, being set, with a little honey, a day or two in the sun, in a little glass, is very excellent against redness, or swarthiness, or anything that breeds in the eyes."

Of the Smelt, Sir Thomas Browne writes :—

"Spirinches, or smelt, in great plenty about Lynn; but where they have also a small fish, called a priames, answering in taste and shape a smelt, and perhaps are but the younger sort thereof." (Vol. iv. p. 330.)   Smelt.

The name smelt was given to it from its having, as some think, the scent of a cucumber or violet. According to Muffett the best smelts were taken " by Kew and Brainford, within eight miles of London, and at Westchester." The sauce recommended for this fish was the juice of Seville oranges.

Harrison gives the various names bestowed on the Pike at the different stages of growth :—   Pike.

" I might here make report how the pike, carpe, and some other of our river fishes are sold by inches of cleane fish, from the eies or gilles to the crotch of the tailes, but it is needlesse : also how the pike as he ageth, receiveth diverse names, as from a frie to a gilthed, from a gilthed to a pod, from a pod to a jacke, from a jacke to a pickerell, from a pickerell to a pike, and last of all to a luce." (*Holinshed*, vol. i. p. 376.)

Randle Holme gives the additional name, in one of the junior stages, of a hurling pick.

Yarrell says that this fish was so rare in the reign of Henry VIII., that a large one sold for double the price of a house-lamb in February, and a pickerel, or small pike, for more than a fat capon. He does not give his authority for these instances, but the numerous instructions for serving and carving the pike which appear in books long before this period, make it probable that it was plentiful, at least in certain districts. Leland speaks of good pikes in the Welsh lakes, and so far back as the time of Edward III. Chaucer writes :—

> " Full many a fair partrich hadde he in mewe,
> And many a breme and many a luce in stewe."
> *(Prologue to Canterbury Tales.)*

The particular fish referred to by Yarrell may have been of unusual size.

Gesner and other learned authorities endeavour to account for the sudden, and even in our own day mysterious, appearance of the pike in ponds far from other water, by the theory that they were produced by the heat of the sun from a weed called, in consequence, pickerel-weed. Izaak Walton repeats this theory, with the remark :—

> "Doubtless divers pikes are bred after this manner, or are brought into some ponds some such other ways as is past man's finding out; of which we have daily testimonies." (Part 1, ch. viii.)

In his description of Lincolnshire, Fuller writes :—

> "Pikes are found plentifully in this shire, being the fresh-water wolves, and therefore an old pond pike is a dish of more state than profit to the owner, seeing a pike's belly is a little fish-pond, where lesser of all sorts have been contained. Sir Francis Bacon alloweth it (though tyrants generally be short lived) the surviver of all fresh-water fish, attaining to forty years... The flesh thereof must needs be fine and wholsome, if it be true what is affirmed, that in some sort it cheweth the cud; and yet the less and middle size pikes are preferred for sweetnesse before those that are greater." (*Worthies*, vol. ii. p. 1.)

The pike has been known to attain to a great age. Gesner records the capture of a monster pike at Heilbron, in Suabia, in 1497, that bore a ring of brass, on which was the following inscription: "I am the first fish that was put into this lake by the hands of the Governor of the Universe, Frederick the Second, on the 5th of October, 1232." The weight of this veteran pike is said to have been 350 lbs.

Lincolnshire pikes were proverbially good:—

> "Ancolme ele, and Witham pike,
> Search all England and find not the like."

Modern writers on angling endorse *Falstaff's* assertion, that "the dace is a good bait for the old pike" (2 *Henry IV.*, iii. 2). This is the only allusion Shakspeare has to the pike under this name. The passage in *Merry Wives of Windsor*, "The luce is the fresh fish, the salt fish is an old coat" (i. 1, 22), has given rise to much conjecture. The generally received opinion is that it has reference to Sir Thomas Lucy of Charlecote, the supposed original of *Justice Shallow:* three silver pikes, or lucies, on a red field, were, what is called, the *canting* arms of the Lucy family. Another explanation is given by Mr. Masey:—

> "Amongst the decorations at the coronation of James I., it is very probable that his arms were impaled with those of his consort, the daughter of the King of Denmark, or hers associated with his collaterally, and so the singular charge of the stock-fish in the Danish arms would be publicly known. It appears to be likely that the words were added in reference to the Queen's arms, and, if not before, *for* the representation before the king in 1604." (*Notes and Queries*, 3rd series, xii. p. 4.)

Mr. Keightley has another suggestion:—

> "*Shallow* had asserted that 'the dozen white luces' was an old coat, and *Sir Hugh* had misunderstood him. He here corrects him, telling him that the luce was an old coat too, alluding, as is supposed, to the arms of the Fishmongers' Company, 'azure, two sea-luces in

saltire with coronets over their mouths;' or he may have only reiterated his assertion, saying 'The same fish is an old coat,' and the printer, misled by 'fresh fish,' may have made it 'salt fish.'"

Garefish. The Sea Pike, Merluce, or Garefish was a curious-looking fish which preceded the mackerel in their annual visit to shallow waters. It was taken in considerable numbers on the east coast. Harrison classes it with congers, eels, and other long fish. Sir Thomas Browne gives a more correct description of it:—

"The *acus major*, called by some a garfish, and greenback, answering the figure of Rondeletius, under the name of *acus primas* species, remarkable for its quadrangular figure, and verdigrease-green backbone."

Stow describes a pageant on the return of Edward I., after his Scotch victory, in which there were "sixe and fortie armed knightes riding on horses, made like luces of the sea." Whether the garefish is here intended is uncertain, and it is somewhat difficult to imagine either a knight or a horse, for it is not quite clear which is meant to represent the fish, being "made up" into such a totally different shape.

The name sea-pike was also given to the hake.

Flying-fish. In Marlowe's *Edward II.*, the *King* inquires of *Lancaster* what device he has chosen for the forthcoming rejoicings upon the occasion of *Gaveston's* return. *Lancaster* replies:—

"My lord, mine's more obscure than Mortimer's.
Pliny reports there is a flying fish
Which all the other fishes deadly hate,
And therefore, being pursued, it takes the air:
No sooner is it up, but there's a fowl
That seizeth it: this fish, my lord, I bear,
The motto this: *undique mors est.*"

Edward, indignant at this implied threat, declares his

intention to uphold his favourite against any attacks or insults :—

> "Though thou compar'st him to a flying fish,
> And threatenest death whether he rise or fall,
> 'Tis not the hugest monster of the sea,
> Nor foulest harpy that shall swallow him." (ii. 2.)

The shoals of Flying-fish are often described by the early explorers. Joseph Acosta writes :—

> "There are other small fishes, which they call flying fishes, the which are found within the tropickes, and in no other place, as I thinke: they are pursued by the ducades; and to escape them they leape out of the sea, and goe a good way in the ayre, and for this reason they are called flying fishes: they have wings as it were of linnen cloath, or of parchment, which doe support them some space in the ayre. There did one flye or leape into the ship wherein I went, the which I did see, and observe the fashion of his wings." (*Purchas*, vol. iii. p. 931.)

Sir Thomas Herbert, writing in 1626, says :—

> "The greatest recreation we had [in the Red Sea] was a view of such large sholes of flying fishes as by their interposing multitude for some time darkned the body of the sun; a fish beautiful in its eye, the body though no larger than a small herring yet big enough for those complemental fins, which so long as moist serve as wings to fly 200 paces or more, and 40 feet high, helping them to avoid the pursuit which sharks, dolphins, bonetaes, albicores, and other sea-tyrants make, and causes them for self-preservation to forsake their proper element. . . . The French call it *aronder dumer*, the swallow of the sea; others a sea bat, or reremouse of the sea." (*Travels*, p. 39.)

Some uncertainty prevails as to the date when the Carp was first introduced into England. Dame Juliana Berners, in her *Treatise on Angling*, printed 1496, writes, "The carpe is a deyntous fysshe: but there ben but fewe in Englonde and therfore I wryte the lasse of hym" (p. 27, ed. 1841). Leonard Mascall, a Sussex gentleman, has had the credit of im-

Carp.

porting the carp into England about the year 1514. This fish was plentiful in Fuller's time:—

"Now as this county [Sussex] is eminent for both sea and river fish, namely an Arundel mullet, a Chichester lobster, a Shelsey cockle, and an Amerly trout; so Sussex aboundeth with more carps than any other of this nation." (*Worthies*, vol. iii. p. 240.)

Mention is made, in the *Privy Purse Expenses* of Elizabeth of York, 1502, of a reward paid for the present of a carp. Harrison refers to the recent introduction of this fish into England. Noticing the number of fish found in the Thames, he writes:—

"Onelie in carps it seemeth to be scant, sith it is not long since that kind of fish was brought over into England, and but of late to speake of into this streame, by the violent rage of sundrie landflouds, that brake open the heads and dams of divers gentlemens ponds, by which means it became somewhat partaker also of this said commoditie, whereof earst it had no portion that I could ever heare." (*Holinshed*, vol. i. p. 77.)

Robert Burton, in his *Anatomy of Melancholy* (vol. i. p. 218), gives us some learned information respecting the carp's place in hygiene:—

"Carp is a fish, of which I know not what to determine. Franciscus Bonsuetus accounts it a muddy fish. Hippolytus Salvianus, in his book *De Piscium Naturâ et Præparatione*, which was printed at Rome in folio, 1554, with most elegant pictures, esteems carp no better than a slimy watery meat. Paulus Jovius, on the other side, disallowing tench, approves of it; so doth Dubravius in his books of fishponds. Frietagius extols it for an excellent wholesome meat, and puts it amongst the fishes of the best rank; and so do most of our countrey gentlemen, that store their ponds almost with no other fish."

The sturgeon, on account of its want of scales, was to the Jews a forbidden fish; a caviare, which was prepared from the roe of the carp, was appreciated by them as a substitute for the genuine article.

The notion alluded to by Ben Jonson, that "the carp

has no tongue" (*Cynthia's Revels*, i. 2), was derived from Aristotle. Gesner follows this classical authority, and says that this fish has only a piece of flesh-like substance in its mouth resembling a tongue, but which should be rather called a palate. Elsewhere Ben Jonson classes the "tongues of carps, dormice, and camel's heels" together as special dainties (*Alchemist*, ii. 1); and Muffett, in his *Healths Improvement*, recommends the tongue of the carp as specially wholesome.

Polonius justifies himself to the spies that he sets upon his son, by the assurance, " Your bait of falsehood takes this carp of truth" (*Hamlet*, ii. 1, 63). This is Shakspeare's only mention of the carp.

The Bream was an inhabitant of the lakes in Cumberland and some of the smaller rivers. It was so plentiful, Leland says, that in a Welsh lake near Brecknock, through which the river Lleveney runs, the breams, which appeared in May, came in such shoals as to break the nets (*Itinerary*, vol. v. p. 66). Walton quotes a French proverb to the effect that "he that hath breams in his pond is able to give his friend welcome," but this may be more on account of their quantity than their quality.

Bream.

It was recorded that the method which the bream, or brenna, adopted for his defence against the pike was to sink to the bottom of the stream and by stirring up the mud to prevent his enemy from observing him. Muffett writes:—

"Breams seem no other than fat carps: yet whiter of flesh, and finer nourishment. There is a kind of bream called *scarus ruminas*, which we call a cudbream, because his lips are ever wagging like a cow chawing the cud." (Page 175.)

The black sea bream, beetle, or old wife, was one of the commonest fish. Muffett says :—

"Olaffes, or rather old wives (because of their mumping and soure countenance), are as dainty and wholesome of substance as they are large in body; it was my chance to buy one about Putny, as I came from Mr. Secretary Walsingham his house about ten years since : which I caused to be boiled with salt, wine, and vinegar, and a little thime, and I protest that I never did eat a more white, firm, dainty, and wholesome fish." (Page 184.)

This author must have had a good memory to be able to recall the flavour of a dish after so many years had elapsed.

Tench. The Tench, on the contrary, was considered unwholesome, or, as one writer expresses it, "of a most unclean and damnable nourishment." It was frequently eaten nevertheless, and was usually served in jelly.

The tench was sometimes called "the physician of fishes," and the touch of a tench was even supposed to have the power of curing the wounds of a human being. Izaak Walton reports that " the tyrant pike will not be a wolf to its physician, but forbears to devour him though he be never so hungry." The cause of this forbearance is thus explained by Harrison :—

"The pike is freend unto the tench, as to his leach and surgeon. For when the fishmonger hath opened his side and laid out his rivet and fat unto the buier, for the better utterance of his ware, and cannot make him away at that present, he laieth the same againe into the proper place, and sowing up the wound, he restoreth him to the pond where tenches are, who never cease to sucke and licke his greeved place, till they have restored him to health, and made him readie to come againe to the stall, when his turne shall come about."

Fuller, in his description of Dorsetshire, writes of the tench :—

" Plenty hereof are bred in the river Stowre ; which is so much the more observable, because generally this fish loveth ponds better than rivers, and pits better than either. It is very pleasant in taste, and is called by some the physician of fishes: though in my opinion he may better be styled the surgeon ; for it is not so much a disease as a wound that he cureth, nor is it any potion but a playster which he affordeth ; viz. his natural unctuous glutinousness, which quickly consolidateth any green gash in any fish. But the pike is principally beholding unto him for cures in that kind; and some have observed that that tyrant, though never so hungry, forbeareth to eat this fish, which is his physician; not that pikes are capable (which many men are not) of gratitude : but that they are indued with a natural policy, not to destroy that which they know not how soon they may stand in need of." (*Worthies,* vol. i. p. 309.)

It has been suggested that this consideration on the part of the pike is due to the difficulty he finds in catching the tench, as the latter keeps generally at the bottom of the water. It was also thought that the tench, unlike other fishes, enjoyed an immunity from all diseases.

The commentators have worried themselves and their readers by their vain endeavours to explain the meaning of the *carrier's* phrase, " Stung like a tench " (1 *Henry IV.,* ii. 1, 17). The smooth appearance of the fish affords no clue to the meaning of the simile. The *Carrier* would doubtless have been as much puzzled as any one, if he had been called on to give a reason for his words, and as this is the only mention of the tench by Shakspeare, we are left rather in the dark as to the amount of the poet's knowledge of its appearance. It may be, however, that the tench has in process of years lost its spots, as the following passage from Sir Thomas Herbert's *Travels* (p. 384) certainly implies that at one period of its existence it possessed them. In his description of the product of the seas around the Island of Mauritius, this author writes :—

" Give me leave to name what fish we took ; dolphins, bonetaes, albicores, cavalloes, porpice, grampasse, which Mr. Sands thinks is the right dolphin, none else being of that opinion; this some call the *susmarinus,* mullet, bream, tench, trout, sole, flounders, tortoise, eels, pike, shark, crab, lobster, oysters, crafish, cuttle-fish (which though its blood be as black as ink caused by a high concoction, is nevertheless meat very delicious), rock-fish, limpits, and a speckl'd toadfish or poyson fish as the seamen from experience named it ; which last-named came first to net and eaten too greedily by the heedless sailors was an error cost some no less than their lives, others for some time their senses; in shape it was not unlike a tench, but more black and deformedly spotted."

Barbel.
"The Barbell, than which fish a braver doth not swim, Nor greater for the ford within my spacious brim [Trent] Nor, newly taken, more the curious taste doth please."
(DRAYTON, *Polyolbion*, song xxvi.)

The barbel was considered of sufficient value in Elizabeth's time to be protected by statute, but modern epicures have nothing to say in support of Drayton's opinion of its gastronomic merits. "The barbell is an evil fysshe to take, for he is so strongly enarmyd in the mouth that there may no weak harnesse hold him," writes Dame Juliana. When caught he makes a brave resistance, and, according to Du Bartas (p. 40), strives vigorously to rid himself of the hook:—

"But timorous barbles will not taste the bit,
Till with their tails they have unhooked it :
And all the baits the fisher can devise
Cannot beguile their wary jealousies."

Izaak Walton quotes from Plutarch's *De Industria Animalium* the statement that the barbel attempts to release himself by striking off the line with his tail. This assertion is repeated by a modern authority, Mr. Frank Buckland, and called in question by Mr. Manley, who writes:—

"I hope I may be pardoned when I say 'I doubt this.' How can Mr. Buckland tell what the barbel does when he is hooked, unless he has encased himself in a diver's dress, and lain in barbel swim, or observed this phenomenon through a glass window on a river's bank?"
(*Notes on Fish and Fishing*, 1877, p. 267.)

According to Chester, this fish was remarkable for fecundity :—

"The barbell that three times in every yeare,
Her natural young ones to the waves doth beare."
(*Love's Martyr*, p. 99.)

Drayton mentions:— **Roach.**

"The Roche, whose common kind to every flood doth fall."
(*Polyolbion,* song xxvi.)

There was a mistaken notion that the Roach possessed an immunity for the various maladies that fish is heir to; whence, according to some, its name. Muffett writes:—

"Roches, or Roch fishes (called so of Saint Roch, that legendary Æsculapius and giver of health) are esteemed and thought incapable of any disease, according to the old proverb, *as sound as a roch."*
(*Healths Improvement,* p. 186.)

The little Dace was also common. Drayton writes:— **Dace.**

"The pretty slender dare, of many called the Dace,
Within my liquid glass, when Phœbus shows his face,
Oft swiftly as he swims, his silver belly shows,
But with such nimble sleight, that ere ye can disclose
His shape, out of your sight like lightning he is shot."
(*Polyolbion,* song xxvi.)

Shakspeare's only reference to this fish is as a bait for pike.

"The Chub, whose neater name, which some a
   chevin call, **Chub.**
Food to the tyrant pike, most being in his power,
Who for their numerous store he most doth them devour."
(*Polyolbion,* song xxvi.)

The chub, chevin, or chavender seems to have been more popular as a dainty in Shakspeare's time than he is in these days. Dame Juliana Berners writes of him, "The chevyn is a stately fysshe: and his heed is a deynty morsell. There is noo fysshe so strongly enarmyd wyth scalys on the body." The chub was called skelly in Cumberland, on account of its large scales, and pollarde in other places. The chief peculiarity about this fish is the roundness of the head and the width of the mouth, which suggests the idea of plumpness. Randle Holme says that the name chub comes from the German *schupfish*. Chubby has grown to mean a smooth-faced plump appearance. Marston writes :—

> "I never saw a fool lean; the chub-fac'd fop
> Shines sleek with full cramm'd fat of happiness."
> (*Antonio's Revenge.*)

Bleak. "The Bleke is but a feble fysshe, yet he is holsom," writes Dame Juliana. The bleak was called from its appearance the fresh-water sprat, and from the rapidity of its movements the water-swallow. According to Walton, bleaks were packed in salt and exported by the Italians as anchovies. Another use to which this fish was put was in the manufacture of artificial pearls. The glittering scales were rubbed off, and formed a silvery paste-like substance, which was made up into balls, or formed the lining of glass beads.

Loach. The name of the next fish, the Loach, is derived by some writers from the French word *locher*, to fidget, from its restless movements, especially during stormy weather.

Shakspeare's only mention of the loach has given rise to some discussion. Mason suggested that the phrase "breeds fleas like a loach" (1 *Henry IV.*, ii. 1, 23) has reference to the great fecundity of this fish. Izaak Walton says that the loach is usually full of spawn, and breeds three times in the year, as Drayton reports of the barbel. He says also that Gesner and other learned physicians recommended this small fish as light and harmless diet for invalids. Reference has been made by some critics to a passage in Pliny (*Nat. Hist.* b. ix. c. xlvii.), showing that in ancient times fishes were supposed to be infested with the parasites that so annoyed the *Carrier*:—

> "Last of all some fishes there be which of themselves are given

to breed fleas and lice; among which the chalcis, a kind of turgot, is one."

The sense of the *Carrier's* remark is by no means obscure; it is simply this, that fleas are abundant, and to attempt precisely to explain the utterances of such a dull-brained fellow is as idle as the "famous inquiry into the probable character of the husband of Juliet's nurse."

> "The dainty Gudgeon, loche, the minnow, and the bleake,
> Since they but little are, I little need to speak
> Of them, nor doth it fit me much of those to reck, **Gudgeon.**
> Which every where are found in every little beck."
>   (*Polyolbion,* song xxvi.)

The facility with which the gudgeon is captured in certain localities is proverbial; things easily won are apt to be lightly regarded. It may be on this account that Gratiano advises Antonio—

> " Fish not with this melancholy bait
> For this fool gudgeon, this opinion."
>   (*Merchant of Venice,* i. 1.)

The gudgeon was considered a wholesome fish, perhaps owing to the possibility of keeping it alive in fresh water till it was required. Muffett writes: "Gulls, guffs, pulches, chevins, and millers thombs are a kind of jolthead gudgins, very sweet, tender and wholesome." The miller's thumb is now placed by naturalists among the spiny-finned fishes, next to the gurnet.

> " And last the little Minnow-fish,   **Minnow.**
> Whose chiefe delight in gravell is."
>   (BROWNE, *Britannia's Pastorals,* book i. song ii.)

The Minnow, Menise, Pink, or Penk, was often used as bait for taking larger fish. Of this small swimmer, Muffett writes :—

" Minoes, so called either for their littleness, or (as Dr. Cajus imagined) because their fins be of so lively a red, as if they were died with the true cinnabre-lake called *minium:* they are less than loches, feeding upon nothing, but licking one another. . . . They are a most delicate and light meat, either fried or sodden." (Page 183.)

In Wynkyn de Worde's *Boke of Kervynge,* minnowes, or menewes, are recommended as an adjunct to stewed porpoise, as we add shrimp sauce to cod.

Coriolanus insolently treats the plebeian senator, the tribune of the people, the tongue of the common mouth, who ventures to oppose him, as a giant among pigmies :—

" Shall remain!
Hear you this Triton of the minnows? mark you
His absolute 'shall'?"

(*Coriolanus*, iii. 1, 87.)

The haughty temper of the consul who would fain have destroyed at one fell swoop the many-headed multitude, as a whale annihilates whole shoals of undistinguished fishes, cannot brook that such small fry should venture to have rights or opinions of their own.

CHAPTER XVI.

THE older naturalists had an idea that the Pilchard, like the herring, was a visitor from distant shores. This is so little true, that the fact is the pilchard is never seen in the Northern Ocean, the resort which they assigned to it, and the few that sometimes wander through the Straits of Dover or the British Channel have evidently suffered from passing so far out of their accustomed limits (*Yarrell*, vol. ii. p. 97). The pilchard is found almost exclusively on the western shores of England and the south of Ireland. Sir Thomas Browne speaks of some stragglers on the Norfolk coast: "Though this sea aboundeth not with pilchards, yet they are commonly taken among herrings; but few esteem thereof, or eat them" (vol. iv. p. 332). Cornwall has always been the chief fishing station for the pilchard; and Camden reports that in his day—

Pilchard.

"a most rich revenue and commoditie they have by those little fishes that they call pilchards, which swarming, as one would say, in mighty great skuls about the shores from July unto November, are there taken, garbaged, salted, hanged in the smoke, laied up, pressed, and by infinite numbers carried over into France, Spain, and Italie, unto which countreys they be very good chaffer, and right good merchandise, and are there named *fumados*."

Chester attributes medical qualities to this fish:—

"The little pilcher,
Whose onely moisture prest by cunning art,
Is good for those troubled with aches smart."
(*Love's Martyr*, p. 100.)

Like the herring, the pilchard will rush through the water with such force as to cause flashes of light. Carew tells us (*Survey of Cornwall*, p. 105) that—

"the pilchards are pursued and devoured by a bigger kind of fish, called a plusher, being somewhat like the dog-fish, who leapeth now and then above water, and therethrough bewrayeth them to the balker [fisherman]. So are they likewise persecuted by the tunny, and he (though not very often) taken with them *damage faisant*."

Herring. "The Herring, king of fish," is thus described by Olaus Magnus (p. 226):—

"Of all fish, almost, this onely lives by water. But taken out of the water he presently dies, and there is no delay between his coming to the ayr, and dying, as can be perceived, so soon as he is drawn forth of the water. His eyes shine in the sea by night: and which is more, you shall perceive as it were lightnings and glitterings over the sea, with the great motion of this fish, and turning of vast sholes of them, causing a reflexion; and this is commonly called herring-lightnings."

The sudden motion of a shoal of herrings might on a moonlight night cause a sparkling effect. The phosphorescent appearance of the open sea, of course, early attracted the notice of travellers, and was ascribed by them to a variety of causes. One of Purchas's pilgrims asserts " that it proved to be cuttle-fish which made this fearful show " (*Purchas*, vol. i. p. 352).

The name herring has been derived by some authors from the German word *heer*, an army, signifying their numbers. The chief biographer of this fish is Nashe, who in his *Lenten Stuffe, or Praise of the Red Herring*, gives it the pre-eminence over all marine inhabitants for usefulness, which honour it deserves even now. His enthusiasm is somewhat amusing :—

"For if Cornish pilchards, otherwise called *fumados*, taken on the shore of Cornewall, from July to November, bee so saleable as they are in France, Spain, and Italy, which are but counterfets to the red-herring, as copper to golde, or ockanie to silver; much more their elbows itch for joy, when they meete with the true golde, the true red-herring itselfe. No true flying-fish but he; or if there be, that fish never flyes but when his wings are wet, and the red-herring flyes best when his wings are dry; throughout Belgia, High Germanie, Fraunce, Spaine, and Italy hee flyes; and up into Greece and Africa, south and southwest, ostrich-like walkes his stations; and the sepulcher palmers or pilgrims, because he is so portable, fill their scrips with them." (*Harleian Miscellany*, vol. vi. p. 165.)

Nashe also gives full particulars of the mode of herring-fishing, and enumerates the towns on the English coast where this trade was chiefly carried on. Yarmouth then, as now, stands first on the list. In a pamphlet on *England's Way to win Wealth*, 1614, an account is given of the best fishing stations. The author begins with Colchester, and will "scarce afford these men of the water the name of fishermen, for that their chiefest trade is dragging of oysters." He moreover charges the inhabitants of this town with catching, under the name of sprats, infinite thousands of young herrings, which are almost worthless as food, and thus destroying the summer harvest. Ipswich, according to him, was the best town in England for the building of *busses*, or fishing smacks, also for keeping them during the winter. Great Yarmouth was the head-quarters of the herring fishery, and boats from Holland, Picardy, and Normandy came "in hundred and two hundred sail at a time together" to bring fresh fish to be turned into red herrings (*Harleian Miscellany*, vol. iii. p. 398).

According to the herring's most recent biographer, Mr. J. M. Mitchell, an idea prevailed in early times that the herring came from the Arctic Circle, or at least from a considerable distance northward of Scotland, in large shoals of some leagues in extent, and divided into lesser shoals on coming towards the north of Scotland, one body proceeding to the west coast of Scotland and to Ireland, and the other to the east coast, each directing its course southward. One author actually affirms that the whale was designed by a kind Providence for the special purpose of, at certain seasons of the year, frightening the herring away from its native seas into those regions where it would be obtainable with greater ease by man; he did not care to inquire what might be the opinion of the herring on the subject. Mr. Mitchell refutes this notion of the shoals migrating from the North, and considers it more probable that, after the herrings have spawned, they return to the seas in the neighbourhood—

"where they continue, and where they feed until the spawning-season again approaches, while the fry, on being vivified, continues near the spawning-ground until it is of sufficient size to venture further." (*The Herring*, 1864, p. 84.)

The title of "king of the sea" was probably conferred on the herring in consequence of the great profit that some nations derived from the fishery. To account for the sovereignty of the herring, Nashe relates the following fable:—A falcon, which had escaped from confinement on its passage from Ireland, not finding its ordinary prey, struck at a fish, and thereby came within reach of a shark, which swallowed her, bells and all, at a mouthful. All varieties of birds, hearing of this murder of one of their aristocracy, determined to revenge the insult, and formed themselves into a league for the purpose of chastising the fishes. Information being carried to the fish by the puffin, they on their side prepared for the danger, and met in council to choose a king. The stronger fish, such as the whale and the dolphin, laughed contemptuously at the idea of peril, so the choice was limited to the weaker kinds. After much deliberation the selection fell on the herring, who was saluted with *Vive le Roy* by all present, with the exception of the plaice and the butte, who sneered at the newly chosen king, and for their mocking have wry mouths ever since. In remembrance of the honour, the herring has since this time worn a coronet on his head. Nashe does not continue the story, or tell us the result of the conflict, but only reports that—

"the herring, from that time to this, hath gone about with an army, and never stirres abroade without it: and when he stirs abroade with it, he sendes out his scowts or sentinels before him, that oftentimes are intercepted, and by theyr parti-coloured liveries descried, whom the mariners, after they have tooke, use in this sort: eight or nine times they swinge them about the maine mast, and bid them bring them so many last of herrings, as they have swinged them times; and that shall be theyr ransome, and so throw them into the sea againe." (*Harleian Miscellany*, vol. vi. p. 170.)

The same writer gives, as the mythological origin of the herring, the story of Hero and Leander, and declares that after the unfortunate termination of the lovers' last attempt to cross the Hellespont, the gods, commiserating the misfortunes of the unhappy pair, transformed Leander into the fish ling, and gave him as a habitation the coast of Iceland; Hero they changed into—

"the flanting Fabian or Palmerin of England, which is Cadwallader Herring: and as their meeting were but seldome, and not so oft as welcome, so but seldome should they meete in the heele of the weeker at the best men's table, upon Fridayes and Saturdayes, the holy time of Lent exempted; and then they might be at meats and meale for seven weekes togither." (Page 169.)

Smoked or red herrings seem to have been a common article of food. It is related that on Maunday Thursday Cardinal Wolsey washed and kissed the feet of fifty poor people, gave each person twelve pence, three ells of good canvas for shirts, a pair of shoes, and a cask of red herrings (*Mitchell*, p. 149). Russell, in his *Boke of Nurture*, 1450, recommends mustard with salt herrings, and with white or fresh herrings, white sugar, which does not sound particularly inviting :—

"Baken herynge, dressid and disht with white sugure ;
That white herynge by the bak a brode ye splat hym sure,

> Bothe roughe and boonus voyded then may youre lorde endure
> To ete merily with mustard that tyme to his plesure."
> (*Babees Book*, p. 38, ed. Furnivall, 1876.)

Shakspeare has several references to the herring, and takes notice of its great resemblance to the pilchard. *Feste* tells *Viola*, "Fools are as like husbands as pilchards are to herrings; the husband's the bigger" (*Twelfth Night*, iii. 1, 38).

Falstaff denounces the cowardice of the *Prince* and *Poins*, and sings his own praises :—

> "Go thy ways, old Jack; die when thou wilt, if manhood, good manhood, be not forgot upon the face of the earth, then am I a shotten herring." (1 *Henry IV.*, ii. 4, 142.)

"A shotten herring" was a phrase used to denote a shabby, underfed fellow. Taylor, the Water Poet, has the same expression :—

> " Though they like shotten herrings are to see,
> Yet such tall souldiers of their teeth they be,
> That two of them, like greedy cormorants,
> Devour more than sixe honest Protestants."
> (Page 5, ed. Hindley.)

Mr. Halliwell-Phillipps, in his *Dictionary*, explains the term " shotten herring " to mean the gutted fish that were dried for keeping. According to other authorities the expression meant herrings that had spawned, and that were consequently in poor condition. Shotten herring might be cured just the same as full fish, but the name applied to the fish and not to the method of preparing them.

Fuller learnedly discourses on the origin of the proverb, " a Yarmouth capon "—

> " that is, a red-herring. No news for creatures to be thus disguised under other names; seeing criticks by a Libyan bear, *sub pelle Libystidis ursæ*, understand a lion, no bears being found in the land of Libya.

And I believe few capons (save what have more fins then feathers) are bred in Yarmouth. But, to countenance this expression, I understand that the Italian friers (when disposed to eat flesh on Fridays) call a capon *pisce è corte*, a fish out of the coop." (*Worthies*, vol. ii. p. 126.)

Mr. Mitchell gives an account of the excitement occasioned among the superstitious of all ranks in 1587, in consequence of marks observed on two herrings caught on the 10th of November of that year, off the coast of Norway, which seemed to exhibit words in Gothic letters :—

"They were brought to Copenhagen, and seven days after their capture presented to King Frederick the Second, who was terrified at their appearance, and thought they predicted his own death. He consulted the wise men of the age, who read the letters, and said they were the following very innocent, and at present true, prophecy, ' You will not fish herrings in future so well as other nations.' But this interpretation did not satisfy the king, and he applied to the learned men of Rostock; but neither the professors there, nor at several of the Universities of Germany who were consulted, could give a satisfactory interpretation of the prophetic budget carved out on the backs of the two ominous fishes; but a learned French mathematician, then at Copenhagen, published a large volume in elucidation of the supposed words. This work would be a curiosity if it were found, as we are not informed what his interpretation was. Another author published his opinions, to the effect that the supposed letters announced the subversion of all Europe." (*The Herring*, p. 152.)

There was an old Highland superstition that the herring quitted the coasts where blood had been shed, and this theory was revived after the battle of Copenhagen, when it was said that they had deserted the Baltic on account of the noise of the guns.

Early authorities on fish considered that the Sprat was the young of the herring or the pilchard, whence it was called *garvie herring*, or garvie. Sprat.
The sprat was formerly held in greater estimation than it is at present. It was thought not unworthy to make its appearance at the Lord Mayor's banquet, and even

now this fish is not considered to be in season until after the 9th of November.

Sir Thomas Browne tells us that among the Norfolk fishes—

" the herrings departed, sprats, or sardæ, not long after succeed in great plenty, which are taken with smaller nets, and smoked and dried like herrings, become a sapid bit, and vendible abroad." (Vol. iv. p. 332.)

Jasper Mayne observes that—

"Since amulets and bracelets,
And love-locks were in use, the price of sprats,
Jerusalem artichokes, and Holland cheese,
Is very much increased."

(*The City Match*, ii. 1.)

Sardine.
Andrew Boorde, in his *Introduction of Knowledge*, written in 1542, tells his readers that in Spain "you shall get kyd, and mesell bakyn, and salt Sardyns, which is a lytle fysshe as bydg as a pylcherd" (p. 198, ed. Early English Text Society, 1870). These were in all probability the true sardines, still taken in large quantities in the Mediterranean, but in most cases any small fish that could be caught were pickled and packed in similar fashion.

Anchovy.
The Anchovy, another fish chiefly found in the Mediterranean, has been occasionally taken on the British coast, and its range extends even as far north as the coast of Norway. Anthonie Parkhurst, writing to Richard Hakluyt, in 1578, concerning the commodities of Newfoundland, mentions a fish "like a smelt, which commeth on shore," which a marginal note explains to be the fish "called by the Spaniards *anchovas*, and by the Portugals *capalinas*." The description of the fish is too slight to warrant this explanation (*Hakluyt*, vol. iii. p. 171).

In the paper of accounts purloined from *Falstaff's*

pocket by the *Prince* and *Peto*, we find that anchovies were appreciated as a relish by the valiant knight. *Peto* reads :—

> "Item, a capon, 2s. 2d.
> Item, sauce, 4d.
> Item, sack, two gallons, 5s. 8d.
> Item, anchovies and sack after supper, 2s. 6d.
> Item, bread, ob.
> *Prince.* O monstrous! but one half-pennyworth of bread to this intolerable deal of sack!"
>
> (1 *Henry IV.*, ii. 4, 584.)

In a discussion between the hostess of an inn and her servant, in Thomas Heywood's play, *The Faire Maid of the West*, this delicacy is again mentioned :—

> "*Clem.* Then for twelve penyworth of anchoves, 18d.
> *Besse.* How can that be?
> *Clem.* Marry, very well mistresse, 12d. anchoves, and 6d. oyle and vineger."

Muffett writes :—

> "Javelings or sea-darts are plentiful in the Venecian Gulf and all the Adriatique Sea, where having taken the young ones, they salt them and send them to Constantinople in infinite numbers for anchovaes; the greater sort they fry and boil at home." (*Healths Improvement*, p. 154.)

Eels were found everywhere, both in fresh and salt water, and were much esteemed. They were generally roasted fresh, but were sometimes salted. The conger was also considered a choice dish.

Eel.

Randle Holme gives the following names for the eel :—

> "An eel, first a fauser, then a grigg, or snigg, then a scaffling, then a little eel; when it is large, then an eel, and when very large, a conger."

The city of Ely is said to have been so named from rents being formerly paid in eels, and Elmore on the Severn obtained its name from the immense number of these fish there taken. Young eels are called elvers in the neighbourhood of that river (*Yarrell*, vol. ii. p. 294). As at this period naturalists were of opinion that eels were without scales, they were included among the forbidden articles of food among the Jews; fortunately for those who like this fish, this restriction has been removed by later investigations.

The conger was considered to be only a large-sized eel, or rather a fresh-water eel that had gone to the sea and remained there long enough to extend its dimensions, whereas the two species are now found to be perfectly distinct. Carew, in his list of fish found on the Cornish coast, more correctly divides eels into two kinds—

"the one *valsen*, of best taste, coming from the fresh rivers, when the great rain floods after September do break their beds, and carry them into the sea: the other, bred in the salt water, and called a *conger eel*, which afterwards, as his bigness increaseth, ventureth out into the main ocean, and is enfranchised a burgess of that vast commonwealth." (*Survey of Cornwall*, p. 97.)

Fuller assigns the palm to Cambridgeshire for the production of eels—

"which, though they be found in all shires in England, yet are most properly treated of here, as most, first, and best; the courts of the kings of England being thence therewith anciently supplied. I will not engage in the controversy, whether they be bred by generation as other fish; or equivocally, out of putrefaction; or both ways, which is most probable; seeing some have adventured to know the distinguishing marks betwixt the one and the other. I know the silver eels are generally preferred, and I could wish they loved men but as men love them, that I myself might be comprised within the compass of that desire." (*Worthies*, vol. i. p. 152.)

Instead of the beef and cheese usually ordered to be provided for the repast at the *month's mind*, which was the thirtieth day after a funeral, a testator of the time of Henry VIII. ordains that eel pies shall be substituted in the event of his month's mind falling in Lent, or on a fast day. The custom of having a grand repast a month after a person's decease probably arose from the inability of the relations to give sufficient importance to the obsequies in the few days which intervened between the death and the funeral. Postal arrangements were by no means rapid, relations and family friends had to be summoned from a distance, and provisions to the required amount could not be obtained without due preparation. Vernon, who wrote in 1561, alludes to the extensive scale on which these feasts were sometimes provided:—

"I should speake nothing, in the mean season, of the costly feastes and bankettes that are commonly made unto the priestes (which come to suche doinges from all partes, as ravens do to a deade carkase), in their buryinges, moneths mindes, and yeares mindes."

Some idea may be gained of the magnitude of these feasts from an account of a meal partaken of by the mourners, on the occasion of the interment of the Duke of Norfolk, at Framlingham, in Suffolk, in the year 1554. Machyn, citizen and merchant-taylor of London, in his *Diary* tells us that on this occasion the following substantial repast was provided: forty great oxen, a hundred sheep, and sixty calves, besides venison, swans, and cranes, capons, rabbits, pigeons, pikes, and other provisions, both flesh and fish (p. 70, ed. Camden Soc., 1848).

There was a notion that eels were bred from the slime of other fish, also that they could be produced by laying horsehair in water. Shakspeare refers to this theory, though it would appear from the context that snakes and not eels were the result of the experiment:—

"Much is breeding,
Which like the courser's hair hath yet but life,
And not a serpent's poison."
(*Antony and Cleopatra*, i. 2, 199.)

Sir Thomas Browne admits that he failed in his attempt thus to produce living creatures: he writes:—

"Besides horseleaches and periwinkles, in plashes and standing waters, we have met with *vermes setacci*, or hard worms; but could never convert horsehairs into them by laying them in water. (Vol. iv, p. 335.)

In *Pericles* we find a reference to the irritability of eels during a thunderstorm.

Sturgeon.

The " feast-famous Sturgeon," or Sturio, was an occasional visitor to our shores, and was always exceedingly welcome :—

"The sturgeon cut to keggs, too big to handle whole,
Gives many a dainty bit, out of his lusty jole."
(*Polyolbion*, song xxv.)

This fish was taken in considerable quantities at the mouth of the Elbe, but its head-quarters were in Russia. Dr. Giles Fletcher, in his account of fresh-water fish caught there, mentions—

" the bellouga, or bellougina, of foure or five clles long, the ositrina, or sturgeon, the severiga and sterlady, somewhat in fashion and taste like to the sturgeon, but not so thick or long. These foure kinds of fish breed in the Volgha, and are catched to great plenty, and served thence into the whole realme for a great food. Of the roes of these foure kindes they make very great store of icary or caveary." (*Purchas*, vol. iii. p. 417.)

The sturgeon was called a " fish royal," and was granted by charter to the mayor and burgesses of Boston, in Lincolnshire. When it came into the Thames it was claimed by the lord mayor, and was usually presented by him to the sovereign. Both fresh and salt sturgeon are mentioned as desirable dishes in Russell's *Boke of Nurture*.

Shark.

" The ravin'd salt sea Shark," the terror of mariners, is thus described by Sir Richard Hawkins, in his voyage in the South Seas, in 1593 :—

" The Sharke or Tiberune, is a fish like unto those which wee call dog-fishes, but that hee is far greater, I have seene of them eight or nine foot long; his head is flat and broad, and his mouth in the middle,

Parental Affection.

underneath, as that of the scate; and he cannot bite of the baite before him but by making a halfe turne; and he helpeth himself with his taile, which serveth him in stead of a rudder; his skinne is rough, like to the fish which we call a rough hound, and russet, with reddish spots, saving that under the belly hee is all white : hee is much hated of sea-faring men, who have a certaine foolish superstition with them, and say that the ship hath seldome good successe, that is much accompanied with them. It is the most ravenous fishe knowne in the sea; for he swallowth all that hee findeth." (*Purchas*, vol. iv. p. 1330.)

Mr. Couch says that the notion that the shark, while ferocious in the extreme to every other living creature, yet exhibited great devotion to its young, and watched over them with tender solicitude, is derived from the Greek poet Oppian, who relates that, when danger threatens, the parent shark opens her mouth and conceals her young ones in the large concave space provided for the purpose, much in the same way as the adder is said to provide for the safety of its offspring. This statement is repeated and confirmed by Rondeletius, a naturalist of eminence, whose work on fishes was the chief authority of this period (*British Fishes*, vol. i. p. 32).

The largest species of shark, and indeed of all true fishes, the Basking Shark, or sun-fish, was formerly often mistaken for the whale, from its habit of floating quietly and peaceably in the sunshine.

The Hammer-head, or Balance Shark, was only occasionally found :—

"The Italians name them *arbalestes*, because they have some resemblance therewith. Others call them hammers, or mallets, for their head resemble that instrument. They are hideous to behold, haveing their two eyes in the ends of that their hammered head, their mouth in the midst, very great, with three rankes of teeth, large and pointed; their tongue as that of a mans, their backe black with four finnes and their tayles divided into two parts. Rondolet describeth them, and sheweth their figure in his 30 booke, chapter ii." (*Learned Summary on Du Bartas*, p. 213.)

The shark was often observed by sailors to be accompanied by a small fish called the Albacore, or Pilot-fish. This little attendant was considered to be a kind of jackal, to provide the prey for his master, and to share in the spoil. Sir Richard Hawkins, in his account of a voyage to the South Sea, in 1593, writes :—

Pilot-fish.

" There doth accompany this fish [shark] divers little fishes, which are called pilats fishes, and are ever upon his finnes, his head, or his backe, and feed of the scraps and superfluities of his preyes. They are in forme of a trowte, and streaked like a mackerell, but that the streakes are white and blacke, and the blacke greater than the white." (*Purchas*, vol. iv. p. 1376.)

The pilot-fish was also thought to have a friendship for man, and to keep close to ships, and to warn them of danger by forsaking them when they came near the shore. It was therefore treated as a guide, and protected from injury by mariners. Mr. Couch suggests that the reason of the dislike of this fish to the neighbourhood of land is probably to be assigned to its objection to encounter any fresh water which may come from the mouth of large rivers.

The Remora, or Sucking-fish, was very common in the Mediterranean. It possesses a flat adhesive disk on the top of the head—

Remora.

" by means of which," says Yarrell, " it is able to attach itself firmly to the surface of other fishes, or to the bottom of vessels, but whether for protection or conveyance or both is a question which has not been satisfactorily ascertained." (*British Fishes*, vol. ii. p. 281.)

Although in reality only a small fish, and not capable of inconveniencing either fish or vessel to any great extent, the obstructive powers attributed to the remora were out of all proportion to its strength, and the word *remora* came to be used to signify an impediment or obstacle. Massinger writes :—

"To swim up to her, and like remoras
Hang upon her keel, to stay her flight."
(*The Renegado*, ii. 5.)

And Du Bartas is still more imaginative:—

"The remora, fixing her feeble horn
Into the tempest-beaten vessels stern,
Stayes her stone-still, while all her stout consorts
Saile thence at pleasure to their wished ports.
Then loose they all the sheets, but to no boot:
For, the charm'd vessell bougeth not a foot:
No more then if three fadome undergrounde,
A score of anchors held her fastly bound."
(Page 42.)

Horace, in the *Poetaster* of Ben Jonson (iii. 1), when victimized by a long-winded "Hydra of discourse," exclaims:—

"Death, I am seized here
By a land remora; I cannot stir,
Nor move but as he pleases."

And in Mayne we find a like comparison:—

"No remora that stops your fleet,
Like serjeants gallants in the street."
(*The City Match.*)

Montaigne also has a story to tell of this strange impediment:—

"Many are of opinion that in the great and last naval engagement, that Anthony lost to Augustus, his admirall gally was stay'd in the middle of her course, by the little fish the Latins call Remora, by reason of the property she has of staying all sorts of vessels, to which she fastens her self. And the Emperor Caligula, sailing with a great navy upon the coast of Romania, his gally only was suddenly stayed by the same fish, which he caused to be taken, fastned as it was to the keel of his ship, very angry that such a little animal could resist both the sea, the wind, and the force of all his oars, by being only fastened by the beak to his galley (for it is a shell-fish) and was, moreover, not without great reason astonished, that being brought to him in the long-boat, it had no more the strength it had without."
(*Essay* liv.)

The curious power of adhesion that the remora possesses was attributed by the ancient writers to supernatural agency, and from these writers also comes the confusion which often occurs in the descriptions of travellers between this fish and the lamprey.

> "Frenchmen, I'll be a Salisbury to you:
> **Dog-fish.** Pucelle or puzzel, dolphin or Dogfish,
> Your hearts I'll stamp out with my horse's heels."
> (1 *Henry VI.*, i. 4, 106.)

Thus threatens *Talbot*, stung to fury, and thirsting to revenge the dying *Salisbury*.

The dog-fish, a species of ground-shark, is chiefly remarkable in modern times for its voracity. It was used by our forefathers as an article of food, and was rendered palatable, or at least eatable, by the addition of a sauce compounded of garlic or mustard, verjuice, and pepper. Chaucer thus alludes to the rough scales of this fish, whence the name Rough-hound:—

> "He lullith her, he kissith hir ful ofte;
> With thikke bristlis on his berd unsofte,
> Lik to the skyn of hound-fisch, scharp as brere,
> (For he was schave al newe in his manere,)
> He rubbith hir about hir tendre face."
> (*Marchaundes Tale.*)

According to Du Bartas (p. 46), the dog-fish, like the adder, swallowed its young in time of danger:—

> "So, in the deep, the dog-fish for her fry
> Lucina's throwes a thousand times doth try,
> For, seeing when the suttle fisher followes them,
> Again alive into her womb she swallows them;
> And when the perill's past, she brings them thence,
> As from the cabins of a safe defence;
> And (thousand lives to their deer parent owing)
> As sound as ever in the seas are rowing."

The theory was often broached, both by classical

writers and by the philosophers of the sixteenth century, that every creature that has life upon the earth or in the air, has its counterpart in the water. Du Bartas puts into rhyme this fanciful notion, which may be found stated in prose by other writers of his time:—

Monk-fish.

> "Seas have (as well as skies) sun, moon, and stars:
> (As well as ayre) swallows, and rooks, and stares:
> (As well as earth) vines, roses, nettles, millions [melons],
> Pinks, gilliflowers, mushroms, and many millions
> Of other plants (more rare and strange than these)
> As very fishes living in the seas:
> And also rams, calfs, horses, hares, and hogs,
> Wolves, lions, urchins, elephants, and dogs,
> Yea men and mayds; and (which I more admire)
> The mytred bishop, and the cowled fryer:
> Whereof, examples (but a few years since)
> Were shew'n the Norways, and Polonian prince."
>
> (Page 39.)

The curiosity referred to in the last two lines was probably the Bishop, or Monk-fish, a species of shark. A specimen of this fish, according to Rondeletius, was taken in the year 1531, in Polonia, and brought alive to the king. After due inspection it was considerately restored to its own habitation. The monk-fish is a strange looking creature, with large wing-like fins. It may be the origin of some of the wonderful stories told by the old chroniclers of seamen. Stow tells us that a bishop-fish which was caught was actually taken as a compliment to the nearest church, where, to the chronicler's astonishment, he "showed no signs of adoration."

> "Fair Queen, forbear to angle for the fish
> Which, being caught, strikes him that takes it *Torpedo.*
>   dead;
> I mean that vile Torpedo, Gaveston,
> That now I hope floats on the Irish seas."
>
> (MARLOWE, *Edward II.*, i. 4.)

The power of imparting an electric shock possessed by the torpedo, or cramp-fish, was known to the ancients. Oppian, the "Izaak Walton" of classical authors, gives a full account of the mode by which this fish defends itself against its enemies. The torpedo, or electric ray, is found occasionally on the British coasts. Montaigne illustrates by the action of the torpedo the knowledge which animals have of their respective faculties, and the ingenuity which they display in putting these faculties to the best possible use.

"The cramp-fish," he writes, "has this quality, not only to benumb all the members that touch her, but even through the nets transmit a heavy dulness into the hands of those that move and handle them; nay, it is further said, that if one pour water upon her, he will feel this numness mount up the water to the hand, and stupifie the feeling through the water. This is a miraculous force; but 'tis not useless to the cramp-fish; she knows it, and makes use on't, for to catch the prey she desires, she will bury herself in the mud, that other fishes swimming over her, struck and benum'd with this coldness of hers, may fall into her power." (*Essay* liv.)

Thornback. The Thornback, mentioned by Harrison in his list of British fish, was very abundant. It was much used as an article of food. It was subjected to heavy pressure, salted, and dried for winter consumption.

The name *maid* was given to several fish of the ray species, but was generally applied to young skates. The name skate, says Couch, is derived from the Saxon word *skitan*, to reject, and was probably bestowed on this fish on account of its being thrown aside as worthless, at least for the market. The fishermen sometimes reserved it for their own use. Willoughby records an instance of a skate weighing two hundred pounds, dressed by the cook of St. John's College, Cambridge, which proved sufficient to satisfy the appetite of one hundred and twenty gentlemen.

"Lamprey, a fish of the sea, and of the sweet water, well knowne, long and sliding; depictured and described at large by Rondolet in his 3 chapter of his fourteenth booke."   Lamprey.

So writes the learned commentator on Du Bartas. Fuller, describing Worcestershire, tells us that—

"lampreys, in Latin *lampetræ*, *à lambendo petras*, from licking the rocks, are plentiful in this and the neighbouring counties in the river Severn. A deformed fish, which for the many holes therein, one would conceive nature intended it rather for an instrument of music than for man's food." (*Worthies of England*, vol. iii. p. 87.)

Drayton writes:—

"The lamprey, and his lesse, in Severn genral be."
(*Polyolbion*, song xxvi.)

The unwholesomeness of the lamprey grew into a proverb in consequence of the tradition that Henry I. owed his death to his partiality for this fish. In the old works on cookery it is recommended that the lamprey be stewed with good wine and herbs.

Du Bartas, in his curious jumble of Greek and Hebrew mythology, writes (p. 42) :—

"His sweetest strokes then sad Arion lent
Th' inchanting sinnewes of his instrument:
Wherewith he charm'd the raging ocean so,
That crook-tooth'd lampreys and the congers row
Friendly together, and their native hate
The pike and mullet, for the time, forgate."

It may not be out of place to quote the poet's apology for this incongruity. In the preface to his chief work, a long poem on the Creation, Du Bartas announces that he presents no profession of his faith, but a poem, which he has adorned "as much as the subjects will permit with all those most excellent jewels plucked and picked out of all sciences and professions." Referring to the then universal practice of introducing heathen deities into a religious work, he calls the attention of his readers to the small use he has made of them :—

"Poesie hath been so long times seasoned and seized of these fabulous termes that it is impossible to dispossesse her but by little and little thereof. I have attempted amongst the first to reform her, some other will come after me that will wholly purge her, and will interdict (as the civilians speake) these monstrous jests from fire and water."

This passage is not in Sylvester's translation, but in the translation of the *Learned Summary on his Works*, by T. L. D., M.P., 1637.

The following conjectural emendation on a passage in *Pericles* has been suggested by Mr. Bell, which has at least the merit of ingenuity :—

"The air-*retaining* lamps, the belching whale,
And humming water must o'erwhelm thy corpse,
Lying with simple shells." (iii. 1, 63.)

"The word *lamps*," writes Mr. Bell, "is here put for one of the lowest, and one of the most loathed species of fish, the lamprey. This animal, as is well known, has seven spiracula or air-holes on its side. These, with the Germans, according to a wide-spread and popular belief, are taken for seven eyes; which, with the two real ones the animal has, make up the Teutonic tale of nine, to give it the only name by which it is known of 'neunagen,' or nine eyes. But consequently, from this view, no orifices remain for respiration; and it follows that, not being able to emit the air, it must retain it: so that by the change of a single letter in the line, we have a perfectly consistent epithet, and a perfect solution. The contrast, too, is forcible, betwixt the lamprey emitting no air, and the whale spouting it so furiously, and in such columns." (*Notes and Queries*, 3rd series, vol. vii. p. 237.)

Dame Juliana Berners, after recommending the minnow and the worm as proper baits for the trout in the month of March, adds, "in Aprill take the same baytes: and also *junaba* other wyse named vii eyes" (*Treatise on Fyshynge*).

CHAPTER XVII.

THE word insect, from the Latin, *in*, and *seco*, to cut, was given originally to such small creatures whose bodies appear to be cut in, or almost divided, or, as Topsell calls them, *cut-wasted*. Insects are included by Topsell in his *General Treatise of Serpents*. He could not place these many-legged creatures with four-footed beast, and was therefore compelled thus oddly to classify them. He thus defines the word *serpent* :—

<small>Insects.</small>

"By serpents we understand in this discourse all venomous beasts, whether creeping without legs, as adders, and snakes, or with legs, as crocodiles and lizards, or more neerly compacted bodies, as toads, spiders, and bees. . . . Aristotle and Galen define a serpent to be *animal sanguineum pedibus orbatum et oviparum*, that is, a bloudy beast without feet, yet laying egges; and so properly is a serpent to be understood. . . . And thus much for the name in general, which in Holy Scripture is Englished a creeping thing." (Page 598, ed. 1658.)

The phrase in Leviticus (xi. 20), "All fowls that creep, going upon all four, shall be an abomination unto you," is thus explained by Professor Bush, in his notes on this chapter:—

"That insects are here meant is plain from the following verse; and, therefore, the sense is, 'all those creatures which fly and also creep, going upon all four,' *i.e.*, creeping along upon their feet in the manner of quadrupeds, such as flies, wasps, bees, etc., together with all leaping insects; these are to be avoided as unclean, with the exceptions in the next two verses."

Bacon makes use of the word *insecta*, but gives a different interpretation; after mentioning several kinds of insect, such as the weevil and gadfly, he writes, " Note that the word *insecta* agreeth not with the matter, but we use it for brevity's sake, intending by it creatures bred out of putrefaction."

Thomas Muffett, or Mouffet, a Frenchman, was physician to the English Court, in the reign of Elizabeth. He wrote a learned and elaborate work on insects, but died before the book was published. This work, *The Theater of Insects*, was brought out by Sir Theodore Mayerne, one of the Court physicians, in the year 1634. Mayerne, in his dedicatory epistle to Sir William Paddy, chief physician to Charles I., looks forward to the time when powerful microscopes shall reveal the wonders of insect forms. He writes:—

" How wilt thou be pleased to see the small proboscis of butterflies wreathed alwaies into a spiral line, after they have drawn forth nutriment from flowers, their extended large wings painted by Nature's artificial pencil, with paints cannot be imitated; to which the very rainbow is scarse comparable—
Which right against the sun a thousand colours shewes.
What a pleasant spectacle will this be when the artificial hands carefully and curiously guide the most sharp penknife, and very fine instrument by direction of the sight."

Muffett's work, which is printed with Topsell's *History of Four-footed Beasts*, in Rowland's edition, 1658, is the chief authority of the time on insects. It would have been far more valuable had the author devoted himself exclusively to obtaining information from personal observation and experiment, instead of quoting at length from Aristotle, Pliny, and other classical authorities, perpetuating their errors and conjectures, as well as their truths.

The use of Cochineal in dyeing is of great antiquity.

Cochineal. Colour-yielding insects are found on various plants in the southern and eastern countries of Europe. The best cochineal comes from Mexico and New Spain, and was first imported by the Spaniards from their Mexican possessions, about the middle of the sixteenth century. The nature of the coccus was, however, quite unknown. By most early writers it is called either the natural fruit of the tree, or an animal product bred of putrefaction. Beckmann, in his *History of Inventions and Discoveries*, writes :—

"As the coccus was gathered at Midsummer [St. John's Day] it was called St. John's blood; probably because the clergy wished by that appellation to make this revenue appear as a matter of religion; and that name is still continued among the country people in Germany. As the monks and nuns carried on various trades, particularly that of weaving, they could employ the St. John's blood to very good purpose."

We read in *Hakluyt* (vol. ii. p. 675), that on—

"the 9th of October, 1589, there arrived in Tercera fourteene ships that came from the Spanish Indies, laden with cochinile, hides, golde, silver, pearles, and other rich wares."

Du Bartas writes (p. 86) :—

"There lives the sea-oak in a little shel;
There grows untill'd the ruddy cochenel:
And there the chermez, which on each side arms
With pointed prickles all his precious arms;
Rich trees, and fruitfull in those worms of price,
Which pressed, yeeld a crimsin-coloured juice,
Whence thousand lambs are died so deep in grain,
That their own mothers know them not again."

On the second line of this passage his commentator has the following note :—

"This is a graine first of all brought from the East; and I have heard that certaine caterpillers doe every yeere cast out the same in a certaine time, as the silk-wormes doe: some likewise hold that it is a part of their bodies. The grain is like a small pease; and being kept (as wee see amongst the dyers) resembleth a little graine of dryed currants. Being grinded, it hath a purple browne colour, and serveth the dyers likewise for purple, which is betweene red and tawny; and is much in use at this day in Europe. The poet surnameth it red, because it is found that it hath a more high colour, and that which he addeth (that it groweth without tillage) may be understood according as I have expounded; except a man will say, that there is another graine of that name which commeth of it selfe: for I know not, whether the other proceeding from the bodie of a creature, may take root and fructifie." (*Learned Summary on Du Bartas*, p. 86.)

Chermes, or kermes-grain, from the Arabic word *kirmiran*, was the name given to the *Coccus ilicis*, an insect found on the ilex or evergreen oak, a tree growing in the south of Europe. Our word *crimson* is derived from this obsolete name, *kermes*.

Cricket.
Queen Mab was indebted to the insect tribes for her dainty chariot and "team of atomies:"—

> "Her waggon-spokes made of long spinners' legs,
> The cover, of the wings of grasshoppers,
> The traces of the smallest spider's web,
> The collars of the moonshine's watery beams,
> Her whip of Cricket's bone, the lash of film,
> Her waggoner a small grey-coated gnat,
> Not half so big as a round little worm
> Prick'd from the lazy finger of a maid;
> Her chariot is an empty hazel-nut,
> Made by the joiner squirrel or old grub,
> Time out o' mind the fairies' coachmakers."
> (*Romeo and Juliet*, i. 4, 59.)

The cricket was often confused with the cicada of the ancient Greeks, especially by those writers whose knowledge of natural history was derived mainly from classical sources. We should probably be correct in substituting the word cicada for the grasshopper in the following remarkable piece of information. The main value of the passage, however, is to show the extreme credulity of the narrator. Giraldus Cambrensis writes:—

"In the districts of Apulia and Calabria there are grasshoppers with wings, which spring from place to place not by any effort of their legs, but by the use of their wings, and have orifices under their throats by which they utter tuneful sounds. It is also reported that they sing sweetest when their heads are cut off, and when they are dead better than when they are alive." (*Topography of Ireland*, 1187, p. 40.)

This vocal accomplishment was confined to the male insect, hence the rhyme, handed down from antiquity :—

"Happy the cicadas' lives,
Since they all have voiceless wives."

Ben Jonson credits the cricket also with tuneful powers: "Walk as if thou hadst borrowed legs of a spinner and voice of a cricket" (*Bartholomew Fair*, i. 1).

It was considered a sign of good fortune to have a cricket chirping by the hearth, and to kill one of these harmless little creatures was looked on as a breach of hospitality.

"The cat, with eyne of burning coal,
Now couches fore the mouse's hole;
And crickets sing at the oven's mouth,
E'er the blither for their drouth."
(*Pericles*, act iii., GOWER.)

Shakspeare has several references to this lover of the fireside, whose monotonous note is so suggestive of cosy comfort. The boy *Mamillius* thus begins a tale of goblins by a winter's fire :—

"*Mam.* There was a man—
Herm. Nay, come, sit down; then on.
Mam. Dwelt by a [churchyard : I will tell it softly ;
Yond crickets shall not hear it."
(*Winter's Tale*, ii. 1, 28.)

This was for some time considered a scientific blunder on the part of the poet, but modern naturalists have demonstrated that the cricket is by no means deficient in the sense of hearing.

Sir Thomas Browne mentions " the *Gryllotalpa*, or

Fen Cricket, common in fenny places; but we have met with them also in dry places, dunghills, and churchyards, of this city [Norwich]" (vol. iv. p. 336).

The Grasshopper was regarded as the type of careless improvidence, of light-hearted enjoyment of the present moment, without thought of the morrow:—

Grasshopper

> "As long liveth the mery man (they say),
> As doth the sory man, and longer by a day:
> Yet the grassehopper for all his sommer piping
> Sterveth in winter wyth hungrie gripyng."
> *(Ralph Royster Doyster.)*

Muffett, in his *Theater of Insects,* says that the grasshopper is the only insect that is without a mouth. It is provided, according to this writer, with a long proboscis, with which it sucks the dew from the grass. This notion he derives from his classical authorities, and quotes from Plato the information that the grasshopper was consecrated to Apollo, and the Muses bestowed upon it this boon, that it should only live by singing, not so much as mentioning the dew. Ben Jonson writes of some careless spendthrift:—

> "Tut, he will live like a grasshopper—on dew,
> Or like a bear, with licking his own claws."
> *(The Staple of News, v. 2.)*

Unfortunately for farmers this theory of the grasshopper's diet is incorrect. It is a vegetable feeder, and in some districts has been known to cause considerable damage to the crops.

According to Ben Jonson, the grasshopper's chirp was more a sound of anger than of pleasure:—

> "And though the impudence of flies be great,
> Yet this hath so provoked the angry wasps,
> Or, as you said, of the next nest, the hornets,
> That they fly buzzing, mad, about my nostrils,

And like so many screaming grasshoppers
Held by the wings, fill every ear with noise."
(*The Poetaster*, act v. apologue.)

The poet's knowledge of natural history was not equal to his skill in classical lore, and he here, as elsewhere, confuses the grasshopper with the cicada of Italy and Greece.

Among whole-bodied insects Harrison includes "beetles, horseflies, turdbugs, or dorres (called in Latine *scarabei*), and the Locust or grasshopper (which to me also seeme to be one thing") (*Holinshed*, vol. i. p. 382). The locust proper is, fortunately, not a visitor to the cornfields of Britain, though the largest species of grasshopper has sometimes received this name.

Locust.

Shakspeare's only use of the word *locust* has reference, in all probability, to the bean and not to the insect: "The food that to him now is as luscious as locusts, shall be to him shortly as bitter as coloquintida" (*Othello*, i. 3, 354).

In 1553 the neighbourhood of Arles, in the south of France, was visited by swarms of these locusts, which caused great distress by their ravages on the standing crops. Sir Francis Alvarez, a Portuguese priest, gives an account of how he excommunicated the locusts in Ethiopia, in the year 1560.

"The number of these creatures," he writes, "is as great as it is incredible, and with their multitude they cover the earth and fill the ayre in such wise that it is an hard matter to be able to see the sun.... These vermine are as great as a great grasshopper, and have yellow wings.... We assembled the people of the towne, and all the priests, and taking a consecrated stone and a crosse, all we Portugals sung the Letanie. I caused them to take up a quantity of locusts, and make of [over] them a conjuration, which I carried with me in writing, which I had made the night before, requiring them, charging them, and excommunicating them, willing them within three houres space to begin to depart toward the sea, or toward the land of the Moores, or towards the desert mountaines, and to let the Christians alone: and if they obeyed me not, I called and adjured the fowles of the heaven, the beasts of the field, and all the tempests, to scatter, destroy, and consume their bodies. And for this purpose I tooke a quantitie of these locusts, and made this admonition to them which were present, in the name of themselves, and of those which were absent: and so I let them goe, and gave them libertie. . . . In the meanwhile, arose a great storm and thunder towards the sea, which lasted three hours, with an exceeding great shower and tempest, which filled all the rivers, and when the water ceased, it was a dreadful thing to behold the dead locusts, which we measured to be above two fathomes high upon the bankes of the rivers in such wise, that on the next morning there was not one of them found alive upon the ground." (*Purchas*, vol. ii. p. 1047).

As this ceremony was so successful, the worthy priest found himself applied to by the neighbouring countries when their fields were threatened in like manner, but he was probably too cautious to risk a failure by frequent repetition of the experiment.

The weird-looking creature, the Praying Mantis, is mentioned by Muffett in his *Theater of Insects* (p. 982). This author seems in all seriousness disposed to give the insect credit for the devotion which its eccentric attitude suggests. He writes, of locusts:—

Mantis.

"I have seen only three kindes very rare, *i.e.* Italian, Greek, and Affrican: they are called *mantes*, *foretellers*, either because by their coming (for they first of all appear) they do shew the spring to be at hand, so Anacreon the poet sang; or else they foretell dearth and famine, as Cælius the scholiast of Theocritus have observed. Or lastly, because it alwaies holds up its forefeet like hands praying as it were, after the manner of their diviners, who in that gesture did pour out their supplications to their gods. Of this Italian *mantis* (whose figure we do here represent), Rondeletius makes mention in his book *De Piscibus*, in these words: It hath a long breast, slender, covered with a hood, the head plain, the eyes bloudy, of a sufficient bignesse, the cornicle short, it hath six feet like the locust, but the foremost thicker and longer than the other, the which for the most part she holds up together (praying-wise), it is commonly called with us

Preque Dieu, the whole body is lean. So divine a creature is this esteemed, that if a childe aske the way to such a place, she will stretch out one of her feet, and shew him the right way, and seldome or never misse. Her tail is two forked, armed with two prickles: and as she resembleth those diviners in the elevation of her hands, so also in likeness of motion; for they do not sport themselves as others do, nor leap, nor play; but walking softly, she retains her modesty, and shewes forth a kinde of mature gravity."

> "We are oft to blame in this,—
> 'Tis too much proved—that with devotion's visage
> And pious action we do sugar o'er
> The devil himself."
>
> (*Hamlet*, iii. 1, 44.)

The so-called pious action of the mantis denotes in reality patient watchfulness for prey, as the cat crouches in silence before the mouse's hole. This insect is specially remarkable for savage ferocity, and will often destroy others of its own species, if they chance to come within range of its sabre-like legs.

An early mention of the singular Leaf Insect occurs in an account given by Antonio Pigafetta of the voyage of Ferdinand Magellan. Magellan sailed from Seville 1519, proceeded along the coast of South America, through the straits which bear his name, among the numerous islands of the South Sea, across the Great Pacific Ocean, and after many adventures arrived at the Ladrone Islands, where the gallant commander was unfortunately slain in a combat with the natives. Though he did not live to see the return of his expedition, Magellan is almost entitled to the claim of the first circumnavigator, as the *Victoria*, one of the three ships that formed the expedition, completed the circuit of the globe, and reached Seville in safety in the year 1522. Pigafetta, who kept a record of the events of this wonderful voyage, writes:—

"Leaving Borneo they came to the Isle Cimbubon, which lies in 8° 7' of north latitude; here they stayed forty days calking their ships, and taking in fresh water and fuel. In the woods of this isle they found a tree, the leaves of which, as soon as they fall on the ground move from place to place, as if they were alive. They resemble mulberry-leaves, and on the sides of them there are certain fibres produced, that seem like little eggs. If they are cut or broken, there is nothing like blood comes forth; but if they are touched they suddenly spring away."

Dr. John Harris, F.R.S., who includes this narrative in his collection of voyages, informs us that Pigafetta kept one of these leaf animals in a dish for eight days. The learned compiler considers it advisable to add as a note:—

"This account is not only improbable, but incredible; yet I have retained it, because, on the credit of Pigafetta, it has been taken into several treatises of natural history." (*Harris's Travels*, vol. i. p. 116, ed. 1764.)

Cockroach. The beetle, only too well known in modern kitchens by the name of Cockroach, is an importation from the West Indies. Captain John Smith, in his history of the Bermudas, or Summer Islands, 1622, mentions this insect under its native name :—

"The musketas or flies are very busie, with a certaine Indian bugge called by the Spaniards, a *cacaroatch*, which creeping into chests by their ill sented dung defile all, besides their eating." (*Purchas*, vol. iv. p. 1801.)

The word *bug*, it is scarcely necessary to note, was in older times, as it still is in America, the name given to beetles of all kinds. Harrison calls the dor-beetle a turd-bug, and Topsell speaks of humble-bees or shorn-bugs.

Beetles. Muffett mentions several species of Beetle: the great stag beetle; the long-horned beetle or goat-chafer; the dung beetle or sharn-bugg, which he describes as a round cat-faced beetle; the oil beetle; the great water beetle; the tree beetle or dorr, and others. Of this last, by which he evidently means the common cockchafer, he writes :—

"The tree beetle is very common, and every where to be met with especially in the moneths of July and August, after sun-set: for then it flyeth giddily in mens faces with a great humming and loud noise, and vexeth cattel. These beetles spoil the leaves of trees, which they do not so much eat as tear in pieces out of an inhred malice; for they feed upon gnats. We call them *dorrs* in English; the Dutchmen, *baumkafer, loubkaefer*; Agricola, *l. de subterr. anim. seukaefer*; the French, *hannetons*. The sheaths of their wings are of a light red colour, and covered as it were with a very fine flower, otherwise they shine but a little; their legs, feet, and prickly tail are of the same colour: its other parts are all over brown: only that the circle about their eyes, and their little horns are yellowish, and of the same colour are they a little above the beginning of their tail, the joynts of their bellies are whitish. In Normandy they are much more numerous every third year, and therefore they call it *l'an des hannetons*. It is recorded in our Chronicles, that in the year of our Lord 1574, on the 24 of February there fell such a multitude of them into the river Severn, that they stopt and clog'd the wheels of the water-mils: and indeed, unless together with the industry of men, the hens, ducks, goat-milkers, castrels, bats, and other birds of prey (which seem to make these their dainties) had afforded their help, the mills had even to this day been choaked and stood still." (*Theater of Insects*, p. 1014.)

Ben Jonson has many references to the desultory uncertain flight of the chafer or dor, and to the blind way in which it frequently dashes itself against the face of a pedestrian or any other obstacle. He uses the verb *to dor* in the sense of to mock, to outwit :—

"Abroad with Thomas! Oh, that villian dors me,
He hath discovered all unto my wife."
(*Every Man in His Humour*, iv. 6.)

" What should I care what every dor doth buz."
(*Cynthia's Revels*, iii. 2.)

Shakspeare's allusion to " the shard-borne beetle with his drowsy hums" (*Macbeth*, iii. 2, 42) has provoked some controversy. Robert Patterson, in his *Natural History of Insects mentioned in Shakspeare's Plays*, 1842, inclines to the opinion that the adjective *shard-borne* here refers to the hard outer coverings of the wings, and that the peculiarity of the insect's flight would be more likely to attract the poet's attention than would its place of nurture.

"These shards or wing cases," he writes, "are raised and expanded when the beetle flies, and by their concavity act like two parachutes in supporting him in the air. Hence the propriety and correctness of Shakspeare's description, 'the shard-borne beetle,' a description embodied in a single epithet."

Mr. Patterson refers any reader interested in this question to a long and interesting note published in the *Zoological Journal*, No. xviii. p. 147.

Bellarius warns the aspiring princes, *Guiderius* and *Aviragus*, that security may best be found under a humble roof:—

"And often to our comfort, shall we find
The sharded beetle in a safer hold
Than is the full winged eagle."
(*Cymbeline*, iii. 3, 19.)

A contrast is here drawn between the case-wings of the beetle, which, while they seem to impede its flight, protect it from harm, and the soft full-fledged pinions of the eagle, which too often carry the bird into danger.

Enobarbus, commenting on the love expressed by *Lepidus* for *Cæsar* and *Antony*, insinuates that this pretended devotion is but assumed as a means of self-aggrandizement. This "slight unmeritable man" seeks to rise by the aid of the superior strength of his colleagues:—

"They are his shards, and he their beetle."
(*Antony and Cleopatra*, iii. 2, 19.)

Other critics consider the word *shard* to refer to the

material usually selected by the parent beetle as a habitation for its offspring. Lyly uses the word in this sense, and writes : " The quaile that forsaketh the mallowes to eat hemlock, or the fly that shunneth the rose to light on a cow-shard " (*Euphues*, p. 240). This reading of the word is supported by Kirby and Spence in their *Entomology* (p. 221, 7th edition).

Ben Jonson notices these sheath-like cases :—

> "The scaly beetles with their habergeons,
> That make a humming murmur as they fly."
> (*The Sad Shepherd*, ii. 2.)

Isabella's appeal to her brother's courage and honour has been frequently quoted as indicating Shakspeare's opinion as to the sensibility of insects. That the dramatist was too large-hearted and tender to be indifferent to pain, even if suffered by so small a creature as a worm, is certain, but the Rev. Mr. Bird has pointed out that in these lines Shakspeare's purpose was to show how little man feels in dying :—

> " Darest thou die?
> The sense of death is most in apprehension;
> And the poor beetle, that we tread upon,
> In corporal sufferance finds a pang as great
> As when a giant dies.'
> (*Measure for Measure*, iii. 1, 76.)

The sting of death lies in the foreknowledge of it, not in the act :—

" Even a beetle, which feels so little, feels as much as a giant does. The less, therefore, the beetle is supposed to feel, the more force we give to the sentiment of Shakspeare." (*Patterson*, p. 79.)

> "The honey-bags steal from the humble-bees,
> And for night-tapers crop their waxen thighs, Glow-worm.
> And light them at the fiery Glow-worm's eyes."
> (*Midsummer Night's Dream*, iii. 1, 171.)

2 D

The mistake of placing the light in the glow-worm's eyes, instead of its tail, has been commented on by Dr. Johnson, and defended by Monck Mason, who writes:—

"Surely a poet is justified in calling the luminous part of the glow-worm the eye: it is a liberty we take in plain prose; for the point of greatest brightness in a furnace is commonly called the eye of it."

It may be observed that as the furnace has no real eyes to begin with, no confusion is likely to ensue from such an expression. Another very excusable error, as to the sex of the insect, occurs in the speech of the *Ghost* in *Hamlet*:—

"The glow-worm shows the matin to be near,
And 'gins to pale his uneffectual fire."
(*Hamlet*, i. 5, 89.)

Spirits cannot be expected to trouble themselves about minute entomological details; besides, the relationship of the male winged beetle to the crawling luminous female was not commonly recognized. Bacon mentions the *lucioli* of Italy and hot countries, which, he says, may be the flying glow-worm. He thinks it probable that the luminous insect of cold countries has not ripened far enough to be winged. He leans also to the doctrine of the generation of this insect from putrefaction (*Nat. Hist.*, century viii.). Muffett (p. 975) gives the names by which the glow-worm is known in a variety of languages. It is called in English—

"*Glow-worm, shine-worm, glass-worm*, i.e., a glistering or shining worm, for here as also in Gasconia, the male or flying glow-worm shines not, but the females which are meer worms. On the other side in Italy, and in the county of Heidelberg, the females shine not at all, and the males do. I leave the reason to be discussed by philosophers."

Lyly makes frequent and poetical use of this little insect: "Dost thou not know that a perfect friend should

be like the glaze-worme, which shineth most bright in
the darke?" (*Euphues*, p. 91).
Again :—

> "And yet, as bright as glow-worms in the night,
> With which the morning decks her lovers hayre."
> (*The Woman in the Moon.*)

Lyly also gives us a curious piece of information :—

> "Where the rainbow toucheth the tree no caterpillar will hang on the leaves; where the gloworme creepeth in the night no adder will goe in the day." (*Epilogue to Campaspe.*)

Webster writes :—

> "Glories, like glow-worms, afar off shine bright,
> But look'd too near have neither heat nor light."
> (*Vittoria Corombona*, act v.)

Fire-flies of various sizes are described by the early explorers. The lantern-fly, found in the West Indies, the Malay Archipelago, and in China, is mentioned by Champlain, in his account of a voyage to the West Indies and Mexico in the year 1599. He writes :—

Fire-fly.

> "There is a kind of little animal of the size of prawnes, which fly by night, and make such light in the air that one would say that they were so many little candles. If a man had three or four of these little creatures, which are not larger than a filbert, he could read as well at night as with a wax light." (*Reprint Hakluyt Soc.*, 1859, p. 35.)

Du Bartas (p. 45) classes this insect among the birds of the New World :—

> "New-Spain's cucuio, in his forehead brings
> Two burning lamps, two underneath his wings:
> Whose shining rayes serve oft, in darkest night,
> Th' imbroderer's hand in royall works to light:
> Th' ingenious turner, with a wakefull eye,
> To polish fair his purest ivory:
> The usurer to count his glistring treasures:
> The learned scribe to limn his golden measures."

On this passage his commentator remarks :—

"Oviedo in the 15 booke of the history of the Indies ch. 8. maketh mention of this little bird, which he found in the ile of Hispaniola and in other neighbouring places. He is very little, as of the thicknesse of a mans thumbe, or thereabouts; he hath two wings very strong and hard under which he hath two other little wings very thin which appeare not, but when he extendeth his other to fly; then are they seene (besides his two eyes shining like two burning candles) yeelding so great light that all about is enlightened. He flyeth not but by night. The Indians make use of them for candles both in time of warre, and of peace, and they yeeld them a farre greater light than our glow-wormes doe. . . . In a word the cucuye is the king of creatures which shine by night." (*A Learned Summary on Du Bartas.*)

Oviedo also informs us that the Indians managed to obtain a phosphorescent paste from the bodies of these flies, with which they smeared their faces. He admits that this statement is somewhat incredible, as the light vanishes with the creature's life. He relates that when Sir Thomas Cavendish and Sir Robert Dudley, son of the Earl of Leicester, first landed in the West Indies, by night, they saw to their astonishment a number of moving candles and torches among the trees. Thinking these lights were caused by an attacking body of Spaniards, they retreated with great haste to their ships, and only by degrees found out their mistake.

Ladybird.
"They shall be of the lady-cow,
The dainty shell upon her back,
Of crimson strewed with spots of black."
(DRAYTON, *The Muses Elysium.*)

The pretty spotted Ladybird, the favourite of country children, has received a great variety of names. It was called cush-cow lady, dowdy-cow, and May-bug or golden-bug. In Forby's *Vocabulary of East Anglia* (p. 130), notice is taken of the strange name sometimes given to this insect, Bishop Barnaby :—

"It is sometimes called Bishop Benebee, sometimes Bishop Benetree, of which it seems not possible to make anything. The name has most probably been derived from the barn-bishop; whether in scorn of that silly and profane mockery, or in pious commemoration of it, must depend on the time of its adoption, before or after the Reformation ; and it is not worth inquiring. The two words are transposed, and *bee* annexed as being perhaps thought more seemly in such a connection than fly-bug or beetle. The dignified ecclesiastics in ancient times wore brilliant mixtures of colours in their habits. Bishops had scarlet and black, as this insect has on its wing covers."

Tusser includes "the bishop that burneth" in his ten unwelcome guests in the dairy. The name *barnaby* has been derived by some authors from the low Dutch *barn-bie*, fire-fly, in allusion to the fiery colour of the wings.

Shakspeare has but two references to the Ant. *Glendower* worries the impatient *Hotspur*—

Ant.

"With telling me of the moldwarp and the ant,
Of the dreamer Merlin and his prophecies."
(1 *Henry IV.*, iii. 1, 149.)

The *Fool* in *Lear* tells *Kent*, " We'll set thee to school to an ant, to teach thee there's no labouring i' the winter" (*Lear*, ii. 4, 67). Mr. Patterson, from this passage, draws the inference that Shakspeare, unlike his contemporaries, was aware that in this country ants lie dormant during the cold winter months, and consequently do not require food. The ant has been held up as a model of industry, wisdom, and foresight, mainly on the authority of Solomon, who bids the sluggard—

"go to the ant, consider her ways and be wise: which having no guide, overseer, or ruler, provideth her meat in the summer, and gathereth her food in the harvest." (Proverbs vi. 6.)

Chester writes:—

" The ant, or emote is a labouring thing,
And have amongst them all a public weale,
In sommer time their meat they are providing,
And secrets mongst themselves they do conceale:

> The monstrous huge big beare being sickly,
> Eating of these is cured presently."
>
> (*Love's Martyr*, p. 115.)

Montaigne illustrates his proposition, that man shares with other inhabitants of the globe every passion he possesses, by reference to the storing propensities of the ant:—

"As to thrift, they surpass us not only in the foresight and laying up, and saving for the time to come, but they have moreover a great deal of the science necessary thereto. The ants bring abroad into the sun their grain and seed to air, refresh, and dry them, when they perceive them to mould and grow musty, lest they should decay and rot; but the caution and prevention they use in gnawing their grains of wheat, surpass all imagination of human prudence: for by reason that the wheat does not always continue sound and dry, but grows soft, thaws and dissolves, as if it were steept in milk, whilst hasting to germination, for fear lest it should shoot, and lose the nature and property of a magazine for their subsistence, they nibble off the end by which it should shoot and sprout. War," he continues, "which is the greatest and most magnificent of human actions," is exemplified in the encounters of such small creatures as bees and ants. Some trifling quarrel, some petty jealousy, may cause a leader to sacrifice the lives of many thousands of men. "This furious monster with so many heads and arms, is yet man, feeble, calamitous and miserable man. 'Tis but an ant-hill of ants disturb'd and provok'd by a spurn." (*Essay* liv.)

Huber, who studied with immense patience ant habits and customs, and published the result of his observations at the beginning of the present century, demolished for a time the claim of these little creatures to the virtues ascribed to them by earlier writers. The grains of corn, he contended, which they were supposed to hoard were in reality the young ants in the pupa stage of development. If we break open an ant-hill in the summer months we shall see that after the first moment of surprise and consternation the chief concern of the ants is for the safety of these small, white, grain-like forms, which they seize and carry off to a place of safety. Corn, he declared,

An Omission in Shakspeare. 407

would be perfectly useless to them, as they feed on soft, generally animal, substances. But more recent investigations have reinstated the ant in its former position of instructor. It is true that in cold countries ants do not collect grain; but in the East, whence these stories had their origin, the warmth of the winter renders hybernation impossible, and a supply of food consequently necessary. Further, though the grains of corn or rice are too hard for the ants' mandibles, they become softened by being kept in the moist underground granaries.

Mr. Patterson considers it strange that the ant is not oftener noticed by Shakspeare, when other insects not more attractive are so frequently introduced. It may be that the qualities which, rightly or wrongly, have been attributed to this insect were not those on which Shakspeare cared to dwell. Mr. H. Green, in his *Shakspeare and the Emblem Writers*, 1870 (p. 147), considers that the dramatist has been guilty of a great omission in neglecting to point out the value of sustained persevering work. He remarks:—

> "Industry, diligence, with their attendant advantages,—negligence, idleness, with their disadvantages,—are scarcely alluded to, and but incidentally praised or blamed.... The idea is in some degree approached in the *Chorus* of *Henry V.* (act i.), and the triumph of industry may also be inferred from the marriage blessing which *Ceres* pronounces in the *Tempest* (iv. 1. 110), yet for labour, industry, diligence, or by whatever name the virtue of steady exertion may be known, there is scarcely a word of praise in Shakspeare's abundant vocabulary, and of its effects no clear description."

"The Bee," writes Batman, "is called *apis*, and is a little short incecti, with many feete, and among all flyes with round bodyes and so shapen he beareth the price [prize] in manye things, hugenesee of wit rewardeth him in littlenesse of body, and though he might be accounted among flyeing flyes, yet for he useth feete, and goeth upon them, he may rightfully be accounted among beastes that goe on grounde." (*Uppon Bartholome*, 1582.)

Bee.

If Shakspeare has little to say in praise of the ant, he makes up for this want of appreciation by his numerous references to the bee. The possibility of obtaining benefit from apparently adverse circumstances is compared by *Henry V.* to the labours of this insect:—

> "There is some soul of goodness in things evil,
> Would men observingly distil it out:
> Thus may we gather honey from the weed."
> (*Henry V.*, iv. 1, 4.)

The poetical description of the economy of a bee-hive in the same play (act i. sc. 2) is not necessarily drawn from personal observation. There is a very similar account of these small creatures in the *Euphues* of Lyly. Lyly was in his turn apparently indebted to Virgil, and other classical writers, for his information. *Fidus* thus addressed *Euphues* and his friend *Philautus*:—

"Gentlemen, I have for ye space of this twenty yeares dwelt in this place, taking no delight in any thing but only in keeping my bees, and marking them, and this I finde, which had I not seene, I should hardly have beleeved. That they use as great wit by indution, and arte by workmanship, as ever man hath, or can, using betweene themselves no lesse justice than wisdome, and yet not so much wisdome as majestie: insomuch as thou wouldest thinke, that they were a kinde of people, a common wealth for Plato. . . . They call a Parliament, wher-in they consult, for lawes, statutes, penalties, chusing officers, and creating their king, not by affection but reason, not by the greater part, but ye better. . . . Every one hath his office, some trimming the honny, some working the wax, one framing hives, an other the combes, and that so artificially, that *Dedalus* could not with greater arte or excellencie, better dispose the orders, measures, proportions, distinctions, joynts and circles. Divers hew, others polish, all are carefull to doe their worke so strongly as they may resist the craft of such drones, as seek to live by their labours, which maketh them to keepe watch and warde, as lyving in a campe to others, and as in a court to themselves. . . . When they go forth to work, they marke the wind, the clouds, and whatsoever doth threaten either their ruine, or raign, and having gathered out of every flower honny they return loden in their mouthes, thighs, wings, and all the bodye, whome they that tarried at home receyve readily, as easing their backes of so great burthens." (Page 262.)

Virgil's fanciful description of the bees' labours was possibly the authority from which both Lyly and Shakspeare quoted :—

> "They only have a common progeny,
> The mansions of a city shared of all,
> And under noble statutes pass their life;
> And they alone a native country know,
> And settled household gods; and mindful of
> The coming winter, in the summer time
> Engage in toil, and for the common stock
> Store up their gains. For some watch o'er the food,
> And by a covenant agreed upon
> Are in the fields employed; others, within
> Th' enclosures of their homes, the tear
> Of daffodil, and clammy from the bark,
> A gum, the first foundations of the combs,
> Lay down; then hang they up th' adhesive wax;
> Others the nation's hope, the full-grown young
> Lead forth; others all virgin honeys pack,
> And with the crystal nectar stretch the cells.
> There are to whom hath fallen out by lot
> The sentry at the gates; and in their turn
> They watch the waters and the clouds of heaven;
> Or they the burdens of those coming in
> Receive, or in battalion formed, the drones,
> A lazy cattle, from the cribs fend off:
> Work glows, and th' odorous honeys smell of thyme.
> *   *   *   *   *
> Unto the aged are the towns a charge,
> To wall the combs, and mould their artful roofs:
> But, jaded, late at night betake them home
> The younger, loaded on their legs with thyme.
> And browse they upon arbutes everywhere,
> And blue-grey willows, and the cassia,
> And blushing crocus, and the gummy lime,
> And rust-hued martagons. With all is one
> The rest from work, with all is one the toil."
>
> (*Georgics*, book iv., Singleton's trans.)

The comparison of a well-governed State to the monarchy of the bees, observes M. Paul Stapfer in his recent work, *Shakespeare and Classical Antiquity* (p. 88), "is met with in Plato's 'Republic,' as well as in a fragment preserved by Augustine of Cicero's long lost treatise, 'De Republica.'" In the reign of Elizabeth there was no translation of Plato, with the exception of a single dialogue by Spenser. M. Stapfer comments on the wonderful power possessed by Shakspeare of grasping an idea, and, from the slightest suggestion of an author's thought, of reproducing it almost in its original shape.

"It must be remembered," he writes, "that the comparison of a well-ordered government to a concert in which every instrument plays its part, or to a bee-hive, has long since become a commonplace in literature. Ever since it was set in circulation by Plato and Cicero in their respective treatises on the 'Republic,' there has probably been no ancient philosopher or poet from whose writings some analogous simile could not be quoted. . . . Lyly, the author of *Euphues*, borrowed the name of his hero from Plato's 'Republic,' and his romance teems with comparisons between human governments and those presented to us in nature, especially in the case of bees. The tedious length of his exemplification places it far below the poetry of Shakespeare's passage, and makes it infinitely less worthy to be compared to the antique model, but it is precisely in such cases as this that we catch a glimpse of genius at work in one of its most marvellous operations, by virtue of which, diving through all the prolixity and exaggeration that a whole host of imitators have lost themselves in, it re-discovers an ancient conception, and makes it live again in all its first freshness and truth: for there is a brotherhood among all great minds, and Shakespeare happening to meet with the enfeebled expression of what had once been a thought of Plato's, was able to re-think it, almost back to its original form."

To return to the insects. Thomas Hyll, in 1593, published a treatise on the right ordering of bees, with instructions for keeping them, and for preparing the wax. His information is gathered almost entirely from the works of Aristotle, Pliny, Varro, and other classical authors. Topsell also perpetuates much ancient lore respecting the habits and nature of the bee. It is remarkable how long writers on natural history were content to repeat at second hand, without caring to verify by experience, the conjectures of their predecessors.

The idea of a king bee instead of a queen prevailed at a time much later than that of Shakspeare. The function of the drone bees was not clearly understood. Shakspeare calls them "lazy yawning drones," treats them as interlopers and even robbers :—

"Drones suck not eagles' blood but rob bee-hives."
(2 *Henry VI.*, iv. 1, 109.)

The yearly slaughter of these helpless members of the community may well have perplexed early naturalists. This "cruel, not unnatural," proceeding is thus explained by Dr. Ludwig Buchner (*Mind in Animals*, 1880, p. 214). The drones, according to this author—

"represent a hereditary peerage, which lets itself be served and fed by an industrious working class without directly contributing anything to the good of the community; from May to August they lead an easy life, devoted to amusement, untouched by care or toil. If, indeed, they could foresee the woful fate which awaits them at the end of this period, their bliss would be less untroubled. Their great number, which far exceeds real necessity, would be a thoroughly incomprehensible and puzzling fact in the otherwise well-ordered bee State, if it were not to be regarded as a legacy from the formerly wild and uncultivated condition of the bees, in which each bee colony lived independently, and partly because of this, partly because of the many dangers threatening the drones on their flight, a very great number of these was requisite for the secure attainment of the object of their existence; to-day, when as a rule many hives stand close together, and the care and providence of men ward off dangers, so large a number of drones no longer seems necessary."

This mistake of nature, however, is corrected by the workers, and on the approach of autumn—

"the famous massacre of the drones takes place, in which the male aristocracy of the State is offered up for the common good, without regard to close family ties between them and the workers."

Before the discovery of spermaceti, wax procured from the hive of the bee was a most important article of commerce. *Jack Cade* refers to its use in sealing letters and documents:—

"They say the bee stings, but a say 'tis the bees' wax; for I did but seal once to a thing, and I was never mine own man since."
(2 *Henry VI.*, iv. 2, 88.)

Imogen makes fond delay over a letter from *Leonatus*:—

" Good wax, thy leave. Blest be
You bees that make these locks of counsel. Lovers
And men in dangerous bonds pray not alike :
Though forfeiters you cast in prison, yet
You clasp young Cupid's tables."
(*Cymbeline*, iii. 2, 35.)

The number of candles required for the various religious services must have been considerable. Wax must have therefore been in great demand, though tallow candles were probably generally used for household purposes. According to Marlowe, wax was put to another use. Describing how *Hero* held aloft a flaming torch to guide her lover in his perilous passage, he writes:—

" Sweet torch, true glass of our society !
What man does good, but he consumes thereby ?
But thou wert loved for good, held high, given show ;
Poor virtue loathed for good, obscured, held low :
Do good, be pined, be deedless good, disgraced ;
Unless we feed on men, we let them fast.
Yet Hero with these thoughts her torch did spend :
When bees make wax, nature doth not intend
It should be made a torch ; but we, that know
The proper virtue of it, make it so,
And when 'tis made, we light it."
(*Hero and Leander*, 6th sestiad.)

Shakspeare illustrates by the same comparison the idea that virtue is wasted that is not diffused :—

" Heaven doth with us as we with torches do,
Not light them for themselves ; for if our virtues

Did not go forth of us, 'twere all alike
As if we had them not. Spirits are not finely touch'd
But to fine issues."
(*Measure for Measure*, i. 1, 33.)

Honey was used in England in the manufacture of ale, and by the Scandinavians in the production of mead, their favourite beverage. It is said that the word *honeymoon* had its origin in the northern custom of drinking honey-wine, *hydromel*, for thirty days after marriage.

The humble-bee is noticed more than once by Shakspeare. *Titania* bids her fairy train be kind and courteous to her hairy love :—

" Feed him with apricocks and dewberries,
  With purple grapes, green figs, and mulberries;
  The honey-bags steal from the humble-bees,
  And for night-tapers crop their waxen thighs."
(*Midsummer Night's Dream*, iii. 1, 168.)

Bottom accordingly sends one of his attendant sprites on the following errand :—

" Mounsieur Cobweb, good mounsieur, get you your weapons in your hand, and kill me a red-hipped humble-bee on the top of a thistle; and good mounsieur, bring me the honey-bag. Do not fret yourself too much in the action, mounsieur; and, good mounsieur, have a care the honey-bag break not; I would be loath to have you overflown with a honey-bag, signior." (iv. 1, 10.)

John Day wrote an allegorical masque, *The Parliament of Bees*, which was printed about the year 1607. Mr. A. H. Bullen, who, in 1881, edited the works of Day, is enthusiastic in his admiration of this composition.

" *The Parliament of Bees*," he writes, " assuredly deserved to have been acted; for a daintier sample of exquisite workmanship in this form of writing could hardly be found. . . . But hear Charles Lamb, the truest and subtlest of all critics :—
               ' The doings,
         The births, the wars, the wooings,

of these pretty little winged creatures are with continued liveliness portrayed throughout the whole of this curious old drama, in words which bees would talk with, could they talk; the very air seems replete with humming and buzzing melodies while we read them. Surely bees were never so be-rhymed before.'" (*Day's Works*, part i. introduction, p. 28.)

In this work Day brings a serious charge against the humble-bee:—

> "A bill preferd against a publique wrong,
> The surly humble bee, who hath too long
> Liv'd like an out-law and will neither pay
> Money nor waxe, do service nor obey;
> But like a fellou, coucht under a weed,
> Watches advantage to make boot and feed
> Upon the top-branch blossomes, and by stealth
> Makes dangerous inroads on your common-wealth;
> Robs the day-labourer of his golden prize
> And sends him weeping home with emptie thighes.
> Thus, like a theefe, he flies ore hill and downe
> And out-law-like doth challenge as his owne
> Your highnes due; nay, pyratick detaines
> The waxen fleet sailing upon your plaines."

Wasp. The Wasp is next arraigned:—

> "*Speaker*. A bill preferd against the waspe; a flie
> Who merchant-like under pretence to buy
> Makes bold to borrow, and paies too.
> *Prorex*. But when?
> *Speaker*. Why, ad kalendas Græcas; never then."

"The wasp," writes Topsell, "is a kinde of insect, that is swift, living in routs and companies together, having somewhat a long body encircled, with four membranous wings (whereof the two former are the greatest), without bloud, stinged inwardly, having also six feet, and a yellow colour, somewhat glistering like gold, garnished with divers black spots all over the body in form of a triangle."

Topsell seems to have made an exception in favour of the wasp, and to have endeavoured to test by personal observation the truth of the information he imparts:—

> "I think that all the whole pack of them have stings in general, although I am not ignorant that some authors hold the contrary, affirming that the breeding female wasps do want them: but thus

much I can say of my own knowledge, that on a time finding a wasps nest, and killing them every one by pouring hot scalding liquor into their holes, because I would bolt out the truth, I plainly perceived by long viewing of their bodies, that there was not one of them all but had a sting, either thrust out evidently, or closely and secretly kept and covered."

Shakspeare has several references to the irritable temper of this insect. *Brutus* refuses to crouch under the testy humour of *Cassius*, and declares :—

"I'll use you for my mirth, yea, for my laughter,
When you are waspish."
(*Julius Cæsar*, iv. 3, 48.)

Wasps as well as bees like honey, and as they do not collect it for themselves, they are under the painful necessity of robbing their more industrious connexions, and frequently commit "flat burglary" in order to obtain this delicacy. *Julia*, having torn to shreds her lover's letter, thus chides herself for her o'erhasty action :—

" O hateful hands, to tear such loving words !
Injurious wasps, to feed on such sweet honey
And kill the bees that yield it, with your stings !
I'll kiss each several paper for amends."
(*Two Gentlemen of Verona*, i. 2, 105.)

Shakspeare has no mention of the Hornet, another marauder on the treasure-house of the poor bees. Of this formidable intruder, Day writes: **Hornet.**

" There's the strange hornet, who doth ever weare
A scalie armor and a double speare
Coucht in his front: rifles the merchants packs
Upon the Rhode; your honey and your waxe
He doth by stealth transport to some strange shoare,
Makes rich their hives and keeps your own groves poor."
(*Parliament of Bees.*)

There was a notion, derived from antiquity, that bees were bred from the carcase of a bull, and wasps and hornets from that of a horse. For much etymological and antiquarian information respecting all these insects the reader curious in such matters is referred to Topsell's *History of Serpents*.

Muffett, in his *Theater of Insects*, mentions, and gives illustrations of, the following varieties of Fly: the Flesh-fly, or Blue-bottle, a frequenter of butchers' stalls; the Dog-fly; the Oxe-fly, or Tabanus; the Horse-fly, or Brees, called in Latin *asilum*; the Whane, Burrel-fly, or Wringle-tail, a fly like a bee, but with a longer body; Hair-tails, or Bristle-tails, which feed on smaller flies and caterpillars (ichneumons); Adders, Boults, Dragon-flies, or Water-butterflies; the Water-fly, whereof the caddis, or cados-worme; and the Tipula, or Crane-fly.

Fly.

We find several of these kinds alluded to by Shakspeare. *Ferdinand* protests that but for the love of *Miranda*, he would—

"No more endure
This wooden slavery than to suffer
The flesh-fly blow my mouth."
(*Tempest*, iii. 1, 61.)

Doll Tearsheet applies the epithet "blue-bottle rogue" to the beadle, probably in allusion to the colour of his uniform.

The Horse-fly of Muffett was probably the gad-fly, so called from the Saxon word *gad*, a sharp point or goad. This winged torment was, according to the classical myth, the instrument chosen by Juno to revenge herself upon her rival Ino. We read in the *Georgics* of Virgil:—

"Alburnus, an abundant winged thing,
Of which Asilus is the Latin name;
Greeks have it Æstros rendered in their tongue;
Fierce, buzzing, shrill; at which all panic-struck
Throughout the woods in all directions fly
The herds: storms gather, with their roars convulsed,
And dry Tanager's forests and his banks.

With this dire creature erst her frightful wrath
Did Juno wreak, when she designed a plague
For the Inachian heifer."
(Book iii. l. 202, Singleton's trans.)

Nestor says truly that in the ray and brightness of summer—

" The herd hath more annoyance by the breese
Than by the tiger."
(*Troilus and Cressida*, i. 3, 48.)

When *Scarus* describes the sea-fight between *Antony* and *Cæsar*, he compares the rash and precipitate flight of *Cleopatra* to the frenzied rush of some terror-stricken herd :—

" Yon ribaudred nag of Egypt,—
Whom leprosy o'ertake !—i' the midst o' the fight,
When vantage like a pair of twins appear'd,
Both as the same, or rather ours the elder,
The breese upon her, like a cow in June
Hoists sail and flies."
(*Antony and Cleopatra*, iii. 10, 10.)

Ben Jonson writes :—

" Gods, you do know it, I can hold no longer,
This brize has pricked my patience."
(*Poetaster*, iii. 1.)

Bacon writes, " The fly called the gad-fly breedeth of somewhat that swimmeth at the top of the water, and is most about ponds " (*Natural History*, century vii.).

Guillim informs us that—

" this fly maketh a great humming noise when he flieth, and of some is called the gad-bee, and of others the dun-fly, brimesey, or horse-fly, which in the summer times do grievously vex cattle, having, (as Ælianus saith) a sting both great and stiff." (*Display of Heraldry*, p. 236.)

Topsell recommends, as a remedy for the stings of flies, the fat of a lion dissolved and clarified. This must

2 E

have been a somewhat expensive cure; it is, moreover, a great indignity that the king of beasts should be boiled down to make an ointment for the stings of flies.

It is evident by the illustration he gives, that by the hair-tail or bristle-tail Muffett means the Ichneumon fly. Though he would probably have been puzzled to give a complete life history of this insect, this author is quite correct in stating that it feeds on smaller flies and caterpillars. A curious instance of how easily an insufficient observation of natural phenomena may lead to a conclusion exactly opposed to the true state of things, occurs in Leigh's *Natural History of Lancashire* (p. 149). The writer here imagines the small ichneumon grubs to be the young of the caterpillar. He says :—

"The caterpillar deposites her eggs in cotton, in the clefts of trees, which are enliven'd by the influence of the sun, at a proper season of the year; I do think she is destroy'd by her young ones, which creep within her to suck, for I have sometimes found them creeping upon cabbages, with twenty young ones within them, and sometimes dead with these within their bodies; they enter them at little orifices like nipples, on either side of the belly, and sometimes creep so far as to be scarce discernible, but most commonly one half of them hangs out, The possum in the West Indies is said after the same manner to convey and nourish its young ones, . . . so various are the methods which different creatures have for the preservation of their species."

After this remarkable conclusion the author sagely observes :—

"Thus we croud our heads with unnecessary and false ideas of things, and neglect the most useful part of learning, which is a true knowledge of the properties of bodies, so far as we can attain to it by experimental learning." (Page 169.)

Those who have reared butterflies and moths know to their cost that caterpillars are frequently destroyed by ichneumon grubs; but these objectionable parasites must in common justice be acquitted of "a wrong something unfilial."

The Water-fly is alluded to by Shakspeare as denoting light-hearted, empty-headed vanity. *Hamlet*, on *Osric's* entrance, asks of *Horatio*, " Dost know this water-fly ? "

Muffett writes of the Caddis-fly, the frequenter of pools and streams :—

"*Phryganide* comes from the little worm *phryganium* (which in English is called cados worm), living in the waters, and in the month of August ascending to the top or superficies of the waters; it hath four wings of a brown colour, the body somewhat long, having two short horns, the tail forked, or rather bristles coming out of the tail. The form or figure of this fly is various, in regard of the great variety of those little cados worms whereof they come." (Page 943.)

Izaak Walton mentions several kinds of caddis, or case-worms, but is ignorant of what sort of flies they turn into. His only interest in them, as in almost every other living organism, is whether or not they can be used " to bait fish withal."

The tipula, called in English the Crane-fly, is thus described by Muffett :—

"Of these flies are four sorts. The first species hath long shanks like a wood spider, the body almost ovall of a whitish ash colour, silver wings, black eyes sticking out, with two very short horns, the tail pointed or piked. It flies (much like the ostrich) hopping with the feet, sometimes it flies in the air but not far nor long. So greedy after the light, that it oftentimes is burnt in the candle. In autumn it is frequently seen in pastures and meadowes. This of the male kinde. The female is almost alike, but somewhat more black, the end of the tail as it were bitten off; these are called in English shepherds, in Latin *opiliones*, because they are most often seen where sheep use to feed. The second sort of tipula hath a great head, eyes standing out, four small horns, the body pleasantly various with the colours yellow and black interchangeably mixt. The third is almost like unto this, saving that the body being all yellow, is better set out with six or seven black spots; both the male and female have a three forked tail. The fourth species is very rare and curious, the head and especially the mouth forked, the shoulders swelling, the feet shorter, the body twice as thick as the rest; the back black, the belly and sides yellow, the tail black and picked." (Page 943.)

While *Titania* sleeps, her attendant fairies warn off from her elfin bower all hurtful intruders:—

> " Weaving spiders, come not here;
>   Hence you, long-legg'd spinners, hence!
> Beetles black, approach not near;
>   Worm nor snail, do no offence."
>   (*Midsummer Night's Dream*, ii. 2, 21.)

Mercutio thus describes *Queen Mab's* equipage :—

> " Her waggon-spokes made of long spinners' legs,
> The cover of the wings of grasshoppers,
> The traces of the smallest spider's web."
>   (*Romeo and Juliet*, i. 4, 59.)

The word *spinner* is generally explained by annotators to mean spider, but it seems probable that in both these instances the crane-fly or daddy-long-legs is referred to. There is a want of imagination in repeating, even under another name, the same creature in the very next line.

Ben Jonson writes, " Walk as if thou hadst borrowed legs of a spinner and voice of a cricket " (*Bartholomew Fair*, i. 1). And again, in the same scene : " *Quar.* Good faith, he looks, methinks, and you mark him, like one that were made to catch flies, with his Sir Cranion-legs." Drayton, however, gives this appellation to a fly :—

> " Four nimble gnats the horses were,
>   Their harnesses of gossamere,
>   Fly Cranion, her charioteer
>   Upon the coach-box getting."
>   (*Nymphidia.*)

Mr. Patterson notices, but does not explain, the curious comparison in *Henry V.* (v. 2, 434):—

> "Maids, well summered and warm kept, are like flies at Bartholomew-tide, blind, though they have their eyes; and then they will endure handling, which before would not abide looking on."

He imagines this allusion to have reference to some forgotten legend, some ancient superstition. By the end of

August, especially if the season be wet, flies seek the shelter of houses in great numbers, and become drowsy and semi-torpid, or, as children call them, tame.

"The small grey-coated Gnat" is often mentioned by Shakspeare. He refers to its habit of dancing, as it were, in the sunbeams:—

Gnat.

> "When the sun shines let foolish gnats make sport,
> But creep in crannies when he hides his beams."
>
> (*Comedy of Errors*, ii. 2, 30.)
>
> "The common people swarm like summer flies;
> And whither fly the gnats but to the sun?"
>
> (3 *Henry VI.*, ii. 6, 8.)

This troublesome little insect was evidently common in England, and precautions were taken against its attacks. We find in an inventory of the goods of the abbey of Sawtre, taken in 1537, among other articles of furniture of the "new chamber—the bedstedd with a net for knattes" (*Archæologia*, xliii. p. 240). This abbey was founded by Simon, Earl of Northampton, in 1146, and was dismantled by Henry VIII.

Muffett quotes from Stow, the chronicler, a strange account of a battle between two giant armies of gnats, observed between the monasteries of Sion and Shene in England; such multitudes of these insects gathered to the fray, that the light of the sun was darkened.

The larger and more venomous gnat, known as the Musquito, is mentioned by Henry Hawks, in a description of New Spain, in the year 1572:—

"This towne [Vera Cruz] is inclined to many kinde of diseases, by reason of the great heat, and a certaine gnat or flie which they call a musquito, which biteth both men and women in their sleepe; and as soone as they are bitten, incontinently the flesh swelleth as though they had bene bitten with some venimous worme. And this musquito or gnat doth most follow such as are newly come into the countrey. Many there are that die of this annoyance." (*Hakluyt*, vol. iii. p. 549.)

Miles Philips, another explorer, relates his adventures on a voyage to the West Indies, in 1568. He writes:—

"We were also, oftentimes, greatly annoyed with a kind of fly which in the Indian tongue is called *tequani*, and the Spaniards call them *musketas*. There are also in the said country, a number of other flies, but none so noisome as these *tequanies* be. You shall hardly see them they be so small; for they are scarce so big as a gnat. They will suck one's blood marvellously, and if you kill them while they are sucking, they are so venomous that the place will swell extremely even as one that is stung with a wasp or bee: but if you let them suck their fill and go away of themselves, they do you no other hurt, but leave behind them a red spot somewhat bigger than a flea-biting." (*Hakluyt's Voyages*, rep. Arber's *English Garner*, vol. v. p. 276.)

The writer of this account met with adversaries more cruel and bloodthirsty than the dreaded mosquito. He and his companions were put ashore by Sir John Hawkins, on account of the failure of provisions. A short time after they landed they were seized by Spaniards, taken to Mexico, and handed over to the mercy of the Inquisition. After about fifteen years of misery and servitude, Philips contrived to make his escape and to return to England.

Butterfly. "There is a differency between a grub and a Butterfly; yet your butterfly was a grub. This Marcius is grown from man to dragon: he has wings; he's more than a creeping thing." (*Coriolanus*, v. 4, 10.)

The transformations of the butterfly were imperfectly understood. Topsell describes several species of caterpillars, in language so quaint as well to repay perusal, but a short extract must here suffice. He writes:—

"If I should goe about to describe and set downe all the differences and varieties of caterpillers, I might perhaps undertake an endlesse and tedious labour. I thinke it therefore fittest to bend my slender skill, and to imploy my best forces, in speaking of such as are more notable and common with us in this country. For some of them in touching are rough, hard, and stiffe; and other-some againe, are soft, smooth, and very tender. Some are horned, either in the head or in the tayle, and againe, others have no hornes at all, some have many feete, and some fewer, and none at all have above sixteen feete. Most of them have a bending swift pace, and like unto waves, and others againe keepe on their way very plainely, softly, by little and little, and without any great haste. Some change their skinnes yeerely, others againe there be that neither change nor cast their old dry skinnes, but keepe them still. Some of them, ceasing altogether from any motion, and giving over to eate any thing at all, are transformed very strangely into a kind of vermin or worms, who beeing covered with a hard crust or shell, lye as it were dead all the winter; and from these come in the beginning of hot weather, our usuall butter-flyes." (Book 3, p. 104.)

The opinions held by Bacon on the subject of insect transformations were somewhat vague. He writes:—

" The caterpillar is one of the most general of wormes, and breedeth of dew and leaves: for we see infinite number of caterpillars which breed upon trees and hedges by which the leaves of the trees or hedges are in great part consumed, as well by their breeding out of the leaf as by their feeding upon the leaf. . . . Greatest caterpillars breed on cabbages which have a fat leaf, and are apt to putrefy. The caterpillar towards the end of summer waxeth volatile and turneth to a butterfly or perhaps some other fly." (*Nat. Hist.*, century viii.)

The entomologist will find some amusing reading concerning caterpillars and their ways in Izaak Walton's *Complete Angler* (part i. ch. 5).

Shakspeare uses this guest of summer as a most appropriate comparison to " translate the stubbornness of fortune :"—

"What the declined is
He shall as soon read in the eyes of others
As feel in his own fall ; for men, like butterflies,
Show not their mealy wings but to the summer."
(*Troilus and Cressida*, iii. 3, 76.)

Valeria tries to console *Virgilia* for her husband's absence by speaking in flattering terms of young *Marcius*:—

" O' my word, the father's son : I'll swear, 'tis a very pretty boy. O' my troth, I looked upon him o' Wednesday half an hour together :

has such a confirmed countenance. I saw him run after a gilded butterfly; and when he caught it, he let it go again; and after it again; and over and over he comes, and up again; catched it again; or whether his fall enraged him, or how 'twas, he did so set his teeth and tear it; O, I warrant, how he mammocked it!
Volumnia. One on 's father's moods." (*Coriolanus*, i. 3, 62.)

Truly, "his father's son!" At the close of the play this childish episode is enacted on a larger scale. *Coriolanus* hotly pursues a painted glory; checked in his career and enraged by his fall, he would tear to pieces, in like ruthless fashion, the city he had professed to love.

Muffett divides butterflies into day-butterflies and night-butterflies, or *phalens*. He gives illustrations and descriptions of several kinds, and is evidently at a loss to find words in which to paint their varied hues. He notices the occurrence of one of those blood showers that are frequently mentioned by medieval writers, and which were always held to foretell misfortune.

"In the year 1553," he writes, "as Sleidanus reports, a little before the death of Mauritius, the duke of Saxony, an infinite army of butterflies flew through great part of Germany, and did infect the grasse, herbs, houses and garments of men with bloudy drops, as though it had rained bloud." (Page 974.)

Moth. The word Moth generally implies some very small insect, and was probably not given to the larger species of night-butterflies. Muffett writes:—

"Moreover there are found in houses a certain sort of little silver coloured *phalens* marked with black spots, which fly to the candles called *mothes* in English, which eat linnen and woollen clothes, and lay eggs, of which come moths, and of the moths again these *phalens*; they are said to come first of all from rose leaves and other herbs putrefying." (Page 966.)

Shakspeare gives the name *Moth* to one of the little fairies attendant on *Titania*, and to the young page of

Armado. The destructive propensities of these small insects are referred to by *Valeria* :—

"You would be another Penelope: yet, they say, all the yarn she spun in Ulysses, absence did but fill Ithaca full of moths." (*Coriolanus*, i. 3, 92.)

Ben Jonson writes :—

"But greatness hath his cankers. Worms and moths
Breed out of too much humour, in the things
Which after they consume, transferring quite
The substance of their makers into themselves."
(*Sejanus*, iii. 3.)

By medieval writers the words *caterpillar, worm,* and *canker* were used synonymously, as denoting the grub stage of any insect. *Viola* relates in a few pathetic words the history of many a lovelorn damsel :—

"She never told her love
But let concealment, like a worm i' the bud,
Feed on her damask cheek."
(*Twelfth Night*, ii. 4, 114.)

Proteus makes use of a similar comparison :—

"Yet writers say, as in the sweetest bud
The eating canker dwells, so eating love
Inhabits in the finest wits of all."

Valentine thus adroitly turns this image against the speaker :—

"And writers say, as the most forward bud
Is eaten by the canker ere it blow,
Even so by love the young and tender wit
Is turn'd to folly, blasting in the bud,
Losing his verdure even in the prime,
And all the fair effects of future hopes."
(*Two Gentlemen of Verona*, i. 1.)

Chester writes :—

"Of wormes are divers sorts and divers names,
Some feeding on hard timber, some on trees,

> Some in the earth a secret cabbine frames,
> Some live on tops of ashes, some on olives;
> Some of a red watrish colour, some of green,
> And some within the night like fire are seen."
> (*Love's Martyr*, p. 116.)

"It was formerly a very prevalent idea," writes Mr. Thistelton Dyer," and one, too, not confined to our own country—that toothache was caused by a little worm, having the form of an eel, which gradually gnawed a hole in the tooth. This notion is still to be met with in Germany, and is mentioned by Thorpe in his *Northern Mythology* (vol. iii. p. 167). Shakspeare, in *Much Ado about Nothing* (ii. 2), speaks of this curious belief:—

> "' *D. Pedro.* What! sigh for the toothache?
> *Leon.* Where is but a humour or a worm.'"
> (*English Folk-Lore*, 1878, p. 155.)

In this passage Mr. Dyer implies that this superstition has died out in England; but only recently a lady who read his work remarked, " It is quite true that toothache does come sometimes from a worm: if you make a person who has this pain inhale boiling water you may see the little worms drop out. I should have thought," she concluded," that a clever man like Mr. Dyer would have known better."

We come next to—

Silkworm.
> " The Silkeworme by whose webbe our silkes are made,
> For she doth dayly labour with her weaving,
> A worme that's rich and precious in her trade,
> That whilst poore soule she toyleth in her spinning
> Leaves nothing in her belly but empty aire,
> And toyling too much falleth to despaire."
> (CHESTER, *Love's Martyr*, p. 116.)

The fabric manufactured from the produce of the silkworm was introduced into Europe from China as early as the sixth century. Silk, interwoven with threads of gold or silver, was known as *baudekyn*, or cloth of Baldeck or Babylon, from whence it was supposed to come. The religious persecutions in France, during the reigns of Elizabeth and James, induced many silk-weavers to leave that country and to bring their families and their trade to England. In the *Harleian Miscellany* (vol. ii. p. 218), there is a reprint of some instructions, published in 1609, for planting mulberry-trees in all the English counties, together with a letter from King James I. to the lord lieutenants of the various shires, commanding each of them to buy and distribute ten thousand mulberry plants, at the rate of three farthings the plant, or six shillings the hundred. For those who found the process of planting inconvenient, a good quantity of mulberry seeds were to be distributed, also at a cheap rate, with complete instructions as to breeding and rearing the silkworms. This appears to have been the first attempt on an extensive scale to introduce this manufacture into England, but some few private individuals had already imported both trees and insects.

Shakspeare has many references to the use of silk in costume. He is guilty of a slight anachronism in mentioning this fabric as worn by the ancient Britons at the time of Augustus Cæsar:—

> "O, this life
> Is nobler than attending for a check,
> Prouder than rustling in unpaid-for silk."
> (*Cymbeline*, iii. 3, 21.)

When *Othello* demands from *Desdemona* the handkerchief, his first gift of love, he declares that it is endowed with supernatural virtues:—

> "'Tis true: there's magic in the web of it:
> A sibyl, that had number'd in the world
> The sun to course two hundred compasses,
> In her prophetic fury sew'd the work;
> The worms were hallow'd that did breed the silk;
> And it was dyed in mummy which the skilful
> Conserved of maidens' hearts."
> (*Othello*, iii. 4, 69.)

Du Bartas (p. 46) falls into the error of transforming the silkworm into a fly :—

> "Yet may I not that little worm pass by,
> Of fly turn'd worm, and of a worm a fly:
> Two births, 2 deaths, heer nature hath assign'd her,
> Leaving a post-hume (dead-live) seed behind her,
> Which soon transforms the fresh and tender leaves
> Of *Thisbes* pale tree, to those slender sheaves
> (On ovall clews) of soft, smooth, silken flakes,
> Which more for us, than for her self, she makes.
> O precious fleece! which onely did adorn
> The sacred loyns of princes heretoforn:
> But our proud age, with prodigall abuse,
> Hath so profan'd th' old honourable use,
> That shifters now, who scarce have bread to eat,
> Disdain plain silk, unless it be beset
> With one of those deer metals, whose desire
> Burns greedy soules with an immortall fire."

"The Spider," says Guillim prettily, "is born free of the weaver's company.". Batman writes:—

Spider.
"The spinner is a little creeping beast with many feet and hath alwaye feet even, and not odde, and among beasts of rounde bodyes the spinner hath best feeling of touch."

Quoting Aristotle, he says that spiders are of many kinds, some small and of divers colours, sharp and swift of moving, some black in colour, whose hind legs are longer than the rest. He here refers to the hunting species. After his discourse on spiders, drawn entirely from classical sources, he concludes his remarks with a most uncomplimentary suggestion :—

> "Besides this large discourse of spiders, it hath beene reported, that in Ireland be many spiders, and some verye great, and that being eaten of the Irishmen, have not performed any shewe of venime: it may be that the greater poyson subdueth the lesse." (*Batman uppon Bartholome*, 1582, p. 347.)

Some foreign species of spiders are mentioned by travellers. In an account of the West Indies written to Charles V. of Spain, 1525, Oviedo remarks :—

"There are also spiders of marveilous bignesse, and I have seene some with bodies and legges bigger than a mans hand extended every way, and I once saw one of such bignesse, that onely her body was as bigge as a sparrow, and full of that laune whereof they make their webbes: this was of a darke russet colour, with eyes greater then the eyes of a sparrow, they are venemous, and of terrible shape to behold." (*Purchas*, vol. ii. p. 970.)

Shakspeare speaks of the spider as poisonous:—

"But let thy spiders, that suck up thy venom,
And heavy-gaited toads lie in their way."
(*Richard II.*, iii. 2, 14.)

In *Edward III.* (iii. 1), a play either written by Shakspeare or by some most successful imitator, we find the same idea:—

"Dare he already crop the flower-de-luce?
I hope, the honey being gather'd thence,
He, with the spider, afterward approach'd,
Shall suck forth deadly venom from the leaves."

In the following passage it would seem that the injury inflicted by the spider was more imaginary than real:—

"There may be in the cup
A spider steep'd, and one may drink, depart,
And yet partake no venom, for his knowledge
Is not infected: but if one present
The abhorr'd ingredient to his eye, make known
How he hath drunk, he cracks his gorge, his sides,
With violent hefts. I have drunk, and seen the spider."
(*Winter's Tale*, ii. 1, 39.)

The belief in the spider's venomous properties was at this time universal. At the trial of the Countess of Essex for the murder of Sir Thomas Overbury it came out, in course of the examination, that the lady had procured from one of the witnesses seven large spiders, as the strongest poison that could be obtained.

We find in early writings many references to a strange disease called *tarantismus*. People infected with this malady were supposed to have been bitten by a venomous spider, which was found chiefly in the vicinity of the city of Taranto in Apulia. Topsell writes:—

"If the speckled *phalangie* of Apulia, which is usually known by the name of tarantula, do bite any one, there will follow divers and contrary accidents and symptoms, according to the various constitutions, different complexion, and disposition of the party wounded. For after they are hurt by the tarantula, you shall see some of them laugh, others contrariwise to weep, some will clatter out of measure, so that you shall never get them to hold their tongues, and othersome again you shall observe to be as mute as fishes: this man sleepeth continually, and another cannot be brought to rest at all, but runneth up and down, raging and raving like a mad man. . . . With others again you shall have nothing but sadnesse, and heavinesse of minde, brown-studies, unaptnesse to do any thing, as if one were astonyed. . . . But let them be affected either with this or that passion, yet this is common to them all, as well to one as to another, that they are generally delighted with musical instruments, and at their sound or noise will so trip it on the toes dancer-like, applying both their mindes and bodies to dancing and frisking up and down, that during the time of any musical harmony, they will never leave moving their members and limbs, like a jackanapes that cannot stand still." (Page 772, ed. 1658.)

The dances and songs composed as a remedy for this malady were called *tarantella*. According to Muffett, this poisonous spider was of a light brown colour, with dark spots, with short thick, hairy, legs.

Muffett has much to say on behalf of the "tame or house spider," and draws many a moral from its industrious ways and parental affection:—

"Aristotle the greatest diver into Nature, saith that this is the most magnificent, and wisest of all insects. And Solomon himself, at whose wisdome all the world admired, amongst those four animals that exceed philosophers for their knowledge, reckons up the spider, dwelling as he saith in kings palaces, and weaving webs that man cannot do the like. . . . I know not whether I were best commend the spider for the gifts of her minde, as wisdom, justice, valour, temperance, humanity, love of poverty, love of works, sufficiency, cunning, cleanlinesse, and her other vertues; or else her admirable art and skill in weaving her webs." (*Theater of Insects*, p. 1065.)

A Cure for Ague. 431

According to Lyly, the bee was impervious to the attacks of the spider, and might enter its web with impunity; "though the spider poyson the fly, shee cannot infect the bee" (*Euphues*, p. 35). The belief that ague could be cured by wearing a spider hung round the neck in a nutshell has been called an "old wives' fable," but Robert Burton, while he admits that he was indebted to his mother for his knowledge of this remedy, yet, in apparent seriousness, endorses her belief in its efficacy himself, and supports it by quotations from other learned authors:—

"I first observed this amulet of a spider in a nut-shell lapped in silke, &c., so applied for an ague by my mother: whom although I knew to have excellent skill in chirurgery, sore eyes, aches, &c., and such experimental medicines, as all the country where she dwelt can witness, to have done many famous and good cures upon divers poor folks, that were destitute of help—yet, among all other experiments, this methought was most absurd and ridiculous: I could see no warrant for it. *Quid araneæ cum febre?* For what antipathy? Till at length, dabbling amongst authors, as often I do, I found this very medicine in Dioscorides, approved by Matthiolus, repeated by Aldrovandus, *cap. de aranæ, lib. de insectis*. I began to have a better opinion of it, and to give credit to amulets when I saw it in some parties answer to experiments." (*Anatomy of Melancholy*, vol. ii. p. 134.)

Well may Mr. Harting ask, "When such men are so credulous, how can we wonder at the superstitions of the illiterate?" Spiders were recommended by medieval physicians for various diseases; among others, for the gout:—

"Also that knotty whip of God, and mock of all physicians, the gowt, which learned men say can be cured by no remedy, findes help and cure by a spider layd on, if it be taken at that time when neither sun nor moon shineth, and the hinder legs pulled off, and put into a deers skin, and bound to the pained foot, and left on for some time."

So writes Thomas Muffett, "a notable ornament to the company of physicians, a man of the most polite and solid learning, and well experienced in most sciences" (*Theater of Insects*, p. 1073). The medicinal virtues of the spider's web are also referred to by Bottom the weaver: "I shall desire you of more acquaintance, good master Cobweb: if I cut my finger, I shall make bold with you" (*Midsummer Night's Dream*, iii. 1, 184).

Another use of these little creatures was to provide a dainty repast for the small monkeys or marmosets, the favourite pets of this period. In Ben Jonson's *Staple of News* (ii. 1), *Almanack* says of old *Penny Boy*, as a skit upon his penuriousness, that he—

> " Sweeps down no cobwebs here,
> But sells them for cut fingers; and the spiders,
> As creatures reared of dust, and cost him nothing,
> To fat old ladies' monkeys."

Mr. Patterson points that though Shakspeare has twice mentioned the silvery threads of gossamer, it is not in connexion with the little being from whom it originates, and with which he was probably unacquainted:

> "A lover may bestride the gossamer,
> That idles in the wanton summer air,
> And yet not fall: so light is vanity."
> (*Romeo and Juliet*, ii. 6, 18.)

The "lash of film," wielded by *Queen Mab's* coachman, was in all probability composed of this delicate material.

Scorpion.

Sir Thomas Herbert, in the account of his travels, begun in the year 1626, gives a description of the Scorpions in Cashan, a city in Persia:—

"But which rages there in no less violence is scorpio; not that in the Zodiak, but real scorpions.which in numbers engender here. A little serpent of a finger long, which makes me marvel at Cedrenus, who says there are scorpions 2 cubits long in the Brachmans countrey, *i.e.* India, like but less than our cray-fish; and is the oncly creature that stings with his tail, some flyes excepted. Of great terrour is the sting; and so inflaming as with their invenomed arrow some die, few avoid madness, at least for a whole day; the sting proving most dangerous when the season is hottest, which is when the Dog-star rages; . . . the execration is, *May a scorpion of Cashan sting thee.* But which is more remarkable, and agreeable to what Pliny in his *Natural History* reports of the scorpions in Mesopotamia; they say, and we found it true; some of them creeping into our rugs as we slept, they seldom or never hurt a stranger." (*Travels*, p. 222.)

Ben Jonson is also indebted to Pliny for his knowledge of the existence of an antidote to this creature's sting :—

"*Tiberius.* I have heard that aconite,
Being timely taken, hath a healing might
Against the scorpion's stroke; the proof we'll give:
That, while two poisons wrestle, we may live."
(*Sejanus*, iii. 3.)

Chester has also some information to impart, drawn from a classical source :—

" The scorpion hath a deadly stinging taile,
Bewitching some with his faire smiling face,
But presently with force he doth assaile
His captive praie, and brings him to disgrace :
   Wherefore 'tis cald of some the flattering worme,
   That subtilly his foe doth overturne.

" Orion made his boast the earth should bring
Or yeeld no serpent forth but he would kill it
Where presently the scorpion up did spring,
For so the onely powers above did will it :
   Where in the people's presence they did see,
   Orion stung to death most cruelly."
(*Love's Martyr*, p. 116.)

The scorpion, used metaphorically, meant the most virulent poison :—

"*Macbeth.* O, full of scorpions is my mind, dear wife!
Thou know'st that Banquo, and his Fleance, lives."
(*Macbeth*, iii. 2, 36.)

2 F

CHAPTER XVIII.

Lobster. "OF the legged kind of fishes," writes Harrison, " we have not manie, neither have I seene anie more of this sort than the polypus, called in English the Lobstar, crafish, or crevis, and the crab."

Harrison here uses the word *polypus* in its literal signification of many-feet.

Nares, in his *Glossary*, takes notice of the strange word that Sylvester coins in his translation of Du Bartas, and adds that, though an explanation is wisely given, the omission of this peculiar verb would have been still better:—

"Thou makest rivers the most deafly-deep
To *lobstarize* (back to their source to creep)."
(*Divine Weekes and Workes*, p. 184.)

Pliny observes that lobsters—

"so long as they are secure of any fear and danger, go directly straight, letting down their horns at length along their sides; . . . but if they be in any fear, up go their hornes straight, and then they creep byas and go sidelong." (*Nat. Hist.*, book ix. ch. 30.)

Du Bartas (p. 43) writes :—

"And lobsters floated fearless all the while
Among the polyps prone to theft and guile."

Shakspeare has no mention of the lobster.

Crayfish.

Crayfish, according to Harrison, were found plentifully in streams and small rivers. Thomas Hyll, in his *Art of Gardening*, 1593, quotes from Democritus a strange use for these little creatures: ten sea or river crevises are to be put into a covered vessel full of water, which is to be set out in the sun for ten days, the seeds of plants are to be soaked in this mixture for eight days, and afterwards sown; and—

Crayfish.

"after the yong plants of those seeds be sprung up, they will not onely drive cattle and other small beasts from the eating of them, but all other creeping things from the gnawing of them." (Page 23.)

Describing the river Severn and its produce, Drayton writes:—

"The dainty gudgeon, loche, the minnow, and the bleake,
Since they but little are, I little need to speak
Of them, nor doth it fit me much of those to reck,
Which every where are found in every little beck;
Nor of the crayfish here, which creeps along my stones,
From all the rest alone, whose shell is all his bones."
(*Polyolbion*, song xxvi.)

The crevis, or cray-fish, was a favourite dish. It was generally minced fine, and served cold with vinegar, cinnamon, and ginger. Randle Holme gives, as the various names under which the crayfish was known, "a crevice, first a spron frey, then a shrimp, then a sprawn, and when it is large then called a crevice."

"Shrimps," writes Muffett, "are of two sorts; the one crookbacked, the other strait-backed: the first sort is called of Frenchmen *caramots de la sante*, healthful shrimps; because they recover sick and consumed persons; of all other they are most nimble, witty, and skipping, and of best juice. . . . There is a great kind of shrimps, which are called *prawnes* in English, and *crangones* by Rondeletius, highly prized in hectick fevers and consumptions; but the crookbackt shrimp far surpasseth them for that purpose." (*Healths Improvement*, p. 168.)

Shrimp.

Shakspeare uses the word *shrimp* to denote something small and insignificant. The pedant *Holofernes*, in his assumed character of *Judas*, thus announces his attendant, *Moth*, who plays the part of *Hercules* :—

> " Great Hercules is presented by this imp,
>   Whose club kill'd Cerberus, that three-headed canis;
> And when he was a babe, a child, a shrimp,
>   Thus did he strangle serpents in his manus."
>   (*Love's Labour's Lost*, v. 2, 592.)

The *Countess of Auvergne* expresses her astonishment at the diminutive stature of *Talbot*, the scourge of France :—

> " Is this the Talbot, so much fear'd abroad
> That with his name the mothers still their babes ?
> I see report is fabulous and false :
> I thought I should have seen some Hercules,
> A second Hector, for his grim aspect,
> And large proportion of his strong-knit limbs.
> Alas, this is a child, a silly dwarf!
> It cannot be this weak and writhled shrimp
> Should strike such terror to his enemies."
>   (1 *Henry VI.*, ii. 3, 16.)

Crab.
" Crab.—A fish in the sea that hath his head upon his brest, whereof Gesner discourseth amply in the fourth booke of his history of fishes, having gathered together in one body, all that which the ancients and modernes have said."

So writes the learned commentator on Du Bartas (*Learned Summary*, p. 211).

"Crabs of the sea," writes Muffett, "be of divers sorts; some smooth-crusted, and some rough-casted as it were and full of prickles, called *Echinometræ* : the first sort hath the two formost clawes very big and long, the other wanteth them. Wherefore as they go side wise, so these move not themselves but round about like a spiral line." (*Healths Improvement*, p. 150.)

Lyly informs us that " the sea crab swimmeth alwayes against the streame ; " also that " the filthy sow when she is sicke, eateth the sea crab, and is immediately recured" (*Euphues*, p. 61). He does not tell how the sow contrives to catch the crab.

The eccentric motion of the crab is humorously alluded to by Webster:—

"Like the irregular crab,
Which, though't goes backward, thinks that it goes right,
Because it goes its own way."
(*Duchess of Malfi*, i. 2.)

And *Hamlet* mockingly tells *Polonius*, "Yourself, sir, should be old as I am, if like a crab you could go backward" (*Hamlet*, ii. 2, 205). The method of locomotion adopted by the crab is more correctly described by Oviedo, in an account of a soft-bodied species, found in South America:—

"There are also a strange kinde of crabbes, which come forth of certaine holes of the earth, that they themselves make: the head and bodie of these make one round thing, much like to the hood of a falcon, having foure feete comming out of the one side, and as manie out of the other; they have also two mouthes, like unto a paire of small pincers, the one bigger then the other; wherewith they bite, but doe no great hurt, because they are not venemous: their skin and bodie is smooth, and thinne, as is the skinne of a man, saving that it is somewhat harder; their colour is russet, or white, or blew, and walke sidelong; they are verie good to be eaten, in so much that the Christians travailing by the Firme Land, have beene greatly nourished by them, because they are found in manner everie where: in shape and forme they are much like unto the crabbe which we paint for the signe Cancer, and like unto those which are found in Spaine and Andalusia in the river Guadalchiber, where it entreth into the sea, and in the sea coasts there they are sometimes hurtfull, so that they that eate of them dye, but this chanceth onely when they have eaten any venemous thing, or of the venemous apples wherewith the cauiball archers poison their arrowes, whereof I will speak hereafter, and for this cause the Christians take heede how they eate of these crabbes, if they finde them neere unto the said apple trees." (*Purchas*, vol. iii. p. 979.)

In Purchas's collection also there is an account of a voyage undertaken by George, Earl of Cumberland, in the year 1594, to the Southern Seas. The earl's chaplain and attendant, Dr. Layfield, who writes a description

of the expedition, tells us that the wild dogs of Porto
Rico live on crabs. He is careful to guard against any
confusion between the crustacean and the apple :—

"I meane not fruits of trees, but an animal, a living and sensible creature, in feeding whereupon, even men finde a delight, not onely a contentednesse. These woods are full of these crabs, in quantitie bigger than ever I saw any sea-crabs in England, and in such multitudes that they have berries [burrows] like conies in English warrens. They are in shape not different from sea-crabs, for ought I could perceive. For I speake not this out of report, but of my owne sensible experience, I have seene multitudes of them both here, and at Dominica. The whitest whereof (for some are ugly black) some of our men did catch, and eate with good liking, and without any harme, that ever I heard complaint of." (*Purchas*, vol. iv. p. 1172.)

In John Russell's *Boke of Nurture*, written about the
year 1450, the following quaintly minute instructions are
given how to dress and carve the crab when served at
table :—

"Crabbe is a slutt to kerve and a wrawd [froward] wight;
Breke every clawe a sondur, for that is his ryght:
In the brode shelle putt youre stuff, but first have a sight
That it be clene from skyn and senow [sinew] or ye begyn to dight.
And what [when] ye have piked the stuff owt of every shelle
With the poynt of youre knyfe, loke ye temper it welle,
Put vinegre thereto, verdjus, or ayselle,
Cast thereon powdur, the better it wille smelle.
Send the crabbe to the kychyn there for to hete,
Agayn hit facche [fetch it] to thy soverayne sittynge at mete;
Breke the clawes of the crabbe, the smalle and the grete,
In a disch them ye lay if hit like your soverayne to ete."
(*The Babees Book*, ed. F. J. Furnivall, 1868, p. 42.)

This delicacy, so carefully prepared, must not be mistaken for the favourite supper dish, referred to by
Puck :—

"And sometime lurk I in a gossip's bowl,
In very likeness of a roasted crab,
And when she drinks, against her lips I bob,
And on her wither'd dewlap pour the ale."
(*Midsummer Night's Dream*, ii. 1, 47.)

"To turne a crab," writes Dr. Drake, "is to roast a wilding or wild apple in the fire for the purpose of being thrown hissing hot into a bowl of nut-brown ale, into which had been previously put a toast with some spice and sugar." (*Shakspeare and his Times*, 1817, vol. i. p. 105.)

In the well-known drinking song which prefaces the second act of the old comedy, *Gammer Gurton's Needle*, first printed in 1551, we read:—

> "I love no rost, but a nut brown toste,
> And a crab layde in the fyre;
> A lytle bread shall do me stead,
> Much bread I not desyre."

The ingenious device employed by the hermit crab in order to gain a habitation, is described by Du Bartas (p. 42):—

> "There would I cease save that this hum'rous song
> The hermit-fish compels me to prolong.
> A man of might that builds him a defence
> 'Gainst weathers rigour and warr's insolence,
> First dearly buyes (for, what good is good-cheap?)
> Both the rich matter and rare workmanship:
> But, without buying timber, lime, and stone,
> Or hiring men to build his mansion,
> Or borrowing house, or paying rent therefore,
> He lodgeth safe: for, finding on the shoare
> Some handsom shell, whose native lord, of late
> Was dispossessed by the doom of fate:
> Therein he enters, and he takes possession
> Of th' empty harbour by the free concession
> Of natures law; who, *goods that owner want
> Alwaies allots to the first occupant.*
> In this new cace, or in this cradle (rather)
> He spends his youth: then, growing both together
> In age and wit, he gets a wider cell
> Wherein at sea his later daies to dwell."

Olaus Magnus gives a quaint account of the Polypus, an early name for what is now known as the octopus:— *Polypus.*

"On the coasts of Norway there is a polypus, or creature with many feet, which hath a pipe on his back, whereby he puts to sea, and he moves that sometimes to the right side, sometimes to the left. Moreover, with his legs as if it were by hollow places, dispersed here and there, and by his toothed nippers, he fastneth on every living creature that come near to him, that wants blood. Whatever he eats he heaps up in the holes wherein he resides: then he casts out the skins, having eaten the flesh, and hunts after fishes that swim to them: also he casts out the shels, and hard out-sides of crabs that remain. He changeth his colour by the colour of the stone he sticks unto, especially when he is frighted at the sight of his enemy, the conger. He hath four great middle feet, and in all eight; a little body, which the great feet make amends for. He hath also some small feet that are shadowed, and can scarce be perceived. By these he sustains, moves, and defends himself, and takes hold of what is from him; and he lies on his back upon the stones." (Page 232.)

Montaigne (*Essay* liv.) distinguishes between the power possessed by the polypus of changing its hue, and the similar faculty of the chameleon :—

"The cameleon takes her colour from the place upon which it is laid; but the polypus gives himself what colour he pleases, according to occasion, either to conceal himself from what he fears, or from that he has a design to seize: in the cameleon 'tis a passive, but in the polypus 'tis an active change."

Nautilus. Thomas Stevens, the first Englishman who was known to have reached India by way of the Cape of Good Hope, describes in a letter written from Goa, in the year 1579, an animal that seems to correspond to the Nautilus. Stevens writes :—

"Along all that coast we oftentimes saw a thing swimming upon the water like a cock's comb (which they call a Ship of Guinea), but the colour much fairer, which comb standeth upon a thing almost like the swimmer [bladder] of a fish in colour and bigness, and beareth under the water, strings, which saveth it from turning over. This thing is so poisonous that a man cannot touch it without great peril." (ARBER's *English Garner*, vol. i. p. 131.)

The Cuttle-fish is noticed by Du Bartas :—

Cuttle-fish. "Even so, almost, the many spotted cuttle Well-neer insnared yet escapeth suttle;

For, when she sees her selfe within the net,
And no way left, but one from thence to get,
She suddenly a certaine ink doth spew,
Which dyes the waters of a sable hew;
That, dazling so the fishers greedy sight,
She through the clouds of the black waters night
Might scape with honour the black streams of Styx,
Whereof already, almost lost, she licks."

(Page 41.)

It is hardly necessary to point out the glaring absurdities of which this author is guilty throughout his poem on the Creation. He delights to describe the various stratagems by which the different creatures escape from snares spread for them by another creature not yet called into existence.

Bacon observes :—

"It is somewhat strange that the blood of all beasts and birds and fishes should be of a red colour, and only the blood of the cuttle should be as black as ink. The cuttle," he adds, "is accounted a delicate meat, and is much in request."

The Calamary, or Squid, often called the Sea-arrow, or Flying-squid, was, and still is, extensively used as a bait by the fishermen of Newfoundland. The body of the common squid is not unlike an old-fashioned inkhorn, whence the name *calamar*. Two long, slender tentacles suggest the idea of pens, and ink is supplied by the creature.

Of the cuttle-fish, Muffett says :—

"They are called also *sleeves* for their shape, and *scribes* for their incky humour wherewith they are replenished, and are commended by Galen for great nourishers; their skins be as smooth as any womans, but their flesh is brawny as any ploughmans; therefore I fear me Galen rather commended them upon hear-say then upon any just cause or true experience."

Sir Thomas Browne writes :—

"The loligo sleve, or calamar, found often upon the shore, from head to tail sometimes about an ell long, remarkable for its parrot-like bill, the gladiolus or celanus along the back, and the notable crystalline of the eye, which equalleth if not exceedeth, the lustre of oriental pearl." (Vol. iv. p. 332.)

Scallop. Drayton enumerates some of the delicacies of the sea:—

> "These nymphs tricked up in tyers, the sea-god to delight
> Of coral of each kind, the black, the red, the white;
> With many sundry shells, the Scallop large and fair;
> The cockle small and round, the periwinkle spare;
> The oyster, wherein of the pearl is found to breed;
> The mussel, which retains that dainty orient seed."
> (*Polyolbion*, song xx.)

Of the mollusks here mentioned, the scallop was chiefly valued in early times on account of its form. Pilgrims to Palestine considered themselves sufficiently equipped for their long journey if they possessed a staff, a wallet, or bag, and scallop or escallop shell. This last article served them as cup, dish, and spoon. The scallop was the special emblem of St. James the Great, of Compostella, the tutelary saint of Spain, and the patron of pilgrims, and was adopted as a badge by these religious travellers. *Ophelia* sings:—

> "How should I your true love know
> From another one?
> By his cockle hat and staff,
> And his sandal shoon."
> (*Hamlet*, iv. 5, 23.)

This beautiful shell was borne as a charge by many families in memory of the real or imaginary exploits of their ancestors in—

> "Streaming the ensign of the Christian Cross
> Against black pagans, Turks, and Saracens."

Oyster. "Canst tell how an Oyster makes his shell?" asks the *Fool* of his royal master, and *Lear* cannot answer the question.

Colchester Oysters. 443

The town of Colchester owed much of its importance and wealth to its valuable oyster fisheries. Mr. Thomas Cromwell, in his *History and Description of Colchester*, states that—

"Richard I. granted to the burgesses the fishery of the river Colne, and the grant was very amply assured and confirmed to them by subsequent charters, especially by that of Edward IV." (Page 290.)

Attempts were repeatedly made by landed proprietors in the neighbourhood to deprive the burghers of Colchester of their ancient rights. The first landowner who endeavoured to gain for himself the privilege bestowed on the town was Lionel De Bradenham, Lord of the Manor of Langinhoe, who, in the reign of Edward III., enclosed parts of the river, and appropriated them to his own use. At a later period John, Earl of Oxford, procured a grant from Henry VI. of this royalty; but the Corporation, rather than surrender their claim, entered into a contest with the earl, and, after some opposition, succeeded in obtaining from the king a confirmation of their rights. Colchester oysters have been celebrated from the earliest period, and have been deemed a valuable present. We find them on several occasions sent both to Leicester and Walsingham in the reign of Elizabeth.

The praises of the Colchester oysters are sounded by Thomas Fuller :—

"The best in England, fat, salt, green-finn'd, are bred near Colchester, where they have an excellent art to feed them in pits made for the purpose. King James was wont to say, ' he was a very valiant man who first adventured on eating of oysters ;' most probably meer hunger put men first on that trial." (*Worthies of England*, vol. i. p. 336.)

We learn, also, from Norden that—

"Some part of the sea shore of Essex yealdeth the beste oysters in England, which are called Walflete oysters : so called of a place in the sea ; but in what place of the sea it is, hath ben some disputation. . . .

Ther is greate difference between these oysters and others which lie upon other shores, for this oyster, that in London and ells wher carieth the name of Walflete, is a little full oyster with a verie greene fynn. And like unto these in quantitie and qualitie are none in this land, thowgh farr bigger, and for some mens diettes better." (*Description of Essex*, 1594, p. 11.)

Tom Coryat, the celebrated pedestrian traveller, relates with great gusto, that, during his stay in Venice, he tasted some oysters that even exceeded in flavour those of Colchester:—

"Here did I eate the best oysters that ever I did in all my life. They were indeede but little, something lesse then our Wainflete oysters about London, but as green as a leeke, and *gratissimi saporis & succi*." (*Crudities*, vol. ii. p. 18.)

Coryat, otherwise known as "the Odcombian leg-stretcher," or "the Peregrine of Odcome," published his *Crudities* in 1611. This book was the result of observations made in five months' travel, mostly on foot, from his native place of Odcome, in Somersetshire, through a great part of Europe. He set out in May, 1608, and returned the same year. He was much ridiculed by some of his contemporaries, and commended by others. His chief fault is his intense vanity, and his constant reference to himself; but his descriptions of the various towns he visited are minute, and tell of careful observation.

Tarlton, the Court jester of Elizabeth's time, passed an unfavourable opinion upon oysters:—

"Certaine noblemen and ladies of the Court, being eating of oysters, one of them, seeing Tarlton, called him, and asked him if he loved oysters. No, quoth Tarlton, for they be ungodly meate, uncharitable meate, and unprofitable meate. Why, quoth the courtiers? They are ungodly, sayes Tarlton, because they are eaten without grace; uncharitable, because they leave nought but the shells; and unprofitable, because they must swim in wine." (*Shakspeare's Jest Book*, ed. W. C. Hazlitt, vol. ii. p. 192.)

Pearls, the product of the oyster, have ever been

highly prized and held in great estimation. Margarite, from the Latin word, *margarita*, was a name sometimes given to the pearl. Drummond of Hawthornden plays on this word in an epitaph on a lady named Margaret :—

> "In shells and gold, pearles are not kept alone,
> A Margaret here lies beneath a stone;
> A Margaret that did excell in worth
> All those rich gems the Indies both send forth."

Antonio de Herrera, of Spain, in his description of the West Indies, gives some account of the pearl fisheries :—

> "There are in the Indian Ocean, an infinite number of fishes, the kindes and properties whereof the Creator onely can declare. Now that we intreate of the great riches that comes from the Indies, it were no reason to forget the pearle, which the ancients called marguerites, and at the first were in so great estimation, as none but royall persons were suffered to weare them : but at this day there is such abundance as the Negres themselves doe weare chaines thereof; they grow in shels of oystres, in eating whereof I have found pearles in the middest of them. These oysters within are of the colour of heaven, very lively. In some places they make spoones, the which they call mother of pearle. The pearles doe differ much in forme, in bignesse, figure, colour and polishing; so likewise in their price they differ much. Some they call *Ave Mariaes*, being like the small grains of beades : others are called *Pater Nosters*, being bigger. Seldome shall you finde two of one greatnesse, forme, and colour. For this reason the Romans (as Plinie writeth) called them *unions*. When they doe finde two that are alike in all points, they raise the price much, especially for eare-rings." (*Purchas*, vol. iii. p. 952.)

Before *Hamlet* attempts to win the wager that his uncle has laid upon his skill in fencing, *Claudius* orders some stoups of wine to be set on the table, and declares that at the first successful hit—

> "The king shall drink to Hamlet's better breath ;
> And in the cup an union shall he throw,
> Richer than that which four successive kings
> In Denmark's crown have worn.
> *   *   *   *   *

Stay ; give me drink. Hamlet, this pearl is thine ;
Here's to thy health."
(*Hamlet*, v. 2, 282.)

Shakspeare has many references to this beautiful and valuable ornament. Antony sends to his Egyptian queen a precious gift : *Alexas*, who bears the offering, reports :—

"Last thing he did, dear queen,
He kiss'd,—the last of many doubled kisses,—
This orient pearl. His speech sticks in my heart.
Cleo. Mine ear must pluck it thence.
Alex.   ' Good friend,' quoth he,
' Say, The firm Roman to great Egypt sends
This treasure of an oyster ; at whose foot,
To mend the petty present, I will piece
Her opulent throne with kingdoms ; all the East,
Say thou, shall call her mistress.' "
(*Antony and Cleopatra*, i. 5, 39.)

Luke, in Massinger's *City Madam*, for years a poor dependant in his brother's household, suddenly becomes possessed of boundless wealth : he describes in glowing language his newly acquired treasures. Gold and silver lay in glittering heaps about the room, and dazzled his sight by their splendour ; diamonds shot forth their beams from the caskets that contained them,—

" And made the place
Heaven's abstract, or epitome !—rubies, sapphires,
And ropes of orient pearl, these seen, I could not
But look on with contempt."
(*City Madam*, iii. 3.)

The history of the oyster, as told by our forefathers, is enlivened by a touch of the marvellous. One William Finch, a merchant, in his description of the coast of Sierra Leone, in the year 1607, gravely informs us that the oyster is the fruit of a tree : —

"There grow likewise within the bayes great store of oysters on trees, resembling willowes in forme, but the leafe broad and of thicknesse like leather, wearing small knops like those of the cypresse. From this tree hang downe many branches, each about the bignesse of a good walking sticke into the water, smooth, lithe, pithy within, overflowne with the tide, and hanging as thicke of oysters as they can sticke together, being the only fruit the tree beareth, begotten thereof, as it seemeth, by the salt water." (*Purchas,* vol. i. p. 416.)

We often read of these oyster-bearing trees in the narrations of the Elizabethan travellers. Pigafetta mentions the close relation of the shell to the tree, although he does not, like the last writer, call it the fruit:—

"In that part of this island, which is toward the maine land [Loanda, off Congo], in certaine low places there grow certaine trees which (when the water of the ocean ebbeth) discover themselves, and at the feet thereof you shall find certaine shel-fishes cleaving as fast to the trees as may bee, having within them a great fish as bigge as a mans hand, and very good meate. The people of the countrey know them very well, and call them *ambiziamatare,* that is to say, the fish of the rocke. The shells of these fishes they use to burne, and they make very good lime to build withall. And being like the corke or barke of the tree, which is called *manghi,* they dresse their oxehides withall, to make their shooe soles the stronger." (*Purchas,* vol. ii. p. 990.)

The Mussel, spelt muscle and muskle, was sometimes called the Conche, or Echeola. Mussels were found in most of the large rivers and ponds in England. The pearl-producing property of these shells was well known. Antonie Parkhurst, in a letter to Richard Hakluyt, mentions, among other commodities of Newfoundland—

Mussel.

"oisters and muskles, in which I have found pearles, above 40 in one muskle, and generally all have some, great or small. I heard of a Portugall that found one worth 300 duckets." (*Hakluyt,* vol. iii. p. 171.)

According to classical writers, pearls were formed by drops of rain falling into the shells of oysters or mussels; this notion long remained uncontradicted. Lawrens Andrews, in his *Noble Lyfe,* writes:—

"Echeola is a muskle in whose fysshe is a precious stone, and be night they flete to the water syde and there they receyve the hevenly dewe, where-throughe there groweth in them a costly margaret or orient perle, and they flete a great many togeder and he that knoweth the water best gothe before and ledeth the other, and whan he is taken, all the other scater a brode, and geteth them away." (*Babees Book*, p. 16.)

Muffett has little to say in praise of the English mussel as an article of diet, but recommends the "lily-white mussel" found on the coast of Holland.

Snail. "*Fool.* I can tell why a Snail has a house.
Lear. Why?
Fool. Why, to put his head in; not to give it away to his daughters, and leave his horns without a case."
(*Lear*, i. 5, 29.)

Shakspeare has many references to the timid garden snail:—

"Love's feeling is more soft and sensible
Than are the tender horns of cockled snails."
(*Love's Labour's Lost*, iv. 3, 337.)

"Or, as the snail, whose tender horns being hit,
Shrinks backward in his shelly cave with pain,
And there, all smother'd up, in shade doth sit,
Long after fearing to creep forth again."
(*Venus and Adonis*, l. 1033.)

Menenius compares the enemy of Rome to this cautious but destructive intruder:—

"'Tis Aufidius,
Who, hearing of our Marcius' banishment,
Thrusts forth his horns again into the world;
Which were inshell'd when Marcius stood for Rome,
And durst not once peep out."
(*Coriolanus*, iv. 6, 43.)

Ben Jonson writes:—

"We have no shift of faces, no cleft tongues,
No soft and glutinous bodies, that can stick
Like snails on painted walls; or, on our breasts,
Creep up, to fall from that proud height to which
We did by slavery, not by service climb."
(*Sejanus*, i. 1.)

Snails eaten Abroad.

According to Bacon—

"the creatures that cast their skin are the snake, the viper, the grasshopper, the lizard, the silk-worm, &c. Those that cast their shell are the lobster, the crab, the craw-fish, the hodmandod, or dodman, the tortoise, &c." (*Nat. Hist.*, century vii.)

This word *hodmandod* has been explained by some writers to mean the shelled snail.

Sir John Mandeville tells of some enormous foreign species:—

"There ben also in that contree [Siam] a kynde of snayles, that ben so grete that many persones may loggen him in here scolles as men wolde done in a lityle hous. And other snayles there ben, that ben fully grete, but not so huge as the other." (*Travels*, p. 193.)

Garden snails were used in medicine as a remedy for an inward bruise. They also formed the foundation of a highly recommended "soothing syrup." They do not seem to have found favour in England as a delicacy for the table, but, according to Muffett, they were eaten in other countries.

"Snailes," he writes, "are little esteemed of us in England, but in Barbarie, Spaine, and Italy they are eaten as a most dainty, wholesome, nourishing and restoring meat." (*Healths Improvement*, p. 190.)

"*Pistol.* Let us to France; like horse-leeches,   Leech.
    my boys:
To suck, to suck, the very blood to suck."
                   (*Henry V.*, ii. 3, 58.)

The use of the Leech in surgery dates back to a very early period. The life of Dionysius, the tyrant of Syracuse, is reported to have been prolonged by means of this remedy.

The soft-bodied marine animal, the sea-anemone, so well known to visitors to the sea-side, may be the creature referred to by Du Bartas (p. 42) in the following lines:—

"And so the sponge-spye warily awakes
The sponges dull sense, when repast it takes."

His commentator has a long and involved note on this passage, but does not succeed in making it quite clear what sort of creature is meant. He writes:—

"This is a little fish (as Plutarch saith in his treatise of the industry of living creatures) like unto a spider of the sea. He guardeth and governeth the spunge (called properly the hollow animal plant) which is not wholly without soule neither without blood and sence: but (as divers other sea-animals) cleaveth to the rocks, and hath a proper motion to restraine her selfe outwardly; but to effect this, shee hath neede of the advertisement and friendship of another, because that (being rare, lither, and soft, by reason of her small vents, and empty for want of bloud, or rather want of sence, which is very dull) shee feeleth not when any good substance fit to be eaten, entreth into these holes, and void spaces, which the spunge there makes her feele, and incontinently she closeth her selfe, and devoureth it." (*Learned Summary*, p. 224.)

"Coral of each kind, the black, the red, the white" (Drayton, *Polyolbion*, song xx.), was well

Coral.

known, though its substance was a sore puzzle to naturalists. The animal nature of coral was only discovered about a hundred and fifty years ago. Bacon says it is a submarine plant:—

"It hath no leaves, it brancheth only when it is under water; it is soft and green of colour; but being brought into the air it becomes hard and shining red as we see. It is said also to have a white berry, but we find it not brought over with the coral." (*Nat. Hist.*, cent. viii.)

Elsewhere he notes, "Coral is in use as an help to the teeth of children." This use of coral is referred to in a poem by G. Fletcher, called "A Canto upon the Death of Eliza." An ocean nymph appeals to the rocks around her to join in lamentations for Britain's queen:—

"Tell me, ye blushing currols that bunch out,
   To cloath with beuteous red your ragged fire,
So let the sea-greene mosse curle round about,
   With soft embrace (as creeping vines doe wyre
   Their loved elmes) your sides in rosie tyre,

So let the ruddie vermeyle of your cheeke
Make stain'd carnations fresher liveries seeke,
So let your braunched arms grow crooked, smooth, and sleeke.

" So from your growth late be you rent away,
   And hung with silver bels and whistles shrill;
Unto those children be you given to play,
   Where blest Eliza raign'd; so never ill
Betide your canes, nor them with breaking spill,
Tell me, if some uncivill hand should teare
Your branches hence, and place them otherwhere;
Could you still grow, and such fresh crimson ensignes beare ? "
               (NICHOLS, *Progresses of James I.*, vol. i. p. 17.)

Coral was brought back by travellers from warm countries. One of Purchas's pilgrims, wandering through Brazil, reports that on the shores of that country they—

"find great store of white stone corrall under water; it groweth like small trees all in leaves, and canes, as the red corrall of India, and if this also were so, there would be great riches in this countrie, for the great abundance there is of it; it is very white, it is gotten with difficulty, they make lime of it also." (*Purchas,* vol. iv. p. 1316.)

And Sir Richard Hawkins, whose travels in the South Seas (1593) are recorded in the same collection, informs us that "the corrall in the sea is soft, but comming into the ayre, becommeth a stone" (vol. iv. p. 1377). Shakspeare poetically introduces this beautiful material into *Ariel's* song :—

   " Full fathom five thy father lies;
      Of his bones are coral made;
   Those are pearls that were his eyes:
      Nothing of him that doth fade
   But doth suffer a sea-change
   Into something rich and strange.
   Sea-nymphs hourly ring his knell.
              Ding-dong.
   Hark! Now I hear them,—ding-dong bell."
              (*Tempest*, i. 2, 396.)

CHAPTER XIX.

IT may perhaps be thought unnecessary to take any notice of creatures that had only an imaginary existence; but while the unicorn supports the arms of England, the dragon of St. George is stamped upon the coin of the realm, and a griffin rampant guards the entry to the City of London, these mythical animals may surely claim a brief mention.

Unicorn. "*Alon.* Give us kind keepers, heavens. What were these?
Seb. A living drollery. Now I will believe That there are Unicorns."
(*Tempest,* iii. 3, 20.)

Of all fabulous animals the unicorn is the most conspicuous, from the position it holds in the English arms. The unicorn was first adopted as a supporter by James IV. of Scotland, and made its appearance as a supporter of the royal shield of England on the accession of James VI. to the English throne, as a token of the alliance between the two countries.

The unicorn of the Greeks and Romans was probably founded upon some exaggerated description of the one-horned rhinoceros; but the unicorn of the Bible, according to Mr. Houghton, had reference to a species of bull. The Hebrew word *reem,* which denotes a two-horned animal, was the wild bull of the Assyrian monuments, an animal common at one time both in Palestine and Syria, and the

Assyrian name for which was *rimu* (*Natural History of the Ancients*, 1879, p. 170).

The heraldic unicorn has gained his horn, according to some authors, from the spike anciently fixed to the head-piece of a war-horse; but as this does not account for the cloven hoofs and slender tufted tail, Mr. Lower (*Curiosities of Heraldry*, p. 101) reverses the inference, and derives the appendage of the charger from the popular notion of the unicorn. Guillim, whose work on heraldry, published about 1600, is at the same time a cyclopædia of natural or unnatural history, gives the following account of this animal:—

"The unicorn hath his name of his one horn on his forehead. There is another beast of a huge strength and greatnesse, which hath but one horn, but that is growing on his snout, whence he is called rinoceros, and both are named *monoceros*, or one-horned. It hath been much questioned among naturalists, which it is that is properly called the unicorn: and some have made doubt whether there be any such beast as this or no. But the great esteem of his horn in many places to be seen may take away that needless scruple. . . . His vertue is no less famous than his strength, in that his horn is supposed to be the most powerful antidote against poison: insomuch as the general conceit is, that the wild beasts of the wilderness use not to drink of the pools, for fear of venomous serpents there breeding, before the unicorn hath stirred it with his horn. . . . It seemeth by a question moved by Farnesius, that the unicorn is never taken alive; and the reason being demanded, it is answered, that the greatness of his mind is such, that he chuseth rather to die than to be taken alive." (*Display of Heraldry*, p. 163, ed. 1724.)

All sorts of myths grew up around this creature's history; it was supposed to live in solitude in the woods, and to be of indomitable courage. No man could succeed in approaching it, but if a pure maiden came near its haunts it would lose its fierceness, lie down at her feet, and suffer itself to be captured. It is to be hoped, however, that few maidens consented so basely to betray the confidence reposed in them. Some say that a young man, dressed in female attire, served equally well for the purpose of alluring the unicorn, but this statement gives the animal little credit for shrewdness. Topsell writes:—

"These beasts are very swift, aud their legges have not articles. They keep for the most part in the desarts, and live solitary in the tops of the mountaines. There was nothing more horible then the voice or braying of it, for the voice is straind above measure. It fighteth both with the mouth and with the heeles, with the mouth biting like a lyon, and with the heeles kicking like a horse." (Page 719.)

Sir Thomas Browne, writing half a century later, doubts the existence of such an animal, in spite of this precise account; but he mentions five kinds of one-horned animals—the Indian ass, the Indian ox, the rhinoceros, the oryx, and the monoceros or unicornis, which last may have been the narwhal.

Thomas Fuller dwells at some length on the vexed question of the unicorn's existence, but adds little of value to the controversy. That such a creature lived at one time he considers clearly proved by the mention of it in Scripture, and as the belief then was that no species could be wholly lost, it was clear to Fuller that the unicorn was to be met with somewhere. With regard to the horn, he writes:—

"Some are plain, as that in St. Mark's in Venice; others wreathed about, as that at Dyonis near Paris, with anfractuous spires, and cocleary turnings about it, which probably is the effect of age, those wreaths being but the wrinkles of most vivacious unicorns. The same may be said of the colour, white, when nowly taken from his head; yellow, like that lately in the Tower, of some hundred years seniority; but whether or no it will ever turn black, as that of Plinie's description, let others decide." (*Worthies*, vol. ii. p. 54.)

The Rev. Edward Topsell visits with true ecclesiastical scorn those sceptical mortals who refuse to accept the traditional accounts of the unicorn, and even dare to doubt its existence. After enumerating the different kinds of animals which are described as having a single horn, he adds:—

"Now our discourse of the unicorne is of none of these beasts, for there is not any vertue attributed to their hornes, and therefore the vulgar sort of infidell people which scarcely beleeve any hearbe but such as they see in their owne gardens, or any beast but such as is in their own flocks, or any knowledge but such as is bred in their owne braines, or any birds which are not hatched in their owne nests, have never made question of these, but of the true unicorne, whereof there were more proofes in the world, because of the noblenesse of his horn, they have ever bin in doubt: by which distraction, it appeareth unto me that there is some secret enemy in the inward degenerate nature of man, which continually blindeth the eies of God his people from beholding and beleeving the greatnesse of God his workes. But to the purpose that there is such a beast, the Scripture it selfe witnesseth, for David thus speaketh in the 92. Psalme: *Et erigetur cornu meum tanquam monocerotis.* That is, My horne shall bee lifted up like the horne of a unicorn; whereupon all divines that ever wrote have not onely collected that there is a unicorne, that as the horne of the unicorne is wholesome to all beasts and creatures so should the kingdome of David be in the generation of Christ; and do we think that David would compare the vertue of his kingdom, and the powerful redemption of the world unto a thing that is not, or is uncertain or fantastical, God forbid that ever any man should so despight the Holy Ghost." (Page 712.)

The Rev. Mr. Topsell is here so angry that he is rather incoherent. The following minute description of the unicorn by an eye-witness may serve to justify this author's indignation:—

"On the other part of the temple [of Mecha] are parkes or places inclosed, where are seene two unicornes, named of the Greekes *monocerotæ,* and are there shewed to the people for a miracle, and not without good reason, for the seldomeness and strange nature. The one of them, which is much hygher then the other, yet not much unlike to a coolte of thyrtye moneths of age, in the forehead groweth only one horne, in maner ryght foorth of the length of three cubites; the other is much younger, of the age of one yeere, and lyke a young colte; the horne of this, is of the length of foure handfuls. This beast is of the coloure of a horse of weesell coloure, and hath the head lyke an hart, but no long necke, a thynne mane hangyng onlye on the one syde: theyr legges are thyn and slender, lyke a fawne or hynde: the hoofes of the fore feete are divided in two, much like the foot of a goat, the outwarde part of the hynder feete is very full of heare. This beast doubtlesse seemeth wylde and fierce, yet tempereth that fiercenesse with a certain comelinesse. These unicornes one gave to the Soltan of Mecha, as a most precious and rare gyfte. They were sent hym out of Ethiope by a kyng of that countrey, who desired by that present to gratifie the Soltan of Macha." (*Hakluyt*, vol. iv. p. 5 62.)

This account occurs in a narrative of the travels of Lewes Vertomannus, "Gentelman of the Citie of Rome, in the yeere of our Lorde 1503. Translated out of Latine into Englyshe, by Richarde Eden, 1576."

"The horne of Windsor," referred to by previous writers, is mentioned also by Shakspearean dramatists as one of the stock curiosities of the time. Paul Hentzner, in his account of a visit to England, in 1598, writes of Windsor Castle.

"We were shewn here among other things, the horn of a unicorn, of above eight spans and an half in length, valued at above 10,000*l*." (*Dodsley's Fugitive Pieces*, vol. ii. p. 244.)

Topsell gives a minute description of this most precious article, which was, in all probability, the horn or tusk of a narwhal.

"I doe also kuow," he writes, "that [horn] the King of England possesseth to be wreathed in spires, even as that is accounted in the Church of S. Dennis, then which they suppose none greater in the world, and I never saw any thing in any creature more worthy praise then this horn.... It is of so great a length that the tallest man can scarcely touch the top thereof, for it doth fully equal seven great feet. It weigheth thirteen pounds, with their assize, being only weighed by the gesse of the hands it seemeth much heavier. The figure doth plainely signifie a wax candle, being folded and wreathed with it selfe, being farre more thicker from one part, and making it selfe by little and little lesse towards the point, the thickest part thereof cannot be shut within one hand, it is the compasse of five fingers, by the circumference, if it bee measured with a thred, it is three fingers and a span. ... That part which is next unto the heade hath not sharpenesse, the other are of a polished smoothnes. The splents of the spire are smooth and not deep, being for the most part like unto the wreathing turnings of snailes, or the revolutions or windings of wood-bine about any wood. But they proceed from the right hande toward the left, from the beginning of the horne, even unto the very ende. The colour is not altogether white, being a long time somewhat obscured. But by the weight it is an easie thinge of conjecture, that this beast which can beare so great burden in his head, in the quantity of his body can be little less then a great oxe." (Page 717.)

Specimens of this curiosity, which are in reality tusks of the narwhal, can be seen in many museums, and two are at the present time exhibited at Gardner's, in Oxford Street.

Spenser not only takes it for granted that the unicorn exists, but describes the mode of warfare adopted by its time-honoured antagonist, the lion :—

"Like as the lyon, whose imperial powre
A proud rebellious unicorn defyes,
T' avoide the rash assault and wrathfull stowre
Of his fiers foe, him to a tree applyes,
And when him ronning in full course he spyes,
He slips aside ; the whiles that furious beast
His precious horne, sought of his enimyes,
Strikes in the stroke, ne thence can be released,
But to the victor yields a bounteous feast."
(*Faerie Queene*, ii. v. 10.)

Shakspeare refers to this method of defeating the unicorn, which was adopted by his human antagonists, as well as by the lion: in his tirade against *Apemantus*, *Timon of Athens* exclaims :—

"Wert thou the unicorn, pride and wrath would confound thee, and make thine own self the conquest of thy fury." (*Timon of Athens*, iv. 3, 337.)

And again, *Decius* declares that *Cæsar*—

"Loves to hear
That unicorns may be betray'd with trees,
And bears with glasses, elephants with holes,
Lions with toils and men with flatterers."
(*Julius Cæsar*, ii. 1, 303.)

Webster mentions the horn, and in reference to its supposed virtues, he tells how men—

> "Make of the powder a preservative circle,
> And in it put a spider."
>
> (*Vittoria Corombona*, act ii.)

Dragon. Out of compliment to his Welsh ancestry, Henry of Richmond adopted the device of the Red Dragon, when he advanced against Richard III. on Bosworth Field. After his coronation he placed the victorious animal as one of the supporters of the English arms. The dragon maintained this position through the reigns of Henry VIII. and Elizabeth, but was superseded on the accession of James I. by the Scotch unicorn. One of the pursuivants in the College of Arms at the present day is called "Rouge Dragon," in commemoration of the Lancastrian victory.

Figures of the heraldic dragon vary considerably, according to the fancy of the draughtsman. The chief characteristics are the head of a wolf, the body of a serpent, four eagle's feet, bat-like wings, and barbed tongue and tail. The dragon's attributes were animation and ferocity.

Lyly was evidently untroubled by any doubt of the existence of this imaginary animal. In support of his assertion that wise counsel is to be regarded, though the speaker may not be virtuous, he points to the "Precious gemme dacromtes [draconites] that is ever taken out of the heade of the poysoned dragon" (*Euphues*, p. 124).

Shakspeare often mentions the dragon, but generally in an allegorical sense. Among the ingredients of the witches' cauldron, however, are included "scale of dragon, tooth of wolf."

Basilisk. "I'll slay more gazers than the basilisk," exclaims Richard (3 *Henry VI.*, ii. 2, 187). And Drayton writes :—

"The basilisk so poisons with the eye,
To call for aid, and then to lie in wait."
(*England's Heroical Epistles.*)

The fatal effect of the glance of the basilisk could only be averted by holding in front of the creature a polished mirror. The terror of its own image caused its instant death.

The basilisk combined the head and body of a cock with the tail of a serpent. A minute description of this creature and other fabulous animals may be found in any good work on heraldry.

The Cockatrice added to the charms of the basilisk a dragon's tail, armed with a sting. It shared with the basilisk the power of destroying by its glance. *Sir Toby Belch* says of the intending duellists, "This will so fright them both that they will kill one another by the look, like cockatrices" (*Twelfth Night*, iii. 4, 214).   Cockatrice.

Juliet, distracted by her nurse, plays thus nicely with her words :—

> "What devil are thou, that dost torment me thus?
> This torture should be roar'd in dismal hell.
> Hath Romeo slain himself? Say thou but 'I,'
> And that bare vowel 'I' shall poison more
> Than the death-darting eye of cockatrice:
> I am not I, if there be such an I."
> (*Romeo and Juliet*, iii. 2, 43.)

In art the cockatrice was an emblem of sin generally, and the special attribute of St. Vitus.

The Wyvern was a more bird-like form of the dragon, having only two legs, an eagle's head, and a scorpion's tail.   Wyvern.

The Fire-drake, or Fire-dragon, was a shining serpent that was supposed to guard hidden treasures. The name was also given to the luminous appearance known as "will o' the wisp."   Fire-drake.

Ben Jonson writes:—

> "The shrieks of luckless owls
> We hear, and croaking night-crows in the air!
> Green bellied snakes, and fire-drakes in the sky."
> (*The Sad Shepherd*, ii. 2.)

In *Henry VIII.* (v. 4, 41) this name is given to a man with an overflorid complexion:—

> "There is a fellow somewhat near the door, he should be a brazier by his face, for, o' my conscience, twenty of the dog-days now reign in 's nose; all that stand about him are under the line, they need no other penance: That fire-drake did I hit three times on the head."

The Griffin, or Gryphon, was a compound animal whose delineation reflects some credit on its inventor. It was supposed to combine the qualities of the king of beasts and the king of birds. Its head, fore legs, and wings were those of an eagle, while the rest of the body resembled that of a lion. It denoted watchfulness and courage, and was often borne as a charge, or more frequently as a supporter. The griffin's wings, unlike those of the dragon, were plumed.

Griffin.

In his prologue to *Sappho and Phæon*, Lyly writes: "The gryffin never spreadeth her wings in the sunne, when she hath any sicke feathers."

Du Bartas has transmitted some legendary lore concerning the griffin's love of gold. To a list of ravenous birds (p. 45) he adds:—

> "The Indian griffin with the glistring eyes,
> Beak eagle-like, back sable, sanguin brest,
> White (swan-like) wings, fierce talons alwaies prest [ready]
> For bloody battails; for, with these he tears
> Boars, lions, horses, tigres, bulls and bears:
> With these our grandams fruitful panch he puls,
> Whence many an ingot of pure gold he culls,
> To floor his proud nest, builded strong and steep
> On a high rock, better his thefts to keep:

The Griffin. 461

> With these he guards against an army bold
> The hollow mines where first he findeth gold;
> As wroth, that men upon his right should rove,
> Or thievish hands usurp his tresor-trove."

This is not the griffin of heraldry, but the gigantic bird known in Eastern fable as the roc, or rukh, to whom Sinbad the Sailor was indebted for his discovery of the "valley of diamonds." Burton writes:—

> "As I go by Madagascar I would see that great bird rucke that can carry a man and horse or an elephant, with that Arabian phœnix described by Adrichomius; see the pellicanes of Egypt, those Scythian gryphes in Asia." (*Anatomy of Melancholy*, vol. i. p. 489.)

Drayton mentions the roc as coming with its feathered comrades to seek the shelter of the ark:—

> "All feather'd things yet ever known to men,
> From the huge ruck, unto the little wren."
> (*Noah's Flood.*)

In England a large kind of eagle was sometimes called the gripe, or griffin; in this sense Shakspeare evidently uses the word in 1 *Henry IV.* (iii. 1, 152). *Hotspur*, when reproved by *Mortimer* for thwarting *Owen Glendower*, exclaims impetuously—

> "I cannot chose: sometimes he angers me
> With telling me of the moldwarp and the ant,
> Of the dreamer Merlin and his prophecies,
> And of a dragon and a finless fish,
> A clip-winged griffin and a moulten raven,
> A couching lion and a ramping cat,
> And such a deal of skimble skamble stuff
> As put me from my faith."

In the passage in *Lucrece* (line 541) the powerful fabulous bird described by Du Bartas is probably meant:—

> "While she, the picture of pure piety,
> Like a white hind under the gripe's sharp claws,
> Pleads, in a wilderness where are no laws,

To the rough beast that knows no gentle right,
Nor aught obeys but his foul appetite."

Chester writes (p. 119) :—

" The griffon is a bird rich feathered,
His head is like a lion, and his flight
Is like the eagles, much for to be feared,
For why, he kills men in the ugly night :
Some say he keeps the smaragd and the jasper,
And in pursuite of man is monstrous eager."

Sphinx. The Sphinx is too well known to need description. It is only once referred to by Shakspeare :—

" For valour, is not love a Hercules,
Still climbing trees in the Hesperides?
Subtle as sphinx ; as sweet and musical
As bright Apollo's lute, strung with his hair."
(*Love's Labour's Lost*, iv. 3, 340.)

"Lord Bacon's original resolution of this fable," writes Dr. E. C. Brewer, "is a fair specimen of what some persons call ' spiritualising the incidents and parables of Scripture.' He says that the whole represents ' science,' which is regarded by the ignorant as 'a monster.' As the figure of the sphinx is heterogeneous, so the subjects of science ' are very various.' The female face ' denotes volubility of speech ;' her wings show that ' knowledge like light is rapidly diffused ;' her hooked talons remind us of ' the arguments of science which enter the mind and lay hold of it.' She is placed on a crag overlooking the city, for ' all science is placed on an eminence which is hard to climb.' If the riddles of the sphinx brought disaster, so the riddles of science ' perplex and harass the mind.'" (*Dictionary of Phrase and Fable*, p. 844.)

Unfortunately Dr. Brewer does not condescend to give any reference for his quotation.

Harpy. The Harpies were imaginary beings of Grecian mythology. According to some writers they were three in number, Ocypete, Aello, and Celeno. They were the personifications of winds and storms. They were depicted with the head and body of a woman and the wings and feet of a vulture or eagle, and symbolized deceit and cruelty. Spenser introduces one of them into the *Faerie Queene* (II. vii. 23):—

> "While sad Celeno, sitting on a cliffe,
> A song of bale and bitter sorrow sings."

Again he writes (II. xii. 36):—

> "The whistler shrill, that whoso heares shall dy;
> The hellish harpyes, prophets of sad destiny."

By *Prospero's* command the delicate *Ariel* assumes the form of one of these savage monsters; the stage directions (*Tempest*, iii. 3) are, "Thunder and lightning. Enter *Ariel* like a harpy; claps his wings upon the table; and, with a quaint device, the banquet vanishes. . . . *Alonso, Sebastian*, &c., draw their swords:"—

> "*Ariel.* You fools! I and my fellows
> Are ministers of fate: the elements,
> Of whom your swords are temper'd, may as well
> Wound the loud winds, or with bemock'd at stabs
> Kill the still-closing waters, as diminish
> One dowle that's in my plume. [*He vanishes in thunder.*
> *Prospero.* Bravely the figure of this harpy hast thou
> Perform'd, my Ariel; a grace it had, devouring."

We find this monster again in *Pericles* (iv. 3, 46):—

> "*Cleon.* Thou art like a harpy,
> Which, to betray, dost, with thine angel's face,
> Seize with thy eagle's talons."

The Minotaur was a fabulous monster of antiquity, half man and half bull. It guarded the labyrinth of Minos, and was destroyed by Theseus, with the assistance of Ariadne, the king's daughter.

Minotaur.

> "*Suffolk.* O, wert thou for thyself! but Suffolk stay;
> Thou mayst not wander in that labyrinth;
> There minotaurs and ugly treasons lurk."
> (1 *Henry VI.*, v. 3, 187.)

Ben Jonson writes:—

> "I am neither your minotaur, nor your centaur, nor your satyr, nor your hyæna, nor your babion, but your mere traveller, believe me."
> (*Cynthia's Revels*, i. 1.)

Centaur. The Centaur was another classical monster, half man and half horse. The battle of the Centaurs with the Lapithæ has been told by Ovid and other authors, as well as by *Theseus*:—

> "*Theseus* [*reads*]. 'The battle with the Centaurs, to be sung
> By an Athenian eunuch to the harp.'
> We'll none of that: that have I told my love,
> In glory of my kinsman Hercules."
> (*Midsummer Night's Dream*, v. 1, 44.)

Chester writes (p. 112):—

> "The Onocentaur is a monstrous beast;
> Supposed halfe a man, and halfe an asse,
> That never shuts his eyes in quiet rest,
> Till he his foes deare life hath round eucompast,
>   Such were the Centaures in their tyrannie,
>   That liv'd by humane flesh and villanie."

Satyr. Satyrs were sylvan demigods, half men, half goats, who attended the revels of Bacchus. *Hamlet* compares his father with his uncle:—

> "So excellent a king; that was to this,
> Hyperion to a satyr."
> (*Hamlet*, i. 2, 139.)

Chimæra. The Chimæra, a mythological monstrosity frequently introduced into medieval architecture, was a creature with a goat's body and three heads, one like a lion, one like a goat, and the third like a dragon. In Christian art it symbolized deliberate cunning or fanciful illusion. The word *chimerical* in modern usage signifies an idle dream, a castle in the air, a project that can have no existence but in the imagination.

A correspondent in *Notes and Queries* (3rd series, vol.

viii. p. 66) gave the name of some brutes, endowed with immortality, that are sometimes referred to in medieval literature:—

"Mahomet allows that into paradise will be admitted Abraham's calf, Jonah's whale, Solomon's ant, Ishmael's ram, and Moses's ox, to these will be added Mahomet's dove, the Queen of Sheba's ass, the Prophet Salech's camel, and Belkis' cuckoo."

The writer asked for some particulars of these highly favoured beasts, but did not receive much information. One gentlemen wrote:—

"By Ishmael's ram is meant 'a noble victim,' (*Koran*, surat xxxvii. p. 369, Sale,) the same which Abel sacrificed, and which was sent to Abraham out of paradise when he offered his son. I can find nothing on the subject of Moses's ox, nor of the Queen of Sheba's (Balkis's) ass. Neither can I find anything of her cuckoo; although the lapwing conveyed messages between her and Solomon." (Page 115.)

To this list of immortal beasts the dog of the Seven Sleepers may be added.

In the play by Wilkins, *The Miseries of Inforced Marriage*, published 1607, we find money-lenders compared to "Mantichoras, monstrous beasts, enemies to mankind, that have double rows of teeth in their mouths. They are usurers, they come yawning for money."

Mantichor.

Topsell obligingly favours us with a description and a drawing of this formidable creature. Unfortunately this author does not give his authority for the portraits he introduces into his work of the various animals. His picture of the mantichor certainly does such credit to the imaginative powers of the artist that it is a pity his name is withheld. A facsimile reprint of this drawing forms the frontispiece of the present volume. The description runs as follows:—

"This beast, or rather monster, as Ctesias writeth, is bred among the Indians, having a treble rowe of teeth beneath and above, whose greatnesse, roughnesse, and feete are like a lyons, his face and eares like unto a mans [even to the carefully trimmed moustachios] his eies gray, of colour red, his tail like a scorpion of the earth, armed with a sting, casting forth sharp pointed quils, his voice like the voice of a small trumpet or pipe, being in course as swift as a hart. . . . Although India be full of divers ravening beastes, yet none of them are stiled with the title *andropophagi*, that is to say, men eaters; except onely this mantichora." (Page 442.)

Topsell sets this remarkable beast down as a kind of hyena, which however it does not resemble in one single particular. If *Othello* had any adventures to tell of encounters with such *anthropophagi* as these mantichors no wonder that *Desdemona* preferred listening to his traveller's tales to attending to her domestic duties.

Phœnix.

" *Sebastian.* Now I will believe
That there are unicorns, that in Arabia
There is one tree, the Phœnix' throne, one phœnix
At this hour reigning there."

(*Tempest*, iii. 3, 20.)

Ancient writers appear to have quite exhausted their imagination in depicting the splendid appearance and attributes of the phœnix. This remarkable bird is thus described by Pliny :—

" By report he is as big as an eagle, in colour yellow, and bright as gold, namely all about the neck, the rest of the bodie a deepe red purple; the taile azure blue, intermingled with feathers among of rose carnation colour: and the head bravely adorned with a crest and pennache finely wrought, having a tuft and plume thereupon right faire and goodly to be seene." (*Holland's Plinie*, book x. c. 2.)

Du Bartas simply paraphrases this passage when he tells us that—

" The heav'nly phœnix first began to frame
The earthly phœnix, and adorn'd the same
With such a plume, that Phœbus, circuiting
From Fez to Cairo, sees no fairer thing;
Such form, such feathers, and such fate he gave her,
That fruitfull nature breedeth nothing braver :

The Phœnix.

Two sparkling eyes : upon her crown, a crest
Of starrie sprigs (more splendid than the rest)
A golden doun about her dainty neck,
Her brest deep purple, and a scarlet back,
Her wings and train of feathers (mixed fine)
Of orient azure and incarnadine."

(Page 44.)

The origin of the phœnix fiction has been traced by some writers to Herodotus, but that author in his turn acknowledges that he knows nothing of the bird, but only writes from report or from pictures. An ingenious explanation has been given of the myth of the revival of the expiring bird from the burning ashes. In Eastern countries sacrifices were frequently offered in the open air, and cremation was also practised. Vultures and other birds of prey, too impatient to wait for the fire to subside, may occasionally have flown off with pieces of smoking flesh, and have either perished on the funeral pile or have set fire to their own nests. There may have been some connexion between the supposed ascension of the purified spirit from the flames and the forms of the birds which hovered round the corpse, albeit the motive of the latter in their attentions was purely carnal.

Lyly informs us that "feathers appeare not on the phœnix under seven months" (*Prologue to Campaspe*). But as time appears to have been of little value to this bird, perhaps the delay thus occasioned in its path to perfection was not of much consequence.

We learn from Fynes Moryson's *History of Ireland* (book i. part 2, ch. i.) that in the sixteenth century the pope supported the Earl of Tyrone, who was then engaged in conflict with the English, and by way of encouragement presented him with a crown of phœnix feathers, "perhaps in imitation of Pope Urban the Third, who sent John, the sonne of King Henry the Second, then made Lord of Ireland, a little crowne woven of peacocks feathers." We have no information, unfortunately, as to how this curiosity was obtained.

The phœnix was the badge of Jane Seymour. It was also a favourite name for Queen Elizabeth. The verse-makers who supplied the dedications of authors to her most gracious Majesty, and the rhymers " who stuck and spangled her with flatteries" whenever she honoured any of her subjects by a royal progress, repeatedly made use of the phœnix in their lines. King James also was universally greeted on his accession as the bird sprung from the ashes of his illustrious predecessor. The author of *Henry VIII.* gives us an example of this " title blown from adulation : "—

> " Nor shall this peace sleep with her : but as when
> The bird of wonder dies, the maiden phœnix,
> Her ashes new create another heir,
> As great in admiration as herself,
> So shall she leave her blessedness to one."
>
> (*Henry VIII.*, v. 5, 39.)

Many examples of this fashion of comparing Elizabeth to the phœnix are given by Dr. Grosart, in the introduction to his edition of Chester's curious poem, *Love's Martyr*, published by the New Shakspere Society, 1878. In this work, Chester describes some other fabulous birds :—

> "The snow-like colour'd bird, *Caladrius*,
>
> **Caladrius.** Hath this inestimable natural propertie,
> If any man in sicknesse dangerous,
> Hopes of his health to have recoverie,
> This bird will alwayes looke with chearefull glance,
> If otherwise, sad in his countenance."
>
> (Page 117.)

> " The gentle birds called the faire *Hircinie*,
>
> **Hircinie.** Taking the name of that place where they breed,
> Within the night they shine so gloriously,
> That mans astonied senses they do feed ;

The Liver.

> For in the darke being cast within the way
> Gives light unto the man that goes astray."
>
> (Page 119.)

> "The birds of Ægypt or Memnonides,   **Memnonides.**
> Of Memnon that was slaine in rescuing Troy,
> Are said to flie away in companies,
> To Priames pallace, and there twice a day
>   They fight about the turrets of the dead,
>   And the third day in battell are confounded."
>
> (Page 120.)

The Liver was a bird of obscure, heraldic origin. The name of the city of Liverpool has been derived from this ornithological curiosity, **Liver.** which in shape is said to have resembled a heron. According to a writer in *Notes and Queries* (4th series, vol. 8, p. 536), "there is an insurance office near Blackfriars Bridge, over the porch of which is a bird as the crest, called the liver."

In his work, *Demonology and Devil-lore* (vol. i. p. 319), Mr. Conway observes that, while a belief in such creatures as were-wolves and sea-serpents has arisen from an exaggerated conception of forms that have at one time existed, the invention of nondescript compound animals is traceable to a more poetic and artistic idea. The portrayal of such creatures as the sphinx and the griffin are—

"a kind of crude effort at *allgemeinheit*, at realisation of the types of evil—the claw principle, fang principle in the universe, the physiognomies of venom and pain detached from forms to which they are accidental."

The adventurous men who faced "the tyrannous breathings of the North," and penetrated the "regions of thick-ribbed ice," may well be **Sea-serpent.** excused if, amid the novelty of the scenes around them, and the hardships they often had to endure, they were sometimes led to exaggerate the wonders of those unvisited seas. One of the marvels described by them has not ceased to be a mystery, even in our own time. Various accounts of the Sea-serpent are given by writers; and, according to the imagination of the narrator, this monster varied in length from one to six hundred feet. One of the most detailed accounts is given by Olaus Magnus, who also draws an augury from its appearance :—

"They who in works of navigation, on the coast of Norway, employ themselves in fishing or merchandise, do all agree in this strange story, that there is a serpent there which is of a vast magnitude, namely 200 foot long, and moreover 20 foot thick; and is wont to live in rocks and caves toward the sea-coast about Berge : which will go alone from his holes in a clear night, in summer, and devour calves, lambs, and hogs, or else he goes into the sea to feed on polypus, locusts, and all sorts of sea-crabs. He hath commonly hair hanging from his neck a cubit long, and sharp scales, and is black, and he hath flaming shining eyes. This snake disquiets the shippers, and he puts up his head on high like a pillar, and catcheth away men, and he devours them; and this hapneth not, but it signifies some wonderful change of the kingdom near at hand ; namely, that the princes shall die, or be banished; or some tumultuous wars shall presently follow. There is also another serpent of an incredible magnitude in a town, called Moos, of the diocess of Hammer; which, as a comet portends a change in all the world, so that portends a change in the kingdom of Norway, as it was seen, anno 1522; this serpent was thought to be fifty cubits long by conjecture, by sight afar off: there followed this the banishment of King Christiernus, and a great persecution of the bishops; and it shew'd also the destruction of the countrey." (Page 235.)

"Experience, O, thou disprovest report!
The imperious seas breed monsters."
(*Cymbeline*, iv. 2, 34.)

INDEX.

Adder, 314
Agouti, 156
Ai, or sloth, 163
Aiochtochth, an animal, 166
Albacore, or pilot-fish, 382
Alcatrazi, or pelican, 288
Amphisbena, 313
Anchovy, 376
Aut, 405
Ant-eater, 167
Antelope, 136
Archangel, or titmouse, 182
Ardluk, or ork, 99
Armadillo, 166
Asp, 315
Ass, 111
Astanapa, or giraffe, 131
Auk, 292
Aurochs, or bison, 132

Badger, 77
Ban-dog, 59
Banks and his horse, 109
Barbel, 364
Baremoe, or ant-eater, 167
Barnacles, 275
Basilisk, 458
Bat, 11
Bawson, or badger, 78
Beagle, 48
Bear, 81, 185
Bear's grease for the hair, 85
Beaver, 151
Bee, 407
Beech-marten, 67
Beetle, 398
Biarataca, or skunk, 80
Biche, a fur, 74
Bird-fowling, 172

Bird of Paradise, 189
Birds, lists of, 171, 174
Bishop or monk-fish, 385
Bison, 132
Bittern, 269
Blackbird, 178
Bloodhound, 45
Bleak, 366
Blindworm, 312
Boa Constrictor, 319
Boar, 115
Bocher, a young salmon, 352
Bonassus, or bison, 132
Bonito, 337
Booby, 278
Boorde (Andrew), notice of, 129
Bovy, a wild ox, 134
Bream, 361
Breese, or gad-fly, 417
Brew, or whimbrel, 259
Brill, 348
Brock, or badger, 77
Buffalo, or buffe, 133
Bugle, a wild ox, 134
Bulldog, 59
Burge, or bogy, a fur, 74
Bustard, 264
Butterfly, 422
Buzzard, 252

Caddis-fly, 419
Caius on dogs, 44
Calabar, or calabrere, a fur, 74
Caladrius, 468
Camel, 117
Canary, 195
Capercaillie, 219
Carp, 359
Cassawary, 296

Cat, 26
Cattle, English, 134
Centaur, 464
Chameleon, 310
Chamois, 138
Char, 353
Cheetah, or hunting leopard, 24
Chermes, 392
Chimæra, 464
Chimpanzee, or engeco, 9
Chisamus, a fur, 75
Chough, 188
Chub, 365
Churchia, or opossum, 168
Cicada, 392
Civet, 32
Coati, or coati-mundi, 80
Cobra, 318
Cochineal, 390
Cock, 225
Cockatoo, 214
Cockchafer, 400
Cockroach, 398
Cod, 341
Coiumero, or manatee, 101
Comforter, a dog, 56
Condor, 231
Coral, 450
Cormorant, 284
Coryat, notice of, 444
Cosset, a house lamb, 142
Cotswold games, 53
Coursing-matches, 51
Crab, 436
Crane, 265
Crane-fly, 419
Crayfish, 435
Cricket, 392
Crocodile, 303
Crossbill, 196
Crow, 183
Cry of hounds, 48
Cuckoo, 205
Cure for ague, 431
Cure for blindness, 30
Cure for gout, 431
Cure for stings of flies, 417
Curlew, 257
Cuttle-fish, 441

Dabchick, 292
D..ce, 365
D...s.und, or badger-dog, 50, 80
I.ant, a species of antelope, 137
D..ier, a war-horse, 108

Dodo, 218
Dog, 40
Dog-fish, 384
Dogs, Huxley on, 41
Dolphin, 95
Dory, 348
Dossus, a fur, 75
Dotterel, 263
Dozado, or dolphin, 96
Dragon, 458
Dromedary, 118
Dugong, 100
Dugong in Palestine, 79

Eagle, 232
East India Company founded, 145
Eel, 377
Egg-hatching in Egypt, 226
Elephant, 146
Elk, 121
Emeu, 296
English love of novelty, 60
Ermine, 64

Falconry, 237
Fallow deer, 125
Ferret, 71
Fewterer, a, 52
Finch, 193
Fire-drake, 459
Fire-fly, 403
Fir-martin, 67
Fish as an article of food, 325
Fish, Harrison's definition of, 87
Fish, lists of, 326
Fishing, Burton on, 330
Fisting-hound, 56
Fitchet, or fitchew, 71
Flamingo, 288
Flounder, 346
Fly, 416
Flying-fish, 338, 358
Foines, or beech-martens, 67
Foulmartin, or foumart, 71
Fox, 62
Friendships of animals, 251
Frog, 320
Fur out of fashion, 69

Gad-fly, 417
Garefish, 358
Gayns, or martens, 67
Galloway horses, 107
Gazehound, 50
Gelert, the dog, 50

Gennet, a Spanish horse, 107
Ger-falcon, 246
Gerfauntz, or giraffe, 130
Giraffe, 130
Glow-worm, 402
Glutton, 75
Gnat, 421
Gnat-snap, or knot, 260
Goat, 145
Goat-sucker, 209
Godolphin, or sea-eagle, 235
Godwit, 260
Goose, 273
Gorilla, or pongo, 9
Goshawk, 251
Gossamer, 432
Grampus, or ork, 99
Grasshopper, 394
Gray, or badger, 78
Grayling, 354
Greyhound, 51
Grice, a cub, 78
Griffin, 460
Grouse, 219
Grymbart, name of badger, 80
Guanaco, 120
Gudgeon, 367
Guinea-fowl, 228
Guinea-pig, 157
Gull, 282
Gurnet, 335
Gwiniad, 354

Hackney horses, 107
Haddock, 343
Hake, 344
Hare, 157
Harpy, 463
Harrier, 47
Hecco, or woodpecker, 203
Havoc! a coursing phrase, 51
Hawking, technical terms of, 7, 238, 248
Hedgehog, 12
Hen-harrier, 248
Herbert, Sir Thomas, notice of, 12
Hermelin, or ermine, 65
Heron, 268
Herring, 370
Hippopotamus, 114
Hircinie, 468
Hobby, 250
Hobby, an Irish horse, 106
Holibut, 347
Hoopoe, 209

Horn, value of, 135
Hornet, 415
Horse, 104
Horsehair laid in water, 379
Humble-bee, 413
Humming-bird, 210
Hunt, a cockney, 48
Hunting, technical terms of, 7, 127
Hyæna, 32

Iceland dog, 60
Ichneumon, 32, 308
Ichneumon fly, 418
Immortal animals, 465
Insect, definition of, 388
Insects, sensibility of, 401
Ireland free from venom, 298

Jaccatray, or hyæna, 33
Jackal, 38
Jackdaw, 188
Jaguar, called the tiger, 21
Jews indifferent to animals, 27
Jews indifferent to natural beauty, 28

Kestrel, 250
Kingfisher, 207
Kinship of man and animals, 1
Kite, 236
Knot, 259
Koumiss, mare's milk, 108

Ladybird, 404
Lamprey, 387
Land-rail, 255
Lanner, 249
Lant, species of antelope, 137
Lark, 198
Laws respecting dress, 63, 66, 74
Lawyers to wear fox or lamb skin, 63
Leaf insect, 397
Lear's allusion to dogs, 57
Leech, 449
Lekat, or ermine, 65
Lemming, 65, 151
Leopard, 22
Lettice, a fur, 66, 69
Ling, 345
Linnet, 196
Lion, 17
Lion, heraldic, 23
Lions hanged as scarecrows, 37
Lituite, a fur, 75

Liver, 469
Lizard, 310
Llama, 119
Loach, 366
Lobster, 434
Lobster, or stoat, 65
Locust, 395
Loon, 281
Losh, or buffe, 133
Lycanthropy, 34
Lynx, 30

Macaw, 215
Machlis, or elk, 122
Magpie, 183
Mallard, 280
Maltese dog, 61
Mamuques, or Birds of Paradise, 189
Manatee, 100
Mantichor, 465
Mantis, 396
Marine animals, 87
Marmoset, 10
Marmot, 154
Marocco, a performing horse, 109
Marten, or Martron, 67
Martin, 192
Mastiff, 58
Mavis, or thrush, 176
Memnonides, 469
Menageries, 5
Merle, or blackbird, 178
Merlin, 250
Mermaid, 97
Mermaid tavern, 103
Migration of birds, 173
Miller's Thumb, 335
Miniver, 73
Minnow, 367
Minotaur, 463
Missel-thrush, 177
Mole, 14
Monedula, the jackdaw, 188
Monkey, 8
Monsters, English love of, 331
Month's mind, a, 378
Moose, or elk, 121
Morse, or walrus, 88
Moryson (F.), notice of, 125
Moth, 424
Mouse, 150
Mousehunt, meaning of, 72
Mullet, 334
Musk deer, 129
Musquito, 421

Mussel, 447
Mythology in poetry, 387
Myths, growth of, 4

Narwhal, 97
Nautilus, 440
Neat, term for oxen, 136
Newt, 320
Night-crow, or night-raven, 188
Nightingale, 178
Nightjar, 209
Northumberland Household Book, 175
Norway rat, 65

Olaus Magnus, notice of, 124
Opossum, 168
Orafle, or giraffe, 130
Ordegale, the beaver's wife, 72
Oriole, 182
Ork, or orca, 99
Ortolan, 197
Oryx, or bison, 132
Osprey, 252
Ostrich, 294
Otter, 76
Ounce, 25
Ouzel, or blackbird, 178
Owl, 253
Oyster, 442
Oyster-catcher, 263

Paca, 157
Paco, or llama, 120
Panther, breath of, 23
Paris Garden, 82
Parrot, 212
Partridge, 220
Peacock, 220
Pearls, 445
Peel, a young salmon, 352
Pelican, 285
Penguin, 289
Perch, 333
Peregrine, 247
Performing animals, 111, 161
Performing birds, 195
Performing dogs, 61
Petit gris, a fur, 75, 77
Petrel, 284
Pheasant, 223
Philo, or elephant, 131
Phœnix, 466
Pigeon, 216
Pike, 355

Index. 475

Pilchard, 369
Pilot-fish, 381
Plaice, 346
Plover, 260
Poaching dog, a, 54
Polecat, 71
Polypus, or octopus, 439
Poor-John, 344
Popinjay, meaning of, 213
Porcupine, 155
Porpoise, 98
Prister, or physeter, 94
Puffin, 293
Puma, 24
Purchas, notice of, 8
Puttock, or kite, 236

Quail, 220

Rabbit, 161
Racing in England, 109
Rat, 149
Rattlesnake, 318
Raven, 185
Red deer, 124
Redshank, 257
Redwing, 177
Reindeer, 122
Remora, 382
Reptile, 297
Rhinoceros, 112
Roach, 365
Robin, 179
Roc, or griffin, 461
Rondes, or sable, 69
Rook, 184
Rosetel, or ermine, 65
Rosmarine, or walrus, 89
Ruff, 259
Ruffe, or pope, 333
Rukenawe, the she ape, 72
Russian furs, 64

Sable, 68
Sables, Hamlet's suit of, 70
St. Anthony's pigs, 116
St. Martin's bird, 187
Saker, 249
Salamander, 319
Salmon, 349
Sardine, 376
Satyr, 464
Scallop, 442
Scamell, or sea-gull, 283
Scented dogs, 56

Scolopendra, 95
Scorpion, 432
Sea-anemone, 450
Sea-calf, or seal, 90
Seal, 90
Seal in Palestine, 79
Sea-monster of *Lear*, 100
Sea-pye, or oyster-catcher, 263
Sea-serpent, 470
Sea-unicorn, or narwhal, 97
Selsey, famous for seals, 90
Serpent, definition of, 388
Setter, 55
Shark, 380
Sheldrake, 281
Sheep, 139
Sheep-dog, 60
Shoveller, 270
Shrew, 15
Shrimp, 435
Silkworm, 426
Siskin, 194
Sismusilis, a fur, 75
Skunk, 80
Slightfalcon, 251
Smelt, 355
Snail, 448
Snake, 316
Snipe, 256
Sole, 347
Sorocucu, a snake, 318
Spaniel, 54
Sparrow, 200
Sparrow-hawk, 252
Species, distribution of, 102
Species, variation of, 21
Spenser's list of monsters, 95
Sphinx, 462
Spider, 428
Spinke, or chaffinch, 194
Sports on Cotswold, 53
Spowe, or sparrow, 201
Spowe, or whimbrel, 201, 259
Sprat, 375
Squid, 441
Squirrel, 152
Starling, 197
Stickleback, 332
Stockfish, 342
Stork, 271
Stot, a young ox, 136
Sturgeon, 380
Suant, or bull trout, 352
Surnapa, or giraffe, 131
Swallow, 191

Swan, 278
Sword-fish, 339

Talbot, 46
Tamandua, or ant-eater, 167
Tarantula, 429
Tatus, or armadillo, 166
Teal, 281
Technical terms, 7
Tench, 362
Terrier, 49
Thornback, 386
Thresher, or ork, 99
Thrush, 176
Tie-dog, 59
Tiger, 20
Timber of furs, u, 69
Titmouse, 182
Toad, 322
Toothache caused by a worm, 426
Torpedo, 386
Tortoise, 300
Toucan, 204
Trials of animals, 36
Trochilus and crocodile, 307
Tropic bird, 288
Trout, 352
Tumbler, 53
Tunny, 336
Turbot, 347
Turkey, 227
Turtle, 301

Unicorn, 452
Uranoscopus, 339

Vair, a fur, 74
Vicuna, 120

Viscacha, 154
Vows on birds, 223
Vulture, 230

Walrus, 87, 95
Wasp, 414
Water birds, abundance of, 170
Weasel, 73
Welsh explorers, 291
Were-wolf myth, 34
Whale, 91
Wheat-ear, 180
Whie, a heifer, 136
Whimbrel, 259
Whirlpool, 94
Whistler, a bird of ill omen, 258, 262
Whiting, 343
Wise men of Gotham, 207
Wolf, 33
Wolf-dog, Irish, 50
Woodcock, 256
Woodlark, 199
Woodpecker, 203
Woodwele, or oriole, 183
Woollen trade, 144
Woolverine, or wood dog, 75
Woozel, or blackbird, 178
Wren, 181
Wyvern, 459

Xaco, or llama, 121

Yellow-hammer, 201

Zebel, or sable, 68
Zebra, 112
Zebu, 134

PRINTED BY WILLIAM CLOWES AND SONS, LIMITED, LONDON AND BECCLES.

www.ingramcontent.com/pod-product-compliance
Lightning Source LLC
Chambersburg PA
CBHW021425300426
44114CB00010B/653